POETICS, PERFORMANCE AND POLITICS
IN FRENCH AND ITALIAN RENAISSANCE COMEDY

LEGENDA

LEGENDA is the Modern Humanities Research Association's book imprint for new research in the Humanities. Founded in 1995 by Malcolm Bowie and others within the University of Oxford, Legenda has always been a collaborative publishing enterprise, directly governed by scholars. The Modern Humanities Research Association (MHRA) joined this collaboration in 1998, became half-owner in 2004, in partnership with Maney Publishing and then Routledge, and has since 2016 been sole owner. Titles range from medieval texts to contemporary cinema and form a widely comparative view of the modern humanities, including works on Arabic, Catalan, English, French, German, Greek, Italian, Portuguese, Russian, Spanish, and Yiddish literature. Editorial boards and committees of more than 60 leading academic specialists work in collaboration with bodies such as the Society for French Studies, the British Comparative Literature Association and the Association of Hispanists of Great Britain & Ireland.

The MHRA encourages and promotes advanced study and research in the field of the modern humanities, especially modern European languages and literature, including English, and also cinema. It aims to break down the barriers between scholars working in different disciplines and to maintain the unity of humanistic scholarship. The Association fulfils this purpose through the publication of journals, bibliographies, monographs, critical editions, and the MHRA Style Guide, and by making grants in support of research. Membership is open to all who work in the Humanities, whether independent or in a University post, and the participation of younger colleagues entering the field is especially welcomed.

Transcript publishes books about all kinds of imagining across languages, media and cultures: translations and versions, inter-cultural and multi-lingual writing, illustrations and musical settings, adaptation for theatre, film, TV and new media, creative and critical responses. We are open to studies of any combination of languages and media, in any historical moments, and are keen to reach beyond Legenda's traditional focus on modern European languages to embrace anglophone and world cultures and the classics. We are interested in innovative critical approaches: we welcome not only the most rigorous scholarship and sharpest theory, but also modes of writing that stretch or cross the boundaries of those discourses.

TRANSCRIPT

1. *Adapting the Canon: Mediation, Visualization, Interpretation*, edited by Ann Lewis and Silke Arnold-de Simine
2. *Adapted Voices: Transpositions of Céline's Voyage au bout de la nuit and Queneau's Zazie dans le métro*, by Armelle Blin-Rolland
3. *Zola and the Art of Television: Adaptation, Recreation, Translation*, by Kate Griffiths
4. *Comparative Encounters between Artaud, Michaux and the Zhuangzi: Rationality, Cosmology and Ethics*, by Xiaofan Amy Li
5. *Minding Borders: Resilient Divisions in Literature, the Body and the Academy*, edited by Nicola Gardini, Adriana Jacobs, Ben Morgan, Mohamed-Salah Omri and Matthew Reynolds
6. *Memory Across Borders: Nabokov, Perec, Chamoiseau*, by Sara-Louise Cooper
7. *Erotic Literature in Adaptation and Translation*, edited by Johannes D. Kaminski
8. *Translating Petrarch's Poetry: L'Aura del Petrarca from the Quattrocento to the 21st Century*, edited by Carole Birkan-Berz, Guillaume Coatalen and Thomas Vuong
9. *Making Masud Khan: Psychoanalysis, Empire and Modernist Culture*, by Benjamin Poore
10. *Prismatic Translation*, edited by Matthew Reynolds
11. *The Patient, the Impostor and the Seducer: Medieval European Literature in Hebrew*, by Tovi Bibring
12. *Reading Dante and Proust by Analogy*, by Julia Caterina Hartley
13. *The First English Translations of Molière: Drama in Flux 1663-1732*, by Suzanne Jones
14. *After Clarice: Reading Lispector's Legacy in the Twenty-First Century*, edited by Adriana X. Jacobs and Claire Williams
15. *Uruguayan Theatre in Translation: Theory and Practice*, by Sophie Stevens
16. *Hamlet Translations: Prisms of Cultural Encounters across the Globe*, edited by Márta Minier and Lily Kahn
17. *The Foreign Connection: Writings on Poetry, Art and Translation*, by Jamie McKendrick
18. *Poetics, Performance and Politics in French and Italian Renaissance Comedy*, by Lucy Rayfield

Poetics, Performance and Politics in French and Italian Renaissance Comedy

Lucy Rayfield

LEGENDA

Transcript 18
Modern Humanities Research Association
2022

Published by Legenda
an imprint of the Modern Humanities Research Association
Salisbury House, Station Road, Cambridge CB1 2LA

ISBN 978-1-78188-512-3

First published 2022

Copy-Editor: Charlotte Brown

CONTENTS

Acknowledgements		ix
Note on Translations and Spelling		xi
Abbreviations		xii
Introduction		1
1	Charles Estienne: France's Innovator of Comic Theatre	13
2	Comic Theory in Thomas Sébillet, Joachim Du Bellay, and Jean-Pierre de Mesmes	41
3	From Page to Stage: The Example of *La Calandra*	59
4	Estienne Jodelle and the Italian Model	89
5	Resistance and Rivalry: Anti-Italianism in the Comedy of Jacques Grévin	115
6	Comedy as Propaganda: Pierre de Larivey and Odet de Turnèbe	149
	Afterword	179
	Bibliography	183
	Appendices:	201
	I Jean-Pierre de Mesmes's Prefatory Letters (1552)	201
	II Timeline of Key Dates	203
	III Plot Synopses	204
Index		209

For my parents,
Sue and Bill;
and in loving memory of my grandparents,
Kit and Jim

ACKNOWLEDGEMENTS

My sincere thanks firstly go to Richard Cooper and Martin McLaughlin, my supervisors for the doctoral thesis on which this book is based. I will always be grateful for their unfailing guidance, support, and commitment to my academic work, and also for their generosity and good humour outside of our supervision sessions, which enhanced immeasurably my experience of postgraduate life. My heartfelt thanks too to my DPhil examiners, Elena Lombardi and John Parkin, as well as to Graham Nelson, Charlotte Wathey, and my anonymous reviewers at Legenda, whose insight and attentive readings have been invaluable. I wish to thank Nico De Brabander, Dirk Imhof, and Silke Geiring at the Museum Plantin-Moretus and Bayerische Staatsbibliothek for their support with archival materials; additionally, I am grateful to Eugene Johnson and Grace McEniry for their permission to reproduce their illustrations in this book. Further thanks are due to the AHRC, whose financial support throughout my doctorate made my research possible; I am also grateful for the bursaries awarded to me by Balliol College, which funded my archival research and conference travel. The 2019 MHRA Research Scholarship in the Modern European Languages gave me a year of editing time at the Centre for the Study of the Renaissance, University of Warwick, which has been crucial to the completion of this book. Since 2019 I have also been lucky enough to hold a Research Associateship of St Benet's Hall, and my findings in this book have been enriched by interactions with the many great minds there.

Over the past few years I have been fortunate to be surrounded by a wonderful network of colleagues and friends. My thanks go to Jennifer Rushworth, Hanna Smyth, and Esther van Raamsdonk for their never-failing advice and encouragement; I must also thank Julia Hartley and Natalya Din-Kariuki for their steadfast support and camaraderie. The humour and friendship of Alice Coombes Huntley, Angharad Jones, Claudia Price, Deborah Price, and Ivo Gruev have made the writing of this book — as well as the series of lockdowns — bearable, as has the generosity of Emanuela Tandello, Richard Cooper, and Emma Herdman. This book was finished while teaching French and Italian at the Universities of Oxford, Exeter, Warwick, and Bristol, and I have been lucky to work with colleagues such as Patrick McGuinness, Fiona Cox, Ingrid De Smet, Clare Siviter-Groschwald, and Rhiannon Daniels, with whom I have enjoyed talking all things laughter, literature, and Latin. My gratitude also goes to Laurence Fleming and Stephen Parry-Jones, who have gone over and above in their roles as teachers, mentors, and friends.

The process of completing this book would have been far more arduous without Adam Cross, my partner and closest friend, whose sense of fun and adventure never ceases to put a smile on my face. I would also like to thank his family, particularly

Kim, Nicki, and Sam, for their kindness and solidarity. Finally, I am endlessly grateful to my own family: my parents Sue and Bill, and my late grandparents Kit and Jim. No words can do justice to the love and support they have shown me: my thanks to them for believing in me and for always encouraging me to reach for the stars.

L.R., Oxford, August 2021

NOTE ON
TRANSLATIONS AND SPELLING

English translations are provided alongside all quotations and titles in the original French, Italian, and Latin. Except where otherwise indicated, all translations are my own. In quotations from early printed books, I have normalised to modern usage the letters *i* and *j*, *u* and *v*, the long *s*, and the ampersand; early modern contractions have also been expanded. Some punctuation has also been modified in my English translations to clarify the meaning of the source text.

ABBREVIATIONS

The following abbreviations are used for the most frequently cited archives and journals:

BAV   Biblioteca Apostolica Vaticana
INHA   Institut national d'Histoire de l'Art
BnF   Bibliothèque nationale de France
BHR   *Bibliothèque d'Humanisme et Renaissance*
PMLA   *Publications of the Modern Language Associations of America*

INTRODUCTION

It is often said that there is nothing funny about comedy. Throughout history, humour has been used as a political weapon, a tension-reliever, and a statement of power; it has also functioned as a means of building communities and as evidence of literary and intellectual prowess. A serious side to laughter can always be found. Yet, it is the lack of laughter in sixteenth-century French comedy which has caused it to be overlooked in scholarship, particularly in relation to its seventeenth-century counterpart. It is true that the comedies of Molière and his contemporaries are more performable than early modern plays, and that the laughable aspects of seventeenth-century drama are more easily transposed to the modern-day stage. Sixteenth-century comedy, then, is often mentioned only in relation to its more celebrated successor, and almost customarily referred to as 'la comédie avant Molière' [comedy before Molière]. Geoffrey Brereton, for instance, has indicated the 'relative poverty of comic theatre before 1630'; Harold Lawton, too, discusses sixteenth-century drama in reference to its 'preparation for the great age of the seventeenth century'.[1] Retrospectively, it is easy to compare unfavourably the work of early modern writers with the plays of Molière and others, and to conclude that 'in France the sixteenth century, the great age of lyric poetry, was not the age of great drama'.[2] This study seeks not to show that these plays constituted great drama, nor even that they were regarded as such when they were written. In the same way, this study does not aim to prove that these plays are or were laughable. Instead, I examine the aforementioned 'serious side' of sixteenth-century French comedy, showing that these plays served at once as literary experiments, political weapons, and nationalistic propaganda, both fighting for a place within French culture and at the same time trying — with varying degrees of success — to make their mark upon it.

This study focuses on the period 1540 to 1580, and presents new readings of a range of texts pertaining to comic theatre in France. These materials include not only plays, but also letters, prefaces, treatises, and commemorative booklets, each of which allow us to build up a clearer picture of the ways in which comic theatre throughout the century was revived and received. In this way, this book brings to light contemporary arguments for and against the reinvention of classical comedy in print and in the vernacular; it also provides critical new perspectives on the impact of court performances on the genre. Additionally, it offers insights into the employment of comic theatre as a political tool, and particularly one which could make a nationalist statement. Each facet of this tripartite framework of poetics, performance, and politics was affected in no small part by the Italians, whose role in the reshaping of comedy in France forms another major line of enquiry in this book. As well as broadening our knowledge of the status of comedy throughout the century, an analysis of the Italian influence on French drama also helps to pioneer a new approach to understanding the turbulent relationship between France and Italy. This book traces the shift from the French admiration and imitation of Italian models in the 1540s to an antagonism which intensified over the next decades, and which saw French writers not only attempting to move away from Italian sources but also to turn their plays against the Italians themselves. The Italians had long employed comedy as a weapon against the French; however, as this book will show, it is largely through the ingenuity of the Italians that the genre was brought to France, and French writers had to make use of increasingly canny techniques to transform Italian inventions into anti-Italian propaganda.[3] The comedy which they produced reveals in greater detail than before the French resentment of Italian innovators, as well as the measures taken by French writers to prove their own cultural and literary superiority.

To avoid cumbersome repetition in this book, the unprefixed term 'comedy' will be used to denote the classical comedy reinvented by the Italians towards the end of the fifteenth century, and which French humanists sought to revive in the next century.[4] Any references to medieval comic theatre — to the farce, *sottie*, or *sermon joyeux*, for instance — will clearly be identified as such; additionally, although this book makes several mentions of the *commedia dell'arte*, any references to this wholly distinct genre will be made explicit.[5] In the same way, the terms 'playwright', 'dramatist', or 'comedian' in this book should not be taken at face value. During the years in question, the creation of comic theatre was never the writer's sole occupation: the drama produced was a pastime or a sideline to other careers.[6] Indeed, most writers of comedy had highly lucrative professions as doctors or lawyers, and others resided at court under the patronage of the nobles, writing in order to please those who paid them. As the professions of these writers might suggest, the comedies examined in this book were not enjoyed by the general public; as Corinne Noirot has also noted, despite the efforts of writers, the new genre of comedy 'never quite reached a sizable audience'.[7] Unlike medieval comic forms, which were created largely for general audiences and performed within the community, the spectators or readers of these plays would have been more affluent or elite individuals with connections to the courts or colleges. The readerships and audiences under discussion in this book constitute only a small part of the population, whereas farce remained both accessible and appreciated throughout the century.

The start date of 1540 coincides with the completion by Charles Estienne of the first translation into French of an Italian play;[8] this is earlier than the majority of studies of sixteenth-century French drama, many of which begin in 1552, the year in which Estienne Jodelle composed the first original comedy in French.[9] Numerous works still claim that comedy in France was absent before this date, an idea which began to circulate over a century ago with the assertions of scholars such as Lucien Pinvert, who wrote that 'avant Jodelle et avant Grévin, le théâtre français n'existait pas' [before Jodelle and Grévin, French theatre did not exist].[10] The earlier start date of this study brings to light Estienne's translation along with his other work on comic theatre, printed in the early 1540s; it also explores some key discussions about comedy which took place later in the decade, as well as a major comic performance in France, staged in 1548, which constituted a turning point in the genre. The end date of this book in 1580 is marked by the completion of Odet de Turnèbe's Italianate play *Les Contens*. This was the final overtly anti-Italianist comedy to be printed in France before interest in the genre diminished, being revived only in the 1620s.

Comic Theatre in Early Modern France

France was well known for its lively farce tradition long before the period in question. Hundreds of performances by itinerant troupes (such as the Basochiens and the Confrérie de la Passion) took place in the fourteenth and fifteenth centuries, and some were so successful that they were printed and performed until well into the 1600s. *La Farce de Maistre Pierre Pathelin* (*c.* 1464), for instance, made its way to Lyons, Paris, and Rouen, and was so popular that two spin-off farces were written for its admirers: *Le Nouveau Pathelin* and *Le Testament de Pathelin*.[11] As noted above, farce performances were written with a general audience in mind; yet, they were also appreciated by those at court: François I was a leading patron of the farce, generously remunerating players such as Jean de L'Espine Du Pont-Allais — also known as Songecreux — and even commissioning a farce to satirize his mother, Louise de Savoie, which was performed in 1523.[12] Another comic genre which thrived in the fifteenth century was the *sottie*, which differed from the farce in its portrayal of allegorical characters. Pierre Gringore made a living out of writing *sotties*, mainly for the Enfans-sans-Souci troupe, which attracted the admiration not only of the general public but also of Louis XII.[13] The comic monologue was also celebrated during this period, the most famous example being the anonymous *Le Franc-archer de Bagnolet* [The Free Archer of Bagnolet] (*c.* 1468);[14] other forms of the monologue, such as the *sermon joyeux*, were also popular. The *sermon joyeux* often parodied the sermon of a Catholic mass, and others critiqued the state.[15] The use of comedy as propaganda in France, which will be a main subject of Part III of this book, has important precedents in medieval comic theatre:[16] writers were used to walking a very fine line between *ridere* [laughter] and *deridere* [derision], as it was understood at the time.[17]

Turning to humanist theatre in France, in the early sixteenth century classical drama was largely synonymous with Terence, whose comedies — deemed models of pure Latin worthy of imitation — had been used as part of grammar-teaching in schools.[18] In 1540 Charles Estienne (1504–64) completed his translation into French of an Italian comedy, which was swiftly followed by his translation into French of Terence's *Andria*. Both translations were accompanied by prefatory materials which made the case for the reinvention of classical comedy in France. The importance and usefulness of comedy was discussed later in the decade by humanists such as Thomas Sébillet (1512–89), Joachim Du Bellay (1522–60), and Jean-Pierre de Mesmes (1516–78), from which a broad proliferation of viewpoints emerge. A turning point came in 1548, with the performance of *La Calandra* by Bernardo

Dovizi da Bibbiena; this inspired a series of Italian performances at the courts in the early 1550s, as well as the composition of Jodelle's *L'Eugène*, which was written at the request of the Italian queen consort of France, Catherine de' Medici. Over the next two decades, writers such as Jacques Grévin (*c.* 1539–70), Pierre de Larivey (1541–1619), and Odet de Turnèbe (1552–81) experimented with the comic theatrical form. Writing against the backdrop of the Wars of Religion, some of their plays constitute religious and political propaganda; others also seek to resist and to rival the increasingly pervasive Italian influence in France, denigrating Italian culture while at the same time minimising the appearance of their reliance on Italian sources. Each author attempts to prove their originality in writing comic drama, forging both a legacy for themselves and accolade for France. It is this narrative — from the first endeavours of Estienne to reinvent the genre, to Turnèbe's employment of the genre as a political weapon — which will be traced in this book.

This study of plays during this period is by no means exhaustive. Many comedies are surely lost to us: both Jacques de La Taille and François d'Amboise, for instance, mention their completion of a number of comedies, all of which have proved irretrievable.[19] Others have been deliberately omitted: Jean de La Taille's *Les Corrivaus* [The Rivals] (1560) and Jean-Antoine de Baïf's *Le Brave* [The Braggart] (1567) are examples of the changing status of comedy throughout the century; however, since neither reveal new angles on the culture of performance or on the complexities of the Franco-Italian relationship, they are not singled out for case studies in this book.[20] In the same way, Gillian Jondorf has already documented in depth the tragic drama of the sixteenth century, which was in any case less prevalent at the courts.[21] It is well known that Catherine de' Medici commissioned a French translation of the Italian Gian Giorgio Trissino's *La Sofonisba* (*c.* 1515), performed at Blois in 1556 and 1559, and that Catherine became greatly superstitious that her presence at the latter performance of *Sophonisbe* had caused her husband's death.[22] As the chronicler Brantôme recounts:

> [Catherine] aimoit fort à veoir jouer des comedies et tragedies; mais depuis *Sophonisbe* [...] elle eut opinion qu'elle avoit porté Malheur aux affaires du royaume [...] elle n'en fit plus jouer [des tragedies], mais ouy bien des comedies et tragi-comedies, et mesmes celles de Zani et Pantalons, y prenant grand plaisir et y riait son saoul.[23]

> [Catherine really loved to see comedies and tragedies acted, but ever since *Sophonisbe* [...] she believed that she had brought ill fortune to the affairs of the kingdom [...] she had no more [tragedies] acted, but enjoyed watching comedies and tragi-comedies, and even those of the Zani and Pantalons, taking great pleasure from them and laughing until she cried.]

The 'Zani et Pantalons' clearly refer to the *commedia dell'arte* actors, not only supported by Catherine but also by her sons: Charles IX, who became king in 1560 after the short reign of his brother François II, enjoyed an especially close friendship with the Italian players.[24] As outlined above, this book does not trace in detail the influence in France of the *commedia dell'arte*, a genre largely separate from the humanist comedy which writers sought to reinvent in France. In the same way, this study does not focus on comic narratives such as those by François Rabelais or Marguerite de Navarre. Some recent works have complicated the term 'drama' in a sixteenth-century context, showing the hybridity of comedy and the fluidity between some comic prose genres and stage-plays: we can take, for example, a narrative depicting performance, such the Chiquanous episode in Rabelais's *Quart Livre* [Fourth Book].[25] However, given that the case studies in this book are adaptations of earlier Italian plays, which have been chosen in light of the complex and often problematic relationship with their models which they reveal, this study considers theatre from the more conventional angle of pieces written entirely for performance before an audience or — as in the case of Estienne — of pieces written to exemplify how narratives could be brought to the stage in the classical style.

This study confirms some findings of Patrizia De Capitani Bertrand, whose comparative work on French and Italian comedy has shown that sixteenth-century playwrights were more than capable of adapting to their contemporary cultural and literary milieux.[26] With its detailed study of the theatrical interventions of Estienne, the present book builds on De Capitani Bertrand's analysis of the contribution of Sienese comedy in France; yet, unlike De Capitani Bertrand, I contend that Larivey's translations of Italian comedy were completed with an element of rivalry in mind, and that other playwrights too competed with their sources. Charles Mazouer's 2002 study of French Renaissance theatre is among the most comprehensive, and also brings to light certain elements of the Italian influence on its French comic counterpart.[27] The bibliographical details provided by Mazouer, as well as his synthesis of medieval comic genres with the new humanist comedy, have been fundamental for the present book, and the detailed case studies which I have included both support and expand on his argument for the significance for the genre of the Italians in France. Émile Chasles's *La Comédie en France au XVIe siècle* (1862) was the first extensive work on sixteenth-century French comedy; this study too remains an important biographical and bibliographical source, although it creates retrospectively a neat and linear narrative of the emergence of comic theatre which this book seeks to unwrite.[28] The series *Théâtre français de la Renaissance*, founded by Enea Balmas and Michel Dassonville, has also made available as modern editions a broad range of plays, each of which are accompanied by framing and contextualising notes.[29] This series has been invaluable not only in making accessible some of the comedies in question in this study, but also in providing detailed and up-to-date readings of each text.

France and Italy

Nineteenth- and early twentieth-century scholarship described a sudden enamourment of French soldiers with Italian women, literature, and culture during the wars led by Charles VIII and Louis XII.[30] Yet, interactions between France and Italy were extensive throughout the Middle Ages, and there were many artistic and literary connections between the two cultures long before the period under discussion in this book. It is true, however, that these connections were strengthened by the repeated French invasions of Italy during the early sixteenth century, led by François I. While François had been raised speaking Italian, as well as learning about his own Italian heritage through his mother Louise de Savoie, Italy's humanist endeavours to rediscover and reinvent classical art and literature made a lasting impression on him. Following his return to France, he invited artists such as Rosso Fiorentino and Francesco Primaticcio to Fontainebleau, rewarding them with generous sums of money; he also introduced into France the *lecteurs royaux*, and began to collect a broad range of Italian writings — such as Boccaccio's *Decameron* — for the royal library.[31]

Yet French humanists grew increasingly resentful of their Italian predecessors. In the same way as Erasmus recommended not simply to reproduce the work of Cicero, but to defeat it and to leave it behind, so did French writers strive to surpass their Italian sources: the literary output of Italy was at once 'an inspiring model and a dangerous rival'.[32] In the second half of the sixteenth century, a number of prominent humanists began openly to challenge the Italian cultural, political, and commercial influence in France, and attitudes towards Italy became ever more hostile. The presence of the Italians in France — which was precipitated by the growing power of Catherine de' Medici — also coincided with the Wars of Religion: it is no coincidence that many of the most famous anti-Italian writers in this period (such as Innocent Gentillet and Henri Estienne) were Protestants, and opposed to the Italians who were broadly synonymous with the Catholics and with Machiavellian policies. It is at this point in the century that French writers focused with a new energy on their attempts to surpass Italian models, and many sought explicitly to overthrow the Italian cultural dominance in Europe. This book will trace this shift in French attitudes towards the Italians, using comic theatre as a lens through which to offer new perspectives on the tense and largely unstable relationship between these two cultures.

While comic theatre has never before been used to document in detail the politics of the Franco-Italian relationship in this period, there have been a great number of more general studies on the rapport between France and Italy. Jean Balsamo's *Les Rencontres des muses* and Lionello Sozzi's *Rome n'est plus Rome* have been indispensable in providing contextual foundations for the claims I make in this book, and both remain key guides to navigating the complex and ever-shifting relations between France and Italy.[33] Despite being completed over a century ago, Émile Picot's *Des Français qui ont écrit en italien au XVIe siècle* and his *Les Français italianisants au XVIe siècle* are still the most extensive accounts of the attempts of French writers to imitate Italian literature; several case studies in the present book — particularly the accounts of the works of Jodelle and Larivey — expand upon Picot's findings.[34] Finally, Henry Heller's *Anti-Italianism in Sixteenth-century France* is a crucial account of France's hostility towards Italy, especially towards the end of the period in question in this book.[35] The story of xenophobia outlined by Heller is retold from the angle not of war, nor of debate, but of comedy: a new set of nationalist tensions emerge from this genre, which was still experimental and which was still testing the boundaries of what drama could convey.

Methods

In this book I employ a dual framework, using both historical and textual exegesis to examine France's relationship with comedy and, in turn, with Italy. As part of my historical analysis I consider the political and cultural conditions of early modern France, including the reigns of various monarchs, the Wars of Religion, and debates surrounding the practice of *imitatio*, asking how these conditions helped to shape the thoughts of playwrights, patrons, and polemicists. Conversely, I employ textual analysis to provide new perspectives on historical context, providing a range of close readings which offer insights into the shifting political and cultural status of early modern France. Much of this textual analysis is comparative, taking into account French adaptations of Italian sources; Part III of this book focuses particularly on adaptations which take a particularly political or nationalist position against their models. This study compares across decades as well as across cultures, broadening our understanding of the move from medieval to humanist drama, which was not always clear-cut; such an approach also provides a more nuanced perspective on the crucial role of the Italians in bringing comedy to France, and on the ever-changing relationship throughout the century between France and Italy. This book thus draws on this reciprocal relationship between text and context, using history to shed light on the writing of comedy, and comedy to offer new insights into history.

Special attention is paid to a number of previously untapped or little-known manuscripts and early printed books. This study presents, for instance, an analysis of Charles Estienne's unpublished manuscript 'Livre des jeux et theatres antiques' [Book of ancient games and theatres], dating from around 1543, which contains the first extant sketches of a theatre completed by a French writer. This manuscript is held in the Vatican Library.[36] As part of this study I have also investigated the copy of the 1562 *editio princeps* of Jacques Grévin's comedies held at the Plantin-Moretus Museum in Antwerp, which contains previously unseen marginalia and corrections completed in the author's own hand.[37] This study thus strikes a balance between examining the comedies themselves and analysing paratexts surrounding the comedies, such as letters and prefaces. Gérard Genette has shown that paratexts are often a mode of entry into the text itself, used to guide and direct the reader's interpretation;[38] as Helen Smith and Louise Wilson have pointed out, however, paratexts are also inseparable from the historical context which informs them.[39] A focus on the paratext, then, complements the wider framework in this study of bringing together textual and contextual considerations.

This book is split into three parts, reflecting and exploring in turn this study's three material conditions of poetics, performance, and politics. Each part contains two chapters, which present various case studies on the condition they explore. Although these conditions are structured so as to create a distinct framework, they are still interconnected; by overlapping and interacting with one another, they create a richer overall picture of the various shifts in comic theatre and in the Franco-Italian relationship. Given that these shifts make it difficult to identify a clear development of the genre throughout the century — indeed, they help to show that no such linear development took place — this book does not follow a wholly sequential timeline of dates, though the structure is for the most part chronological.

Part I focuses on poetics, and concentrates on the period 1540 to 1552. It traces the first endeavours of writers to reinvent comedy in France, examining their attempts to establish the genre as a viable mode of humanist literary production — or indeed their efforts to prevent this from happening. The two chapters in this part consider not the comic plays, but the writings surrounding comedy, using close readings of prefatory and theoretical materials to assess early approaches to comic theatre in France before any ideas were put into practice. Chapter 1 explores the attempts of doctor and translator Charles Estienne to promote classically-inspired comic theatre in France in the early 1540s, and the innovative, if not entirely successful, arguments he proposes to convince humanists of its superiority to medieval theatre. I focus especially on his relationship with classical and Italian sources, also analysing a previously undiscovered manuscript to show that discussions about comic theatre, as well as about the usefulness of the Italian dramatic model as a crucial intermediary between ancient and contemporary, were far more prominent than has previously been thought. By comparing and contrasting the proliferation of viewpoints surrounding comic theatre in the mid-century, Chapter 2 further illustrates the forward-and-backward movement of comedy in France. This chapter explores in detail the treatment of comedy in the first full-length French poetic treatises, Thomas Sébillet's *Art poétique françoyse* [French Poetic Art] (1548) and Joachim Du Bellay's *Deffence, et illustration de la langue francoyse* [Defence and Illustration of the French Language] (1549); it also assesses the preface to Jean-Pierre de Mesmes's 1552 French translation of Ariosto's Italian comedy *I suppositi* [The Exchanged Ones]. Despite Estienne's exhortations for the reinvention of comedy in France, particularly by way of imitating Italian models, I propose that humanists remained both unfamiliar with the genre and unconvinced of its ability to enrich French literature.

Part II moves from poetics to performance, focusing on the period 1548 to 1558. In this part, I consider the effects on comic theatre of the increased Italian presence in France, paying special attention to the influence of this presence in the context of the French court. Both chapters in Part II explore a range of performances of Italian comedy in France and also look in detail at the Italian patrons of theatre at the courts: each chapter shows that the Italians in France played a fundamental role not only in persuading French writers to accept comedy as a viable mode of literary production, but also in prompting them to experiment with comic theatre. Chapter 3 provides an in-depth study of the 1548 performance of Bernardo Dovizi da Bibbiena's *La Calandra*, organised in celebration of the royal entry of Henri II and Catherine de' Medici into Lyons. By exploring a number of records of this event, this chapter asks how this performance put into practice many of the features which Estienne had outlined earlier in the decade, astonishing its spectators and setting a new standard at the courts for comic theatre. Chapter 4 offers close readings of two Italian comedies acted at the courts in the wake of *La Calandra*; it also analyses Estienne Jodelle's attempt to produce the first original comedy in French as well as a set of *mascherate* [masquerades], both of which at once imitate and compete with the Italian model. In this way, while both chapters identify the interactions of performance with poetics, looking back to the theoretical implications of comedy explored in Part I, they also look forward to the politics of comic writing and of cross-cultural exchange, the subject of Part III.

In Part III we turn to the years 1561 to 1580, when the violence and schism caused by the Wars of Religion were intensifying and when humanists were still seeking to forge a place for France in the European literary sphere. This part centres on the final material condition of politics, which in the context of this study denotes the unstable and increasingly hostile state of Franco-Italian relations. As outlined above, the admiration for Italian culture which characterised French poetics in earlier decades was being replaced by an antagonism and xenophobia which manifested themselves in resistance and rivalry across French writings. By examining in detail a range of comedies, focusing particularly on techniques such as characterisation, language, and deliberate manipulation of Italian sources, Part III provides new perspectives not just on the changing status of comedy towards the end of the century but also on the relationship between France and Italy. Chapter 5 examines Jacques Grévin's *Les Esbahis* (1561), France's first explicitly anti-Italian comedy. Although this play was based closely on Italian models, it both resists and rivals Italian culture to create an entirely unflattering picture of Italy, while at the same time promoting French culture and the achievements of its writers. Chapter 6 assesses Pierre de Larivey's *Les Six Premieres Comedies facecieuses* [The First Six Facetious Comedies] (1579) and Odet de Turnèbe's *Les Contens* [The Happy Ones] (1580), comparing and contrasting the increasingly innovative techniques used by playwrights to make a nationalist statement and to turn Italian comedy into a weapon against the Italians themselves.

This book seeks to complicate the standard narrative which has traditionally been told of the development of comic theatre in sixteenth-century France. Studies have often constructed a timeline of a neat and linear progression of humanist comedy, claiming that this progression led ultimately to an autonomous literary genre by the end of century. Yet, comedy during this period walked a knife edge of cultural and political sentiment, meeting variously with resistance from French writers and with artfulness as dramatists sought to transform it into a nationalist weapon. Although the relationship between France and Italy was productive — this book shows in more detail than before that the Italians played a crucial role in shaping French perspectives on and approaches to comedy — this relationship was also fraught with tensions which manifest themselves increasingly forcefully and in ever more inventive ways within the plays. While dramatists aimed to establish themselves as originators of the genre, they also aimed to compete with their Italian models in a way which at times left them open to failure, as in the case of Jodelle. Indeed, we see a substantial decrease in comic production towards the end of the century, which did not pick up again until the 1620s. This book, then, brings to light the complexity of the genre's emergence in France: it tells not a story of success, but one of experimentation, contest, and dispute.

Notes to the Introduction

1. Geoffrey Brereton, *French Comic Drama: From the Sixteenth to the Eighteenth Century* (London: Methuen, 1977), p. 7; Harold Lawton, *French Renaissance Dramatic Theory* (Manchester: Manchester University Press, 1949), p. 27.

2. Elliott Forsyth, 'Discussion: French Renaissance Tragedy and its Critics: A Reply to Donald Stone, Jr', *Renaissance Drama*, 2 (1969), 207–22 (p. 211).

3. See for example Niccolò Machiavelli's *La Mandragola* [The Mandrake Root], which blamed the French invasions for bringing an end to Italy's golden age ('In capo di dieci cominciorono, per la passata del re Carlo, le guerre in Italia, le quali ruinorono quella provincia' [Ten years ago the wars in Italy, which ruined this province, started with the invasion of King Charles]). Niccolò Machiavelli, *La Mandragola, Clizia*, ed. by Ezio Raimondi and Gian Mario Anselmi (Milan: Mursia, 1984), p. 72 (I.1). Pietro Aretino's *Il Marescalco* [The Master of the Horse], which accuses the French of bringing syphilis into Italy, dubs it the 'mal francioso' ('Il mal francioso con tutte le solennità delle gome, delle bolle e delle doglie' [The French disease, with all its solemnities of boils, swellings, and pains]). Pietro Aretino, *Il Marescalco*, in *Teatro*, ed. by Giovanna Rabitti, Carmine Boccia, and Enrico Garavelli, 2 vols (Rome: Salerno, 2010), II, 38 (I.6).

4. This comedy has come to be termed by many scholars as 'erudite comedy', following from the Italian stylisation as *commedia erudita*. Although others have called it 'neoclassical comedy', this term is too often associated with seventeenth-century theatre to appropriately describe its sixteenth-century counterpart.

5. An up-to-date study of the influence on the *commedia dell'arte* on sixteenth-century French comedy is long overdue. The most detailed work on this subject is still Armand Baschet's *Les Comédiens italiens à la cour de France sous Charles IX, Henri III, Henri IV et Louis XIII: d'après les lettres royales, la correspondance originale des comédiens, les registres de la trésorerie de l'épargne et autres documents* (Paris: Plon, 1882).

6. Only Robert Garnier made a living out of writing theatre; however, he showed little interest in comic plays. He wrote one tragi-comedy, but is best known for his tragedies.

7. Corinne Noirot, 'French Humanist Comedy in Search of an Audience: The Case of Jean de la Taille', in *French Renaissance and Baroque Drama: Text, Performance, Theory*, ed. by Michael Meere (Newark: University of Delaware Press, 2015), pp. 83–100 (p. 84).

8. For plot synopses of each major case study in this book, see Appendix III.

9. See for instance Brian Jeffery's *French Renaissance Comedy, 1552–1630* (Oxford: Clarendon Press, 1969), which has long been considered the standard work on the subject to be printed in the English language.

10. Lucien Pinvert, *Jacques Grévin (1538–1570): sa vie, ses écrits, ses amis, étude biographique et littéraire* (Paris: A. Fontemoing, 1899), p. 132.

11. Anon., *Le Nouveau Pathelin* (Paris: Jean Saint-Denis, 1530); Anon., *Le Testament de Pathelin* (Paris: Denys Janot, [n.d.]). For more information on the farce, as well as a vast compilation of the most popular French farces, see the *Nouveau recueil des farces françaises des XVᵉ et XVIᵉ siècles*, ed. by Kristoffer Nyrop and Émile Picot (Paris: Damascène Morgand et Charles Fatout, 1880); see also *Recueil des farces (1450–1550)*, ed. by André Tissier, 13 vols (Geneva: Droz, 1986–2000).

12. Arthur Tilley, *The Literature of the French Renaissance*, 2 vols (Cambridge: Cambridge University Press, 1904), II, 56; see Sara Beam, *Laughing Matters: Farce and the Making of Absolutism in France* (New York: Cornell University Press, 2007), p. 46.

13. More information on the *sottie* can be found throughout *Le Comique verbal en France au XVIe siècle: actes du colloque organisé par l'Institut d'Études Romanes et le Centre de Civilisation Française de l'Université de Varsovie*, ed. by Halina Lewicka (Warsaw: Warsaw University Press, 1981); Picot also edited a collection of France's best-known *sotties*: *Recueil général des sotties*, ed. by Émile Picot, 3 vols (Paris: Firmin Didot, 1902–12).

14. Charles Lenient, *La Satire en France au Moyen âge* (Paris: Hachette, 1893), p. 351. This monologue influenced a number of sixteenth-century writers, as Part III of this book will explore.

15. More information on the *sermon joyeux* can also be found in Armand Strubel, *Le Théâtre au Moyen Âge: naissance d'une littérature dramatique* (Rosny-sous-Bois: Bréal, 2003), p. 127. For a

collection of these *sermons joyeux*, see *Recueil des sermons joyeux*, ed. by Jelle Koopmans (Geneva: Droz, 1988).

16. A concise summary of medieval comedy as political propaganda is given by Jessica Milner-Davies, 'Farce', in *Encyclopedia of Humor Studies*, ed. by Salvatore Attardo, 2 vols (London & New York: SAGE Publications, 2014), I, 233–36.

17. See Lucy Rayfield, 'Rewriting Laughter in Early Modern Europe', in *The Palgrave Handbook of Humour, History, and Methodology*, ed. by Hannah Burrows and Daniel Derrin (London: Palgrave Macmillan, 2021), pp. 71–91.

18. The use of classical comedy as a language-learning tool is discussed in Kristian Jensen, 'The Humanist Reform of Latin and Latin Teaching', in *The Cambridge Companion to Renaissance Humanism*, ed. by Jill Kraye (Cambridge: Cambridge University Press, 1998), pp. 63–81 (p. 67).

19. See Raymond Lebègue, 'Tableau de la comédie française de la Renaissance', *BHR*, 8 (1946), 278–344 (p. 294).

20. Jean de La Taille, *La Famine, ou les gabeonites, tragedie prise de la Bible et suivant celle de Saül, ensemble plusieurs autres oeuvres poëtiques de Jehan de La Taille de Bondaroy* (Paris: Frédéric Morel, 1573), ff. 65^v–99^v; Jean-Antoine de Baïf, *Le Brave*, ed. by Malcolm Quainton, in *Œuvres complètes*, ed. by Malcolm Quainton and Elizabeth Vinestock, 3 vols (Paris: Champion, 2017), III.

21. Gillian Jondorf, *French Renaissance Tragedy: The Dramatic Word* (Cambridge: Cambridge University Press, 1990).

22. Salvatore Di Maria, *The Italian Tragedy in the Renaissance: Cultural Realities and Theatrical Innovations* (Lewisburg, PA: Bucknell University Press, 2002), p. 211; Raymond Lebègue, *La Tragédie française de la Renaissance* (Brussels: Office de Publicité, 1954), p. 72.

23. Pierre de Bourdeille, seigneur de Brantôme, *Vies des dames illustres françoises et etrangères*, ed. by Louis Moland (Paris: Garnier, 1868), p. 44.

24. See Thomas Lawrenson, *The French Stage in the XVIIth Century: A Study in the Advent of the Italian Order* (New York: AMS Press, 1986), p. 85. Excerpts of the letters detailing generous payments given by the King to various Italian troupes in the 1570s are provided in William Howarth's comprehensive edited volume *French Theatre in the Neo-classical Era, 1550–1789*, ed. by William Howarth (Cambridge: Cambridge University Press, 1997), pp. 82–83.

25. One such work is Michael Meere's *French Renaissance and Baroque Drama: Text, Performance, Theory* (Newark: University of Delaware Press, 2015), esp. pp. xv–xxxi ('Introduction') and pp. 39–62 (Meere and Caroline Gates's chapter 'Farce, Community, and the Performativity of Violence in Rabelais's *Quart Livre*: The Chiquanous Episode').

26. Patrizia De Capitani Bertrand, *Du spectaculaire à l'intime: un siècle de 'commedia erudita' en Italie et en France* (Paris: Champion, 2005).

27. Charles Mazouer, *Le Théâtre français de la Renaissance* (Paris: Champion, 2002).

28. Émile Chasles, *La Comédie en France au seizième siècle* (Geneva: Slatkine Reprints, 1969).

29. *Théâtre français de la Renaissance*, ed. by Enea Balmas and others, 3 series, 21 vols (Florence: Olschki, 1986–2018). In this book I employ both series *La Comédie à l'époque d'Henri II et de Charles IX* and *La Comédie à l'époque d'Henri III*, and reference each individual volume accordingly.

30. See for example Jules Michelet, *Histoire de France*, 17 vols (Paris: Chamerot, 1855), VII, 1–40; Alfred Forbes Johnson, *Sixteenth-century French Printing* (London: E. Benn, 1928), p. 5.

31. Robert Knecht, *Francis I* (Cambridge: Cambridge University Press, 1984), pp. 264–66. Even Baldassare Castiglione's 1528 *Il libro del Cortegiano* [The Book of the Courtier] recognises François's endeavour to replicate the Italian humanism in France: 'Se la buona sorte vuole, che Monsignore d'Angolen (come si spera), succede alla corona, estimo, che si come la Gloria dell'arme fiorisce, e risplende in Francia; cosi vi debba ancor con supremo ornamento fiorir quelle delle lettere' [If good fortune wishes it so, that Monseigneur d'Angoulême rises to the crown, as it is hoped, in the same way as the glory of arms is flourishing and shining in France, so too will the glory of letters flourish in the supreme state]. Baldassare Castiglione, *Il libro del Cortegiano*, ed. by Giulio Preti (Turin: Einaudi, 1965), p. 70.

32. Erasmus, *Il Ciceroniano*, ed. by Angiolo Gambara (Brescia: La Scuola, 1965), p. 116, cited in George Pigman, 'Versions of Imitation in the Renaissance', *Renaissance Quarterly*, 33.1 (1980),

1–32 (p. 24); Eric MacPhail, *The Voyage to Rome in French Renaissance Literature* (Saratoga, CA: Anma Libri, 1990), p. 34.

33. Jean Balsamo, *Les Rencontres des muses: italianisme et anti-italianisme dans les lettres françaises de la fin du XVIᵉ siècle* (Geneva: Slatkine, 1992); Lionello Sozzi, *Rome n'est plus Rome: la polémique anti-italienne et autres essais sur la Renaissance; suivis de 'La dignité de l'homme'* (Paris: Champion, 2002).

34. Émile Picot, *Des français qui ont écrit en italien au XVIᵉ siècle* (Paris: E. Bouillon, 1902), and *Les Français italianisants au XVIᵉ siècle*, 2 vols (Paris: Champion, 1906).

35. Pauline Smith, *The Anti-courtier Trend in Sixteenth-century French Literature* (Geneva: Droz, 1966); Henry Heller, *Anti-Italianism in Sixteenth-century France* (Toronto: University of Toronto Press, 2003).

36. I identified this manuscript together with Richard Cooper, of the University of Oxford. Charles Estienne, 'Livre des jeux et theatres antiques', Biblioteca Apostolica Vaticana (BAV), *Reg. Lat.* 1697.

37. Jacques Grévin, *Le theatre de Jaques Grevin de Cler-mont en Beauvaisis, à tres illustre et treshaulte princesse ladame Claude de France, Duchesse de Lorraine. Ensemble, la seconde partie de L'Olimpe & de la Gelodacrye* (Paris: Vincent Sertenas and Guillaume Barbé, 1562), Museum Plantin-Moretus, R 19. 34.

38. See Gérard Genette, *Seuils* (Paris: Seuil, 1987), esp. pp. 7–21.

39. See *Renaissance Paratexts*, ed. by Helen Smith and Louise Wilson (Cambridge: Cambridge University Press, 2014), esp. pp. 1–14.

PART I

The Poetics of Comedy in Renaissance France (1540–52)

CHAPTER 1

Charles Estienne: France's Innovator of Comic Theatre

J'espere que la trouverez telle, que si Terence mesmes l'eust composée en Italien, à peine mieux l'eust il sceu diter, inventer ou deduyre.

[I hope that you find it such, that if Terence himself had written it in Italian, he would hardly have been able to improve on its expression, invention, or ability to amuse.]

(Charles Estienne, in *Les Abusez*, 1540)

Humanist and doctor Charles Estienne is celebrated in historiography for his anatomical publications, and his guide to dissection remains famous for its detailed wood engravings and annotations.[1] Estienne is also remembered for his discovery of the canal running along the spinal cord, and for his unprecedented description of the condition now known as syringomyelia.[2] His anatomical work has so far eclipsed his status as a forerunner of comic theatre: few critics have paid attention to Estienne's translations of ancient and Italian drama, and even fewer have examined his accompanying thoughts on comedy. Although he was a talented doctor, Estienne was also the first to make the case for comic drama, promoting it not as a money-spinner for teaching Latin in schools, but as an autonomous literary genre to be recognised as such by humanists and playwrights. In 1540, at around the same time as he finished studying for his medical degree, Estienne completed a French translation of the 1532 Italian comedy *Gl'ingannati* [The Deceived] by the Accademia degli Intronati [Academy of the Stunned],[3] the first translation of an Italian play to be completed in any language.[4] Estienne prefaced his translation, entitled *Les Abusez*, with a dedicatory letter to the Dauphin of France, in which he discusses the position of French comedy in relation to its medieval, classical, and Italian counterparts. A year later Estienne began editing Terence's *Andria*, and in 1542 he translated it into French, thus making available the first translation of an ancient comedy in French prose.[5] Estienne prefaced this translation — entitled *L'Andrie* — with his own treatise on comedy, the first to be written in the French language.[6] As we will see in this chapter, several ideas from this treatise are reproduced from his earlier letter to the Dauphin. In around 1543 Estienne also composed a brief guide to classical theatre, which he entitled 'Livre des jeux et theatres antiques'. This guide was never printed and until now has been unknown to scholars; however, it is extant in manuscript form, and contains the earliest French sketches of a theatre,

drawn by Estienne himself.[7] Although he is by no means a skilled artist, his sketches
— discussed for the first time in the present volume — afford us a clearer insight
into the role of classical and Italian playwrights in the reinvention of drama in
France, as well as into contemporary debates surrounding the principle of *imitatio*.
Close readings of Estienne's largely forgotten treatise and letter also allow for a
new story to be told about the status of humanist comic theatre in France in its
earliest stages, providing new evidence that attempts to revive the classical theatrical
tradition in France were well and truly underway over a decade earlier than had
been previously thought.

Estienne and the Classical Models

Terentian comedy was considered in France to be an excellent vehicle of good Latin,
and Terence's plays had long been used as language manuals for schoolchildren,
as well as at the University of Paris. Readings and performances of Terence's
comedies had certainly taken place, aimed not only at language-learning but also
at providing training for public speech, composure, and diction.[8] Although it is
true that numerous French writers (such as Jodelle and Grévin) must have been
inspired by performances or readings which they witnessed at school, many did
not deem Roman comedy to be suitable entertainment, perhaps because of its
association with pedagogy or the lack of availability of the plays in French.[9] A 1502
public performance of Terence's *Andria* recited in the original Latin by students at
the Cour de l'Evêché, for instance, bored spectators to the point that they chased
the students off the stage.[10] The editions most commonly used for educational
purposes had been printed by Robert Estienne, Charles's brother.[11] In 1532 Robert
claimed that the clarifications and corrections made in his most complete edition
for schools 'permettent desormais de comprendre Terence' [allow for Terence now
to be understood];[12] however, the treatise, letter, and sketches completed by Charles
sought to show that classical comedy was still being appreciated for the wrong
qualities. His aim, instead, was to elevate ancient comedy from the discourse of
language-learning tool to the literary canon, worthy of revival not only in schools
but also on the stage.

Estienne's intentions to redefine the cultural worth of comedy are underscored
even in the titles of his translations. Previous editions of Terence had emphasized
the plays' potential to teach language or oration (e.g., the *Ex Terentii comoediis
optimae, copiosissimae atque certissimae loquendi formulae* [The Best, Richest and Most
Reliable Turns of Phrase from the Comedies of Terence] and the *Ex Terentii
comoediis colloquendi formulae ceu Flosculi* [Turns of Phrase in the Style of Flosculus
from the Comedies of Terence]);[13] even the subtitle of Estienne's own previous
Latin edition of Terence had given prominence to its pedagogical value: 'Addita est
constructionis ratio, tum vulgaris, tum etiam latina, item scholia, quae selectiorum
vocabulorum vim et bene latinarum locutionum formulas contineant' [In addition,
an explanation of constructions is offered, both for the Latin and the vernacular,
and there is also a commentary which provides the meaning of the more difficult

words as well as the rules pertaining to good Latin lexis].[14] Yet in the title of his 1542 French translation, Estienne omits all references to Latin-learning or to diction, claiming instead that his translation will be of interest to 'des bons espritz, studieux des antiques recreations' [excellent minds, who pore over ancient pastimes]: he will draw attention to comedy as a long-established form of entertainment. In the opening lines of his treatise, Estienne reiterates this same emphasis on the content and not the language of Terence's comedies, setting out his reasons for translating the *Andria*: '[Je] l'ay faict principalement afin que l'on prenne desormais quelque goust à l'autheur, qui entre les anciens a esté tousjours estimé le bien eloquent, et tres excellent compositeur de Comedies' [I did it mainly so that appreciation would finally be shown for the author, who was, among the ancients, always regarded as the most eloquent and excellent composer of comedies] (*L'Andrie*, p. 349). Given the early modern significance of the term *auteur* as related to 'authority', Estienne asserts that attention should be turned to Terence's status as the creator of comic theatre, and to the genre of comedy itself, instead of focusing solely on his model Latin.[15] Estienne then compares the work of Terence with other forms of comic theatre, which consisted mainly of the farce: '[Notre ouvrage] est tumbé en telle ignorance et cecité, que ce qu'il faict pour le present en telles matieres, ne sent rien moins que sa comedie' [Our work has fallen into such ignorance and blindness, that what it currently produces resembles nothing of his comedy] (*L'Andrie*, p. 349). Here Estienne suggests that the quality of theatre has diminished precisely because of a lack of knowledge about ancient drama. He proposes to help his readers by enlightening them on Terence's methods for composing comedy, focusing on 'la maniere qu'il avoit à bien disposer et ordonner le sens et la matiere dont il escrivoit' [the way in which he arranged and ordered his meanings and the subjects of which he wrote] (*L'Andrie*, p. 349). It is only through overturning his readers' 'ignorance and blindness' that Estienne might enable them to implement Terence's methods in their own work, thereby restoring comedy to its former excellence.

Conversely, while it is clear from Estienne's comments on contemporary comedy that only the farce was widely regarded as suitable entertainment, Estienne does imply that certain peers had recently shown an interest in ancient comic theatre: '[P]lusieurs me semblent beaucoup travaillez à entendre la rayson et maniere des Comedies anciennes' [It seems to me that a few people are eager to understand the functions and foibles of ancient comedies] (*L'Andrie*, p. 349). As a member of the family of Paris's most prominent printer-booksellers — his brother had recently been named *Imprimeur du Roy pour le latin et l'hébreu* [the King's official printer of works in Latin and Hebrew] — Estienne was well connected to the foremost humanists of his day, editing the works of Lazare de Baïf and tutoring Baïf's son, travelling across France with Ronsard, and printing works by prominent writers such as Jean Du Bellay.[16] Some of Estienne's contemporaries had shown an interest in classical tragedy (Baïf, who translated Sophocles' tragedy *Electra* in 1537, had proposed to use classical tragedy to reinvent the morality play); yet, the only writer to mention comedy during these years was Jacques Peletier du Mans, who translates Horace's section on comedy as part of his 1541 French edition of the *Ars poetica*.[17] Estienne's comment — as well as his title, drawing the attention of those who 'pore over ancient pastimes' — suggests that discourse surrounding the status of comedy was present in the early 1540s, most likely among his fellow humanists: his interest in classical theatre was thus not an anomaly, but part of an ongoing conversation. Nonetheless, given that these humanists would have been accomplished in Latin, Estienne's decision to provide a French translation of the *Andria* alongside his treatise indicates that he wanted to popularise Roman comedy also outside of the literary and cultural elite, allowing those who were not fluent in Latin the opportunity to engage with Roman comedy. Additionally, the circulation of the comedy in the inexpensive pocket-sized (16mo) format suggests that the text was intended to be available not just to pedagogues but also to a broader audience: perhaps not quite a 'popular readership', as the category is set out in Henri-Jean Martin and Roger Chartier's study of print history, but possibly schoolchildren.[18] As well as deepening knowledge of and appreciation for Roman comedy among learned circles, then, Estienne's translation sought to reach and to inspire interest in a younger and more general audience, who may previously have been familiar only with forms such as the farce.

Estienne and the Italian Models

Like many of his humanist peers, Estienne understood the requisites of contemporary writing through reading and replicating its classical counterpart, seeking, in a well-known paradox, to imitate ancient rhetorical and poetic techniques in order to introduce new genres into his national literature. By the time that Estienne started work on his translation of *Gl'ingannati* (*Les Abusez*) in 1540, the Italians were widely regarded as crucial intermediaries between ancient and contemporary, having already reinvented several literary categories, such as the epic poem. Guillaume de Postel commented in 1542 that the Italian descendants of Pliny and Lucretius (the Italians being the inheritors of ancient Roman culture, according to the notion of *translatio studii*) were revered by French courtiers almost as demi-gods.[19] Estienne too was an Italophile, having studied in Padua and Bologna during his late twenties (1530–34) and moving back to Italy at the end of the 1530s to work as tutor to the seven-year-old Jean-Antoine de Baïf.[20] Estienne was fluent in Italian, had made many prominent Italian friends (such as the Venetian scholar-printer Paolo Manuzio),[21] and was keen to popularise Italian literature in France: soon after taking joint ownership of his father's print shop, for instance, he printed the first edition in French of Niccolò Machiavelli's seminal 1532 *Il Principe*; he also translated into French and printed the *Paradossi* (1543), Ortensio Lando's controversial collection of *sententiae*.[22] Estienne was no doubt aware of the Italian development of humanist comic theatre: it is likely that he had seen one of the many university performances of Roman and Italian comedy during his studies, and print editions of such plays were readily available, with the comedies of Ariosto leading the way in terms of popularity.[23] It is possible that Estienne acquired a copy of *Gl'ingannati* during his stay in Venice in 1540, where it had been printed three years prior.[24]

Prior to Estienne's translation, *Les Abusez*, no Italian comedies had been printed across the French border, and troupes of Italian comic actors had not yet reached French towns.[25] As well as being the first writer to translate into French prose an ancient comedy, Estienne's bid to make available and accessible an Italian play in France was unprecedented. As reflected by the full title of his translation, *Comedie à la maniere des anciens, et de pareille matiere, intitulée Les Abusez* [Comedy in the Style of the Ancients, and of the Same Subject Matter, entitled *Les Abusez*], he aims to draw attention to the Italians' successful replication of classical theatre in their own language and context. This idea of the Italians as important intermediaries between classical and contemporary is one which he reiterates in his prefatory letter to the Dauphin: 'J'espere que la trouverez telle, que si Terence mesmes l'eust composée en Italien, à peine mieux l'eust il sceu diter, inventer ou deduyre' [I hope that you find it such, that if Terence himself had written it in Italian, he would hardly have been able to improve on its expression, invention, or ability to amuse] (*Les Abusez*, p. 9).[26] Here Estienne asserts that the Italians have reinvented ancient theatre so successfully that their comedy is indistinguishable from the works of Terence: Italian dramatists and their classical predecessors are discussed on equal terms, and the former are presented as an ideal, and more immediate, model for imitation. Given that learned circles would already have understood Italian, it is again clear that Estienne's translation and accompanying letter were intended for a more popular readership, such as the merchant classes or school or college attendees.[27] Estienne's intention to show that classical comedy was worthy of attention and imitation stretched to an audience beyond those who 'travaillez à entendre [... les] Comedies anciennes', and it is possible that he sought to reach a broader spectrum of readers who may decide not only to write, but also to watch or to act in a play.

Reinventing Classical and Italian *dispositio* in Comic Theatre

Medieval writers had frequently misinterpreted how classical comedies should be performed. Initially, it was judged that plays should be read aloud by one person from a pulpit-style structure, while actors mimed the accompanying gestures below.[28] Although it was recognised in the mid-1400s that actors should recite the lines themselves as well as performing suitable gestures, the style of standing still and delivering a speech continued in the fifteenth and sixteenth centuries, manifesting itself in sub-branches of comedy such as the *sermon joyeux*. Estienne criticises the verbosity of contemporary French playwrights, suggesting that they should again take as examples the comedies of their classical ancestors, who understood the importance of brevity: 'N'ayants [pas] encor' observé la maniere de taire et suplier, ce que facilement sans exprimer se pourrait entendre: qui est un des poinctz en quoy les anciens facteurs mettoient plus de peine' [They have not yet observed how best to keep quiet and to compensate for words, for that which could be very easily understood without speaking aloud; this is one of the elements over which the ancient writers took most care] (*Les Abusez*, p. 2). Other medieval experimentations with drama had adopted an opposite style. The farce, for example, centred not on words but on exaggerated gestures, such as chases or beatings. Estienne writes that this focus on movement often resulted in a poorly-constructed plot, which he condemns as 'quelque badinage, sans autre invention' [a bit of nonsense, without other invention] (*Les Abusez*, p. 2). Advising playwrights to abandon this style of overblown action and to instead imitate the ancients, Estienne points out that it was only when classical comedians had removed the excessively physical elements from their plays that they were able to find success and to greatly delight their audiences: 'Les anciens abolirent telles folies, comme pernicieuses et plustot incitatives de noyses et debatz que de plaisir et delectation [...] au lieu desquelles folies, trouverent la Comedie, qu'ils apelloient nouvelle' [The ancients abolished such idiocies, judging them to be harmful and more likely to incite boredom and quarrels than pleasure and delight [...]; in place of such foolishness, they discovered Comedy, which they called new] (*Les Abusez*, p. 3). Here Estienne refers to the so-called 'new' comedy which had replaced the coarse, Aristophanic 'old' comedy, its chief exponents being Menander in Greek and Terence in Latin.[29] By striking a balance between the words and actions of their plays, relying too heavily on neither and looking to the classical writers as suitable models for imitation, Estienne suggests that French writers could incite a similar 'plaisir et delectation' in their spectators.

Following his encouragement for a balance between the use of words and action, in his letter Estienne provides, for the first time in the French language, instructions on how both should be structured in comedy. Again, he draws on classical theatre as a foundation for his advice, praising the *dispositio* of ancient comic writers: 'Je ne puis assez louër, mon Seigneur [...] la façon de disposer et poursuyvre leur sens et argument' [I can't praise enough, my Lord [...] the way in which they arranged and pursued their meanings and argument] (*Les Abusez*, p. 1).[30] He later specifies that classical comedy was arranged into acts and scenes: 'Toutes comedies estoient divisées en cinq ou six actes' [All comedies were divided into five or six acts] (*Les Abusez*, p. 6). Peletier's aforementioned translation of Horace's *Ars poetica* has previously been thought to be the first description in the French language of this structure; however, Estienne's description precedes Peletier's by a year. In this way, Estienne's comment also consists of the first known use of the French terms *acte* and *scène* to denote divisions in drama. Additionally, it is clear from Estienne's discussion — which provides definitions of the act and scene — that neither was a well-known concept in France: 'Quand deux personnages ou troys avoient devisé, et tenu propos ensemble, et que l'on se retiroit, ou qu'il en venoit un autre en nouveau propos, ilz apelloient cela une scene' [When two or three characters chatted and made conversation together, and one left; or when another turned up to discuss something different, that was called a scene] (*Les Abusez*, p. 6). As well as clarifying for his reader how to identify a scene, Estienne also sets out its usefulness: 'Et par ce moyen jamais ne demeuroit l'eschaffault vuyde, en n'y avoit personnaige sur le pulpit, qui n'y fust necessaire, ou pour parler, ou pour escouter les autres à quelque intention' [And in this way the stage was never left empty, and there was never an unnecessary character present, who did not need to speak or listen to the others for some reason] (*L'Andrie*, p. 355). By explaining the importance of clearing the stage,

Estienne considers comic theatre from a visual perspective, again emphasising the idea that classical comedy should be brought to life, rather than remain only in textbooks.

Estienne's account of the division of a comedy into acts and scenes is clearly founded on classical poetics. Yet his conception of a scene's dual purpose — never to leave the stage empty, and to remove any superfluous characters — has no precedent in ancient writings, and instead appears to be derived from an Italian source. Giovanni Battista Giraldi Cinzio's *Discorso intorno al comporre delle commedie e delle tragedie* [Discourse on Composing Tragedies and Comedies] (printed in 1554, though written and circulated in various forms far earlier), describes a similar function of the scene, and outlines the audience's frustration at redundant actors on stage when such a structure is lacking: 'Cosa veramente sconvenevole, perchè il vedere gli istrioni in iscena che non favellino, e si stiano tuttavia negli occhi degli spettatori, reca fastidio' [This is a very displeasing thing, because seeing actors on stage who are not speaking, but who are in any case blocking the view of the spectators, causes great annoyance].[31] Acts and scenes had been employed in Italy since the early 1500s, and Estienne would have witnessed first-hand their functions during his travels; it is also possible that Estienne had read Giraldi Cinzio's *Discorso* in manuscript form while in Venice. Having explained and justified this use of *dispositio* in theatre, Estienne draws a direct contrast with the lack of structure in medieval French farces and morality plays: '[La disposition] est une des choses, en laquelle plus nous faillons et que plus je trouve inepte en noz jeux et saintes comedies' [Dispositio is one of the things in which we fail the most, and which I find most foolish in our farces and sacred plays] (*Les Abusez*, p. 7). Estienne uses his prefatory material not just to discredit medieval drama, but also to provide a framework for imitation, based on the classics and also on more recent Italian innovations. His discussion of comedy's visual impact also sets out a trajectory for its reinvention not only in written form, but also on the stage.

Another facet of *dispositio* in classical comic theatre promoted by Estienne is the interval, which he describes in his letter to the Dauphin: 'On voyoit des menestriers, buffons, sotereaux, et autres telz [...] qui par les intervales des actes delectoient le peuple' [One would see musicians, fools, acrobats, and others of their kind [...] who would delight the audience during intervals] (*Les Abusez*, p. 6).[32] The interval had been reintroduced towards the end of the fifteenth century in Italy as a theatre practice, most often in Ferrara and Mantua, and in the *sacre rappresentazioni* as well as in comedy.[33] Possibly inspired by the Italian term *intermezzo* (in use since the early 1500s and popularised by writers such as Machiavelli), this is the first recorded instance of the word *intervale* in French referring to a break in a play, which was later to become standard in French theatrical lexis.[34] In the same way as Estienne defines the terms *acte* and *scènes*, which seem to have been largely unknown in French, Estienne provides a clarification for his readers of the term *intervale* by adding 'des actes', ensuring that his readers understood the point at which intervals would have taken place. As well as enlightening his readers as to the function of the interval, Estienne encourages its reinvention in French drama. Not only does he insist that the interval is successful in evoking pleasure (it would 'delect[e] le peuple' [delight the audience] and 'recréer les espritz' [reinvigorate their minds]); in his treatise accompanying *L'Andrie*, he goes so far as to claim that acts were invented precisely to accommodate the interval: '[L'acte] fut inventé [...] pour recréer les espritz par intervalles' [The act was invented [...] to reinvigorate their minds with intervals] (*L'Andrie*, p. 355). There are no recorded precedents for this idea — indeed, no classical or Italian writers assert that the act and the interval are mutually supportive — and it is likely that Estienne himself devised this notion as a means of promoting its revival in France.

Making his final point on the interval, Estienne again turns his focus from written style and structure to the visual impact of comedy. He praises the skills of classical actors who performed during intervals, and provides definitions of types of performers such as the *Ludi* and the *Aretalogi*.[35] Estienne draws particular attention to the *Pantomimi*, pointing out their versatility: 'Un Pantomimus seul jouoit une grande part d'une Tragedie ou Comedie, en changeant souvent de masque, d'habit, et de voix, ainsi que font aujourd'huy en Italie, ceulx que lon apelle Boufons' [Just one *Pantomimus* played a big part in a tragedy or comedy, often changing their mask, costume, and voice, just as they do today in Italy, the ones who call themselves fools] (*L'Andrie*, p. 353). Estienne's comparison of the classical *Pantomimus* with the contemporary Italian fool is a further example of Italy's status as an intermediary between ancient and contemporary. As well as having been able to write comedy that is indistinguishable from Terence, they have also successfully replicated a prominent category of ancient performer: again, they are set out by Estienne as an important, and more immediate, comic model for France, worthy of imitation not only in print but also in practice.

Translatio, *imitatio*, and *paraphrasis* in Comic Theatre

As considered above, Estienne advocates a reliance on the Italian example — via the vital influence of the ancients — to facilitate the reinvention of comic theatre in France. Yet occasionally, he favours the work of Italian playwrights over their classical counterparts. A major aspect of classical comedy improved on by the Italians, Estienne claims, is their literary form. Like ancient theatre, the majority of French drama in the Middle Ages (for instance, the *Farce de Maistre Pierre Pathelin*) had been composed in verse. A number of Italian comic writers rejected this form, instead choosing to adopt a prosaic style, a decision which Estienne praises in his letter to the Dauphin:

> Tous noz Françoys se sont contraints aux rithmes de leur langue: comme aussi les anciens, ont tousiours fait à leurs metres. Mais les bons personnages compositeurs de ceste Comedie, voyants que les vers ostent la liberté du langage, et proprieté d'aucunes phrases: ont beaucoup mieux aymé faire reciter leur Comedie en belle prose (pour mieux monstrer l'efait et sens d'icelle) que de s'assubietir à la rithme. (*Les Abusez*, pp. 9–10)[36]

> [All of our French writers have constrained themselves to the rhymes of their language, just as the ancients always adhered to their own metre. But the great

composers of this comedy, recognising that verse impedes the freedom of language and the attributes of some expressions, much preferred to have their comedy acted in delightful prose (to better show the effects and meanings therein), and not to subject it to rhyme.]

Here Estienne uses the contrasting images of subjection and freedom to express the strain that verse places on comedy, as opposed to the increased clarity offered by the use of prose. According to Estienne, verse in comic drama imposes three main limits: firstly, on a playwright's ability to use language freely; secondly, on language's many nuances; and thirdly, on the possible meanings and arguments which a writer intends to convey with their comedy. The verb *s'assubietir* also suggests that these limits are artificial and unnecessary. By contrast, the unrestricted use of language that prose affords comedy will improve the clarity and impact of a play's meaning and the language it uses. Estienne's message, then, is that the style of the Italians — who successfully freed comedy from the constraints of verse — should be favoured by French writers over the classical comic form.

Estienne's advice for French authors to improve on the ancient style reflects contemporary debates on imitative rhetoric, which focused largely on the power of emulation over imitation. A well-known collection of debates on the improvement of the classics by Italian writers such as Giovanni Francesco Pico della Mirandola and Pietro Bembo had recently been printed in France by Estienne's stepfather Simon de Colines, sparking heated arguments among French humanists.[37] Instructions for writers not to follow but to surpass their forerunners began to emerge throughout discussions of *imitatio* in France, and while Estienne's advice for comic authors to improve on the ancients is the first of its kind in French, it follows on from many such exhortations in Italy.[38] For instance, Lodovico Dolce set out in the prologue to his comedy *Fabritia* extensive arguments for overshadowing and not just imitating the classics. One protagonist claims that 'E se bene gli antichi tolsero le Comedie da' Greci; non ne segue però [...] che gli intelletti de' moderni non possano in questa parte avanzarli, come gli hanno similmente avanzati in altre cose' [And if even if the ancients borrowed the comedies of the Greeks, there is no reason that [...] the learned of our day cannot surpass them in this field, just as they have done in others].[39] Like Estienne, Dolce provides the example of the Italian replacement of verse with prose as one major improvement on the ancients:

Le solevano finalmente che gli antichi compor tutte in versi: e hoggidì la maggior parte de' nostri ve l'hanno date, e ve ne danno in prosa [...]. Non sapete voi quel detto: che si deve lodare i tempi passati, e viver secondo l'uso de' presenti?[40]

[A final opposition was that the ancients composed everything in verse; nowadays, the majority of comedies which have been and are given to you are in prose [...]. Don't you know that saying, that we must praise past times, and live according to customs of the present?]

Drawing on the discourse of emulation, which was instigated and upheld by many Italian contemporaries, Estienne suggests that French theatre can also improve on its first, ancient models.

Subsequently, Estienne translates into prose the *Andria*, which had originally been written in verse. In his treatise he again juxtaposes freedom with subjection and constraint to reiterate the strain that verse imposes on a play:

> Je ne l'ay point mise en rithme [...] pour autant que la liberté d'un traducteur, tel que les Grecz appelloient *Paraphraste* (c'est a dire, qui rend le sens, la phrase, et l'esprit d'une matiere, sans contrainte du langage) facilement se pert soubz la subjection du vers. (*L'Andrie*, p. 349)

> [I did not render it into rhyme [...] in as such that the freedom of a translator, which is what the Greeks called *Paraphraste* (that is to say, the person who gives the meanings, expressions, and spirit of a subject, without being constrained by language), is often lost under the subjection of verse.]

Drawing on the classical convention of paraphrase, Estienne urges the translator to reject verse translations, which restrict the freedom of language to convey properly a play's subject. While Estienne observes that *paraphrase* is originally a Greek term, his stance is clearly modelled on an argument by the Roman Cicero, who had defended the utility of paraphrasing a text, especially in terms of rendering into prose the verse original.[41] Although the frontiers between translation, imitation, and paraphrase were often fluid in sixteenth-century France, Estienne's argument does reflect contemporary discourse surrounding *imitatio* and *translatio*.[42] Estienne would have been well aware of his brother Robert's definition of *paraphrasis* in his 1531 *Dictionarium*, one of the most prominent Latin dictionaries of the century, which detailed that the paraphrast 'non literam ex litera, sed sensum e sensu transfert, quasi iuxta loquens' [does not put one letter into another; he puts one meaning into another, exactly as though he were talking along with his model].[43] Estienne, too, suggests that the meaning of the play — rather than the precise words used — should be a translator's priority. He would also have been familiar with Estienne Dolet's 1540 guide *La Maniere de bien traduire d'une langue en autre* [How to Successfully Translate from One Language to Another], which had, like Estienne's treatise and letter, used imagery of freedom and subjection to convince translators to move away from restrictions of the source text: 'Je ne veulx taire icy la follie d'aulcuns traducteurs: lesquelz au lieu de liberté se submettent à servitude [...] ilz sont si sots, qu'ilz s'efforcent de rendre ligne par ligne, ou vers par vers' [I cannot keep quiet about the madness of some translators, who, instead of freedom, subject themselves to servitude [...] they are so foolish that they try to translate line by line, or verse by verse].[44] Estienne's promotion of paraphrase over translation, as well as his reiteration that classical verse in comic theatre is not only unnecessary, but often undesirable, at once draws on and contributes to contemporary theories of imitation.[45] He provides a framework for dramatists and translators to follow in their own work, with the intention not only of creating comic theatre in France, but — in typical humanist style — of improving on what has already been done elsewhere.

Estienne very openly employs paraphrase by rejecting classical verse and adopting the modern Italian prose style. Yet, he makes another substantial edit which he does not acknowledge in his prefatory writings, and which has seldom been noted by critics:[46] in *Les Abusez*, he entirely omits a character, the braggart soldier Giglio. This character presents a highly offensive caricature of the Spaniards: he is unintelligent and cowardly, and speaks in an Italo-Spanish jargon which is regularly mocked by the comedy's native Italian protagonists. Despite instructing the reader that the sense of a comedy must always be conveyed in translation, the distinct anti-Spanish sentiments of the source text are removed. It has been suggested that Estienne omits this character because Giglio's macaronic Italian would be 'a feat almost impossible to replicate'; however, given that Estienne was an accomplished and highly versatile translator of several languages, it is unlikely that he was simply incapable of rendering into French Giglio's dialogue.[47] Rather, it is probable that — especially in light of the volume's dedication to the Dauphin, and Estienne's responsibilities on a number of diplomatic missions — Estienne did not want to risk causing tension with Spain, with whom France was at last enjoying a harmonious and prosperous relationship.[48] As early as the 1540s, then, there existed an awareness of the political ramifications of adapting comic theatre into one's own language and context. This idea of comedy as a polemical weapon will be returned to in Part III of this book, as will Estienne's omission of a plainly xenophobic character.

Bringing to Life Comic Theatre: Estienne, the Italians, and Stage Design

Staging requirements for medieval French theatre were minimal: farces were acted on moveable platforms transported from village to village, and required only a curtain behind which the actors could conceal themselves. Previous to Estienne, French writers had not considered bringing to life classical staging, and the famous set of woodcuts commissioned to portray Terence's comedies for Johannes Trechsel's 1493 edition fuse ancient architectural devices with a medieval setting; they depict, for instance, farce stages with classical columns (figure 1.1).[49]

Estienne was interested in many forms of architecture. His *L'Agriculture, et maison rustique* [Agriculture and Rural Housing], for example, proposes to enlighten the reader on 'tout ce qui peut estre requis pour bastir maison champestre' [all that might be required to build rural lodgings].[50] While some of his architectural writings have attracted scholarly attention, there has been little work on Estienne's vision of sets and staging. First and foremost, he provides an innovative description of a theatre space in his letter to the Dauphin: 'Il vous convient sçavoir que le lieu auquel les spectateurs des Comedies anciennes estoient commodement assiz, s'appeloit Theatre' [It is right for you to know that the place in which spectators of ancient comedies so comfortably sat was called a theatre] (*Les Abusez*, p. 3). He adds that the theatre was 'fait à demy rond' [built in a half-round]; in other words, spectators would sit facing the stage, on tiers raised incrementally (*Les Abusez*, p. 3). While this theatre layout is of course very familiar to a modern readership, it did not exist at the time in France, and previous to Estienne's letter, there is no record of the term *théâtre* in French as denoting the physical seating from which performances could be watched. As with his descriptions of the *acte*, *scène*, and *intervale*, Estienne further provides a vocabulary for his readership to use when discussing comic drama, setting out words which would become common in later lexis.

FIG. 1.1. Example of a woodcut from Terence, *Terentii Comoediae sex, a Guidone Juvenale explanatae, et a Jodoco Badio, cum annotationibus suis, recognitae*, ed. by Guido Juvenalis and Jodocus Badius Ascensius (Lyons: Johannes Trechsel, 1493), fol. H4[r].
BnF, Rés. m-Yc-384

Since Vitruvius is the source of many of Estienne's architectural explorations, such as the aforementioned *L'Agriculture*, scholars have also attributed Estienne's ideas on staging to Vitruvius.[51] It is true that Estienne does take inspiration from Vitruvius: he describes, for example, that 'à l'opposition dudit Theatre, estoit eslevé un eschafault de la hauteur de cinq piedz, et non plus' [opposite this theatre was erected a stage no more than five feet high] (*Les Abusez*, p. 5); this is directly imitated from Vitruvius's prescription in his *De architectura* that 'eius pulpiti altitudo sit ne plus pedum quinque' ('the height of the stage is to be no more than five feet').[52] Yet, we have seen that Estienne holds up the Italians as models of several aspects of comedy in performance (praising, for instance, the high quality of their actors); in the same way, he uses the Italian example to promote the idea of a professional acting space in France. A key, previously unidentified, influence on Estienne's staging ideas is the Italian architect Sebastiano Serlio (1475–c. 1554). At one point in his treatise Estienne refers directly to Serlio as an influence: 'Au dessus dudit Theatre [...] estoient des

Scena Comica.

FIG. 1.2. 'Scena comica'. Sebastiano Serlio, *Le premier livre d'Architecture et le second livre de Perspective de Sebastien Serlio Bolognois, mis en langue françoise, par Jehan Martin* (Paris: Jean Barbé, 1545), fol. 66^{v}. Bibliothèque numérique de l'INHA, Bibliothèque de l'Institut National d'Histoire de l'Art, collections Jacques Doucet, NUM 4 RES 1476.

voylles estanduës [...] à la maniere que demonstre l'Architecteur Sebastian Serlio au portraict de l'amphitheatre de Rome, et celuy de Pole' [Above this theatre [...] there hung ceiling drapes [...] in the way that the architect Sebastiano Serlio demonstrates in his picture of the amphitheatres in Rome and Pula] (*L'Andrie*, p. 357). It is clear from his description of the ceiling drapes which adorned ancient theatres that he is familiar with a range of Serlio's work, and that he has used Serlio's drawings as a particular model for his own ideas on staging.

As is well known, Vitruvius in his *De architectura* presents a description of comic, tragic, and satiric sets.[53] Yet he does not provide illustrations of these sets, and his discussion of each is brief, including that of his comic set: 'Comicae autem aedificiorum privatorum et maenianorum habent speciem profectusque fenestris dispositos imitatione communium aedificiorum rationibus' [The comic

[sets] have the appearance of private buildings and balconies and projections with windows made to imitate reality, after the fashion of ordinary buildings].[54] Better known today is Serlio's development of the Vitruvian sets, including his 'scena in prospettiva' [perspective set] for comedy, which consisted of an illustration depicting houses, balconies, pillars, doors, and windows (figure 1.2).

Serlio does not accompany his illustration with a lengthy description, instead instructing potential comic writers that they themselves must find a use for this set: 'S'io volesi scrivere di tutti gli advertimenti che mi abbondano circa a tal' cose, io sarei forsi tenuto prolisso, perho io le lassaro nel'intelletto di coloro che in tal'cose, si voranno essercitare' [If I wanted to write about all of my many thoughts on this subject, I would be writing endlessly, so I leave that to those who want to put these things into practice].[55] Providing only an illustration, he explicitly leaves the comic set in practice to his readers' imagination.

The first writer to respond to Serlio's offer may well have been Estienne. He too describes a comic set in his treatise: 'Peu au derriere desdites colonnes [...] se voyoient certaines portes, comme entrées de diverses maisons' [Just behind the aforementioned pillars [...] certain doors could be seen, which acted as the entrances to various houses] (*Les Abusez*, p. 5). Since features such as pillars and doors are absent from Vitruvius's description, Estienne clearly draws on Serlio, and not Vitruvius, as a source for his own ideas. Estienne then follows Serlio's suggestion and imagines how this set might be employed: picturing the possible functions of doors, for instance, he describes how all characters used them only to enter and exit their own houses, keeping them otherwise shut: 'Desquelles [portes] sailloient les joueurs, et auxquelles se retirioient, selon ce qu'il apartenoit [...] et ne s'ouvroient, sinon quand un joueur entroit leans, puis soudain se refermoient' [From these [doors] the actors emerged, and they went back through them when it was their turn [...] and they did not open the doors except for when an actor entered through them, then they were shut straightaway] (*Les Abusez*, p. 5). Turning to the function of windows, he proposes that characters might shout out of them, and provides a specific example of a character responding from a window when another knocks on the door below: 'Par les fenestrages susditz, au dessus des colonnes, l'on voyoit quelque fois les personnages parler, comme quand l'on buquoit à la porte de quelques uns, et celuy qui estoit leans, respondoit par la fenestre' [From the aforementioned windows, above the pillars, characters could sometimes be heard speaking, such as when one character knocked on the door of another and the person inside answered from the window (*Les Abusez*, p. 5). While Estienne no doubt has in mind Serlio's 'scena comica' when writing this description — Serlio's doors, pillars, and windows accommodate exactly the actions imagined by Estienne — it is also possible that Estienne was inspired by another Italian source. Alessandro Piccolomini (1508–79) was the most prominent member of the Accademia degli Intronati, the academy which wrote *Gl'ingannati*, the Italian comedy translated by Estienne. Piccolomini also wrote comedies as a sole author, the most famous being *L'amor costante* [Constant Love], performed in 1536 for Emperor Charles V, with an elaborate set designed by Domenico Beccafumi.[56] In a memorable scene from this comedy, the servant Agnoletta bangs on the door of the cook Cornacchia's house, who responds angrily from the window:

AGNOLETTA	Tic toc, tic toc, toc, tic toc.
CORNACCHIA	Chi diavol bussa si forte?
AGNOLETTA	Apre [...] voglio una cosa.
CORNACCHIA	Dimmela di costi.
AGNOLETTA	Non si può dir dalla finestra![57]
[AGNOLETTA	Bang, bang, bang.
CORNACCHIA	Who the devil is knocking so loudly?
AGNOLETTA	Open up [...] I want something.
CORNACCHIA	Tell me what it is.
AGNOLETTA	I can't tell you through the window!]

First printed in Venice in 1540, towards the end of Estienne's tenure there as tutor to the young Baïf, it is plausible that Estienne picked up a copy of this play (or indeed witnessed a university performance), and was inspired to use it as an example of a Serlian set in practice.[58]

While Estienne does base some ideas on Vitruvius, his notion of set and stage design is derived mainly from Italian models, with Serlio as a key influence: again, contemporary Italian works are presented as successful, and even superior, rein-ventions of the ancients. Yet, Serlio's *Second livre* — the volume which contains his illustration of the perspective 'scena comica' — was not printed until 1545, several years after Estienne discusses staging in his letter and treatise. In 1540 Serlio moved to Paris after having been invited to Fontainebleau by François I to work as a royal architect. Previous to this, Serlio lived in Venice at the same time as Estienne, and likely moved in the same academic circles which had first informed François of Serlio's reputation (such as Serlio's patron Ippolito d'Este, or Estienne's employer Lazare de Baïf, the former French ambassador to Venice). Given Estienne's reliance on Serlio's sketches, and his close physical and social proximity to the architect in both Venice and Paris, it is likely that Estienne had seen Serlio's unpublished sketches or discussed the comic set with him. Franco-Italian collaboration in relation to comic theatre was, then, taking place as early as 1540, with Italian sources present in France and offering inspiration. Perhaps Serlio himself was one of the 'plusieurs' described by Estienne, who were seeking to understand ancient comedy. In any case, this likely collaboration provides further evidence that comic theatre in this period was a greater area of discussion in France than has previously been imagined.

Further Italian Imitation: Exploring Estienne's Manuscript

Appended to Estienne's 1542 edition of *L'Andrie* is a short discussion entitled the 'Brief recueil de toutes les sortes de jeux, qu'avoient les anciens Grecz & Romains' [Brief collection of all kinds of games played by the ancient Greeks and Romans]. Estienne's descriptions focus not on theatre but on the use of animals and gladiators for entertainment. He concludes the discussion by promising to print a volume of illustrations of classical phenomena, which he will sketch himself: 'Vivras en esperance d'avoir de ceste mesme main quelques beaulx portraictz et plates formes de diverses antiquitez' [You may expect soon to see some beautiful portraits and plates of various antiquities, by this same hand] (*L'Andrie*, p. 377). This book was never printed and Estienne's promise of these drawings has long been forgotten; however, his aforementioned 'Livre des jeux et theatres antiques' manuscript is likely to be this volume he pledged to create, in which he started but failed to complete these drawings. This manuscript (Reg. lat. 1697) has now been digitized by the Vatican Library, and each of the sketches discussed in this chapter can be viewed by visiting the page cited in the Bibliography. The manuscript is unfinished, of around fifty pages in length; however, since his sketches in all depict ancient theatrical structures, we can gauge that his 'Livre' was aimed not as a guide to general 'antiquitez' but more specifically to classical theatre. It is also probable that he began working on this manuscript soon after his treatise was printed; he replicates much of the same material for his guide, although he omits references to modern works to focus only on classical theatre. For instance, he includes his discussion of the ancient *Pantomimus*, but removes his praise of the modern Italian equivalent, which we explored earlier (fol. 4.1^r).

Although Estienne removes direct references to Italian influence in his 'Livre', he still relies heavily on the Italian model. Given that Estienne draws on Serlio's architectural designs in his treatise and letter, we may expect further influence to be taken from Serlio for the 'Livre'. In fact, we find that Serlio's *Terzo libro* (printed in Venice in 1540, during Estienne's stay there) is the direct model for the vast majority of Estienne's sketches.[59] One of Estienne's largest drawings is labelled 'profil du theatre', and claims to show the amphitheatre at Pula. Yet this is clearly copied from Serlio's 'profilo del teatro' of the same amphitheatre in his *Terzo libro* (fol. 24^v); see figure 1.3.

FIG. 1.3. 'Profilo del teatro', in Sebastiano Serlio, *Il terzo libro di Sabastiano serlio Bolognese, nel qual si figurano, e descrivono le antiquità di Roma, e le altre che sono in Italia, e fuori d'Italia* (Venice: Francesco Marcolini, 1544), p. 51. Bibliothèque numérique de l'INHA, Bibliothèque de l'Institut National d'Histoire de l'Art, collections Jacques Doucet, NUM 4 RES 1476. (Owing to the scarcity of the 1540 edition, images in this book are from the 1544 edition.)

Estienne had already referred to the Pula amphitheatre in his treatise, when discussing his representation of ceiling drapes; in the *Livre*, then, he expands on his previous work by providing a sketch for readers interested in seeing a representation of this theatre. Although it was at this point in his treatise that Estienne mentioned Serlio by name, he never cites Serlio in the 'Livre', even when he imitates not just the illustrations but also Serlio's corresponding descriptions. In the next example, Estienne discusses the Corinthian designs on the classical theatrical stonework, depicting nine drawings of columns, arches, and cornices (fol. 25^r; see figure 1.4).

As we can see by examining Serlio's text, not only does Estienne imitate Serlio's drawings, but he also copies their enumeration (from A to X) and translates into French the description which accompanies them. Here Estienne employs a very faithful translation style, rather than that of paraphrase which he had advised for theatrical translation: for example, 'grande richesse de beaulx parementz de pierre vive aornées [*sic*] d'ouvraiges corinthe' [very rich with beautiful decorations of brilliant rock adorned with Corinthian work] translates closely from the Italian 'molto ricco di ornamenti tutto di pietra viva, e di opera Corintia molto bene e riccamente lavorato'.[60] While Estienne portrays the promised 'antiquitez', he again uses a modern Italian source as an intermediary, without changing any details or elaborating on Serlio's ideas.

We might at this point wonder whether Estienne's sketches and translations were private or preliminary, and if he had indeed considered reworking them for publication. Yet throughout his translation he makes one consistent set of edits to Serlio's text: he ensures that any specialist vocabulary and context are comprehensible to a French and non-expert readership. We can take, for example, Estienne's discussion of the Ferentium amphitheatre. Again basing his sketches on Serlio, Estienne discusses the orchestra (referring to the space in which music was played) of the theatre as well as the pillars and the *cunei* which formed the seating area (fol. 22^v; see figure 1.5).

Estienne's translation (which can be seen directly below his sketches) is mostly faithful to the Italian:

> Ce plan fut mesuré au piet antique. L'orchestre du theatre, qui estoit à demy rond, avoit de diametre 141 pietz et demy. Tout le corps du theatre, à sçavoir les coings, que les anciens nommoient cunei, et aussi les portiques avec le pilastre angulaire sont en tout et pour tout 35 pietz.[61]
>
> Questa pianta fu misurata col piede antico [...] A la quale è di mezzo circolo, il suo diametro è piedi cento quaranta uno e mezzo, tutto al corpo del theatro, cioè i cunei con tutto il portico, e il pilastro angulare, è piedi trenta cinque.[62]
>
> [This floor was measured in the ancient foot. The orchestra of the theatre, which was in a half-round, was one hundred and forty-one and a half feet. The body of the theatre, that is to say the wedges, which the ancients called 'cunei', and also the porticos with the angular pillar, are all in all thirty-five feet.]

In his translation, Estienne provides a definition of the term *cuneus* — clarifying that this denotes a 'wedge' — a detail which is absent from the original Italian text. 'Cuneo' was a term already incorporated into Italian from the Latin, which would have been largely comprehensible to an Italian readership; however, the modern

FIG. 1.4. Serlio's original illustrations, in Sebastiano Serlio, *Il terzo libro di Sabastiano serlio Bolognese, nel qual si figurano, e descrivono le antiquità di Roma, e le altre che sono in Italia, e fuori d'Italia* (Venice: Francesco Marcolini, 1544), p. 53. Bibliothèque numérique de l'INHA, Bibliothèque de l'Editions National d'Histoire de l'Art, collections Jacques Doucet, NUM 4 RES 1476.

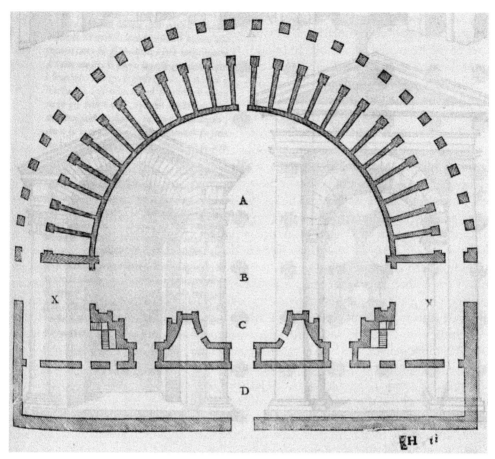

FIG. 1.5. Serlio's illustrations of the orchestra, seating, and stage area, in Sebastiano Serlio, *Il terzo libro di Sabastiano serlio Bolognese, nel qual si figurano, e descrivono le antiquità di Roma, e le altre che sono in Italia, e fuori d'Italia* (Venice: Francesco Marcolini, 1544), p. 55. Bibliothèque numérique de l'INHA, Bibliothèque de l'Editions National d'Histoire de l'Art, collections Jacques Doucet, NUM 4 RES 1476.

French equivalent of *cuneo* (*voussoir*) was not yet in usage, and Estienne does not assume that his readership will be familiar with the Latin. As with his previous translations of the *Andria* and *Gl'ingannati*, this clarification ensures accessibility to a readership broader than the French learned circles, who would have had an excellent command of Latin vocabulary. Similarly, Serlio's opening description of this Ferentium amphitheatre is: 'A Ferrento città molto antica presso a Viterbo sono li vestigi d'un theatro molto ruinato' [At Ferrento, a very ancient city close to Viterbo, are the traces of a very ruined theatre],[63] which is translated by Estienne as: 'A Ferente, cité fort antique aupres Viterbe, apparoissent encor les vestiges et ruynes d'ung theatre fort ruyné [At Ferrento, a very ancient city close to Viterbo, the traces of a very ruined theatre can still be seen].[64] The addition of 'encor' in the French text once again makes it accessible for a French readership who may not, unlike their Italian counterparts, realise that that the remains of the Ferentium theatre were still very much visible. Given that travel to Italy was a fundamental part of the humanist education, and that this theatre was (and still is) on one of the most popular tourist routes between Rome and Florence, many of Estienne's peers would have known about Ferentium, or may perhaps have paid a visit. Not only did Estienne intend to print his 'Livre' — clearly, this was not a private exercise in sketching or translation — his edits also indicate that he had considered in some detail his intended audience, which was to be non-specialist as well as academic.

It is possible that despite Estienne's promise to print his own illustrations, he aimed to print his French translation of the Italian text with Serlio's original drawings alongside them. This would explain the rudimentary nature of his sketches, which were clearly completed in haste. The result would be a volume containing Estienne's own assessment of ancient comedy (largely lifted from his treatise), interspersed with a presentation in French of Serlio's work on classical theatre. However, Jean Martin — secretary to Cardinal Robert de Lenoncourt, a colleague and close friend of Serlio's patron Ippolito d'Este — was in 1545 commissioned to translate into French the first two of Serlio's books.[65] It is possible that Estienne decided to abandon his plans for the 'Livre' when he heard of Martin's work on Serlio's text. In any case, this manuscript containing Estienne's sketches again testifies to his aim of enriching knowledge of classical theatre in France, not only among learned circles but also more general audiences, again perhaps schoolchildren. This is indicated by his clarifications for a non-specialist audience, and also by his decision to present illustrations, which, as Hester Lees-Jeffries has observed, provide 'alternative points of entry to the text', and are more accessible to a broad readership than text.[66] Like much of his treatise and letter, Estienne's manuscript also affirms his interest in comic theatre in performance. Not only does he consider how comedy could be reinvented in written form; he also has in mind how it might appear on stage. Again, for inspiration he draws not on the classical model, but on his Italian contemporaries. This manuscript thus provides further evidence that even in the 1540s, and before Serlio had come to attention or even been printed in France, the Italians were providing an example for the contemporary revival of classical theatre, forming a far earlier foundation for humanist French comedy than we had previously assumed.

Charles Estienne — whose work will be revisited throughout this book — is a key figure in French comedy in its earliest stages. He was the first French writer to make the case for the revival of classical comic theatre, and to advise that the Italians should be regarded as crucial intermediaries between ancient and modern drama. His was also the first French translation of an Italian comedy, and of a classical comedy in prose, the style which was to be favoured by most future French playwrights. He provided a new theatrical lexis, and many terms which would later become common (e.g., *acte*, *scène*, *théâtre*), thereby enabling later writers to discuss these concepts with clarity and ease. Estienne also presented a practical framework for aspiring playwrights: for example, he promotes the utility of striking a balance between words and action; the use of acts, scenes, and intervals; the training of professional comic actors; and the replication of Italian prose over classical verse. He himself relies on the Italians far more heavily than has previously been thought, drawing not on Vitruvius but on Serlio for his discussion of performance space, and taking inspiration from contemporary Italian comedies and theoreticians.

Yet, Estienne's work on theatre does not appear to have come quickly to the attention of readers. After the printing of his treatise, it was another six years before another French theoretician wrote about comic theatre and, as we will see in Chapter 2, those considering comic theatre in the 1540s and early 1550s provide no real evidence that they had read Estienne's work. Although Estienne died in Le Châtelet debtors' prison in 1564, having lost the support of family, friends, and patrons, his defence of comic theatre did gain impetus later in the century: his treatise, for example, was produced in three separate editions in Paris in the 1570s alone, and even formed the basis of a 1566 edition of Terence in Antwerp.[67] His work also directly influenced a number of French playwrights. Jean de La Taille's preface to his 1560 comedy *Les Corrivaus* reproduces verbatim Estienne's discussion of classical *dispositio* in comedy, and is also the first original French comedy to employ prose;[68] Jacques Grévin — who was at one point engaged to Estienne's daughter, the famous humanist and poet Nicole Estienne — also models his comedy on Estienne's ideas, as we will see in Chapter 5. Still, it is clear from Estienne's work that discussions about comic theatre were taking place even in the early 1540s: while his treatise and letter were unprecedented, they appear to have been responding to a demand by his peers for an examination of comedy. Also evident from Estienne's work is the importance of seeking to surpass one's comic theatrical models. While it is well known that humanists had urged for emulation, rather than imitation, of predecessors in other literary genres, it has gone unnoticed that this same ambition was present in discourse on comic theatre even in this early period. Crucially, it is this element of rivalry which acted as a main catalyst in the emergence of comic theatre in France. This notion of competing with one's models will recur in each chapter, and culminates in a more detailed discussion in Part III, which assesses the ways in which French playwrights managed at once to draw on and to turn against their Italian models.

Notes to Chapter 1

1. Charles Estienne, *De dissectione partium corporis humani libri tres* (Paris: Simon de Colines, 1545).
2. *History of Anatomy: An International Perspective*, ed. by Shane Tubbs and others (New York: John Wiley & Sons, 2019), p. 93.
3. The Accademia degli Intronati was an acclaimed literary academy based in Siena, which included members such as Alessandro Piccolomini.
4. Accademia degli Intronati, *Comedie à la maniere des anciens, et de pareille matiere, intitulée Les Abusez. Composée premierement en langue Tuscane, par les professeurs de l'academie Senoise, nommez Intronati, et depuis traduicte en nostre langaige Françoys, par Charles Estienne* (Paris: Denis Janot for Pierre Roffet, 1540) (hereafter referred to as *Les Abusez*). Since no modern edition of Estienne's prefatory letter to this play exists, references throughout will be to the 1549 reprint by Estienne Groulleau: *Comedie à la maniere des anciens, et de pareille matiere, intitulée Les Abusez*, trans. by Charles Estienne (Paris: Estienne Groulleau, 1549).

5. Terence, *Premiere comedie de Terence, intitulée L'Andrie, nouvellement traduicte de Latin en François, en faveur des bons espritz, studieux des antiques recreations*, trans. by Charles Estienne (Paris: André Roffet, 1542) (hereafter referred to as *L'Andrie*). The only previous translations of Terence's comedies into French are in verse, and were completed anonymously (though they are likely by Gilles Sibille) towards the end of the 1400s: see the *Therence en françois* (Paris: Antoine Vérard, [n.d.]). For more information on this verse edition, see Ludmilla Evdokimova, 'La Traduction en vers des comédies de Térence dans l'édition d'Antoine Vérard: le choix du style et du destinataire', in *'Pour acquerir honneur et pris': mélanges de moyen français offerts à Giuseppe Di Stefano*, ed. by Maria Colombo Timelli and Claudio Galderisi (Montreal: Ceres, 2004), pp. 111–21.

6. This prefatory material is reproduced in *La France des humanistes: Robert et Charles Estienne: des imprimeurs pédagogues*, ed. by Bénédicte Boudou, Judit Kecskeméti, and Martine Furno (Turnhout: Brepols, 2009). This is the edition of Estienne's treatise cited throughout this book.

7. Estienne, 'Livre des jeux et theatres antiques'.

8. Céline Candiard, 'Roman Comedy in Early Modern Italy and France', in *The Cambridge Companion to Roman Comedy*, ed. by Martin Dinter (Cambridge: Cambridge University Press, 2019), pp. 325–38 (p. 325).

9. This question is discussed throughout Harold Lawton, *Contribution à l'histoire de l'humanisme en France: Térence en France au XVI siècle, éditions et traductions* (Geneva: Slatkine, 1970).

10. For more information on this performance, see William Wiley, *Early Public Theatre in France* (Cambridge, MA: Harvard University Press, 1960), p. 33.

11. See for example Terence, *Comoediae sex, tum ex Donati commentariis*, ed. by Robert Estienne (Paris: Robert Estienne, 1529).

12. Cicero, *Ciceronis Epistolae familiares. Tertia editio*, ed. by Robert Estienne (Paris: Robert Estienne, 1532). Reproduced in *La France des humanistes*, ed. by Boudou, Kecskeméti, & Furno, p. 80.

13. Terence, *Ex Terentii comoediis optimae, copiosissimae atque certissimae loquendi formulae* (Paris: Chrestien Wechel, 1530); *Ex Terentii comoediis colloquendi Formulae ceu Flosculi* (Paris: Chrestien Wechel, 1533).

14. Terence, *P. Terentii Afri comici Andria*, ed. by Charles Estienne (Paris: Simon de Colines and François Estienne, 1541).

15. Edmond Huguet, *Dictionnaire de la langue française du seizième siècle*, 7 vols (Paris: Didier, 1925–67), I, 412.

16. See for example Jean Du Bellay, *Defense pour le roy treschrestien contre les calomnies de Jacques Omphalius* (Paris: Charles Estienne, 1554).

17. Horace, *L'Art poétique d'Horace*, trans. by Jacques Peletier du Mans ([Paris(?)]: [n.pub.], 1541). For more information on this translation, see Lucy Rayfield, 'The Poetics of Comedy in Jacques Peletier du Mans's *Art poëtique* (1555)', *Classical Receptions Journal*, 13.1 (2021), 31–48.

18. See Roger Chartier, 'Stratégies éditoriales et lectures populaires, 1530–1660', in *Histoire de l'édition française*, ed. by Henri-Jean Martin and Robert Chartier, 4 vols (Paris: Promodis, 1982–86), I, 584–603.

19. Guillaume de Postel, *De orbis terrae concordia*, 2 vols (Paris: Gromors, 1544), I, s.n.; also cited in Smith, *The Anti-courtier Trend in Sixteenth-century French Literature*, p. 122.

20. Estienne was taught by Lazzaro Buonamici. Erich Lau, *Charles Estienne: Biographie und Bibliographie* (Leipzig: Vertheim Bechstein, 1930), pp. 11–13.

21. Patrizia De Capitani Bertrand notes that the Estiennes are 'les homologues en France' [the French counterparts] of the Manutius printing family. *Du spectaculaire à l'intime: un siècle de commedia erudita en Italie et en France* (Paris: Champion, 2005), p. 75.

22. Niccolò Machiavelli, *Le Prince de Nicolas Machiavelle secretaire et citoien de Florence. Traduit d'italien en françoys par Guillaume Cappel*, trans. by Guillaume Cappel (Paris: Charles Estienne, 1553); Ortensio Lando, *Paradoxes, ce sont propos contre le commune opinion*, trans. by Charles Estienne (Paris: Charles Estienne, 1553).

23. Richard Andrews, *Scripts and Scenarios: The Performance of Comedy in Renaissance Italy* (Cambridge: Cambridge University Press, 1993), pp. 31–36.

24. See Robert Melzi, 'Gl'ingannati and its French Renaissance Translation', *Kentucky Foreign Language Quarterly*, 12.3 (1965), 180–90 (p. 185).

25. Peg Katritzky discusses the timeline of the arrival of Italian troupes throughout *The Art of 'Commedia': A Study in the 'Commedia Dell'Arte' 1560–1620 with Special Reference to the Visual Records* (Amsterdam: Rodopi, 2006).
26. The translation of *invention* refers throughout to *inventio*, the first tenet of classical rhetoric, denoting the practice of compiling suitable materials and ideas to create one's own work.
27. Lyndan Warner, in *The Ideas of Man and Woman in Renaissance France: Print, Rhetoric, and Law* (Farnham: Ashgate, 2011), provides an excellent discussion of book prices in the early sixteenth century, and argues for possible readerships of a range of volumes. See in particular Chapter 2 (pp. 25–50).
28. For more information on this misinterpretation of classical drama, see Jonas Barish, 'The Problem of Closet Drama in the Italian Renaissance', *Italica*, 71.1 (1994), 4–30 (p. 6).
29. The work of Aristophanes had first been printed in France in 1528, by Gilles de Gourmont. More on the reception of Aristophanes in France can be found in Malika Bastin-Hammou, 'Teaching Greek with Aristophanes in the French Renaissance, 1528–1549', in *Receptions of Hellenism in Early Modern Europe*, ed. by Natasha Constantinidou and Han Lamers (Leiden: Brill, 2019), pp. 72–93.
30. *Dispositio* is the second tenet of classical rhetoric, referring to the structuring or arrangement of one's work.
31. Giovanni Battista Giraldi Cinzio, *Discorso intorno al comporre delle commedie e delle tragedie*, ed. by Giulio Antimaco (Milan: Daelli, 1864), p. 86.
32. The term 'interval' in this book refers not to its modern significance of comfort break, but to its early modern equivalent, which denoted short theatrical pieces or musical interludes.
33. Bonner Mitchell, 'Les Intermèdes au service de l'état', in *Les Fêtes de la Renaissance*, ed. by Jean Jacquot and Elie Konigson, 3 vols (Paris: Centre national de la recherche scientifique, 1956), III, 117–31 (p. 117).
34. Huguet does not consider the word *intervale* in relation to theatre, explaining that it referred only to a generic period of time or space between two objects. See *Dictionnaire*, IV, 672.
35. 'Il y avoit d'aultres joueurs, qui se nommoient Ludi: mais ceulx là recitoient motz pour rire, et se trouvoient principalement aux bancquets des seigneurs par passetemps. Aultres s'appelloient Aretalogi, lesquelz disoient aussi motz joyeux: mais graves' [There were other actors who called themselves *Ludi*, but they recited words to induce laughter, and were mainly found entertaining royal banquets. Others called themselves *Aretalogi*, who also recited joyful words, but which were at the same time serious], *L'Andrée*, p. 353.
36. In the early sixteenth century, the terms *rhythme* and *rime* were interchangeable.
37. Jacobus Omphalius, *De elocutionis imitatione ac apparatu* (Paris: Simon de Colines, 1537). For more information on these debates, see Martin McLaughlin, *Literary Imitation in the Italian Renaissance: The Theory and Practice of Literary Imitation in Italy from Dante to Bembo* (Oxford: Clarendon Press, 1995), especially pp. 187–228.
38. For a detailed examination of emulation in sixteenth-century Italian theatre, see Salvatore Di Maria, *The Poetics of Imitation in the Italian Theatre of the Renaissance* (Toronto: University of Toronto Press, 2013), pp. 3–25.
39. Lodovico Dolce, *Fabritia* (Venice: Gabriel Giolito, 1560), p. 4. While this comedy was first printed in 1549, it was likely written around a decade earlier.
40. Ibid.
41. Cicero's argument was included in a collection printed several years earlier, again by Estienne's stepfather. Cicero, *De finibus bonorum et malorum libri quinque, cum brevibus annotationibus Petri Joanis Olivarii Valentini* (Paris: Simon de Colines, 1537). Cicero's argument in this volume is summarised in Glyn Norton, *The Ideology and Language of Translation in Renaissance France and their Humanist Antecedents* (Geneva: Droz, 1984), p. 196.
42. See Marc Bizer, *La Poésie au miroir: imitation et conscience de soi dans la poésie latine de la Pléiade* (Paris: Honoré Champion, 1995), p. 35.
43. Robert Estienne, *Dictionarium, seu Latinae linguae thesaurus* (1531), cited in Chris Stamatakis, *Sir Thomas Wyatt and the Rhetoric of Writing: 'Turning the Word'* (Oxford: Oxford University Press, 2012), p. 72. Robert Estienne's approach to paraphrasis has been examined in detail by Terence

Cave in his *The Cornucopian Text: Problems of Writing in the French Renaissance* (Oxford: Clarendon Press, 1979).

44. Estienne Dolet, *La maniere de bien traduire d'une langue en autre* (Lyons: Estienne Dolet, 1540), p. 13. For more information on this guide, see Valerie Worth–Stylianou, 'Translatio and Translation in the Renaissance: From Italy to France', in *Cambridge History of Literary Criticism*, ed. by Glyn Norton, 9 vols (Cambridge: Cambridge University Press, 1999), III, 127–35 (p. 128).

45. Joachim Du Bellay, for example, was to defend imitation but reject translation in his *Deffence et illustration de la langue françoyse* of 1549. For more information on these debates, see Glyn Norton, 'Translation Theory in Renaissance France: The Poetic Controversy', *Renaissance and Reformation*, 11 (1975), 30–45.

46. The most recent edition of *Les Abusez*, edited by Luigia Zilli, does not mention this omission, and remarks that the translation has 'le mérite d'introduire en France dans toute sa pureté le modèle comique italien' [the merit of introducing into France the Italian comic model in all its purity]. *La Comédie à l'époque d'Henri II et de Charles IX*, ed. by Luigia Zilli, 1.6 (1996), 3–20.

47. Florindo Cerreta, 'A French Translation of *Gl'Ingannati*: Charles Estienne's *Les Abusez*', *Italica*, 54.1 (1977), 12–34 (p. 20).

48. Estienne had, in this same year of 1540, accompanied Lazare de Baïf and Ronsard on an important diplomatic mission to Haguenau. See Malcolm Quainton, 'The Mysterious Case of the Missing Source Edition of Jean-Antoine de Baïf's *Le Brave*', in *Court and Humour in the French Renaissance: Essays in Honour of Professor Pauline Smith*, ed. by Sarah Alyn Stacey (Oxford: Peter Lang, 2009), pp. 127–46 (p. 131).

49. Terence, *Terentii Comoediae sex, a Guidone Juvenale explanatae, et a Jodoco Badio, cum annotationibus suis, recognitae*, ed. by Guido Juvenalis and Jodocus Badius Ascensius (Lyons: Johannes Trechsel, 1493).

50. Charles Estienne, *L'Agriculture et maison rustique*, ed. by Jean Liebault (Paris: Jaques Du Puys, 1564), p. 1.

51. Penelope Hobhouse and Patrick Taylor show Vitruvius to be the source of Estienne's *L'Agriculture* in their chapter 'The Gardens of Northern Europe: France', in *The Gardens of Europe*, ed. by Penelope Hobhouse and Patrick Taylor (London: George Philip & Son, 1990), pp. 70–151 (p. 72). Ludger Schwarte mentions the Vitruvian sources of Estienne's theatre work in his chapter 'Anatomical Theatre as Experimental Space', in *Collection, Laboratory, Theatre: Scenes of Knowledge in the Seventeenth Century*, ed. by Jan Lazardzig, Helmar Schramm, and Ludger Schwarte, 2 vols (Berlin: Walter de Gruyter, 2005), I, 75–103 (p. 99, n. 64).

52. Vitruvius, *On Architecture*, trans. by Frank Granger, 2 vols (Cambridge, MA: Harvard University Press, 2014), I, 283.

53. Ibid., I, 289.

54. Ibid.

55. Sebastiano Serlio, *Le premier livre d'Architecture et le second livre de Perspective de Sebastien Serlio Bolognois, mis en langue françoise, par Jehan Martin* (Paris: Jean Barbé, 1545), p. 67.

56. More information on this performance can be found in Javier Berzal de Dios, *Visual Experiences in Cinquecento Theatrical Spaces* (Toronto: University of Toronto Press, 2019), p. 38.

57. Alessandro Piccolomini, *L'amor costante*, in *Commedie del Cinquecento*, ed. by Nino Borsellino, 2 vols (Milan: Feltrinelli, 1962), I, 374–75 (III.2.1–13)

58. Alessandro Piccolomini, *L'amor costante, comedia del Stordito Intronato, composta per la venuta dell'Imperatore in Siena l'anno del MDXXXVI* (Venice: Andrea Arrivabene, 1540).

59. Sebastiano Serlio, *Il terzo libro di Sabastiano serlio Bolognese, nel qual si figurano, e descrivono le antiquità di Roma, e le altre che sono in Italia, e fuori d'Italia* (Venice: Francesco Marcolini, 1544).

60. Serlio, *Il terzo libro*, p. 54.

61. Estienne, 'Livre des jeux et theatres antiques', fol. 22^v.

62. Serlio, *Il terzo libro*, p. 54.

63. Ibid.

64. Estienne, 'Livre des jeux et theatres antiques', fol. 22^v.

65. On the relationship between Lenoncourt and Ippolito, see *The Papacy: An Encyclopaedia*, ed. by Philippe Levillain, 3 vols (London: Routledge, 2002), II, 1126.

66. Hester Lees-Jeffries, 'Pictures, Places, and Spaces: Sidney, Wroth, Wilton House and the *Songe de Poliphile*', in *Renaissance Paratexts*, ed. by Smith and Wilson, pp. 185–203 (p. 187).
67. Bernard Weinberg discusses these later editions of Estienne's treatise in 'Charles Estienne and Jean de la Taille', *Modern Language Notes*, 61.4 (1946), 262–65 (p. 263).
68. Ibid., p. 264.

CHAPTER 2

Comic Theory in
Thomas Sébillet, Joachim Du Bellay,
and Jean-Pierre de Mesmes

*Vous allez promener au mont de Parnase avec les muses mignardes et par
especial avec les Italiques.*

[You will stroll on Mount Parnassus with the graceful Muses, and especially
with the Italians.]

(Jean-Pierre de Mesmes, in Lodovico Ariosto, *La comedie des supposez*, 1552)

The late 1540s and early 1550s brought with them further shifts in the French approach to comic theatre. While there is no evidence that theoreticians in this period read Estienne, a number of works examining the reinvention of comedy appeared in the wake of his 1540 and 1542 discussions. Some, like Estienne, urged for the revival of classical comedy as a means of enriching the French literary canon. Yet others argued for the value of medieval French comedy, encouraging readers to embrace the style of immediate, native predecessors, and to reject the theatre of the ancients. Although theories of comic theatre during these years are scant, few parallels can be drawn between the approaches they take, particularly regarding the sources recommended for imitation. The Italian model, for example, was still praised by some, but writers do not explicitly suggest its replication in comedy. Others, who were familiar with Terence's work only in the classroom, were unconvinced that classical comedy was capable of entertaining a contemporary audience. There was a broad proliferation of viewpoints in poetic discussions of comedy in this period, and no agreement could be reached on the status of comic theatre. There was also a six-year hiatus in between the composition of Estienne's work on theatre and subsequent theoretical writings on the subject. While this is not to say that theatre was forgotten during this period, it is clear that Estienne's appeal for comic theatre to be reinvented did not make an immediate impact. The lack of responses to Estienne's work, as well as the complex and contradictory nature of discussions about comedy during this period, complicate the narrative of a linear development of sixteenth-century comic theatre which some scholars have sought to trace.

This chapter presents three case studies which illustrate this complexity: Thomas Sébillet's *Art poétique françoyse* (1548), Joachim Du Bellay's *Deffence, et illustration de la langue francoyse* (1549), and Jean-Pierre de Mesmes's *La Comédie des supposez* (1552).[1] The first two are literary treatises, written with the explicit aim of elevating French literature and culture: they each discuss a number of major literary genres, including comic theatre. Mesmes's *Les Supposez* is a translation into French of Ariosto's *I suppositi*, the second French prose translation of an Italian comedy after Estienne's edition of *Gl'ingannati*.[2] This translation is accompanied by two prefatory letters, the first to his cousin and the second to his readers. *Les Supposez* is also the first ever Italian-French parallel text, with the Italian dialogue printed on the verso and the corresponding French translation on the facing recto. In comparison to their writings about other literary genres, Sébillet and Du Bellay say little about comedy, and their work on theatre has consequently been overlooked. Mesmes's translation and letters have not been printed since the sixteenth century, and copies of his *editio princeps* are scarce; his approach to comic theatre, as well as his perspective on the Italian models, has not yet been examined.[3] For the purposes of this book, the Bayerische Staatsbibliothek allowed me to examine a copy held in their collections and to provide a transcription and translation of Mesmes's two letters, which are included as an Appendix.

Sébillet's *Art poétique* (1548)

Thomas Sébillet was the first French author to attempt the creation of a comprehensive treatise defining in turn each major literary genre, such as the sonnet, the ode, and the epistle. His work explores how new and reinvented forms of writing are capable of enriching and enhancing French culture, also providing practical advice for aspiring authors of these genres. Sébillet presents a range of models for imitation from two main paradigms — the classical authors and the Italians — often contrasting them with supposedly inferior medieval French writers. Yet elsewhere, Sébillet shows adherence to the earlier *Marotique* humanism, praising what we might call today the 'Grands Rhétoriqueurs', his immediate literary ancestors (such as the authors of the ballad and the *chant royal*), and claiming that some had already successfully amplified French literature. For example, in his discussion of the ode he names Mellin de Saint-Gelais and Clément Marot alongside Pindar and Horace, bridging the gap, as Ehsan Ahmed has noted, between 'foreign and ancient pagan poets on the one hand and the national and contemporary ones on the other'.[4] Still, we may expect for the *Art poétique* — the first French commentary on drama since Estienne wrote his treatise and letter — also to dismiss medieval theatre in favour of classically-inspired work. Sébillet's section on comedy is grouped under the heading of 'La Farce', and opens with a comment that farce and Roman comedy have little in common: 'la Farce retient peu ou rien de la Comedie latine' [Farce retains little to nothing of Latin comedy].[5] Comparing contemporary comedy to the work of Terence, Estienne's treatise had opened in a similar way six years prior: '[C]e qu'il faict pour le present en telles matieres, ne sent rien moins que sa comedie' [What it currently produces resembles nothing of his comedy] (*L'Andrie*, p. 349). Estienne had drawn this comparison as a means of urging readers to abandon the farce in favour of classical comedy; conversely, Sébillet's comment is intended as praise of medieval comic theatre. He subsequently uses his section on comedy to prove the superiority of medieval theatre over its ancient counterpart, and proposes that two particular features of the farce are evidence of its pre-eminence. While he may not have read Estienne, Sébillet's arguments in favour of these two features are distinctly at variance with a number of statements made by Estienne in his treatise and letter.

The first feature examined by Sébillet is the *dispositio* of classical comedy. By 1548, the idea of acts and scenes had been popularised in France by the second edition of Jacques Peletier du Mans's translation of Horace's *Ars poetica* (1545), which was far more prominent than the first.[6] As we have seen, Estienne too had provided definitions of acts and scenes; he had also explained their functions of removing superfluous characters, ensuring that the stage was never left empty, and allowing intervals to take place. Sébillet, on the other hand, claims that such a structure is useless: '[A] vray dire, pour ce a quoy elle sert, ne serviroient rien les actes et scenes' [To tell the truth, in terms of usefulness, acts and scenes are good for nothing].[7] Rather than urging for the reinvention of classical *dispositio*, he discourages writers from using this structure in their comedies. Estienne had also specifically praised the ancients' structuring of words and action, claiming that they had achieved the perfect balance; he drew a direct comparison with medieval genres such as the *sermon joyeux*, the writers of which had not yet learned 'la manière de taire' [how best to keep quiet] (*Les Abusez*, p. 2). In contrast, Sébillet criticises the ancients' verbosity, claiming that their plays contain a 'prolixité ennuieuse' [boring prolixity].[8] While Sébillet was by no means the last French writer to complain that classical and neoclassical comedy was long-winded — a year later, François Rabelais (c. 1494–1553) wrote of his boredom at the 'longueur et mines Bergamasques assez fades' [long and quite dull *bergamasques*] which he witnessed in Rome — Sébillet is the first to criticise so explicitly the classical comic style, and to encourage the continuation of action-based medieval French comedy in place of reinventing the ancients.[9]

Sébillet then moves to his second argument for the superiority of medieval comedy. He was writing for a largely humanist readership, and clearly anticipated some resistance to his dual criticism of ancient comedy and defence of medieval work (which, as we shall see in the section on Du Bellay, he was right to expect). In an attempt to show that medieval theatre was deserving of a place within French culture, he uses a hypothesis obviously intended to appeal to his audience, and claims a strong reliance of farce on antiquity, again seeking to bridge the gap between ancient and contemporary: 'Nos Farces sont vrayement ce que les Latins ont appellé Mimes ou Priapées [...] pource toute licence et lascivie y estoit admise, comme elle est aujourd'huy en nos Farces' [Our farces are really what the Latin writers called mimes or *priapeia* [...] because these forms permitted all kinds of liberties and lasciviousness, just as our farces today do].[10] Sébillet's argument that farce is directly inherited from the mime is likely inspired by Cicero, who was a major influence in other chapters in the *Art poétique*. Yet while Cicero pointed out the mime's lasciviousness, he also praises its other features — such as its quick wit

— which were not commonly associated with the farce, and which Sébillet does not mention.[11] Similarly, the *priapeia* (a collection of erotic Latin poems, possibly written by Ovid or Virgil) resembles the farce only in its obscenity.[12] Sébillet is also wrong to imply that classically-inspired comedy does not allow 'licence et lascivie'. The comedies of Plautus, for instance, are often highly obscene — his work was condemned for this quality by a number of sixteenth-century French writers — and the recently reinvented Italian comedy by writers such as Pietro Aretino were well known for their sexual and scatological humour.[13] As Sébillet must have known, the farce was directly inspired neither by the farce nor the *priapeia*, and the one feature they all have in common — obscenity — was also characteristic of the classical comedy he sought to undercut. Nonetheless, his argument does testify to the authority of classical influence when defending the worthiness of a genre. Evidently, if the farce were thought to have roots in ancient work, humanist readers would be more easily convinced that it deserved a place within French literature.

We might finally enquire as to the source of Sébillet's hostility towards classical comedy. Firstly, it is likely that Sébillet was familiar with ancient theatre only in the classroom. Although it is true that comedy was mainly employed as Latin-learning material, Terence would also have been used for teaching good morals, as advocated by Erasmus and many other leading humanists.[14] Sébillet's experience of reading Terence only in an educational setting may account for a final criticism he makes of classical comedy. He claims that it is unable to please:

> Le vray suget de la Farce ou Sottie Françoise, sont badineries, nigauderies, et toutes sotties esmouvantes à ris et plaisir. Le suget de la Comédie Gréque et Latine estoit tout autre: car il y avoit plus de Moral que de ris.[15]

> [The true subjects of the French farce or *sottie* are nonsense, tomfooleries, and all kinds of silliness which moves one to laughter and pleasure. The subject of Greek and Latin comedy was entirely different, since they contained more morals than laughter.]

We saw in Chapter 1 that Estienne had praised the ancients' ability to evoke 'plaisir et delectation' in their audience, an end which could be achieved by contemporary playwrights if they rejected the *badinage* of medieval drama, which he considered to bore spectators (*Les Abusez*, p. 3). Again in contrast to Estienne — and almost (perhaps unknowingly) echoing his choice of wording — Sébillet asserts that the source of pleasure in medieval comedy is precisely their 'badineries', praising its liveliness and tomfoolery. However, classical comedies could be extremely physical, inspiring in part the *commedia dell'arte*, a theatrical form which relied heavily on movement and expression. Sébillet's emphasis only on the edifying function of classical drama reflects the same stress that would have been placed on these comedies during his education. In the same way, Sébillet's lack of experience with classical comedy in performance may account for the unusual absence of references to Italian models in this section. Sébillet recommends a range of Italian sources elsewhere in the *Art poétique*, and was convinced that imitation of Italian models would help to enrich French literature. A year before writing the *Art poétique*, for instance, he had travelled briefly to Italy, where he bought and later translated

Battista Fregoso's *Anteros*: in the prefatory letter of this translation he claims that imitation of the Italians would support the 'accroissement, l'enrichissement, et la splendeur de nostre Françoise langue' [growth, enrichment, and splendour of our French language].[16] Still, there is no evidence that he saw an Italian comedy performed, and he may not have had the opportunity to read one (the only Italian comedy in print in France was still Estienne's translation of *Gl'ingannati*). Even though Sébillet was close friends with Jean Martin, who had translated into French Serlio's work on architecture, Serlio does not focus only on theatre and does not explain how a comedy would have functioned, unlike Estienne's previous work and proposed volume on theatre.[17] Sébillet's criticism of the verbosity, structure, and moral emphasis of classical comedy may then be accounted for by a discouraging experience with the plays at school, combined with an unfamiliarity with how they might be performed or reinvented in a contemporary context.

On the other hand, Sébillet was clearly very familiar with the medieval comic style, and may have appreciated it for personal and professional reasons. The vast majority of medieval comedies were written and acted by law clerks: the Basochiens were a society specialising in farces, and the Enfants-sans-Souci most often performed *sotties*; many of these plays also centred around law or the courts, such as the *Farce de la Pipée* [The Farce of Luring] (c. 1480) and the renowned *Pathelin*.[18] As a practising lawyer, Sébillet would have witnessed first-hand many of these plays, and may well have had the opportunity to act in them himself. It is probable that he was aware of some kind of threat to medieval drama, not just from humanists who wanted to leave behind forms such as the farce and *sottie*, but also from the Parlement de Paris, whose members were negotiating an *arrêt* on the mystery play. Although the *arrêt* did not come into effect until November 1548, five months after Sébillet's work had gone to press, his omission of the mystery play from his section on theatre indicates that he was aware of the controversy surrounding religious performances.[19] His defence of the farce and the *sottie*, and his reminder that — in supposed contrast to classical comedy — they brought laughter and joy to many contemporary audiences, may have formed part of an attempt to protect these plays from censorship by those who opposed them on artistic or religious grounds. Consequently, Sébillet's defence of his own native theatre does suggest that conversations about comedy had been ongoing since Estienne completed his treatise: as Barthélémy Aneau wrote after reading Du Bellay's *Deffence*: 'Il n'est point defense sans accusation precedente' [There is no defence without a previous accusation].[20] Just as Estienne composed his theatrical work in response to interest from his peers, Sébillet, too, must be writing in response to public opinion: with no threat to, or call for change in, theatrical forms, there would be no need to defend so overtly the existence of medieval drama.

Sébillet's discussion of comic theatre in the *Art poétique* is a clear justification of the worthiness of medieval forms; at the same time, he dismisses classical comedy, portraying it as long-winded, poorly structured, and unable to evoke pleasure in its spectators. It is likely that Sébillet regarded ancient comedy only as a scholarly exercise for learning Latin or morals, or else aimed to safeguard the medieval dramatic forms with which he was most familiar, and in no way can we claim that his approach encouraged or helped to promote the reinvention of classical comedy in France. On the contrary, Sébillet, consciously or not, undermines several key points made by Estienne earlier in the decade, seeking to show the superiority of medieval drama in areas such as *dispositio* and to prove that the farce, too, could boast of classical ancestry. Sébillet's treatise poses significant difficulties to the standard narrative about the emergence of comic drama in sixteenth-century France, and — as Du Bellay's treatise will also show — the reinvention of classical theatre was by no means unanimously supported.

Du Bellay's *Deffence* (1549)

By 1549, a year after Sébillet's treatise was printed, the twenty-seven-year-old Joachim Du Bellay was already one of France's foremost humanists, and was closely allied with writers such as Jean Dorat (1508–88), Peletier, and Marc Antoine Muret (1526–85), who had composed a Latin tragedy (*Julius Caesar, c.* 1547).[21] He had also formed with Ronsard the up-and-coming literary circle, La Brigade, which was later to be known as the Pléiade. Like the *Art poétique*, Du Bellay's *Deffence* describes and promotes a range of literary genres for creation and replication, with the ultimate aim of elevating French literature and culture.[22] However, although he does not refer directly to Sébillet in the *Deffence*, his treatise is clearly intended as a counter-attack to the *Marotisme* displayed throughout the *Art poétique*.[23] Like Sébillet's section on comedy, Du Bellay's treatise is also a defence (as suggested by the title); however, what it seeks to protect is the French language against the long-standing domination of Latin in literary production.[24] The second part of the treatise's title indicates its aim to bring glory or lustre ('illustration') to French language and culture.[25] While Sébillet had encouraged the imitation of some medieval and contemporary French writers, Du Bellay strongly urges his readers to reject their immediate literary predecessors, maintaining that these writers 'corrompent le goust de nostre langue et ne servent sinon à porter tesmoignage de nostre ignorance' [corrupt the taste of our language and serve only to testify to our ignorance].[26] The sole sources of inspiration, Du Bellay advises, should be the Greek, Latin, and modern Italian writers: 'Je veux bien avertir ceux qui aspirent à ceste gloire d'immiter les bons aucteurs Grecz et Romains, voyre bien Italiens' [I would strongly advise those aiming for this glory to imitate the excellent Greek and Latin authors, and even the Italians].[27] Du Bellay praises the Italians' 'conversion to their maternal tongue' and their ability to enrich not only their language, but also vernacular literature; additionally, he claims that in some genres, the Italians have equalled the work of the ancients.[28] In a way which recalls Estienne's comment on the indistinguishability of Italian comedy from the work of Terence (*Les Abusez*, p. 9), Du Bellay asserts that the Italian epic (clearly referring to Ariosto's *Orlando furioso*) equals its Greek and Roman models: '[Il faut] s'egaler aux superbes langues Greque et Latine, comme a faict de nostre Tens en son vulgaire un Arioste Italien que j'oseroy [...] comparer à un Homere, et Virgile' [We must bring ourselves to equal the superb Greek and Latin languages, like in our time the Italian Ariosto has done in his vernacular, which I would dare [...] to compare to Homer or Virgil].[29] The aim is to equal the classical models, following the achievements of the Italians, who have had what Marc Bizer calls a 'shared point of departure' in the Greek and Latin languages.[30] To some extent, Du Bellay's own treatise is a case in point, since it uses as a main source the treatise of Italian humanist Sperone Speroni, as well as the works of Giovanni Battista Gelli and Pietro Bembo.[31]

In this way, we might expect Du Bellay to provide a detailed account of the requisites of comic theatre, justifying the need for a reinvention of ancient comedy and providing a range of models or plays for imitation. Instead, we find that he devotes to drama one single sentence of his treatise:

> Quand aux Comedies, et Tragedies, si les Roys, et les Republiques les vouloint restituer en leur ancienne dignité, qu'ont usurpée les Farces, et Moralitez, je seroy bien d'opinion, que tu t'y employasses, et si tu le veux faire pour l'ornement de ta Langue, tu scais ou tu en doibs trouver les Archetypes.[32]

> [As for comedies and tragedies, if kings and republics want to restore them to their ancient dignity, which farces and moralities have usurped, I truly think that you should set your minds to it, and if you want to do it for the ornament of your language, then you know where you should find the archetypes.]

Perhaps due to its brevity, little attention has been paid to Du Bellay's statement. Some have also suggested that if Du Bellay had decided to write a chapter on theatre, 'it would probably not have differed radically from Sébillet'.[33] Yet a close reading of Du Bellay's comments on theatre does give us an insight into Du Bellay's stance on theatre, revealing five of his ideas, which differ entirely from Sébillet's approach to comedy. Firstly, it is clear from Du Bellay's statement that, unlike Sébillet, he wholly supports the reinvention of classical drama, and considers it to be an important task. Secondly, he explicitly advises against the continuation of medieval forms, claiming that farces and moralities have usurped the ancient dignity of classical drama. His choice of the verb *usurper* — denoting the act of wrongfully and forcefully taking the place of something else — suggests that medieval theatre has, unjustifiably, succeeded a far worthier form. 'Ancienne dignité' is an ambiguous phrase, which has been interpreted by Donald Stone as meaning *copia* of rhetoric.[34] In sixteenth-century French, *dignité* most often denoted a worthiness, originating in an exalted rank or form;[35] it is possible that Du Bellay is praising the elevated style and subject matter of the ancients, in contrast to medieval drama, which most often relied on action, using a simple lexis and plot to reach a broader audience. Like Estienne, then, Du Bellay is advocating a balance between words and action in drama, urging writers to leave behind the 'badineries, nigauderies, et toutes sotties' which Sébillet had judged to be a crucial element of comic theatre.

Thirdly, by advising writers to reinvent theatre 'pour l'ornement de ta Langue' — the idea of 'ornement' denoting decoration or embellishment — Du Bellay suggests that drama has the potential to enrich the French language. Throughout his treatise Du Bellay instructs that various genres, such as the epic, can also elevate French, and dedicates much of one chapter to the usefulness of neologisms in enriching the language.[36] His statement indicates that drama, too, is a vehicle which can be used by writers to enrich and enhance French. Fourthly, Du Bellay claims that the reader will know where to find their 'Archetypes', suggesting that there are a number of obvious models that must be employed by the playwright to restore theatre to its ancient dignity. As the sources recommended by Du Bellay throughout his *Deffence* are the ancient Greek and Roman writers, as well as the Italians, these are quite clearly the same models to which he refers in his statement on theatre. Finally, Du Bellay implies that 'les Roys, et les Republiques' are largely in control of the reinvention of theatre: it is only at their will that writers will turn their minds to drama. This is perhaps an acknowledgement that performances, and the costumes and staging that go with them, are costly, and would need funding from a particular source; it may also suggest that the revival of theatre is not currently a priority, since writers would only turn their attention to plays if it were requested. This was, in fact, an entirely accurate prediction, as we shall see in the discussion in Part II of Estienne Jodelle, France's first writer of original comedy.

While a close reading of Du Bellay's comments on theatre does offer a sharper insight into his thoughts on theatre and comedy, it also reveals, equally significantly, what he does not know about drama. He claims that writers should seek to restore its ancient dignity; yet, he does not explain how this might be done, nor does he describe what a play should look like: in the same way, he praises the 'ancienne dignité' of drama, but provides no gloss on this dignity. Similarly, while Italian theoreticians were clear about how comic drama could enhance the vernacular, through its varied register, colloquialisms, and words transplanted from classical theatre — in some instances, Italian comedy was even used as a resource for teaching new words to native speakers of the language — Du Bellay does not explain how the revival of drama might also enrich and amplify French.[37] Du Bellay refers to the 'Archetypes' to follow in the reinvention of comic drama, which, while denoting the ancients and Italians, suggests that the precise models will be so obvious to the reader that there is no need to specify them. Yet elsewhere in the *Deffence* he is far more exact in his recommendation of sources: for example, in this same chapter containing the section on drama he insists on the imitation of Ovid, Tibullus, and Propertius for the elegy.[38] Additionally, few classical and Italian playwrights were known at this stage in France. Terence was very familiar to French readers through schoolwork, but, in contrast to Italy, little interest was taken in Plautus, and the edition of this writer's works printed in 1530 by Robert Estienne was far less successful than his edition of Terence; as for Italian drama, Estienne's translation was still the only edition available in France of an Italian play.[39] It is possible that Du Bellay himself was unsure of which precise sources to recommend.

Du Bellay's encouragement for the reader to abandon medieval forms in favour of their classical ancestors more clearly echoes Estienne than it does Sébillet, and is characteristic of the stricter approach to medieval comic models that humanists were to take in the years to come. Still, the brevity and vagueness of Du Bellay's discussion indicate that he understood little about classical drama, and that he had scant knowledge of the comedy reinvented by the Italians. Some scholars have argued that the treatise was hurriedly composed; it is possible that Du Bellay had no time to explore theatre in detail.[40] Yet there is no evidence in his discussion that he had encountered Estienne's work on theatre; he does not refer to the Italian performance of *La Calandra*, staged in Lyons as he began composing the *Deffence*; and there is no mention of Muret's tragedy *Julius Caesar*, of which he must have been aware. Du Bellay's treatise, then, suggests that even the most prominent advocates of the reinvention of classical literature, and those who most promoted Italian sources, did not judge comic theatre to be a priority. Du Bellay's insinuation that theatre would be written only at royal request provides further evidence of their indifference, relative to genres such as the epic poem. While Du Bellay appears superficially to support the development of comic theatre in France, there is little substance to his comments, and although the *Deffence* became the best-known literary manifesto in sixteenth-century France, it presents little which would truly benefit or encourage an aspiring writer of drama.

Mesmes's *Les Supposez* (1552)

Jean-Pierre de Mesmes (*c.* 1516–78) is relatively unknown today, yet in the mid-sixteenth century he was France's leading Italianist. His command of Italian was celebrated in letters and reports throughout the century, and was thought to rival that of even the best native speakers. The poet Olivier de Magny (himself an accomplished Italian speaker), for instance, wrote of Mesmes:

> Il [est] capable de congnoistre toutes les délicatesses de ceste langue estrangère, et mesme de la parler et de l'escrire avec autant de grâce et d'ornement que s'il fust né sur les rives du Pau ou sur les bords du Tybre.[41]

> [He has a complete grasp on all of the subtleties of this foreign language, and speaks it and writes it with such embellishment and grace that one might think he were born on the edges of the Po or the banks of the Tiber.]

Mesmes was well connected to a number of eminent Italian humanists, such as Ettore Fregoso;[42] he composed his own poetry in Italian; and in 1548 he completed a handbook of Italian grammar, *La Grammaire italienne, composée en françoys* [Italian Grammar, Composed in French].[43] This volume met with immediate success, becoming the most prominent French guidebook to the Italian language, and was reprinted until well into the eighteenth century.[44] Mesmes worked closely with many of France's foremost humanist writers: in 1550 he was invited to write a preliminary sonnet for Pierre de Ronsard's *Odes*, and he collaborated with other Pléiade members for *Le Tombeau de Marguerite de Valois*, translating into Italian its Latin poetry while others focused on translations of Greek and French.[45] In 1552 he printed his French translation of Ariosto's *I suppositi*, as well as two prefatory letters accompanying the translation, *Les Supposez*.

Mesmes makes it clear in several of his writings that his main aim is to facilitate and encourage France's rising interest in Italian language and culture: we can take as just one example the prefatory letter to his *Grammaire*. In this letter he advises his readership that an Italian speaker in France is held in especially high esteem; he also reminds them that Italian is the most useful language in business and commerce:

> Je priseray beaucoup un Gentilhomme Françoys, un marchand, et tout homme
> de lettres, qui sçait et entend les langues Italienne, Germanique, et Angloise:
> et par especial la premiere, comme celle qui est [...] pour le jour d'huy plus
> commode pour les affaires de la rep. Françoyse, et Italienne.[46]

> [I would hold in high respect a French gentleman, a merchant, and every
> man of letters, who knows and understands the Italian, German, and English
> languages, and particularly the first, as this is [...] today most useful for the
> business of the French and Italian republics.]

As well as promoting a knowledge of the Italian language for commercial reasons,
his letter is an example of cultural diplomacy. He describes the Greek and Roman
nations, and their decision to learn the other's language; in so doing, he claims,
they have achieved a dual aim of enriching their own culture and maintaining a
harmonious relationship: 'Les enfants Romains [...] parvenuz en age employoient la
meilleure partie de leurs ans aux letres Græques, tant pour enricher les Latines, que
pour entretenir en bonne amytié la gent Græque' [The Roman children [...] coming
of age, spent a good part of their years studying Greek letters, both to enrich Latin
literature and to maintain friendly relations with the Greek people].[47] Mesmes
draws parallels with the present-day relationship between France and Italy, often
synonymous with Tuscany at this time. Given that the French and Italians have
exchanged highly different languages and characteristics, they too have enjoyed a
mutual elevation of their cultures:

> D'avantage celà me fait dire, et quasi affirmer, que non sans cause on a ceu et
> voit on encor' entre les Françoys et florentins une amytié ferme et ancienne,
> laquelle n'eust esté si entiere, estants leurs langages autant differents, que leurs
> meurs et facons de faire.[48]

> [Moreover that makes me say, and almost affirm, that not without cause we
> have known, and continue to see, a firm and ancient friendship between the
> French and the Florentines. This friendship would not have been so entire if
> their languages had not been so different, as well as their manners and ways of
> life.]

Mesmes describes a unity and synthesis between Italy and France which has been
promoted by linguistic and literary exchange and enrichment. While his *Grammaire*
is aimed at facilitating the widespread learning of the Italian language, then, Mesmes
also intends to enhance the cultural alliance between France and Italy, encouraging
the influx of Italian literature and language into France, and vice versa.

We might expect Mesmes's Ariosto translation to form part of this bid for
cultural enrichment through Italian influence. Estienne had, a decade prior, advised
the elevation of French literature using modern Italian comedy; Du Bellay had
also (albeit vaguely) noted the ability of theatre to elevate the French language,
through the use of appropriate models. Du Bellay too singled out Ariosto himself
as a particularly excellent writer and source for imitation. In some respects, Mesmes
does appear to be using his translation to promote comedy and thereby enrich
French literature. Like the full title of Estienne's translation *Les Abusez*, the title of

Mesmes's translation emphasises his reliance on Italian sources, drawing attention to Arioso as the author: *La comedie des supposez de M. Louys Arioste.* Ariosto's work was well known in France at this time, and Mesmes evidently anticipated that such a title would generate interest in his translation. Yet it is also possible that Mesmes is promoting knowledge in France of Ariosto's status as a comic writer, since he was famous only as the Italian creator of the epic.[49] In the prefatory letter to his cousin (see Appendix I), he also states that he is printing the translation in order to 'donner [...] contentement aux curieux espritz' [bring [...] satisfaction to curious souls].[50] Clearly, he knew either of a current interest in comedy, or was accommodating for those studying Italian. In either case, Mesmes had identified a potential readership for his translation, and intended for it to be enlightening.

The 'cousin' to whom he is writing is Henri de Mesmes, the future French representative of Siena and an enthusiast of Italian culture.[51] As Neil Kenny has shown, it is possible that Henri was actually his illegitimate brother, or even his father.[52] Whichever the case may be, in his letter, Mesmes reminds Henri of their mutual love of Italian literature and culture, and promises that the reading of this comedy — and the Italian models within — will allow him to forget his worries: 'Vous allez promener au mont de Parnase avec les muses mignardes et par especial avec les Italiques, lesquelles vous sont familieres et privées, voire autant ou plus que les Grecques et Latines' [You will stroll on Mount Parnassus with the graceful Muses, and especially with the Italians, with whom you are familiar and intimate, even more so than the Greeks and Latins].[53] Mesmes's reference to Mount Parnassus and the Muses follows a convention popularised by Pindar and later classical poets, who invoke the inhabitants of Parnassus for poetic inspiration. This conceit was widely employed by early modern French authors: Marot, for example, described how 'plus d'esprits de noble Poesie' [more spirits of noble Poetry] had sprung forth from the 'double Mont des Muses' [twin peaks of the Muses];[54] Ronsard, too, opens his *Franciade* by invoking Calliope, the Muse of epic poetry, to oversee his work:

> Muse qui tiens les sommets de Parnasse,
> Guide ma langue, et me chante la race
> Des Roys Françoys yssuz de Françion.[55]

[The Muse who holds Parnassus's summits, | Guide my tongue, and sing me the race | Of the French Kings born from Francus.]

Mesmes claims that in reading the comedy, Henri will be able to ascend Parnassus 'avec les Italiques': he elevates Italian work to the most prominent literary position, to the location that the Muses and Apollo, god of poetry, are meant to inhabit, and the place towards which French poets had been aspiring. The Italians are portrayed as key sources of inspiration which the French, too, should embrace if they seek to reach the highest literary position. The Italians are even superior to the ancients: they are esteemed by Henri 'voyre autant ou plus que les Grecques et Latines' [even more so than the Greeks and Latins].[56] Since a main part of Mesmes's prefatory letter is aimed at reminding the readers of the literary achievements of the Italians — whose innovation and ambition allowed them to surpass even the ancients — he may have sought to promote an appreciation in France of the new, successfully reinvented comic genre. Yet it is also possible that he aimed simply to raise interest in learning the Italian language (and, by extension, to increase demand for his parallel-text translation) by pointing out the accomplishments of the culture that created this comedy.

Although Mesmes's letter is brief, it does also indicate that he considered important the potential of Italian comedy to bring joy. Just as Estienne had illustrated the ability of comedy to evoke 'delectation' (*Les Abusez*, p. 3), Mesmes describes classical comedy as 'delectable' (according to Huguet, both 'pleasurable' and 'cheerful'),[57] and advises that it will distract Henri from the burdensome study of law: '[Je l'ay mis] en lumiere avec sa source Italienne pour donner [...] à vous plus de passetemps, mesme quant serez ennuyé de l'estude de la tetrique Jurisprudence qui demande (comme j'ay tousjours ouy dire) l'homme tout à soy' [I brought it to light along with its Italian source. It will bring [...] more recreation to you, when you are bored of studying austere Jurisprudence which demands (or so I have always heard) all of a man's time].[58] In contrast to Sébillet, who argued that classical comedy had only an edifying function, Mesmes emphasises the suitability of comedy for entertainment and distraction. It is also possible that, like Estienne, Mesmes wanted to draw attention to his use of prose, and not verse, in the translation of this comedy. In his letter to the readers (see Appendix I), he stresses the importance of paraphrase over translation, explaining that his translation does not correspond 'mot pour mot à l'Italien [...] car le Traducteur ne s'est voulu tant assubiettier ny contraindre' [word-for-word with the Italian [...] for the translator did not want to subject nor constrain].[59] The reference to paraphrase might indicate Mesmes's general approach to translation, which would echo the advice of theoreticians such as Du Bellay (though in practice, Mesmes's translation follows the original very closely).[60] However, Mesmes had taken the major decision to translate the earlier, discarded prose version of *I suppositi*, and not Ariosto's revised verse comedy.[61] In his description of paraphrase, Mesmes draws on the same allegory of *subjection* and *contrainte* that Estienne had used when discussing verse and prose translations (*Les Abusez*, p. 2); he also emphasises his priority for the translation to remain 'au plus pres de l'intention de l'Autheur' [as close as possible to the author's intention], again recalling Estienne's idea that verse impedes the meaning a writer intends to convey with their comedy.[62] Although Mesmes does not refer specifically to prose in his letter, it is possible that, like Estienne, he seeks to show the superiority of the freer prose to the constraint of verse in comedy, thereby justifying his decision to translate the unrevised and lesser-known version of Ariosto's play.

Although Mesmes suggests that there may have been a current interest in comedy, a technique used in his letter also indicates that it was still a little-known genre. His letter to Henri opens by disclosing that this is a translation he completed some years ago: '[E]n revisitant ces jours passez les vieilles compositions de ma premiere jeunesse, je trouvay (sans y penser) la presente traduction' [In recently revisiting the old compositions of my first youth, I found (without planning to) the present translation].[63] His translation, however, is unlikely to be the work of a young student still learning Italian: he translates with no issue a range of registers,

s a n. *Merce del gentilhuomo che vedi là, ma laßa le buffonerie, guardati, & cosi dico à voi al= tri, guardateui tutti de dire che siamo Sanesi, o di chiamarmi altrimenti che Philogono di Catania.*

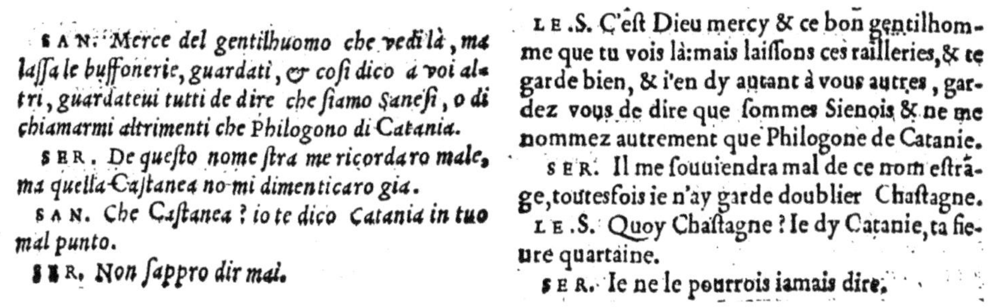

ser. *De questo nome stra me ricordaro male, ma quella Castanea no mi dimenticaro gia.*

s a n. *Che Castanea ? io te dico Catania in tuo mal punto.*

ser. *Non sappro dir mai.*

le .s. *C'est Dieu mercy & ce bon gentilhom- me que tu vois là:mais laissons ces railleries,& te garde bien, & i'en dy autant à vous autres , gar- dez vous de dire que sommes Sienois & ne me nommez autrement que Philogone de Catanie.*

ser. *Il me souuiendra mal de ce nom estra- ge,toutesfois ie n'ay garde doublier Chastagne.*

le .s. *Quoy Chastagne ? Ie dy Catanie,ta fie- ure quartaine.*

ser. *Ie ne le pourrois iamais dire.*

Fig. 2.1. Lodovico Ariosto, *La comedie des supposez de M. Louys Arioste, en italien et françoys*, trans. by Jean-Pierre de Mesmes (Paris: Estienne Groulleau, 1552), ff. 28[v] and 29[r]. Bayerische Staatsbibliothek P.o.it. 82 m., II. 2, urn:nbn:de:bvb:12-bsb11264764-1. 17–22.

idioms, and wordplay, the nuances of which might not have been grasped, as for example when the Italian servant character repeatedly mistakes 'Catania' (the city) for 'Castanea' (chestnut). Mesmes innovates in French with another malapropism, replacing 'Catanie' with 'Chastagne', again meaning 'chestnut' (figure 2.1).

It is likely that Mesmes translated *I suppositi* shortly before it went to print, or at least edited and corrected his previous work. We can infer, then, that Mesmes's comments form part of the widely-practised modesty topos, a form of *captatio benevolentiae* proposed by Cicero in his *De inventione*. This display of humility was a convention most often aimed at protecting the writer from the censure of their readers, employed when engaging with a little-known literary genre or one which could attract controversy.[64] Mesmes's show of modesty — and the anticipation of a critical reaction which the use of this technique would imply — suggests that comic theatre in this period may have been unfamiliar or even unwelcome. The humility shown by Mesmes is also indicative of his own reluctance overtly to urge for the reinvention of classical theatre in France. Mesmes's presentation of his work as a hasty and forgotten exercise of his youth — rather than as a conscious effort to revive a classical genre, by way of the Italian example — is at odds with Estienne's instructions ten years prior for writers to turn their minds to comedy as a means of enriching literature. In no way does Mesmes present his own comedy as a viable mode of humanist writing; on the contrary, he insinuates that this work is inconsequential and insignificant, providing no encouragement for readers themselves to attempt the writing of comedy.

Mesmes's decision to print the volume as a parallel text may even indicate that he intended for the comedy to be used mainly as a language-learning manual. In the early sixteenth century, parallel texts were frequently employed as a means of teaching Latin, as was comic theatre.[65] It is plausible that Mesmes was experimenting with a combination of the two, using Italian comedy in parallel-text format as a means of enhancing the Italian language-learning tools available in France. Given that Mesmes's translation was reprinted in 1585 with its title modified to reflect its language-learning properties (*La comedie des supposez de M. Louys Arioste, italien et françois. Pour l'utilité de ceux qui desirent sçavoir la langue italienne* [The Comedy of *I suppositi* by Lodovico Ariosto, in Italian and French: To Assist Those Who Wish to Learn the Italian Language]), the first edition may well have been used primarily for this purpose.[66] Estienne had previously emphasised that comedies should be appreciated for their literary worth, rather than for their usefulness for language teaching; nonetheless, it is possible that in the early 1550s these plays were used mainly by aspiring linguists, and that the idea of comedy as a worthy literary genre was still dismissed.

Mesmes's translation is a landmark in that it is only the second translation of an Italian comedy into prose, making available in France another Italian play. A close reading of Mesmes's prefatory letters reveals that there was some contemporary interest in comedy, or else in Italian language-learning; additionally, we can infer that Mesmes intended to promote the Italians as linguistic and literary exemplars, if not as models for comic writing. Mesmes's letters also suggest that he appreciated the entertainment value of classically-inspired comic theatre, and that he preferred the Italianate prose comedy to its verse equivalent. However, his modest claim to have rediscovered this translation from his youth (whether or not this is true), as well as the brevity of references to comic theatre itself, do little to inspire or to benefit any humanist readers with a particular interest in drama. The parallel-text format of *Les Supposez* also indicates that it was aimed not at enriching French literature through the reinvention of comic drama, but at language-teaching, or at fulfilling a general interest in Italian language or literature. There is little correlation in Mesmes's prefatory letters with the writings of Estienne or Du Bellay, and although he has provided a piece of classically-inspired theatre, created by paradigms that he clearly advocates, he does not actively promote a bid to reinvent comedy in France. In this way, it is perhaps unsurprising that Mesmes shows no interest in theatre in his *Grammaire*, illustrating his points only with references from canonical writers such as Dante and Petrarch. It has even been suggested that the translation was intended to be confidential, read only by Henri.[67] However, given Mesmes's reference to the 'curieux esprits' in his letter, and dynamic promotion of the Italians — not to mention his decision to print the volume as a parallel text — he had clearly aimed for *Les Supposez* to be shared more widely, and had considered in some detail a possible readership. Mesmes's text does help to enhance our understanding of the status of comic theatre in France at the time, as well as of the French reception of Italian literature and language; yet, while its translator spent his career seeking to forge a cultural and literary alliance between France and Italy, *Les Supposez* was not fundamental to the development of comic theatre in France, nor is there any evidence that Mesmes intended it to be such.

The 1540s and 1550s present a variety of approaches to theatre, though they are similar in one respect: none indicates that humanist comic drama was thriving in this period, and none is clearly aimed at helping to promote the genre. Sébillet favours medieval drama over its classical or Italian counterpart, and argues against the importance of reinventing comedy in France; Du Bellay states the urgency of reviving classical theatre, but provides no practical advice for playwrights, nor any sources for imitation; Mesmes discusses the Italians' literary achievements and presents a new translation of a comedy, but does not explore theatre in any detail, nor does he push for its reinvention. While we can gather from these theoretical and prefatory materials that there was some interest in comic theatre in this period, little seems to have been understood about it, and even claims for the importance of its reinvention are without substance. Some of Estienne's ideas are, probably indirectly, supported (or indeed contradicted); yet, no writings expand on his promotion of the genre, and there is no reference to the more detailed advice that he provides, for instance on intervals, music, actors, or staging. No cohesive approach to comic theatre in the mid-sixteenth century can be mapped, and neither can we situate a linear continuity or development of the genre since the writings of Estienne. Indeed, brief comments of other humanists in this period complicate the narrative even further: Guillaume des Autelz's *Replique aux furieuses defenses de Louis Meigret* [Reply to the Furious Defences of Louis Meigret], for instance, judges to be snobbish the views of Du Bellay, and thus urges for the continuation of the medieval morality play in place of the newly reinvented comedy.[68] As is shown by the complexity of discussions about comedy in this period — which were characterised either by confusion, apathy, or resistance — the emergence of the genre in France was anything but straightforward.

Part II explores how performance, and not poetics, was to have the greatest influence on the reinvention of comic theatre in France, and will show that the Italian colony at the courts was largely responsible for this shift. The next two chapters assess the series of comic performances — as well as the intervention of ambitious patrons and the experimentation of young writers — which helped to forge a place for comic theatre in France, popularising the Italian model and making a more impactful claim for the genre's worthiness.

Notes to Chapter 2

1. Thomas Sébillet, *Art poétique françois*, ed. by Francis Goyet (Paris: Nizet, 1988) (further references are to this edition unless otherwise stated); Joachim Du Bellay, *La Deffence, et illustration de la langue francoyse*, in *Œuvres complètes*, ed. by Richard Cooper and others, 2 vols (Paris: Honoré Champion, 2003), 1 (further references are to this edition unless otherwise stated); Lodovico Ariosto, *La comedie des supposez de M. Louys Arioste, en italien et françoys*, trans. by Jean-Pierre de Mesmes (Paris: Estienne Groulleau, 1552) (hereafter referred to as *Les Supposez*).

2. Jacques Bourgeois had in 1545 printed a verse translation into French of Ariosto's *I suppositi*. This was probably never performed. Lodovico Ariosto, *Comedie tres elegante en laquelle sont contenues les amours recreatives d'Erostrate fils de Philogone de Catania en Sicile et de la belle Polymneste fille de Damon bourgeois d'Avignon*, trans. by Jacques Bourgeois (Paris: Guillaume de Marnef, 1545). A modern edition of this verse translation, along with an introduction and contextualising notes, can be found in *La Comédie à l'époque d'Henri II et de Charles IX*, ed. by Mariangela Miotti, 1.6 (1994), 247–340.

3. Eight known copies of this comedy survive. In *Les Français italianisants* (1, 302), Picot refers to the first of these letters and provides a partial transcription, though he does not critically examine this letter.

4. Ehsan Ahmed, *The Law and the Song: Hebraic, Christian and Pagan Revivals in Sixteenth-century France* (Birmingham, AL: Summa, 1997), p. 27.

5. Sébillet, *Art poétique*, p. 164.

6. Horace, *L'Art poétique d'Horace traduit en vers françois par Jacques Peletier du Mans* (Paris: Michel de

Vascosan, 1545). More information on this edition can be found in Jean-Charles Monferran, *L'Amour des amours* (Paris: Société des Textes Français Modernes, 1996), p. 4.

7. Sébillet, *Art poétique*, pp. 164–65.

8. Ibid.

9. The *bergamasque* was a type of *commedia dell'arte* incorporating masked, dialect-speaking *zanni* from the city of Bergamo. Rabelais witnessed this comedy at a banquet given by the Cardinal d'Armagnac, and writes of his extreme relief that the festivities for the baptism of the Duke of Orléans lasted too long for another comedy to be performed. 'La Sciomachie et festins faits à Rome au Palais de mon seigneur reverendissime le Cardinal Du Bellay, pour l'heureux naissance de mon seigneur d'Orleans', in François Rabelais, *Œuvres complètes*, ed. by Mireille Huchon (Paris: Gallimard, 1994), pp. 967–75 (p. 974).

10. Sébillet, *Art poétique*, p. 165.

11. Cicero, *De oratore*, ed. by Harris Rackham, trans. by Edward William Sutton (Cambridge, MA: Harvard University Press, 2014), pp. 273–74 (book II); *Epistulae ad familiares*, ed. by David Roy Shackleton Bailey (Cambridge: Cambridge University Press, 1977), p. 214 (book VII, letter xi); Cicero, *Epistulae ad Atticum*, ed. by David Roy Shackleton Bailey (Stuttgart: Teubner, 1987), pp. 1–2 (book XIV, letter ii). For a lengthier discussion on Cicero and the mime, see Costas Panayotakis, *Decimus Laberius: The Fragments* (Cambridge: Cambridge University Press, 2010), p. 15.

12. For several well overdue studies of the *priapeia*, see *Eros et Priapus: érotisme et obscenité dans la littérature néo-latine*, ed. by Philip Ford and Ingrid De Smet (Geneva: Droz, 1997); see also '*Les vers du plus nul des poètes': nouvelles recherches sur les Priapées: actes de la journée d'étude organisée le 7 novembre 2005 à l'Université Lumière-Lyon II*, ed. by Frédérique Biville, Emmanuel Plantade, and Daniel Vallat (Lyons: Maison de l'Orient et de la Méditerranée, 2008).

13. In 1555, for example, Peletier (clearly inspired by Horace) condemned Plautus's work for its outrageousness: 'Plaute est facecieus quasi jusques a scurrilite' [Plautus is facetious to the point of indecency]. Jacques Peletier du Mans, *L'art poétique départi en deux livres* (Lyons: Jean de Tournes, 1555), fol. 71ᵛ.

14. Robert Black, *Humanism and Education in Medieval and Renaissance Italy: Tradition and Innovation in Latin Schools from the Twelfth to the Fifteenth Century* (Cambridge: Cambridge University Press, 2001), p. 26. Erasmus claimed that 'modo recte legantur, non modo non ad subvertendos mores, verum etiam ad corrigendos maximopere valere, certe ad Latine discendum plane necessarias judicaverim' ('I am convinced that these [comedies of Terence], read in the proper way, not only have no tendency to subvert men's morals but even afford great assistance in reforming them'). Erasmus, *Opus epistolarum Des. Erasmi Roterodami*, ed. by Percy Stafford Allen and others, 12 vols (Oxford: Clarendon Press, 1906–2002), I, 125 (Epistola 31); *The Correspondence of Erasmus*, trans. by R. A. B. Mynors and D. F. S. Thomson, 16 vols (Toronto: University of Toronto Press, 1974), I, 60. Cited in David McPherson, 'Roman Comedy in Renaissance Education: The Moral Question', *The Sixteenth Century Journal*, 12.1 (1981), 19–30 (p. 20).

15. Sébillet, *Art poétique*, p. 165.

16. Battista Fregoso, *Contramours: L'Anteros ou Contramour*, trans. by Thomas Sébillet (Paris: Martin le Jeune, 1581), pp. 4–5 (prefatory letter 'a tout Franc et débonnaire François' [to every frank and debonair Frenchman]). Sébillet's translation is discussed throughout the collected volume *Anteros: actes du colloque de Madison*, ed. by Ullrich Langer and Jan Miernowski (Orléans: Paradigme, 1994).

17. Together with Martin, Sébillet was artistic lead of the festivities surrounding Henri II's 1549 entry into Paris.

18. More information on the law-related themes of these farces can be found in Richard Cooper, 'Le Juge comme personnage littéraire à la Renaissance', in *L'Intime du droit à la Renaissance*, ed. by Max Engammare and Alexandre Vanautgaerden (Geneva: Droz, 2014), pp. 451–77.

19. Félix Gaiffe wrongly noted that the *arrêt* had already come into effect by the time the *Art poétique* was printed. Thomas Sébillet, *Art poétique*, ed. by Félix Gaiffe (Paris: Droz, 1932), p. 162, n. 2.

20. Barthélémy Aneau, *Quintil Horatien*, in Joachim Du Bellay, *La Deffence, et illustration de la langue françoyse*, ed. by Jean-Charles Monferran (Geneva: Droz, 2001), p. 307.

21. Jan Bloemendal, 'Tyrant or Stoic Hero? Marc-Antoine Muret's *Julius Caesar*', in *Recreating Ancient History: Episodes from the Greek and Roman Past in the Arts and Literature of the Early Modern Period*, ed. by Karl Enenkel and others (Leiden: Brill, 2001), pp. 303–19 (p. 304).

22. François Cornilliat has correctly noted that though the title of the *Deffence* may suggest its subject to be language, the focus of the treatise is in fact on literature. Cornilliat, 'From "Defense and Illustration" to "Dishonor and Bastardization": Joachim Du Bellay on Language and Poetry', *Modern Language Notes*, 130.4 (2015), 730–56 (p. 732).

23. It is possible that Du Bellay completed his treatise in retaliation for being excluded from the group of poets — led by Sébillet and Martin — who organised the King's 1549 entry. On the disappointment experienced by the Brigade, see Ian McFarlane, *The Entry of Henri II into Paris, 16 June 1549* (Binghamton, NY: Medieval and Renaissance Texts and Studies, 1982), p. 59.

24. Margaret Ferguson shows that Du Bellay's treatise produces both an offensive and a defensive stance in relation to the ancients. Ferguson, 'The Exile's Defense: Du *Bellay's La deffence et illustration de la langue françoyse*', *PMLA*, 93.2 (1978), 275–89.

25. Walter Pater, *The Renaissance* (New York: The Modern Library, 1934), p. 132.

26. Du Bellay, *Deffence*, p. 54 (book II, ch. 4). Sébillet's *Marotisme* is discussed in relation to Du Bellay's criticism of immediate literary predecessors in the introduction to Joachim Du Bellay, *The Regrets, with the Antiquities of Rome, Three Latin Elegies, and The Defense and Enrichment of the French Language,* ed. and trans. by Richard Helgerson (Philadelphia: University of Pennsylvania Press, 2006).

27. Du Bellay, *Deffence*, p. 26 (book I, ch. 4).

28. Margaret Ferguson, *Trials of Desire: Renaissance Defenses of Poetry* (New Haven, CT: Yale University Press, 1983), p. 24.

29. Du Bellay, *Deffence*, p. 57 (book II, ch. 5).

30. Marc Bizer, 'Qui a païs n'a que faire de "patrie": Joachim Du Bellay's Resistance to a French Identity', *Romanic Review*, 91.4 (2000), 375–95 (p. 377).

31. Hassan Melehy, *The Poetics of Literary Transfer in Early Modern France and England* (Abingdon: Routledge, 2016), p. 24. See also Ignacio Navarrete, 'Strategies of Appropriation in Speroni and Du Bellay', *Comparative Literature*, 41.2 (1989), 141–54. For Du Bellay's borrowings from Battista Gelli and Bembo, see Pierre Villey, *Les Sources italiennes de la 'Deffence et illustration de la langue françoise'* (Paris: Champion, 1908).

32. Du Bellay, *Deffence*, p. 56 (book II, ch. 4).

33. Marvin Carlson, *Theories of the Theatre: A Historical and Critical Survey, from the Greeks to the Present* (New York: Cornell University Press, 1993), p. 70.

34. Donald Stone, *French Humanist Tragedy: A Re-assessment* (Manchester: Manchester University Press, 1974), p. 67.

35. *Dignité* was also used to mean 'relic', which does not fit in with this context. Huguet, *Dictionnaire de la langue française du seizième siècle*, III, 183–84.

36. This is the sixth chapter of the second book of the *Deffence*, entitled 'D'inventer des mots, et de quelques autres choses qui doit observer le poète françois' [On inventing words, and other things that the French poet must observe].

37. See Bianca Finzi-Contini Calabresi, '"Bawdy Doubles": Pietro Aretino's *Commedie* and the Appearance of English Drama', *Renaissance Drama*, 36 (2010), 207–35, which also describes how an annotated edition of Pietro Aretino's *Il marescalco* (1533) was used as a resource for teaching Italian vocabulary.

38. Du Bellay, *Deffence*, p. 54 (book II, ch. 4).

39. Plautus was not printed in French translation until over a century later. Candiard, 'Roman Comedy in Early Modern Italy and France', p. 327. See also Marie Delcourt, *La Tradition des comiques anciens en France avant Molière* (Liège: Faculté de Philosophie et Lettres, 1934), pp. 34–48.

40. Henri Chamard, for example, suggests that the treatise was written in haste. Joachim Du Bellay, *La Deffence et illustration de la langue françoyse*, ed. by Henri Chamard, 2nd edn (Paris: Didier, 1966), p. vi.

41. Olivier de Magny, *Hymne sur la naissance de Madame Marguerite de France, fille du roy Henri II, en l'an 1553, par Olivier de Magny, avec quelques lyriques de luy* (Paris: Abel L'Angelier, 1553). Magny's

praise of Mesmes is also discussed in Guillaume Colletet, *Vie de Jean-Pierre de Mesmes* (Paris: M. Ph. Tamizey de Larroque, 1878), p. 14.

42. Fregoso was the Bishop of Agen and the son of eminent Italian diplomat and scholar Cesare Fregoso. It is to him that the *Grammaire* is dedicated. More information on Fregoso can be found in Picot, *Les Français italianisants au XVIᵉ siècle*, I, 298.

43. Jean-Pierre de Mesmes, *La Grammaire italienne, composée en françoys* (Paris: Gilles Corrozet, 1548).

44. For more information on the reception of Mesmes's *Grammaire*, see Nicole Bingen, 'Sources et filiations de la *Grammaire italienne* de Jean-Pierre de Mesmes', *BHR*, 46.3 (1984), 633–38 (p. 633).

45. Mesmes's translation of Ronsard's Latin poetry is discussed in Philip Ford, *The Judgement of Palaemon: The Contest between Neo-Latin and Vernacular Poetry in Renaissance France* (Boston: Brill, 2013). pp. 127–59.

46. Mesmes, *La Grammaire italienne*, pp. 2–3 ('Aux Amateurs de la Langue Tuscane').

47. Ibid., p. 3.

48. Ibid.

49. Ariosto's fame in France primarily as a writer of the epic is discussed throughout Alexandre Cioranescu, *L'Arioste en France: des origines à la fin du xviiie siècle* (Paris: Presses modernes, 1938).

50. *Les Supposez*, p. 1.

51. Janet Espiner-Scott has written about Henri de Mesmes's Italian interests in 'Note sur le cercle de Henri de Mesmes et sur son influence', in *Mélanges offerts à M. Abel Lefranc par ses élèves et ses amis*, ed. by Jacques Lavaud (Paris: Droz, 1936), pp. 354–58.

52. Neil Kenny, *Born to Write: Literary Families and Social Hierarchy in Early Modern France* (Oxford: Oxford University Press, 2020), p. 139.

53. *Les Supposez*, p. 1.

54. Clément Marot, 'Enfer', in *Œuvres*, ed. by Alfred Philibert-Soupé, 2 vols (Lyons: Louis Perrin, 1869), I, 63, (l. 388).

55. Pierre de Ronsard, *La Franciade*, in *Œuvres complètes*, ed. by Paul Laumonier, Raymond Lebègue, and Isidore Silver, 18 vols (Paris: Nizet, 1914–75), XVI, 46 (ll. 1–3). More on the early modern approach to the Muses can be found in Stella Purce Revard, *Pindar and the Renaissance Hymn-ode, 1450–1700* (Tempe: Arizona Centre for Medieval and Renaissance Studies, 2001).

56. *Les Supposez*, p. 1.

57. Huguet, *Dictionnaire de la langue française du seizième siècle*, II, 769.

58. *Les Supposez*, p. 1.

59. Ibid., p. 6.

60. Du Bellay's theory of paraphrase is outlined in 'Response à quelques objections' [Reply to Some Objections], the ninth chapter of the first book of the *Deffence*.

61. Italian humanists had discovered that Terence's comedies were in verse and not prose only several years before Ariosto wrote his prose version; he then decided to rewrite it, creating a comedy which was more faithful to the classics. See Martin McLaughlin, 'The Recovery of Terence in Renaissance Italy: From Alberti to Machiavelli', in *The Reinvention of Theatre in Sixteenth-century Europe: Traditions, Texts and Performance*, ed. by Tom Earle and Catarina Fouto (Oxford: Legenda, 2015), pp. 115–39.

62. *Les Supposez*, p. 6.

63. Ibid., p. 1.

64. Susanna de Schepper discusses these purposes of the modesty topos in her ' "For the Common Good and for the National Interest": Paratexts in English Translations of Navigational Works', in *Renaissance Cultural Crossroads: Translation, Print and Culture in Britain, 1473–1640*, ed. by Sara Barker and Brenda Hosington (Leiden: Brill, 2013), pp. 185–208 (p. 207).

65. Valerie Worth-Stylianou, 'Reading Monolingual and Bilingual Editions of Translations in Renaissance France', in *Translation and the Transmission of Culture between 1300 and 1600*, ed. by Jeanette Beer and Kenneth Lloyd-Jones (Kalamazoo, MI: Kalamazoo Press, 1995), pp. 331–58.

66. Lodovico Ariosto, *La comedie des supposez de M. Louys Arioste, italien et françois. Pour l'utilité de ceux qui desirent sçavoir la langue italienne*, trans. by Jean-Pierre de Mesmes (Paris: Hierosme de Marnef, 1585).

67. Balsamo, *Les Rencontres des muses*, p. 54.

68. Guillaume des Autelz, *Replique de Guillaume des Autelz, aux furieuses defenses de Louis Meigret* (Lyon: Jean de Tournes, 1551).

PART II

The Performance of Comedy in Renaissance France (1548–58)

CHAPTER 3

From Page to Stage:
The Example of *La Calandra*

Circa alla sodisfatione della comedia, non pur sua Maestà che lo disse piu
d'una volta, ma ancora i Signori e Gentilhuomini di Corte per una voce tutti
affermavano non haver mai veduto il piu bello spettacolo.

[In terms of appreciation for the comedy, it was not just his Majesty who
voiced his own admiration, but also the lords and gentlemen of the court, who
collectively affirmed that they had never seen a greater spectacle.]

(Francesco Mazzei, in Maurice Scève, *La magnifica et triumphale entrata del
christianiss. re di Francia* [The magnificent and triumphal entry of the most
Christian King of France], 1549)

Part II moves from poetics to performance, turning the focus from written theories
of comedy to the stagings of plays which took place in France from 1548 to 1558.
This chapter centres on a performance of the comedy *La Calandra*, which was staged
in Lyons as part of the 1548 celebrations organised for the royal entry of Henri II and
Catherine de' Medici, the new queen consort of France.[1] *La Calandra* was written
in around 1507 by Bernardo Dovizi da Bibbiena (1470–1520) and first performed
in Urbino as part of the 1513 carnival celebrations. The 1548 Lyons play is one of
the earliest performances of a comedy in France, and the first to be described and
documented in detail by contemporaries. Richard Cooper has collated facsimiles
of some of these sources in his edition of Maurice Scève's *Entry of Henri II into
Lyon: September 1548*, including Scève's *livret* commemorating the Lyons entry, and
the long-forgotten Italian translation of this *livret*, completed by the Florentine
merchant Francesco Mazzei. This translation includes a lengthy section on the
performance of *La Calandra* entitled 'Particolare descrizione', which was absent
from Scève's text: both sources have proved indispensable to this study.[2]

The Entry of Henri II into Lyon makes available a number of essential core texts,
as well as providing an excellent general overview of the performance; however,
Cooper's study focuses on the entire entry, and does not therefore analyse the
comedy in close detail. This chapter assesses the performance in context, comparing
it with other contemporary theatrical writings and identifying the features which
made it an innovation in France, including the use of sets and staging, intervals,
professional actors, and prose. This chapter also helps to determine the Italian
influence on this play, the extent of which has been underestimated. Not only was

La Calandra written by an Italian, but the Lyons staging took place in the original language; was masterminded by a range of Italian patrons; and was brought to life by Italian architects, composers, and performers. In contrast to French theoreticians, such as Estienne and Du Bellay, these Italian innovators were not so concerned with the enrichment of French language and culture, as with pleasing the king and queen, thereby advancing their own agenda. As a figure in *Il Cortegiano*, Bibbiena himself had argued that comedy could be employed by the king as a canny tool to win the popularity of his people; conversely, the Italian colony in France used *La Calandra* as a means of gaining favour with the nobility.[3] In a nod to Part III of this book, this chapter will also examine the political motives for writing comedy, and the techniques used by the Italians to achieve their desired outcomes. As we will see in this chapter, a close reading of source materials reveals in sharper focus the novelty of this early performance, the Italian role in its success, and the exploitation of comedy for political gain.

Theatre as Celebration: The Italian Influence

While figures such as Estienne had struggled to promote their praise of classical theatre, some prominent members of the French nobility had, for some time, shown an interest in ancient and Italian drama. As early as 1518, possibly during his visit to Milan, François I acquired a copy of Lelio Manfredi's 'La Philadelphia', an undated Italian comedy which existed only in manuscript form and which was based closely on the classical writers;[4] Henri II added to his father's collection a compilation of Ariosto's theatre.[5] Lazare de Baïf's aforementioned translation of the *Electra* was possibly read aloud before the nobles,[6] and Marguerite de Navarre commissioned France's first sixteenth-century translation of Boccaccio's *Decameron*, a work which was to inspire numerous comedies in France and beyond.[7] Marguerite also wrote some of her own *comédies* (which, despite the name, are more medieval in style) and produced the first French imitation of the *Decameron*, entitled *L'Heptaméron*, a collection of stories, many of which are comic.[8] This interest in theatre and comedy coincided with an ever accelerating vogue at the French court for Italian culture, a trend which has been well documented by scholars such as Picot, Balsamo, and Sozzi.[9] By the 1540s the Italians were themselves well aware of their influence on the French court; in 1543, for example, the foremost anti-courtier propagandist Pietro Aretino (1492–1556) attempted to dissuade the poet Claude Chappuys from returning to the French court, on the basis that it had become indistinguishable from its Italian counterpart.[10] This Italianisation of the French court intensified in 1547 when Catherine de' Medici became queen consort, and when her *fuorusciti* Italian supporters began to infiltrate the court in far greater numbers.[11]

It had long been customary in France to perform *saynètes* (brief theatrical scenes) along the route of a royal entry. François I, for example, had enjoyed a series of playlets acted for him by a group of 'joueurs de farces et moralitez' [farce and morality actors] in celebration of his entry into the commune of Villers-Cotterêts.[12] Meanwhile, the Italians — and the Medici family in particular — were known for their elaborate celebrations, regularly organising festivities which often included a minimum of one classically-inspired theatrical performance, in imitation of the famously generous hospitality offered by the Greeks and Romans.[13] Given the increasing French awareness of classical theatre, combined with the rising fascination for Italian culture, it is unsurprising that we witness in the 1540s a new emphasis on theatrical performance as celebration. There is evidence that two performances of Italian comedies took place in Lyons for the carnival festivities in 1541 and 1542: these appear to have been organised by the Florentine presence there, and may have been acted for the Florentine Cardinal Niccolò Gaddi in the Abbey of Ainay and at the palace of Ippolito d'Este.[14] Although we know very little about these stagings (there is no record even of which comedies were acted), they do signal the emergence in France of a new trend, and also indicate that it was the Italian presence in France which helped to inaugurate classical and Italian performance as celebration.

Other Theatrical Performance at the Lyons Entry

The organisers of the 1548 entry went to great lengths to recreate the famous Medicean theatrical festivities, not only in their arrangement of the comedy but also in several other performances, of which three examples will suffice. Henri arrived several days before Catherine, and was regaled with games, religious services, and feasts. He was firstly entertained with a *saynète* based on classical mythology, which depicted the Roman goddess Diana hunting a lion. While this *saynète* was clearly an attempt to stage a classically-inspired performance, it was also deeply symbolic: the lion was the symbol of Lyons, and the hunter goddess Diana an allegory for Henri's mistress Diane de Poitiers winning the king's heart. As Cooper notes, Diane was at her closest to the king during this period, having recently been given the duchy of Valentinois; it is likely that the Lyons consuls, who had enlisted Diane to help them evade the annual tax, aimed to flatter her with this representation, thus winning greater favour.[15] A second *saynète*, performed for the king and then again for the queen's entry, featured a mock-battle between Neptune and Pallas. Again, this style of mock-battle has its origins in classical literature and culture; it had also recently been reinvented in Italy as the *battagliola*, and was used as festival entertainment.[16] In the month before the Lyons entry, for example, the king had visited Piedmont, where he was entertained with a *battagliola* comprising over 1,700 participants.[17] This *saynète*, however, was clearly also inspired by another Italian source: a recent etching of Athena and Poseidon by the Bolognese Antonio Fantuzzi (see figure 3.1).[18] Fantuzzi's etching was produced *c.* 1545 at Fontainebleau, imitating designs which decorated the palace. Again, the organisers show close attention to detail in tailoring the performances to the royal couple and to the Medici heritage, as well as relying both on Italian traditions and direct sources.

Finally, an elaborate *naumachia* (naval battle) was performed on the Saône. The *naumachia* was a tradition of Lyons; yet, this performance was far more sophisticated than previous enactments of sea battles. The arrangement of ships, as Margaret

FIG. 3.1. Antonio Fantuzzi, 'Contest between Athena and Poseidon', etching, Fontainebleau, *c.* 1545. Now held in the Metropolitan Museum of Art, The Elisha Whittelsey Collection, The Elisha Whittelsey Fund, 1949 New York City.

McGowan has observed, was modelled on Serlio's engraving of the Belvedere Court at the Vatican Palace;[19] the best fencers were employed to train twelve *gladiateurs* to fight on the galleys which were, according to the royal historiographer Denis Sauvage, 'tellement painctes, pannocellées, enrichies et garnies de soldards braves et fors' [elaborately painted, panelled, enriched and decorated with brave and strong soldiers] (see figure 3.2).[20]

Again, the performance of a sea battle had been inspired by ancient tradition and revived in Italy, where it was a fixture at the Medici court.[21] As well as pleasing Catherine with its imitation of Italian culture, the reinvention of classical entertainment functions as a reminder to Henri that Lyons had its roots in antiquity: it had been a key Roman city in Gaul, known as Lugdunum. The first printed bulletin of the entry emphasises the potential of the Lyons festivities to rival those held for the ancient Roman *triumphus*: 'Qui feirent [les Lyonnois] si bien leurs apprestz, et meirent si bon ordre, que l'entrée fust tres magnifique. Et ne puis croyre, que le triumphe tant renommé de Cesar, fust de si grande valeur et estime que cestuy cy' [The Lyons inhabitants made their preparations so well, and proceeded with such precision, that the entry was very magnificent. The widely renowned *triumphus* of Caesar could not possibly be so worthy and esteemed as this one].[22] Scève, too, points out that the Lyons consuls were magnificent hosts precisely because of their Roman ancestors: 'Parquoy Messieurs de la Ville, ne voulant degenerer à leur antique generosité Romaine, comme descenduz d'icelle,

FIG. 3.2. Woodcut by Bernard Salomon representing the 'Gallere blanche et verte' of the *naumachia* staged at Lyons, in Maurice Scève, *La magnificence de la superbe et triumphante entree de la noble et antique Cité de Lyon faicte au Treschrestien Roy de France Henry deuxiesme de ce nom, et à la royne Catherine son Espouse le XXIII. de Septembre M.D.XLVIII* (Lyons: Guillaume Rouillé, 1549), fol. L2ʳ. BnF, Bibliothèque municipale de Lyon, Rés 355882.

se resolurent unanimement d'estrendre leur debvoir' [Since the consuls of the city, not wanting to forsake their ancient Roman generosity, being descended from them, unanimously resolved to extend their welcome] (*La magnificence*, fol. A2ʳ). By reminding Henri and Catherine of Lyons's Roman legacy, as well as using a running theme of battle, the royal couple are invited to recall Lyons's cultural achievements as well as its former military glory. Non-comic performance, then, was employed not only to please its spectators but also as a tool for gaining favour, which would set the city — and its individual organisers — in good stead for future recompense.

Noble Support of *La Calandra*

Bibbiena's *La Calandra* was one of the most well-known comedies in sixteenth-century Italy. The play's debut in Urbino was the talk of courts throughout the peninsula, and it was reprinted in no fewer than twenty-three editions between 1521 and 1586.[23] Yet it is likely that Bibbiena's links with the Medici family, above all, made it a suitable choice for the Lyons entry. Bibbiena had in 1512 helped to bring the Medici family back to Florence, whence they had been in exile since 1494; he was also secretary to Cardinal Giovanni di Lorenzo de' Medici, and was promoted to Papal Treasurer — and finally created a cardinal — when Giovanni became Pope Leo X.[24] Bibbiena built on his rapport with the Medici by acting as ambassador to France, even bringing to Fontainebleau as a gift for Catherine's father-in-law François I — who collected paintings of female beauty 'designed for his delectation' — Raphael's portrait of the famously alluring Isabel de Requesens, wife of the viceroy of Naples.[25] A performance of *La Calandra*, which had also been acted in Rome for Pope Leo, Catherine's great-uncle, would be a fitting nod to the Medici heritage and one of the family's key supporters. Mazzei's *Particolare descritione* also indicates that the comedy was chosen on account of Catherine, alluding to its link with the Medici: 'La Comedia [...] era nata nella patria loro di Toscana e [...] alzata dalla Chiarissima casa della Maestà Christianissima della Regina sua Consorte' [the Comedy [...] was born in their native land of Tuscany and [...] raised by the illustrious house of her most Christian Majesty the Queen and her consort] (*La magnifica et triumphale entrata*, fol. N4ʳ). It seems as though Catherine herself had been told about the choice of play and especially looked forward to the performance: papal correspondence in the months leading up to the performance of *La Calandra* pass on Catherine's encouragement for Cardinal Farnese to see this comedy: 'La Nation florentine prepare une belle comedie qui sera jouée à cette occasion [...] la Reine voudroit que le cardinal Farnese vint à Lyon pour ces fetes' [The Florentine nation is preparing an excellent comedy which will be performed for this occasion [...] the Queen would like Cardinal Farnese to come to Lyons for these festivities].[26] Catherine was evidently aware of — and had greatly anticipated — the performance of *La Calandra* in Lyons.

While classical and Italianate performance was clearly intended to be an important part of the festivities, the decision to include *La Calandra* may also be due to the king, who seems himself to have requested for a comedy to be performed. Mazzei's translation provides three indications that Henri made a special request for a comedy. Firstly, the full title of the translation, 'Particolare descritione della comedia fatta recitare in Lione da la natione fiorentina à richiesta di sua Maestà Christianissima' [Specific Description of the Comedy Put on in Lyons by the Florentine Nation, at the Request of his Most Christian Majesty], describes unequivocally the King's desire for a comedy at the entry. Secondly, Mazzei praises the 'cortese benignità con laquale [la sua Maestà] si era degnata comandare che fusse recitata davanti a lui' [courteous kindness with which [his Majesty] had deigned to command it to be performed for him] (*La magnifica et triumphale entrata*, fol. N4ᵛ). Finally, Mazzei describes the haste in which the Italian acting troupe was obliged to prepare the comedy, 'havendo al principio di luglio sua Maestà domandata la Comedia per mezzo Agosto' [the king having requested the comedy at the beginning of July, for performance in mid-August] (*La magnifica et triumphale entrata*, fol. N4ᵛ). The king and queen, then, were not passive witnesses to the play, and their role in the first major comic performance in France is not insignificant. While they clearly did not play a part in its organisation, the comedy may have been chosen on Catherine's behalf, and she looked forward to the performance and sought to invite spectators; Henri, too, was evidently eager to see such a performance, and there is sufficient evidence in Mazzei's translation to indicate that he himself had requested one for the entry.

Organising *La Calandra*: Possible Italian Co-ordinators

Lyons was an appropriate city in which to host this performance. Many early styles of comedy took place in Paris and in the provinces; yet Lyons was also known for its comic tradition. Barnabé Chaussard (*c.* 1460–1527), based in Lyons, printed more farces than anyone else in France; Barthélémy Aneau's *Lyon marchant* (1541), a melting pot of the farce, *sottie*, and mystery play, is also one of the first French examples of a college-led performance. France's first purpose-built theatre was constructed by merchant Jean Neiron in Lyons in 1539, where the townsfolk performed 'les histoires du viel et nouveau Testament, avec la farce au bout' [stories of the Old and New Testament, with a farce at the end].[27] Yet Lyons's main advantage was its many Italian inhabitants, who were crucial in ensuring the success of *La Calandra*. While Scève was the *maestro delle preparazioni*, organising much of the entry as well as documenting it in his *livret*, there is no evidence to suggest that he was involved in arranging the comedy. Scève specialised in preparing banquets, religious services, and gardens; he showed little interest in theatre, dedicating only a few lines to the performance in his *livret*, and not even mentioning the comedy by name. The brevity of his discussion of the comedy has led some to believe that he did not even attend the performance.[28] As we have just seen, both the papal correspondence and Mazzei's translation attribute the organisation of the comedy to 'la Nation florentine'; though they mention few names, there is other evidence to suggest the identity of the Italians involved.

1. Ippolito d'Este

Ippolito was not a Florentine; yet, much of the impetus behind the performance of *La Calandra* clearly came from him. Ippolito had been Archbishop of Lyons since 1540, and was protector of France in the Roman court;[29] he was also popular with the king and everyone at court, most famously the women.[30] Ippolito was well known as a patron of theatre: his family had supported comic performance for many years, and was largely responsible for the introduction of theatre into Ferrara in the early Cinquecento.[31] Soon after his arrival at Fontainebleau, he began to organise Italian-style *mascherate*:[32] in 1541, for instance, he arranged a play in which the Duke of Orléans appeared as a *zingaro* [gypsy] and the King of Navarre, together with Ippolito himself, were 'stranamente vestiti [e] i più burloni della schiera' [oddly dressed [and] the silliest of the lot].[33] The comedy also took place in Ippolito's Lyons palace, where the royal couple was staying.

Given his family history of patronising comedy, connection with Lyons, and interest in pioneering performances in France, Ippolito was well placed to assist with *La Calandra*; indeed, evidence suggests that the choice of comedy fell to him, as well as the decision to fund the performance. In the months leading up to the entry, Ippolito's accounts record that he ordered eight comedies to be specially picked out by a representative in Venice and sent to his residence in France.[34] This would suggest not only that Ippolito was to decide on the comedy, but also that he had considered at length a number of options. A play by Ariosto, who was already well known transnationally, would have been more obvious: *I suppositi* was in fact performed by members of the Accademia degli Intronati this same year for the Spanish wedding of Maximilian II to Maria of Spain.[35] Ariosto was also Ferrarese, and had been chamberlain to Alfonso I d'Este (Ippolito's father) and patronised by Isabella d'Este (Ippolito's aunt); however, Ippolito also had links with Bibbiena. Isabella was a friend of Bibbiena, and *La Calandra* had been performed with great success in Rome in 1514 for her sister-in-law, Elisabetta Gonzaga.[36] Crucially, Ippolito would also have been aware of Catherine's family connections with Bibbiena, and the knowledge that this particular comedy would please her may well have convinced him of its suitability.

Cooper has noted that according to his accounts, Ippolito spent a total of ten thousand ducats on the play, which corresponds exactly to the chronicler Brantôme's later report that the comedy cost ten thousand *écus*.[37] It seems likely, then, that Ippolito made a major financial contribution to the play, although this is not mentioned in Scève's *livret* nor in the *Particolare descritione*. Yet a final comment from Brantôme again suggests that Ippolito had a crucial part in bringing *La Calandra* to the stage. Brantôme describes the comedy which 'ce grand et magnifique cardinal de Ferrare, primat de la Gaule et archevesque de Lyon, fit représenter' [this great and magnificent Cardinal of Ferrara, Primate of the Gauls and Archbishop of Lyon, had performed], explicitly crediting the organisation of this play to Ippolito.[38] The performance would have been witnessed first-hand by Brantôme's mother and grandmother, who had accompanied Marguerite de Navarre to the entry: clearly, information concerning Ippolito's involvement had been directly passed down, and we have no reason to believe that the spectators had purely invented these ideas. We might gather from Brantôme's statement — as well as from Ippolito's other theatrical enterprises, order of eight comedies, and swiftly depleting accounts — that Ippolito played a larger role behind the scenes of *La Calandra* than has previously been assumed. It is also plausible that Ippolito, who was a shrewd and skilled negotiator, viewed this performance as an important investment in his rapport with Catherine and Henri. He had already profited from royal favour, being compensated for his political and cultural efforts with generous pensions, periods abroad, and an advantageous position at the court: the impressive spectacle of a comedy he had partly financed and chosen specifically to please the queen was no doubt an important opportunity to earn further rewards.

2. Lucantonio Ridolfi (1510–70)

Turning to Lyons's 'nation Florentine', Ridolfi was one of the city's foremost Florentine *fuorusciti* and a distant relative of Catherine de' Medici.[39] He was also a prominent humanist, who would be known later in the sixteenth century for editing a dialogue between Alessandro degli Uberti and Claude d'Herberé on language in Boccaccio's *Decameron*: this topic was extremely popular among French learned circles in the mid-century, as we will see later in this chapter.[40] Ridolfi played an important part in *La Calandra* by recommending the production of the Italian translation of Scève's *livret*, with its special focus on the comic performance, which is the fullest remaining evidence of the play. In a letter written to Ridolfi by Lyons printer Guillaume Rouillé, who printed the translation, Rouillé describes Ridolfi's encouragement in producing this text: 'Mosso da tale vostra persuasione, feci nella detta lingua tradurre e stampare l'entrata del Re qui in Lyone insieme colla descrittione della comedia: laqual mia impressione penso che se non in tutto almeno in qualche parte vi sodisfacessi' [Moved by your persuasion, I had the entry of the king here in Lyons, together with the description of the comedy, translated into the said language and printed: I believe that you will be satisfied if not by all of it, then by some of it].[41] Ridolfi's request for an Italian translation of the booklet, along with a detailed description of the comedy, indicates that Italian contemporaries living in Lyons and perhaps also in his native city of Florence had wanted to read about the festivities and keep a record of the achievement. Such an interest in this account clearly indicates that this entry — and particularly, this comedy — was not solely a French effort, but the result of a collaboration with other Italians in Lyons. As well as providing further evidence of the Italian contribution to the comedy, Ridolfi's recommendation for this account to be created also implies that he was involved in the production of *La Calandra*, as the later section on staging will suggest.

3. Gondi and Guadagni

The Gondi and Guadagni families, both part of the Florentine business colony, were among the most affluent in Lyons. They were both also linked to the Medici: the Guadagni family had been exiled at the same time as the Medici, and were sympathetic to Catherine;[42] the Gondi family had been supporters and business partners of the Medici for several centuries.[43] It is well known that Ridolfi 'gardait les yeux fixés vers Florence' [kept his eyes turned towards Florence]; however, many members of merchant families were also anxious to return to their native city, and had much to gain by pleasing the king and queen.[44] Catherine was in a powerful position to support their cause for a return to Florence, and even if she did not directly help, it would be beneficial to gain the advocacy of the Florentine Piero Strozzi. Strozzi was their highly influential marshal in Lyons and a long-time favourite of Catherine, and may have been able to exercise political leverage in their favour.[45] Given the links of the Gondi and Guadagni with Lyons's foremost humanists (they were closely connected with Ridolfi, for example), they would certainly have been aware of preparations for the upcoming comedy. Although no contemporary reports suggest that these families helped with the organisation of the performance, we shall see in later sections the likelihood of their financial contribution, as well as their possible involvement of protégés.

Bringing *La Calandra* to Life: Sets and Staging

1. Serlio

The Italians were well known as pioneers in Europe of sets and staging. Almost a century before the performance of *La Calandra*, the Italian humanist and architect Leon Battista Alberti had set out an argument for the similarity of Italian theatre to its Roman predecessor, repeatedly describing the Roman set as *noster* and indicating that the constructions of his contemporaries could rival those of the ancients.[46] Italian architects were internationally respected: as we saw in Chapter 1, Serlio had been enticed from Italy by the French king and patronised by Ippolito. By the time of the Lyons entry in 1548, Serlio was living in Ippolito's lodgings and had designed much of his Italianate residence at Fontainebleau, dubbed 'Le Grand Ferrare'. There is no mention in contemporary accounts of Serlio's contribution to architectural work for *La Calandra*; yet, it is probable that he designed the theatre in which the comedy took place. The theatre was built in the 'Salle Saint-Jean' in Ippolito's Lyons palace, which Brantôme describes as an initially unappealing room: it was 'une chose vaste, layde et sans aucune forme de beauté ny gentillesse, comm'un certain galletas' [a vast, ugly thing, with no beauty, form, or grace; something of a hovel].[47] Using the dimensions provided in the Florentine *braccia* by Mazzei, Eugene Johnson and Grace McEniry have produced a visual reconstruction of this theatre (see figure 3.3).[48]

With its ten pilasters and arches, each displaying a different feature, the walls of this reconstruction strongly resemble those designed by Serlio for the Château d'Ancy-le-Franc in Yonne; in turn, Serlio's arches are possibly themselves imitated from the nave that Alberti designed for the Basilica of Sant'Andrea in Mantua.[49] Additionally, the painted steps leading up to the stage clearly recall Serlio's design of the *scena comica* examined in Chapter 1 (see figure 1.2), and recommended for use by Charles Estienne.[50] Serlio had previously designed a theatre for Ippolito's Fontainebleau lodgings (now demolished); he also attended the Lyons entry as a

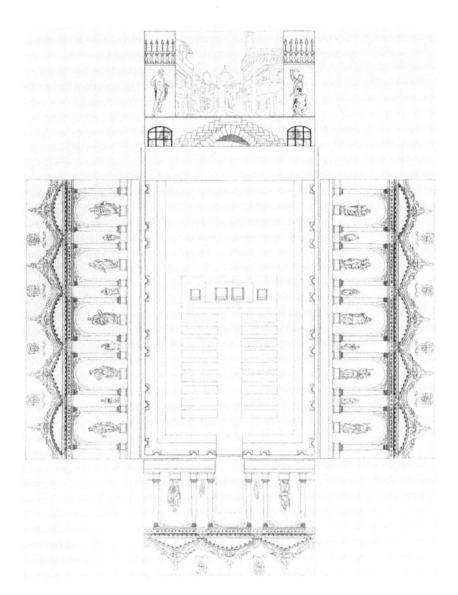

FIG. 3.3. Serlio's possible theatre plan for *La Calandra*, designed by Eugene Johnson and illustrated by Grace McEniry, in Eugene Johnson, 'The Theater at Lyon of 1548: A Reconstruction and Attribution', *Artibus et Historiae*, 35.69 (2014), 173–202 (p. 174, figure 1). Reproduced with the kind permission of the author.

guest of the cardinal.[51] Given his position as royal architect, the similarity of his previous designs with the transformed theatre space in Ippolito's palace, his work on a theatre for Fontainebleau, and his presence at the entry, we can reasonably credit Serlio with the design of the theatre space, which is the first known dedicated theatre to house a comedy in France. Yet, he does not appear to have designed the perspective set itself, a task which was undertaken by another Italian.

FIG. 3.4. Andrea del Sarto, *Sacra Famiglia Medici* (1529),
Galleria Palatina, Inv. Palatina n. 89, Gallerie degli Uffizi, Florence. Reproduced
by permission of the Ministero per i beni e le attività culturali e per il turismo;
all rights reserved

2. Nannoccio della Costa San Giorgio (dates unknown)

While no mention is made of Serlio, Mazzei's *Particolare descritione* outlines that the perspective set was painted by a certain 'maestro Nannoccio che qua si trova gia sono piu anni al servitio del Cardinale di Tornon' [maestro Nannoccio who has been here for a few years already, in the service of the Cardinal of Tournon] (*La magnifica et triumphale entrata*, fol. M2^r). No further description is provided; however, this was most likely to be Nannoccio della Costa San Giorgio.[52] Nannoccio was resident artist for Cardinal François de Tournon, who in 1551 took over from Ippolito d'Este the role of Archbishop of Lyons. Nannoccio had been introduced to Cardinal de Tournon by his longtime supporter Tommaso Guadagni, who may also have recommended his services for the painting of this set.[53] Nannoccio, however, was not simply chosen to paint this set because he was in Lyons: again, his role in the production was aimed at pleasing Catherine. Nannoccio was a fellow Florentine, and connected to the Medici family through his teacher Andrea del Sarto. Del Sarto was an ally of the Medici and had been commissioned by Catherine's cousin Ottaviano to paint the famous 'Sacra Famiglia Medici', which he completed at the time of his tutorship to Nannoccio (see figure 3.4).[54]

As well as choosing an artist who would showcase Florentine talent and links with the Medici, the organisers aimed to flatter Catherine with the only significant edit made to the original text of *La Calandra*: the setting is switched from Rome to Florence. Scève mentions only in passing that the comedy had a 'perspective de Relief' [relief perspective], lending further evidence to the argument that Scève did not attend the play (*La magnificence*, fol. K3^r); however, Mazzei describes the realism and accuracy with which the set depicts the city of Florence (*La magnifica et triumphale entrata*, fol. M2^v). He praises how Nannoccio manages to portray not just Florence's smaller buildings, but also the city's major landmarks, with such success that the spectator might believe themselves to be in Florence: the set is 'figurata per Firenze così bene che per non dire delli altri minori edificii: la cupola, il campanile di santa Reparata, quello del Palazzo Ducale hareste detto che fussimo stati veramente quivi' [made to appear so much like Florence, not just in the smaller buildings but also in the dome, the bell-tower of Santa Reparata, and that of the ducal palace, that the spectators might have thought themselves truly to be there] (*La magnifica et triumphale entrata*, fol. M2^r). Writing to the Duke of Mantua, his ambassador Giorgio Conegrani also emphasises the realism of the cityscape: 'Si fece la scena apparve ad un tratto la città di Firrenza benissimo et molto artificiosamente fatta' [The stage all of a sudden portrayed the city of Florence, very finely and artfully done].[55] The perspective set was an innovation for France, and despite the instructions of Estienne in his writings on theatre, had never before been included in a performance in France. While native spectators would no doubt have been fascinated by the set, the praise of the Italians — whose stage artists prided themselves above all on the realism of their sets — confirms that the scene must have been impressively ornate and detailed.[56] No doubt the convincing depiction of Florence and the glory of its many buildings, completed by a Florentine himself, would also have had a flattering effect on Catherine, portraying to the spectators the majesty of her hometown. The particular incorporation of the ducal palace mentioned by Mazzei — the residence of Catherine's cousin Cosimo, who had been Duke of Florence since 1537 — must also have been intended as a reminder to the spectators of the new queen's distinguished family. The inclusion of a perspective set, then, was aimed largely at impressing and exalting the queen; additionally, we can determine that this set, designed by Serlio and painted by Nannoccio, who may in turn have been recommended by the Guadagni, was once again an Italian enterprise. As we shall see in Chapter 4, this set was also to be the start of a long French tradition of stage design.

3. Zanobi Lastricati (1508–90)

While Scève makes a brief mention that there was an elevated stage — 'une platte forme de deux piedz de haulteur' [a two-foot high platform] — no further references are made to the stage itself (*La magnificence*, fol. E1^v). Instead, the decorative statues which helped to prepare the Salle Saint-Jean for the comedy are singled out for attention in the majority of accounts. Scève does not identify the sculptor, but Mazzei describes the work as 'di mano di maestro Zanobi scultore fatto venire in diligenza di Firenze per questo effetto solamente' [of the hand of the sculptor maestro Zanobi, diligently brought over from Florence for this very task] (*La magnifica et triumphale entrata*, fol. M3^v). As Cooper has noted, this is undoubtedly Zanobi Lastricati, a Florentine sculptor and contemporary of Vasari.[57] Again, it is likely that Lastricati was chosen both on the recommendation of a Lyons Florentine, and as a result of his connections with the Medici family. Lastricati was closely associated with Ridolfi, and had already sculpted 'un Mercurio in bronzo' [a bronze Mercury] for Lorenzo di Piero Ridolfi;[58] it is not unimaginable that Lucantonio Ridolfi recommended his work and invited him to Lyons. Lastricati had also been a protégé of the Medici family, and had been commissioned to create several works in bronze for them.[59]

The most elaborate of Lastricati's statues was that of a young girl, described by Mazzei. She was placed in the antechamber and stood next to the door of the Salle, presumably as a figure for welcoming spectators to the performance (*La magnifica et triumphale entrata*, fol. M1^v). She held a red lily and the pedestal on which she stood was inscribed with the words 'LILIA MAGNA PRECOR, NOSTRUM NE TEMNITE PARVUM' [I beg the big lilies not to look down on our little lily] (*La magnifica et triumphale entrata*, fol. M2^r). This statue was no doubt intended as a means of enhancing the aesthetics of the initially unappealing Salle; yet, she also functioned as a statement of Italian deference. The red lily, which she held, was the emblem of Florence; however, this red lily also refers to the single lily, which begs to be supported by the larger lilies of France. Despite the apparent innocence of this statue, it suggests — in a gesture clearly flattering to Henri — that France's military and cultural powers are beginning to overtake those of their Italian counterparts.

Yet conversely, this statue also invites spectators to consider Catherine's role in bringing Florentine culture to France, especially in light of the comedy they are imminently to witness. The symbol of the lily subsequently reappears in the comedy, where Catherine is presented during an interval with 'une grande fleur de lys en or sur laquelle sont gravés des lys rouges' [a large golden lily on which red lilies are engraved] (*La magnificence*, fol. K3ʳ). This gift is again heavily allegorical: it is a merging of the red lily on a field of silver with the golden lily on a field of blue, which had historically symbolised the alliance between Florence and France. This symbol would have been easily recognised by the spectators, having gained particular renown with Jean Lemaire de Belges's retelling of the founding of Florence by Charlemagne, who had established the city as a heraldic device so that 'toute Ytalie sera à jamais concordée avecques France' [all of Italy will be forever allied with France].[60] The cost of this extravagant gift (which totalled two hundred and fifty écus) was covered by the Florentines: Mazzei describes 'il presente che la Natione Fiorentina fece alla Regina' [the gift made to the queen by the Florentines] (*La magnifica et triumphale entrata*, fol. O3ᵛ). Ippolito's accounts contain no record of this amount, and it is possible that it was the Gondi or Guadagni families who had funded this gift: indeed, they were the most important stakeholders in the Lyons economy, and their wealth was so well known that the phrase *riche comme Gadagne* [as rich as Guadagni] became almost proverbial.[61] This heavily symbolic gift, as well as the statue, was clearly aimed at reminding Catherine of her status as a connection between Italy and France, and — if the gift was indeed made by the Gondi or Guadagni — may well have constituted another attempt to encourage political reward for the Florentines in Lyons.

The statues decorating the Salle itself were designed to draw attention to Tuscan cultural and military successes. Twelve statues depicting Florentine worthies were placed around the room, half depicting poets and half soldiers. Mazzei identifies the six statues portraying poets as Dante, Petrarch, Claudian, Boccaccio, Ficino, and Accursius, and also notes that the military statues represent Lorenzo di Piero de' Medici, Giovanni delle Bande Nere, Filippo Buondelmonti degli Scolari, Farinata degli Uberti, Federico Folchi, and Giovanni Strozzi (*La magnifica et triumphale entrata*, ff. M4ᵛ and M5ʳ). Apart from Claudian, who, as Giannozzi Manetti wrote in his famous fifteenth-century biography of Petrarch, had been the last to wear the laurel crown before Petrarch, all of the poets were born in or associated with Florence.[62] Although Scève tells us that these statues were 'toguez à l'antique et coronez de Laurier' [dressed in ancient togas and crowned with laurels], Mazzei specifies that only Dante and Petrarch wore laurel crowns (no doubt alluding to their real-life attainment of the wreath); Boccaccio wore an oak crown and the others were bareheaded (*La magnificence*, fol. K3ʳ; *La magnifica et triumphale entrata*, fol. N1ʳ). The imagery of the Florentines as the most accomplished ancient poets, as well as the inclusion of the last Roman poet to wear the crown, draws clear parallels between them, indicating that Tuscan writers have equalled the work of their ancient predecessors. Turning to the military statues, Lorenzo's presence among the warriors can be explained by his dual status as Catherine's father and the first Medici to marry into France, and the five others are glorified *condottieri* who battled outside Florence: this representation both flatters Catherine and celebrates the Florentine *fuorusciti* who had found success in Lyons.[63] Johnson is correct to point out that the Lyons theatre space was 'a celebration largely of Tuscany'.[64] These statues were certainly successful in enhancing the aesthetics of the theatre space. Mazzei recounts how the spectators lingered to admire the statues even after the comedy had ended: 'Stetteno tutti Fermi à rimirare buon pezzo di poi lo apparato ilquale nel vero faceva un bellissimo e suntuosissimo vedere' [They all stopped to marvel again at the display, which made truly for a beautiful and sumptuous sight] (*La magnifica et triumphale entrata*, fol. M5^r). Yet these statues also worked to flatter Henri and Catherine, reminding them of the Florentines' diverse and far-reaching talent: not only had they fulfilled the humanist aim of reinventing — and even equalling — classical literature and culture, but they had also secured military victories across Europe. Thus much of the design produced for the comedy, carried out by a fellow Florentine and protégé of the Medici, was focused on strengthening royal favour, constituting a persuasive and political act. This potential of comedy to acquire allies — or, conversely, to insult an enemy — will be an important subject of this book's remaining chapters.

Bringing *La Calandra* to Life: The Interval

As well as the lavish theatre space and set design, which were innovations for France, *La Calandra* was also the first performance to comprise a series of intervals: as Mazouer notes, this was one of the major elements which made the performance 'une révélation' for its French spectators.[65] As we saw in Chapter 1, the interval had been reintroduced in Italy towards the end of the 1400s. The Medici family were particularly well known for their patronage of intervals, employing figures such as Bernardo Buontalenti and Giovanni Bardi to devise impressive and original performances.[66] The intervals which took place during Antonio Landi's comedy *Il commodo* at the 1539 wedding of Cosimo de' Medici and Eleonora di Toledo in Florence were a landmark in the practice.[67] There were seven intervals in total, which were extensive, lavish, and specially written for the occasion: judged by many to be the comedy's most impressive feature, they set an important precedent for *La Calandra*.[68] The organisers commissioned original performances for the 1548 intervals, and had incorporated elaborate music, costumes, and a script. The intervals were clearly striking for the audience, and their novelty in particular is emphasised in several reports: Scève for example stresses that this feature was 'une nouvelle mode, et non encor usitee aux recitementz des Comedies' [a new practice, and never before employed in comic performance] (*La magnificence*, fol. K3^r). Clearly, he anticipated that his readership would be unfamiliar with how an interval worked: calling them 'intermedies des actes', he clarifies, like Estienne, that these performances would have taken place in between each act of the comedy (*Les Abusez*, p. 6; *La magnificence*, fol. K3). In addition to his praise of the interval's novelty, Scève's clarification also suggests that the interval was still a little-known feature in France, eight years after Estienne had advised their reinvention.

Neither Scève nor Mazzei refer to the author of the intervals. Based on the discovery of a document referring to the 'Intermedi alla comedia del 46 di Palla Strozzi', Judith Bryce has suggested that it may have been the Florentine humanist Palla di Lorenzo Strozzi who contributed to the 1541 Lyons comic production.[69] Yet Strozzi's intervals are dated to 1546, two years before the Lyons intervals, which were clearly specially written to incorporate, for example, the presentation of Catherine's golden lily. Bonner Mitchell has argued that the author of the intervals will remain anonymous, and that it is not possible even to identify whether he was French or Italian.[70] Yet Scève's Italianism of *intermedies*, based more closely on *intermezzi* than Estienne's *intervales*, suggests that the author was an Italian, who had perhaps discussed the feature in his native language. Additionally, Conegrani's dispatch, brought to light by Cooper, clearly states that 'ne era lo authore M.r Luigi Allamani' [their author was Luigi Alamanni].[71] Conegrani had taken a close interest in these intervals, and even recalled who delivered each line: it is highly unlikely that he simply fabricated Alamanni's involvement, especially since his was an official dispatch to the Duke of Mantua.

Luigi Alamanni (1495–1556) was a Florentine poet, who had been at Fontainebleau since 1530. He had experience in theatre, having attended performances of comedy during his youth in Italy as well as completing the first Italian translation of Sophocles's *Antigone*.[72] Having been popular with François I, Alamanni was also favoured by his successor Henri, who admired his writings and granted him several distinguished positions, such as ambassador to Genoa.[73] Alamanni was also patronised by Ippolito d'Este, who loaned him money without interest, undertook trips to Italy with him, and granted him lodgings at Fontainebleau, together with Serlio.[74] The third of Alamanni's prestigious protectors was Tommaso Guadagni, whose family, as noted above, almost certainly helped to co-ordinate the performance.[75] Given his popularity at Fontainebleau, the choice of Alamanni was no doubt aimed at pleasing the king, and while it is likely that Alamanni was given the role by Ippolito, Guadagni may well have supported this decision. It also seems as though Guadagni chose the musician who composed the score for and conducted these intervals, who was, as Mazzei tells us, 'Piero Manucci qua organista della Natione Fiorentina' [Piero Manucci, organist here of the Florentine nation] (*La magnifica et triumphale entrata*, fol. P1v). Manucci, an unrenowned musician of whom little is known, appears at first to be a strange choice: however, he was employed at this same time as the organist of Tommaso Guadagni's chapel.[76] Again, the Florentine presence in France was instrumental both in organising this innovation of the interval, and in bringing it to life.

As we saw in Chapter 1, Estienne considered the interval to be particularly able to 'delect[er] le peuple' [delight the audience] and to 'recréer les espr.z' [reinvigorate their minds] (*L'Andrie*, p. 355): a number of accounts of the 1548 intervals also draw attention to these functions. Brantôme notes that the intervals 'contenterent infiniment le roy, la reyne et toute leur court' [infinitely delighted the king, the queen, and all the court];[77] Scève also praises how the intervals commanded 'grandissime attention et plaisance de tous spectateurs' [the utmost attention and pleasure of all the spectators] (*La magnificence*, fol. K4r). The music of the intervals (now lost) appears to have been particularly well received. In the same way as Estienne had singled out the ability of musicians to delight the audience during intervals, Scève describes the 'recreation de la diversité de la Musique' [enjoyment of the many kinds of music] (*Les Abusez*, p. 7; *La magnificence*, fol. K3^r); Conegrani also refers to the pleasure they evoked: 'Ad ogn'uno medesimamente piacque la armonia che li accompagnava' [The harmony that accompanied them pleased one and all].[78] Although Estienne was the first in France to point out the ability of the intervals to please, Alamanni and Manucci were pioneers in bringing to life this idea, and, by all accounts, did so with resounding success.

Yet, as with other Italian involvement in the performance, this innovation was also founded on politics. Alamanni's relationship with the Medici was a problematic one: he had first fled to France after assisting with the notorious 1522 plot to overthrow Pope Clement VII, formerly Giulio de' Medici and Catherine's great-uncle.[79] The composition of intervals for the new queen's entry presented an excellent opportunity to smooth relations with Catherine, and by extension the Medici. The final set of intervals, for example, describe the attainment of the Age of Gold, having passed through the seven ages from the Age of Iron (*La magnifica et triumphale entrata*, ff. N1^r–O3^v). This is a typically humanist representation, depicting the apparent dark ages of literature and culture in contrast with the sublimity considered to have been achieved by contemporary writers and artists.[80] It is at this strategic moment in the final interval, when the peak of artistic achievement has been reached, that Catherine is presented with her golden lily (*La magnifica et triumphale entrata*, fol. O3^v). This presentation is accompanied by the figure of Apollo, addressing Catherine to invoke 'la pace inseno | Al vostro patrio Italico terreno' [Peace at the heart | Of your native Italian lands] and praising the coupling of Florence with France which has been achieved by this marriage: 'Et qual gloria haggia il Tosco fior vermiglio | Di vagheggiar il Franco aurato giglio' [And what glory has the Tuscan vermilion flower | To yearn for the French golden lily] (*La magnifica et triumphale entrata*, fol. O1^r). The inference is that the combined effort of France and Italy, created by the new king and queen, has successfully restored the former glory of classical culture, giving rise in France to 'l'età dell'oro' [the Age of Gold] (*La magnifica et triumphale entrata*, fol. P3^r). As well as being an Italian innovation in France, then, the interval functioned again as a means of gaining royal favour, flattering the spectators with the representation of their role in enhancing and elevating the national culture.

Bringing La Calandra to Life: Professional Performers

There is little evidence to suggest that professional troupes had performed in France before 1548.[81] As we saw in Chapter 2, actors were often lawyers, who performed as part of the plays they had themselves written; members of the nobility also acted in plays, such as Ippolito's aforementioned *mascherate*. Marguerite de Navarre, too, documented the enjoyment of her ladies in acting out medieval comic plays at the Château de Nérac: 'Nous y passons nostre temps à faire mommeries et farces' [We spent our time there acting out mummeries and farces].[82] Estienne had in his 1542 treatise praised the classical actors, drawing special attention to the skills of the Italian 'Boufons' who had successfully reinvented this comic acting style in the present day (*L'Andrie*, p. 353). There is no mention in Scève's *livret* of the delivery of *La Calandra* by a professional troupe, nor does it refer to any involvement of Italian actors. Conegrani's dispatch observes that Henri attended 'una Comedia che dovean far' gli Firrentini' [the comedy that the Florentines put on], which may denote a performance by Florentine actors; however, this may equally be a second reference to the funding of the play by the Florentine colony in Lyons.[83] Yet Mazzei's Italian translation makes a brief reference to a certain 'Barlacchi': 'il Barlacchi, e li altri strioni che di Fierenze si feciono venire' [Barlacchi, and the other actors who were brought from Florence] (*La magnifica et triumphale entrata*, fol. P2[r]). This is without doubt the Florentine Domenico Barlacchi (*c.* 1490–1559) and his troupe 'la Compagnia della Cazzuola' [the Troupe of the Trowel].[84]

The Cazzuola was a shrewd choice of troupe. It was comprised of some of Florence's best-known humanists — including the aforementioned Del Sarto, who painted the sets for the comedy performed at their annual feast — and had performed a range of comedies from Ariosto's 1508 *La cassaria* to Machiavelli's 1525 *Clizia*.[85] The troupe had also already performed *La Calandra*:[86] seeing as the actors were apparently given only six weeks to put together the performance and travel to Lyons (as we have seen, Mazzei explains that notice was provided in July for a performance in mid-August), the organisers clearly judged that a troupe with prior experience of the comedy would be a safe choice. Barlacchi, too, would have been particularly well received by Catherine. He was a prominent Florentine in the service of the Medici as a herald of the Signoria, where he had been called upon to undertake diplomatic missions and act as master of ceremony. He had been involved in numerous Medici festival performances, such as the 1514 plays commissioned by Catherine's father Lorenzo II de' Medici for the Feast of San Giovanni, and a 1518 'Commedia in versi' by Strozzi, acted at Palazzo Medici for the wedding of Catherine's parents.[87] Indeed, a performance by Barlacchi may well have been requested by Catherine herself. The anonymous *Facezie, motti, buffonerie et burle del Piovano Arlotto* [Piovano Arlotto's Quips, Jokes, Buffooneries and Pranks] of 1565 observes that: 'Fu il Barlacchia, oltre all'essere piacevole e faceto, eccellente dicitore a comedie, et massime facendo le parti di un vecchio, et per questo fu egli una volta chiamato in Francia dalla Regina, dove fu benissimo visto e largamente presentato' [It was Barlacchi, who was more than a witty and pleasant man, being a skilled actor of comedies, especially when playing the part of an old man: it was for this reason that the queen called him to France, where he was well received and bountifully rewarded].[88] This account shows knowledge of Barlacchi's generous reward (to be examined in the following pages), as well as suggesting that Barlacchi played an old man: this may well be the eponymous part of Calandro, a much sought-after role. Since the part played by Barlacchi is not specified in any contemporary reports, it is possible that Barlacchi was known to the anonymous author themselves. The new idea that Catherine herself requested Barlacchi's skills may, then, be founded on information provided directly by the actor or his troupe. Not only was a group of Florentines instrumental in bringing comedy to life on the French stage, but Catherine herself may have been more influential than we have previously believed.

While this is the first recorded performance of a professional or semi-professional troupe in France, another key innovation is the inclusion of female actors. We have seen that Marguerite de Navarre, for example, took part in all-female performances of playlets; however, these were private, and were intended only to pass the time among friends. The idea of women acting on a stage before a large audience would have been entirely novel.[89] In this respect, the 1548 performance of *La Calandra* is, as Pamela Allen Brown has noted, an innovation not just in France but also in Italy.[90] Until the 1560s, most women in comedies in Italy and beyond were confined to the wings or to the windows of their houses, with the main female comic roles performed by men.[91] Women did also act in other performances organised for the entry, such as the Diana playlet: however, the comedy was the largest in scale and most prominently featured women; it also received the highest praise from spectators.[92] Brantôme distinguishes between the 'comédiens et comédiantes', pointing out that the latter were 'très belles [et] parloient très-bien et de fort bonne grâce' [most beautiful and spoke extremely well and gracefully].[93] The actors all wore specially made costumes, which were, as Scève notes, constructed from 'satin et velours cramoisy, drap d'or, et d'argent, broché d'or' [crimson satin and velvet, golden and silver cloths, brocaded with gold] (*La magnificence*, fol. K3^r). Again expanding on Scève's description, in his translation Mazzei adds that 'tutti li Strioni furono [...] vestiti richissamamente alla Fiorentina' [all of the actors were [...] richly dressed in the Florentine style] (*La magnifica et triumphale entrata*, fol. P2^r). It is possible that female, Florentine actors were included in the performance specifically to please Catherine, as a symbol of her own power and independence as an Italian woman representing the French court. The actors' costumes, too, would function as a reminder to the spectators of the play's new setting in the queen's native Florence. As the only participants in the comedy who were, as Mazzei tells us, generously rewarded — with five hundred *scudi* from the king and an additional three hundred from the queen's own pocket — the actors were clearly one of the comedy's most successful elements (*La magnifica et triumphale entrata*, fol. P2^r). Estienne had suggested six years previously that the inclusion of specially trained comic performers would enhance immeasurably the quality of a play; indeed, the 1548 *La Calandra* was to signal the start of a long tradition of professional Italian acting in France.

Bringing *La Calandra* to Life: Prose vs Verse

Finally, although no accounts refer to the use of prose in *La Calandra*, it was the first comic play performed in France to employ this style. French writers such as Estienne had considered the superiority of prose over verse in comic theatre, as well as the Italians' improvement on the ancients in this regard; Mesmes, too, was to translate the prose version of *I suppositi*, disregarding its revised verse edition. With the exception of Ariosto, by 1548 Italian writers far more frequently favoured prose in their comedies. *La Calandra* was known in Italy as one of the very first plays to employ this style, and Bibbiena made public his own support of prose; he opens the Prologue of the comedy by calling attention to the novelty and superiority of this style: 'Voi sarete oggi spettatori d'una nova commedia intitulata *Calandra*: in prosa, non in versi; moderna, non antiqua; vulgare, non latina' [Today you will be spectators of a new comedy called *Calandra*: in prose, not in verse; modern, and not old; in the vernacular, and not in Latin].[94] By juxtaposing prose with verse, Italian with Latin, and new with ancient, Bibbiena shows how the classical style had been usurped by modern writers, setting a precedent for his contemporaries.[95] The decision by Ippolito to stage a comedy well known for the effectiveness of its prose may have been influenced by a desire to showcase a new style, innovated by the Italians, which would be entirely new to a French audience.

Additionally, one of the statues decorating the Salle alludes to the comedy's use of prose. While Dante and Petrarch are adorned with laurels, Boccaccio wears an oak crown, symbolising his own innovation of the prose style.[96] The dominance of prose in Italian comedy was no doubt also influenced by Boccaccio's *Decameron*, the style of which was becoming ever more popular in France, due to translations such as the one commissioned in 1545 by Marguerite de Navarre. In a famous argument in the *Ragionamento havuto in Lione*, for example, Ridolfi praised Boccaccio's prose; François I was also known for his appreciation of the 'poeta in prosa'.[97] Bibbiena, too, had clearly been influenced by Boccaccio, not just in his use of prose but also in the creation of his eponymous hero Calandro, which is closely based on Calandrino, one of the most popular characters in the *Decameron*.[98] The representation of Boccaccio wearing an oak crown in the Salle itself may well have been intended as a reminder of the Florentine development of this prose style, developed in the novella and subsequently incorporated into theatre. This comedy was a resounding success among spectators — many of whom would have been unable to understand Italian — which testifies to the ability of the prose style to please the audience. As we shall see in subsequent chapters, prose was later to monopolise comic drama also in France, as yet another Italian innovation to change the course of French comedy.

Only several weeks after Sébillet's treatise had claimed that comic theatre could not please, and that French writers should focus exclusively on the medieval style, *La Calandra* became one of the most celebrated elements of the royal entry.[99] The King requested a second performance of the comedy at the end of the week, and it had to be acted a third time for those who had had not seen the other performances:

> Le soir sa Magesté voulut encor ouir reciter la Comedie pour la seconde foys.
> Laquelle fut aussi de rechief rejoüee le Lundy apres pour Messieurs du grand

Conseil, et autres de la Ville, qui n'avoient peu entrer aux premiers recitementz. (*La magnificence*, K3)

[That evening his Majesty wanted to see the comedy acted for a second time. It was also acted once again the following Monday for the members of the consul, and other townsmen, who had been unable to attend the first performances.]

Mazzei adds that the comedy was the best that the court had ever seen, and that the second performance improved even on the first:

Circa alla sodisfatione della comedia, non pur sua Maestà che lo disse piu d'una volta, ma ancora i Signori e Gentilhuomini di Corte per una voce tutti affermavano non haver mai veduto il piu bello spettacolo [...] la [seconda] Comedia, che durò quatro hore, ò davantaggio e ando sempre tanto bene che non vi segui mai pure un minimo errore dallaquale poi partendosi sua Maestà disse essersi piaciuta ancora più che la prima volta. (*La magnifica et triumphale entrata*, fol. P1ᵛ)

[In terms of appreciation for the comedy, it was not just his Majesty who voiced his own admiration, but also the lords and gentlemen of the court, who collectively affirmed that they had never seen a greater spectacle [...] the [second] comedy, which lasted for four hours or even longer, went so well that it contained not a single error, and his Majesty, upon leaving, remarked that it had pleased him even more than the first.]

In addition to the praise of his Majesty and the court, the greatly extended timespan of this second performance suggests that it contained regular improvisation, laughter, and applause, again indicating that the comedy was extremely well received. Catalogues of the royal library also show that Henri subsequently acquired a copy of *La Calandra* for his personal collection, another testament to the positive reception of the comedy.[100]

As this chapter has shown, the success of this performance can be attributed largely to the Italians, who collaborated to organise, fund, and bring to life the comedy. The network involved in this performance was mostly, but not all, Florentine, and included Ippolito d'Este, Ridolfi, the Gondi and Guadagni families, and protégés such as Alamanni, Serlio, Nannoccio, and Manucci. There are many indications that these collaborators tailored the performance specifically to please the king and queen, for example bringing in Florentine performers dressed in native styles, changing the setting to a beautiful and highly realistic Florence, and incorporating elaborate Italianate intervals, complete with a gift to Catherine symbolising the Franco-Italian alliance. The lead performer Barlacchi, as well as Lastricati, the sculptor of the statues, and Bibbiena, the author of the comedy itself, would have been known to Catherine; Alamanni, who wrote the intervals, and Serlio, who designed the theatre, were also favourites of Henri. By pleasing the comedy's most important spectators, the organisers would increase their prospects of financial or political reward, or even push a more specific agenda: to heal a past rift, to elevate one's position at the court, or to facilitate the return from Lyons to Florence. There was much to gain by winning the favour of the royal couple, and comedy, in this respect, could function as a political or a persuasive tool. While we know only of a reward made directly to the Florentine actors, there is no reason to believe that others were not recompensed. Indeed, the careers of those involved continued to thrive throughout their lifetimes: for instance, Ippolito and Serlio remained generously pensioned and firmly established in the royal households; Alamanni was made Catherine's steward a number of months later, and given more prominent diplomatic responsibilities; Ridolfi, too, was able eventually to return to Florence.[101] We shall see in subsequent chapters that the political function of comedy would continue to be exploited, particularly as French authors themselves grew increasingly adept at dramatic writings.

Although Estienne had emphasised the importance of using theatre to enrich French culture, there are no indications that this was an aim of the Italian organisers. Yet this performance, which introduced into France a range of features, played a crucial role in importing comedy from south of the Alps. This achievement was recognised by a number of contemporary writers, such as Brantôme, who both pointed out its success and called attention to its Italian influence:

> [La comedie estoit] chose que l'on n'avoit encores veu, et rare en France; car paradvant on ne parloit que des farceurs, des connardz de Rouan, des joüeurs de la Basoche, et autres sortes de badins et joüeurs de badinages, farces, mommeries et sotteries: mesmes qu'il n'y avoit pas longtemps que ces belles tragédies et gentilles comedies avoient estré inventées, jouées et représentées en Italie.[102]

> [Comedy was something that had not yet been seen, being unusual in France. Before that one spoke only of farce players, the Rouen idiots, the Basoche players, and other sorts of nonsense, along with foolish actors of buffooneries, farces, mummeries, and stupidities. They spoke of these even though beautiful tragedies and fine comedies had recently been invented, acted, and staged in Italy.]

La Calandra provided visual evidence of comedy's entertainment value, something that Estienne's work and printed editions of Terence had been unable to accomplish. Again, this complicates the traditional narrative of the development of comedy in France: the Italians, and not French writers, succeeded in bringing the genre to wider attention, although their aim was not necessarily to do so. In the wake of *La Calandra*, French writers began themselves to experiment with innovations such as sets, staging, costumes, and prose, particularly after the Italian performances which were patronised at the French court following the 1548 performance. This new phase of theatrical production in France will be the subject of the next chapter, providing further evidence that performance, and not poetics, played a key role in the emergence in the mid-century of French comic drama.

Notes to Chapter 3

1. In previous scholarship this play has been referred to both as *La Calandra* and as *La Calandria*; however, Giorgio Padoan, in the most authoritative edition of the play, has convincingly shown the correct title to be the former. Bernardo Dovizi da Bibbiena, *La Calandra: commedia elegantissima per Messer Bernardo Dovizi da Bibbiena, testo critico annotato a cura di Giorgio Padoan* (Padua: Antenore, 1985), p. 5.

2. Maurice Scève, *The Entry of Henri II into Lyon: September 1548*, ed. by Richard Cooper (Tempe: Medieval and Renaissance Texts and Studies, 1997); *La magnificence de la superbe et triumphante entree de la noble et antique Cité de Lyon faicte au Treschrestien Roy de France Henry deuxiesme de ce nom, et à la royne Catherine son Espouse le XXIII. de Septembre M.D.XLVIII* (Lyons: Guillaume Rouillé, 1549) (hereafter referenced in main text as *La magnificence*); *La magnifica et triumphale entrata del christianiss. re di Francia Henrico secondo, Colla particulare descritione della Comedia che fece recitare in Lione la Natione Fiorentina a richiesta di sua Maestà Christianissima*, trans. by Francesco Mazzei (Lyons: Guillaume Rouillé, 1549) (hereafter referenced in main text as *La magnifica et triumphale entrata*). Cooper has persuasively argued that Mazzei is the Italian translator, though he is referred to on the title-page only as 'F.M.'. Scève, *The Entry of Henri II into Lyon*, p. 139.

3. Castiglione, *Il libro del Cortegiano*, p. 152.

4. Leonardo Terrusi, 'La Philadelphia di Lelio Manfredi: una commedia italiana del primo Cinquecento nella biblioteca del re di Francia', in *Letteratura italiana, letterature europee: atti del Congresso Nazionale dell'Associazione degli Italianisti Italiani*, ed. by Guido Baldassari and Silvana Tamiozzo (Rome: Bulzoni, 2002), pp. 333–39 (pp. 334–35).

5. Henri Omont, *Anciens inventaires et catalogues de la Bibliothèque nationale* (Paris: E. Leroux, 1908).

6. Sophocles, *Tragedie de Sophocles, intitulée Electra*, trans. by Lazare de Baïf (Paris: Estienne Rosset, 1537). Bernard Weinberg discusses this tragedy in his *Critical Prefaces of the French Renaissance* (Evanston, IL: Northwestern University Press, 1950), pp. 73, 105–09.

7. Giovanni Boccaccio, *Le Decameron de Messire Jehan Bocace Florentin, nouvellement traduict d'Italien en Francoys par Maistre Anthoine le Macon conseiller du Roy et tresorier de l'extraordinaire des guerres*, trans. by Antoine Le Maçon (Paris: Estienne Roffet, 1545). The only previous French translation of this work was by Laurent de Premierfait, which is undated, though was certainly completed well over a century previously. More on the reception of the *Decameron* in France can be found in Lionello Sozzi, *Boccaccio in Francia nel cinquecento* (Geneva: Slatkine Reprints, 1999), especially pp. 9–22.

8. Marguerite d'Angoulême, Queen of Navarre, *Heptaméron*, ed. by Simone de Reyff (Paris: Garnier Flammarion, 1982). For more information on the medieval influence of her plays, see Navarre, *Œuvres complètes*, ed. by Nicole Cazauran, Geneviève Hasenohr, and Olivier Millet, 4 vols (Paris: Champion, 2002), IV, 12–13.

9. Picot, *Les Français italianisants au XVIᵉ siècle*; Balsamo, *Les Rencontres des muses*; Sozzi, *Rome n'est plus Rome*.

10. See Claude Chappuys, *Discours de la Court: présenté au Roy par M. Claude Chappuys, son libraire et Valet de Chambre ordinaire* (Paris: André Roffet, 1543). Cited in Smith, *The Anti-courtier Trend in Sixteenth-century French Literature*, p. 31.

11. For details on these supporters, see Lucien Romier, *Le Royaume de Catherine de Médicis: la France à la veille des guerres de religion*, 2 vols (Paris: Perrin, 1922), I, 20.

12. See Léon de Laborde, *Les Comptes des bastiments du roi*, 2 vols (Paris: Libraire de la Société, 1880), II, 270, and Alan Knight, *Aspects of Genre in Late Medieval French Drama* (Manchester: Manchester University Press, 1983), p. 45.

13. For a comprehensive study of these early performances, see Alois Maria Nagler, *Theatre Festivals of the Medici, 1539–1637* (New Haven, CT: Yale University Press, 1964).

14. The 1541 and 1542 performances are discussed in Richard Cooper, 'Scève, Serlio et la Fête', in *Maurice Scève: le poète en quête d'un langage*, ed. by Vân Dung Le Flanchec, Michèle Clément, and Anne-Pascale Pouey-Mounou (Paris: Classiques Garnier, 2020), pp. 339–53.

15. Scève, *The Entry of Henri II into Lyon*, p. 81. Also cited in Georges Guigue, *La Magnificence de la superbe et triumphante entree de la noble et antique cité de Lyon* (Lyons: Société des Bibliophiles Lyonnais, 1927), p. 201.

16. More information on the *battagliola* can be found in Elvira Garbero Zorzi, 'Court Spectacle', in *Italian Renaissance Courts*, ed. by Sergio Bertelli, Franco Cardini, and Elvira Garbero Zorzi (London: Sidgwick & Jackson, 1986), pp. 127–89 (especially pp. 169–72).

17. For more information see Richard Cooper, 'The Theme of War in Renaissance Entries', in *Ceremonial Entries in Early Modern Europe: The Iconography of Power*, ed. by Maria Ines Aliverti, Ronnie Mulryne, and Anna Maria Testaverde (Farnham: Ashgate, 2015), pp. 15–46.

18. Scève, *The Entry of Henri II into Lyon*, p. 84.

19. Margaret McGowan, *The Vision of Rome in Late Renaissance France* (New Haven, CT, & London: Yale University Press, 2000), pp. 326–27.

20. Denis Sauvage's Appendix to Nicolas Gilles, *Le second volume des Croniques et annales de France* (Paris: R. Anvil for J. de Roigny, 16 Aug. 1549), fol. CXLV. Included in the Appendix to Scève, *The Entry of Henri II into Lyon*, pp. 325–26. Margaret McGowan has described in detail the training of 'gladiators', and the rehearsals which took place, in 'Lyon: A Centre for Water Celebrations', in *Waterborne Pageants and Festivities in the Renaissance: Essays in Honour of J. R. Mulryne*, ed. by Margaret Shewring (Oxford: Taylor & Francis, 2016), pp. 37–50 (pp. 40–41).

21. The early modern Italian *naumachia*, and its reinvention by the Medici, can be found in Patrick Eyres, 'British Naumachias: The Performance of Trial and Memorial', in *Performance and Appropriation: Profane Rituals in Gardens and Landscapes*, ed. by Michel Conan (Washington, DC: Dumbarton Oaks Research Library and Collection, 2007), pp. 171–94 (p. 172).

22. This printed bulletin is anonymous: *Le grand triumphe faict à l'entrée du Treschrestien et tousiours victorieux Monarche, Henry second de ce nom, Roy de France, en sa noble ville et cite de Lyon. Et de la Royne Catherine son espouse* (Paris: B. de Gourmont, 1548). Provided as a facsimile in Scève, *The Entry of Henri II into Lyon*, pp. 276–98.

23. Vincenzo Pacifici writes about the debut in *Ippolito II d'Este, Cardinale di Ferrara: da documenti originali inediti* (Tivoli: Società Storia e d'Arte, 1984), pp. 99–100. Information on the many Italian editions of the play can be found in Pamela Stewart, 'A Play on Doubles: The *Calandra*', *Modern Language Studies*, 14.1 (1984), 22–32 (p. 22).

24. For more information on Bibbiena's role in returning the Medici to Florence, see Jack D'Amico, 'Drama and the Court in *La Calandra*', *Theatre Journal*, 43.1 (1991), 93–106 (p. 96).

25. *Doña Isabel de Requesens y Enríquez de Cardona-Anglesola* (1518), now held in the Musée du Louvre, Paris. See Joanna Woods-Marsden, 'Portrait of the Lady, 1430–1520', in *Virtue and Beauty: Leonardo's 'Ginevra de' Benci' and Renaissance Portraits of Women*, ed. by David Alan Brown (Washington, DC: National Gallery of Art, 2001), pp. 62–87 (pp. 80–81); Ivan Cloulas, *Henri II* (Paris: Fayard, 1985), pp. 210–11.

26. The correspondence is of Hieronimo Dandino, the Papal Nuncio in France, and Michele della Torre, an Italian bishop. 'Dandino e della Torre au Cardinal Farnese', ff. 205ᵛ–209ʳ. BAV, 14.092. Reproduced in *Correspondance des nonces en France: Dandino, Della Torre et Trivulto (1546–1551)*, ed. by Jan Lestocquoy (Paris: E. de Boccard, 1966), p. 347.

27. Claude de Rubys, *Histoire veritable de la ville de Lyon, contenant ce, qui a esté obmis par maistres Symphorien Champier & autres, auec vn sommaire recueil de l'administration politicque de ladicte ville. Ensemble vn petit discours de la maison illustre des Medicis de Florence* (Lyons: Bonaventure Nugo, 1604), p. 371. Samuel Pogue has reproduced a list of the plays which may have been performed in this theatre, discussed throughout *Jacques Moderne: Music Printer of the Sixteenth Century* (Geneva: Droz, 1969).

28. For example Bonner Mitchell, 'Firenze illustrissima: l'immagine della patria negli apparati delle Nationi fiorentine per le feste di Lione del 1548 e di Anversa del 1549', in *Firenze e la Toscana dei Medici nell'Europa del '500: Relazioni artistiche; il linguaggio architettonico*, ed. by Giancarlo Garfagnini, 3 vols (Florence: L. S. Olschki, 1983), III, 995–1004 (p. 997).

29. Jean Balsamo, 'L'Italianisme lyonnais et l'illustration de la langue française', in *Lyon et l'illustration de la langue française à la Renaissance*, ed. by Bernard Colombat and Gérard Defaux (Lyons: ENS, 2003), pp. 211–29 (p. 212).

30. Carlo Sacrati, the ambassador to the Duke of Ferrara, even reports that Ippolito was once greeted by five of the most beautiful royal French women naked in a bath. 'Ambasciatori Francia', busta 34, Carlo Sacrati, 18 June 1540, Archivio di stato Modena. Also cited in Pacifici, *Ippolito II d'Este, Cardinale di Ferrara*, p. 64.

31. See Bonner Mitchell, 'Circumstance and Setting in the Earliest Italian Productions of Comedy', *Renaissance Drama*, 4 (1971), 185–97 (p. 188).

32. A series of playlets which often retold classical myths with the use of masks.

33. See 'Ambasciatori Francia', busta 256, Carlo Sacrati, 6 February 1541, Archivio di stato Modena. Cited in Pacifici, *Ippolito II d'Este, Cardinale di Ferrara*, p. 66.

34. Richard Cooper, 'Court Festival and Triumphal Entries under Henri II', in *Court Festivals of the European Renaissance: Art, Politics and Performance*, ed. by Elizabeth Goldring and Ronnie Mulryne (Abingdon: Routledge, 2002), pp. 51–75 (p. 64).

35. See Robert Henke, 'Border-crossing in the Commedia dell'Arte', in *Transnational Exchange in Early Modern Theater*, ed. by Robert Henke and Eric Nicholson (Aldershot: Ashgate, 2008), pp. 19–34 (p. 22).

36. Sarah Cockram, *Isabella d'Este and Francesco Gonzaga: Power Sharing at the Italian Renaissance Court* (London: Routledge, 2016), p. 45.

37. Scève, *The Entry of Henri II into Lyon*, p. 103. It was Ercole d'Este's envoy to the French Court, Giulio Alvarotti, who noted the cost of the comedy to Ippolito. Giulio Alvarotti's letters to the Duke of Ferrara, 1548, 'Ambasciatori Francia', busta 25, fol. 187, Archivio di stato Modena. Brantôme, *Œuvres complètes*, ed. by Ludovic Lalanne, 12 vols (Paris: Jules Renouard, 1864–82), III, 256.

38. Ibid.

39. Catherine's great-aunt Contessina dei Medici was Piero Ridolfi's wife. See Richard Cooper, 'Le Cercle de Lucantonio Ridolfi', in *L'Émergence littéraire des femmes à Lyon à la Renaissance: 1520–1560*, ed. by Michèle Clément and Janine Incardona (Saint-Étienne: Université de Saint-Étienne, 2008), pp. 29–50 (p. 29, n. 6).

40. Lucantonio Ridolfi, *Ragionamento havuto in Lione da Claudio de Herbere, Gentil'huomo Franceze, et da Alessandro degli Uberti, Gentil'huomo fiorentino, sopra alcuni luoghi del cento novelle del Boccaccio* (Lyons: Guillaume Rouillé, 1557). For more information on this volume, see Glyn Norton and Marga Cottino-Jones, 'Theories of Prose Fiction and Poetics in Italy: novella and romanzo', in *Cambridge History of Literary Criticism*, ed. by Glyn Norton, 9 vols (Cambridge: Cambridge University Press, 1999), III, 322–38 (p. 324).

41. Guillaume Rouillé, prefatory letter, in Francesco Petrarca, *Il Petrarca*, ed. by Antonio Brucioli (Lyons: Guillaume Rouillé, 1550). Cited in Scève, *The Entry of Henri II into Lyon*, p. 139.

42. Dale Kent, *The Rise of the Medici: Faction in Florence, 1426–1432* (Oxford: Oxford University Press, 1978), pp. 175–76.

43. The link between the Gondi and Medici families is discussed throughout Joanna Milstein, *The Gondi: Family Strategy and Survival in Early Modern France* (Abingdon: Routledge, 2018).

44. Balsamo, 'L'Italianisme lyonnais et l'illustration de la langue française', p. 224.

45. Virginia Scott and Sara Sturm-Maddox, *Performance, Poetry and Politics on the Queen's Day: Catherine de Médicis and Pierre de Ronsard at Fontainebleau* (London: Routledge, 2007), p. 45.

46. Leon Battista Alberti: 'Sed theatra Graeca ab Latinis differebant ea re, quod illi choros et scenicos saltatores media in area perducentes pulpito indigebant minore; nostri, quod totis ludionibus fabulam agerent in pulpito, id ea de re habere laxius voluere' ('Greek theatres differed from Latin ones in the size of their stage: they required a smaller one, because the chorus and theatrical dancers performed in their central area, whereas we preferred a larger stage, because all our action took place there'). *L'Architettura [De re aedificatoria]*, ed. by Giovanni Orlandi and Paolo Portoghesi, 2 vols (Milan: Il Polifilo, 1966), II, 731; *On the Art of Building in Ten Books*, trans. and ed. by Joseph Rykwert, Neil Leach, and Robert Tavernor (Cambridge, MA: MIT Press, 1988), p. 270.

47. Brantôme, *Œuvres complètes*, III, 256. Also cited in Scève, *The Entry of Henri II into Lyon*, p. 102.

48. Eugene Johnson, 'The Theater at Lyon of 1548: A Reconstruction and Attribution', *Artibus et Historiae*, 35.69 (2014), 173–202.

49. Eugene Johnson, *Inventing the Opera House: Theater Architecture in Renaissance and Baroque Italy* (Cambridge: Cambridge University Press, 2018), p. 80.

50. Ibid., pp. 186–88.

51. On rooms built specifically for entertainment in Ippolito's lodgings, see Eelco Nagelsmit, 'Visualizing Vitruvius: Stylistic Pluralism in Serlio's Sixth Book on Architecture', in *The Transformation of Expression in the Early Modern Arts*, ed. by Joost Keizer and Todd Richardson (Leiden: Brill, 2012), pp. 339–72 (p. 352), and Sebastiano Serlio, *Sebastiano Serlio on Domestic Architecture: Different Dwellings from the Meanest Hovel to the Most Ornate Palace: The Sixteenth-century Manuscript of Book VI in the Avery Library of Columbia University*, trans. and ed. by Myra Nan Rosenfeld (New York: Architectural History Foundation, 1978), p. 23.

52. See Scève, *The Entry of Henri II into Lyon*, p. 110; Elsa Kammerer, 'Une sainte femme desirée: le

Magdalon de la Madalena de Jean de Vauzelles', in *L'Émergence littéraire des femmes*, ed. by Clément and Incardona, pp. 69–88 (p. 83).

53. For more on Guadagni's relationship with Nannoccio, see Dominique Thiebaut, 'Un artiste florentin au service du Cardinal de Tournon: Giovanni Capassini', in *Kunst des Cinquecento in der Toskana*, ed. by Monika Cämmerer (Munich: Bruchmann, 1992), pp. 176–85 (p. 178).

54. Giorgio Vasari, *Le vite de' più eccellenti pittori, scultori ed architetti*, ed. by Fernandino Ranalli, 2 vols (Florence: Batelli, 1848), II, 1261.

55. Giorgio Conegrani's dispatch to the Duke of Mantua: 'Descrittione dell'entrate delle Maestadi del Re et Regina in Lione', 4 October 1548, ff. 234^r–246^v, Archivio Gonzaga, Serie E, busta 641, Archivio di stato Mantua. Included in the Appendix of Scève, *The Entry of Henri II into Lyon*, pp. 301–15.

56. More information on the importance of realism in early modern stage design, see Fabio Finotti, 'Perspective and Stage Design, Fiction and Reality in the Italian Renaissance Theater of the Fifteenth Century', *Renaissance Drama*, 36 (2010), 21–42.

57. Scève, *The Entry of Henri II into Lyon*, p. 104.

58. Vasari, *Le vite de' più eccellenti pittori*, p. 498.

59. See Cristina Acidini Luchinat, *The Medici, Michelangelo, and the Art of Late Renaissance Florence* (New Haven, CT: Yale University Press, 2002), p. 214.

60. Jean Lemaire de Belges, *La Concorde des deux langages* (Paris: Droz, 1947), p. 45 (ll. 295–98). For more information on this narration, see Robert Cottrell, 'Allegories of Desire in Lemaire's *Concorde des deux langages*', *French Forum*, 2.1 (1998), 261–300 (pp. 291–92). Also cited in Scott and Sturm-Maddox, *Performance, Poetry and Politics on the Queen's Day*, p. 46.

61. Richard Gascon, *Grand commerce et vie urbaine au XVIe siècle: Lyon et ses marchands*, 2 vols (Paris: Mouton, 1971), I, 108.

62. Giannozzo Manetti, *Vite di Dante, Petrarca e Boccaccio*, ed. by Angelo Solerti (Milan: Vallardi, 1904). See also Patrick Baker, *Italian Renaissance Humanism in the Mirror* (Cambridge: Cambridge University Press, 2015), p. 107.

63. Scève, *The Entry of Henri II into Lyon*, p. 106.

64. Johnson, *Inventing the Opera House*, p. 79.

65. Charles Mazouer, *Le Théâtre français de la Renaissance* (Paris: Champion, 2002), p. 193.

66. Ronald Martinez, 'Spectacle', in *The Cambridge Companion to the Italian Renaissance*, ed. by Michael Wyatt (Cambridge: Cambridge University Press, 2014), pp. 239–59 (p. 241).

67. Another example would be the intervals performed during the five Plautine plays staged for the wedding of Lucrezia Borgia to Alfonso d'Este, which were vastly preferred by Isabella d'Este to the plays themselves. See John Shearman, *Mannerism* (London: Pelican, 1967), p. 105.

68. For more information on the intervals performed at this wedding, see Roy Strong, *Art and Power: Renaissance Festivals, 1450–1650* (Berkeley: University of California Press, 1984), pp. 133–34.

69. Judith Bryce, 'The Theatrical Activities of Palla di Lorenzo Strozzi in Lyon in the 1540s', in *Theatre of the English and Italian Renaissance*, ed. by Ronnie Mulryne and Margaret Shewring (New York: St Martin's Press, 1991), pp. 55–72 (pp. 58–59).

70. Mitchell, 'Les Intermèdes au service de l'état', p. 130.

71. Conegrani, 'Descrittione dell'entrate', fol. 246.

72. Élie Borza, 'Catalogue des travaux inédits d'humanistes consacrés à Sophocle, jusqu'en 1600', *Humanistica Lovaniensia: Journal of Neo-Latin Studies*, 52 (2003), 196–216 (p. 197).

73. Lucien Romier, *Les Origines politiques des guerres de religion: Henri II et l'Italie (1547–1555)*, 2 vols (Geneva: Slatkine-Megariotis, 1974), I, 147.

74. Pacifici, *Ippolito II d'Este*, p. 84.

75. Mitchell, 'Firenze illustrissima', p. 996.

76. Scève, *The Entry of Henri II into Lyon*, p. 116.

77. Brantôme, *Œuvres complètes*, III, 256.

78. Conegrani, 'Descrittione dell'entrate', fol. 246.

79. Melissa Meriam Bullard, *Filippo Strozzi and the Medici: Favour and Finance in Sixteenth-century Florence and Rome* (Cambridge: Cambridge University Press, 1980), p. 73.

80. Scève, *The Entry of Henri II into Lyon*, p. 119.

81. Baschet, *Les Comédiens italiens à la cour de France sous Charles IX, Henri III, Henri IV et Louis XIII*, pp. 2–9.
82. See her 1542 letter to Guillaume Féau, sieur D'Izernay. Marguerite d'Angoulême, *Lettres de Marguerite d'Angoulême, sœur de François I, reine de Navarre*, ed. by Jules Renouard, 2 vols (Paris: Jules Renouard, 1841), I, 381.
83. Conegrani, 'Descrittione dell'entrate', fol. 244^{v}.
84. Scève, *The Entry of Henri II into Lyon*, p. 114.
85. Vasari, *Le opere di Giorgio Vasari*, ed. by Gaetano Milanesi, 9 vols (Florence: G. C. Sansoni, Editore, 1878), VI, 618.
86. Ibid.. Also cited in Antony Cummings, *The Maecenas and the Madrigalist: Patrons, Performers and the Origins of the Italian Madrigal* (Philadelphia: American Philosophical Society, 2004), p. 99.
87. More information on Barlacchi's history with the Medici can be found in Cummings, *The Maecenas and the Madrigalist*, p. 105.
88. Anon., *Facezie, motti, buffonerie et burle del Piovano Arlotto* (Florence: I Giunti, 1565). Also cited in Scève, *The Entry of Henri II into Lyon*, p. 114.
89. This question of novelty is discussed throughout Virginia Scott, *Women on the Stage in Early Modern France: 1540–1750* (Cambridge: Cambridge University Press, 2010).
90. Pamela Allen Brown, 'The Traveling Diva and Generic Innovation', *Renaissance Drama*, 44.2 (2016), 249–67 (p. 254).
91. Jane Tylus, 'Women at the Windows: *Commedia dell'Arte* and Theatrical Practice in Early Modern Italy', *Theatre Journal*, 49.3 (1997), 323–42.
92. As noted by Daisy Black, 'Theatre and Performance', in *The Routledge History of Women in Early Modern Europe*, ed. by Amanda Capern (Abingdon: Routledge, 2019), pp. 357–85 (p. 362).
93. Brantôme, *Œuvres complètes*, III, 256.
94. Bibbiena, *La Calandra*, p. 61 ('Prologue').
95. For a detailed exploration of Bibbiena's use of prose, see Ronald Martinez, 'Etruria Triumphant in Rome: Fables of Medici Rule and Bibbiena's *Calandra*', *Renaissance Drama*, 36 (2010), 69–98.
96. Scève, *The Entry of Henri II into Lyon*, p. 107.
97. See Emilio Ferretti's prefatory letter to Le Maçon's translation of the *Decameron*. *Le Decameron de Messire Jehan Bocace Florentin*, ã iijr. Cited in Glyn Norton, 'Theories of Prose Fiction in Sixteenth-century France', in *Cambridge History of Literary Criticism*, ed. by Norton, III, 305–13 (p. 308).
98. Further borrowings from Boccaccio by Bibbiena can be found in Anna Fontes-Baratto, 'Les Fêtes à Urbin en 1513 et la *Calandra* de Bernardo Dovizi da Bibbiena', in *Les Écrivains et le pouvoir en Italie à l'époque de la Renaissance*, ed. by André Rochon (Paris: Université de la Sorbonne Nouvelle, 1974), pp. 69–75.
99. Sébillet, *Art poétique*, pp. 164–65.
100. Omont, *Anciens inventaires et catalogues de la Bibliothèque nationale*, p. 105.
101. Balsamo, 'L'Italianisme lyonnais et l'illustration de la langue française', p. 224.
102. Brantôme, *Œuvres complètes*, III, 256.

CHAPTER 4

Estienne Jodelle and the Italian Model

Jodelle heureusement sonna
D'une vois humble et d'une vois hardie
La Comedie, avec la Tragedie,
Et d'un ton double, ore bas, ore haut,
Remplit premier le François échafaut.

[Jodelle happily announced
With one humble and one bold voice
Comedy, with tragedy,
And in a double tone, now low, now high,
Was the first to fill the French stage.]
(Pierre de Ronsard, 'À Jean de La Péruse', 1552)

By the 1550s, Italian comedy was a fixture at Fontainebleau. Following the 1548 staging of *La Calandra*, performances were regularly commissioned as modes of entertainment and celebration, and many still were tailored to please the king and queen. French writers witnessed first-hand this trend and, in turn, changed their approach to comic theatre, seeking to write their own plays and even to rival the comedies which had inspired them. Continuing the focus on performance, this chapter assesses the position of comedy at Fontainebleau and beyond in the period 1552 to 1558. We begin with two brief studies of Italian theatre at the court, providing an insight into the practice and reception of comedy during this period; subsequently, this chapter turns to a French innovator of comic drama, Estienne Jodelle, examining his attempts to write and stage original theatre based on Italian models. By drawing parallels between Jodelle's work and previous performances and writings on comic theatre, as well as with the cluster of Italian plays staged at the court during these years, we can gain new perspectives both on the status of French drama in the mid-century and on the crucial role of Italian performances in the emergence of comedy in France. Such a study also offers us new angles on the increasingly complex relationship in this period between French dramatists and their Italian sources.

The two Italian performances surveyed in this chapter are Agnolo Firenzuola's *I Lucidi*, written in around 1543 and first performed in 1554, and Luigi Alamanni's *La Flora*, written in 1549 and first performed in 1555. Although these stagings took place after Jodelle's comedy was performed, they are largely representative of the Italian plays which dominated the French court during these years; they are also documented in fuller detail than some other performances.[1] The prologue to

Jodelle's *L'Eugène* (1552), the first original comedy to be written in French, is the main case study in this chapter.[2] Owing to a comment by Estienne Pasquier (1529–1615) in his sixteenth-century *Des recherches de la France* that Jodelle composed 'deux Comedies, *La Rencontre* et *l'Eugène*' [two comedies, *La Rencontre* and *L'Eugène*], it has long been thought that *La Rencontre* is a second, lost play;[3] however, it is likely that they are the same play, and therefore that Jodelle only wrote one comedy.[4] It is in the prologue to *L'Eugène* that Jodelle sets out his reasons for writing comedy and his ambitions for the genre; it is also where he at once outlines and rejects his models. A final, shorter case study in this chapter will be Jodelle's 1558 series of Italian-style *mascherate*, which he wrote for the celebrations of Henri II's triumphant return to Paris after recapturing Calais from the English troops. These plays are not strictly comic; yet, they reveal in greater detail the status of Italian theatre in France during this period, as well as helping us to understand the shifting approach of French playwrights to their Italian counterparts. These masquerades are documented in the *Recueil des inscriptions, figures, devises, et masquarades* [Collection of Inscriptions, Figures, Mottos, and Masquerades], which Jodelle himself wrote to commemorate the festivities. Although their volume does not focus in detail on the masquerades, Victor Graham and William McAllister-Johnson have made available in a modern edition the *Recueil* in its entirety, which has facilitated the examination of Jodelle's personal account of the plays for this study.[5]

Italian Theatre at Fontainebleau: *I Lucidi* (1554)

As we are told in a letter by the Italian diplomat and writer Stefano Guazzo, Firenzuola's comedy *I Lucidi* was performed before the king and the rest of the court at Fontainebleau in 1554. While these details have been noted in scholarship, Guazzo's letter has otherwise been overlooked: it is examined only by Lucien Romier, who wrongly comments that Guazzo was a 'comédien'.[6] A closer look at Guazzo's letter — written on 5 March 1555 to Sabino Calandra, the *châtelain* of Mantua — reveals a number of key features of the comedy. We learn that it was put on as part of a celebration, that it was performed in the original Italian, and that it was performed by Italian actors:

> Questo Natale si recitorno *I Lucidi*, comedia del Firenzuola, innanzi a Sua Maestà, della quale io ne dissi una parte, e il simile ho fatto in una comedia del Sig. Luigi Alamanni, intitolata *Flora*, laquale si recitò già otto giorni a Fontanableo, con grandissimo piacere di Sua Maestà et tutta la Corte.[7]

> [This Christmas they acted before his Majesty *I Lucidi*, a comedy by Firenzuola, in which I performed a part; I did the same in a comedy by Sig. Luigi Alamanni, entitled *Flora*, which was acted eight days ago at Fontainebleau, to the greatest pleasure of his Majesty and of all the court.]

Given that the comedy took place at Christmas, we can infer that it was performed as part of the Epiphany festivities. Guazzo's reference to 'questo Natale' also suggests that performances had taken place at previous Epiphany celebrations, and were therefore regular events: following the success of the performance of *La Calandra* to commemorate the royal entry, it may have become customary to include a comic play as part of a festival, as had long been the case in Italy. Since Guazzo was invited to act in the play, the comedy evidently took place in the original Italian; his role also indicates that it was performed by an Italian troupe, who routinely delighted their audience by giving roles to well-known spectators, and often invited other audience members up on stage to perform.[8] Almost fifteen years later, for example, the Gelosi troupe, led by the actor-manager Zan Ganassa, were invited to perform for the 1572 marriage of Henri de Navarre to Marguerite de Valois, in which Catherine helped to play Columbine, the Cardinal of Lorraine Pantalone, and the Duke of Guise Scaramuccia. This occasion, shown on the front cover of this book, is the earliest known depiction of a *commedia dell'arte* performance, apparently painted by François Bunel in the 1570s.[9]

As well as forming part of a tradition of comedy as celebration, the performance of *I Lucidi* clearly relied on the Italian model, in its language as well as in its actors. Additionally, Firenzuola was — like the writer of *La Calandra* and Catherine herself — a Florentine. Although the play is set in Bologna, Firenzuola was a celebrated humanist and writer closely associated with Florence; it is possible that the play was chosen to promote the work of the queen's compatriots, especially as the French court became increasingly Italianised during this period. The comedy may even have been chosen by the Florentine Alamanni, by then Catherine's steward: Alamanni was a close friend of Lazzaro Buonamico, who had first been persuaded to turn to comedy by his mentor Firenzuola.[10]

I Lucidi was well placed to demonstrate the talent of Florentine comic writers. The play was well known among Italian authors as one which lent itself to successful performance:

> Leggetela adunque [...] e cosi venite inganando il desiderio, che forse hora havete d'udire alla presenza gli argutissimi poemi di questa qualità, i quali a noi nella vostra leggiadra lingua, e nella vostra fioritissima patria di questa lieta stagione è concesso ascoltare.[11]

> [Read it then [...] and you will be overcome with the desire, which you may already have, to see in person the wittiest poems of this quality, which are ours in your graceful language, and which your flowery homeland of this happy season has allowed us to see.]

This 1552 prefatory letter of the Florence edition of *I Lucidi*, written by the Italian humanist Lodovico Domenichi to the prominent Florentine Aldighieri della Casa, praises not only the performability of the play but also the Tuscan 'leggiadra lingua', which may refer to the playwright's use of prose. Firenzuola — known as a 'scrittore leggiadrissimo di prosa ed assai mediocre nel verso' [most elegant writer of prose and mediocre in verse] — was celebrated throughout Italy for his witty, Boccaccian-style prose, which characterised his comedies as well as his satirical writings, such as the *Ragionamenti amorosi* [Amorous Reasonings] (an imitation of the *Decameron*).[12] The description of the 'fioritissima patria' may be a further reminder of Florentine talent, alluding to the symbolic lily of the city. As well as being suited to performance, then, *I Lucidi* showcases at its best the innovative

Italian comic prose. It is also the first comedy performed in France to be imitated directly from Plautus, and not the well-known Terence: based on a series of misunderstandings caused by long-lost male twins, it takes its plot and resolution from the *Menaechmi*.[13] Plautus was still largely obscure in France, and inaccessible to those who did not read Latin until 1658, when it was first printed in French translation.[14] It is plausible that the organisers of the Fontainebleau performance of *I Lucidi* intended to bring a further novelty into France, again showcasing the Italians' theatrical accomplishments. It may also be for this reason that Firenzuola's other, more famous comedy *La Trinuzia*, which was a close imitation of *La Calandra*, was not chosen for this occasion. This play demonstrated well the range of the Italians' achievements; yet, being imitated from Plautus, *I Lucidi* was also famously obscene, which was certain to please the king. By this period, Henri was well known for his appreciation of all things licentious, as the Venetian ambassador to France, visiting this same year, ironically remarks: 'Non gode finalmente altra sorte di piaceri che onesti, se per avventura non procedesse si cauto che a nessuno fosse manifestato' [He enjoys only the most honest pleasures; well, he is very keen to make people think that to be the case, anyway].[15]

We can ascertain from this performance of *I Lucidi* that the tradition of performing comedies as part of celebrations or festivals was thriving; we can also infer that the Florentine colony at Fontainebleau was still involved in the organisation of plays for such events. It is clear from Guazzo's letter that this comedy was performed in the original Italian language and also by an Italian troupe, who characteristically invited the audience to lend their acting skills and participate in the drama. Additionally, this performance might be interpreted as an attempt to demonstrate the Italian achievements in comic drama: *I Lucidi* was based not on Terence, but on Plautus, a Roman writer still largely unappreciated in France; the organisers also decided to avoid Firenzuola's better-known *La Trinuzia*, possibly on account of its marked similarity to *La Calandra*. Firenzuola was also a Florentine, who was celebrated for his Tuscan comic prose: such a play was certain at once to please Catherine and to indulge the vogue for Italian innovations at Fontainebleau. While the staging of *La Calandra* six years previous to *I Lucidi* was clearly a catalyst for comic performance at the court, comedy was still considered to be an Italian practice, and it was still brought to life by Italian pioneers.

Italian Theatre at Fontainebleau: *La Flora* (1555)

Guazzo's letter notes his role in a second comedy, Alamanni's *La Flora*. He observes that the play was performed 'già otto giorni' [eight days ago]; it took place, then, in late February 1555, six weeks after the staging of *I Lucidi*. Since this would coincide with the carnival festivities, we can gather that *La Flora* was performed as part of these celebrations, lending further evidence to the idea that comic theatre was becoming a regular part of festival culture. Guazzo's participation in *La Flora* again suggests that the play was performed in the original Italian language, and by an Italian troupe; additionally, it is likely that the author himself helped to organise the performance of his comedy. Alamanni — who, as we have seen, may also have helped to put together the performance of *I Lucidi* — often took charge of courtly entertainments and events, particularly if they involved Italian collaboration. Like *I Lucidi*, *La Flora* appears to have been brought to life largely with the help of Italian innovators.

While *La Flora* has never been examined in detail, a close reading of the play, and particularly of its prologue, gives us an insight into its performance in France.[16] Firstly, it is clear that like *La Calandra*, the performance incorporated specially-made costumes. In the prologue Alamanni refers to the actors' 'rozzi veli' [rough attire] and 'negletto habito' [neglected outfits];[17] although the costumes are not luxurious like those included in *La Calandra*, they are representative of the characters in the play, who belong to the lower classes: indeed, their status is integral to the plot.[18] Secondly, it is clear that Alamanni wrote this play with a view to calling the attention of the French court to Florence. The title of the comedy, as well as its eponymous heroine, brings the focus to the city: by this stage in Alamanni's career, the name 'Flora' itself had become synonymous with Florence, as part of the folk etymology of 'Fiorenza';[19] Flora's father Geri claims in the comedy that he gave her this name 'per amore alla patria' [for love of his hometown].[20] A letter written at Fontainebleau by Bernardo Buoninsegni, the Sienese ambassador, also suggests that the comedy was entitled 'Flora' to give prominence to the city: 'Domane si recita a Fontanableò una bella commedia del signor Luigi Alamanni intitolata Flora per rappresentar Firenze' [Tomorrow at Fontainebleau a brilliant comedy will be acted, written by Sig. Luigi Alamanni, and called Flora to symbolise Florence].[21]

The importance of the city of Florence is outlined throughout the comedy's prologue. Alamanni reminds the spectators that the action takes place in Florence, and invites them to imagine that they themselves are in this city, especially given that they are in the presence of one of Florence's foremost representatives: 'Questa è Fiorenza [...] vi debbe essere per la divina sua pianta, che è qui' [This is Florence [...] you must yourselves be there, for Florence's own divine plant is present].[22] Here Catherine, 'la pianta', is herself presented as Florence's emblem of the lily: as in the performance of *La Calandra*, Alamanni reminds the spectators that Catherine is the link between France and Florence, having united the two cultures with her marriage to Henri. In the next lines of the prologue, Alamanni asks the spectators to recall 'la sincera fede, e [...] l'amore humile che a gigli d'oro porta' [the sincere faith [...] and the humble love that she brings to the golden lilies].[23] Here Alamanni reintroduces the topos of the golden lily which he incorporated into his *Calandra* interludes, where Catherine was presented with this same gift, engraved with the Florentine red lilies, to symbolise the alliance between France and Florence. As well as harking back to the success of the entry performance, this reference again reminds the audience of Catherine's role in bringing Florentine culture to France. In another nod to Florence, *La Flora* is, like *La Calandra*, based on the Florentine *Decameron*.[24] As we have seen, the *Decameron* was well known in France by this time, largely due to the translation commissioned by the king's aunt, Marguerite de Navarre. Although *La Flora* was written in Italian and by an Italian author, it is the first of many plays composed in France to be imitated from Boccaccio's text, as we shall see in Part III.

Alamanni's prologue indicates specifically that the king, queen, and Marguerite de France (Henri's sister) were present at the performance: the speech is directed to 'Henrico invitissimo' [most invited Henri], 'Catherina Cristianissima' [most Christian Catherine], and 'Margherita unica' [unique Marguerite].[25] Yet we may infer from the Florentine focus of the play, as well as from the reminder of Catherine's symbolic golden gift, that Alamanni had composed the comedy mainly with Catherine in mind. As we have seen, Alamanni's specially-written intervals for *La Calandra* were greatly successful in pleasing the royal couple: the king had since called on Alamanni to act as an intermediary in Italian affairs in France, as well as commissioning him to write the nationalistic and chivalric poem *Gyrone il cortese* [Giron the Courteous]; the queen had also made Alamanni her personal steward.[26] It is no coincidence that with *La Flora*, Alamanni uses comedy to please the queen for a second time, and it may even be that *La Flora* was composed only several months after the resounding success of the entry performance and Alamanni's appointment as Catherine's steward. A letter written in early 1549 from Alamanni to Benedetto Varchi describes a comedy he had recently completed, and while this performance of *La Flora* with a full Italian cast did not take place until 1555, it is not unfeasible that the play was recited informally before the king and queen well before this, like Baïf's French translation of Sophocles's *Electra*.[27] Although we know little about the reception of the 1555 performance, it seems as though it was successful in pleasing the royal couple and the rest of the spectators: Guazzo's letter states that it was met with 'grandissimo piacere' [the greatest pleasure];[28] additionally, although it was never printed in France, it very quickly made its way to Florence, where it was printed in 1556 and performed for the carnival there that year.[29] While the comedy was apparently smuggled out without the permission of Alamanni, who was by this stage ill and had only a few weeks left to live, the Florence carnival performance does testify to the success of the 1555 Fontainebleau staging, the news of which had clearly travelled to the Italian city.

Evidence surrounding the 1555 performance of *La Flora* helps to enrich our understanding of the status of comedy at the French court in the mid-century. As well as most likely being organised by Alamanni, *La Flora* was again performed by an Italian troupe, indicating the appreciation at the French court of Italian actors, and also suggesting that invitations to them were regular. The plays were evidently well received, even though they were performed in the original Italian, which may not have been understood by every spectator. Like *La Calandra* and *I Lucidi*, *La Flora* was acted as part of festivities, which suggests that the custom of performing comedies at special occasions was coming into practice in France, as had long been the case in Italy. Alamanni also incorporated a number of features which had been seen in *La Calandra*, such as the inclusion of costumes; he also emphasised its Florentine setting and based the plot on *La Calandra*, most likely with the aim of pleasing his royal spectators. Given Alamanni's endeavour to use the comedy to flatter, we can also gather that drama still offered the potential for political or monetary reward, as it had with *La Calandra*. Yet French writers, too, were beginning to acknowledge the potential of comic theatre — and they desired literary, and not financial, recognition.

A Transitional Play: Estienne Jodelle's *L'Eugène* (1552)

By the mid-century, French humanists had shown little interest in reinventing comic theatre, with the notable exceptions of Estienne and, to a far lesser extent, Du Bellay and Mesmes. In 1552, however, the twenty-year-old Estienne Jodelle (1532–73), who had recently arrived as a writer at Fontainebleau, composed an original comedy in French, *L'Eugène*. This was not his own idea, but the suggestion of Catherine de' Medici, who had, along with her sister-in-law Marguerite, commissioned of Jodelle a comedy and a tragedy: 'Je fis responce que j'avois et des tragédies et des comedies [qui] m'avait été commandée par la Reyne et par Madame seur du Roy' [I replied that I had tragedies and comedies [which] had been requested of me by her Majesty, and by the King's noble sister] (*Recueil*, p. 74). In autumn 1552, just three months after Mesmes's translation of Ariosto's comedy was printed, *L'Eugène* was performed before the king and queen at the Hôtel de Reims, and was acted for a second time in January 1553 at the Collège de Boncourt. The first was a courtly performance, and took place just before Jodelle's Italianate tragedy, *Cléopâtre captive*, was performed:[30] as Noirot has pointed out, although the Hôtel de Reims was geographically independent, it was still linked to and owned by the court.[31] The second was a *collège* performance, the first in France and, as we shall see, the start of a tradition of university comedy. While there are few contemporary accounts of the performances of *L'Eugène*, Jodelle's prologue provides an insight into his motives for attempting to write France's first comedy; it also offers a new perspective on Jodelle's relationship with ancient and Italian models, which differs entirely from Estienne's own approach to these authors, outlined a decade previously.

First and foremost, Jodelle is preoccupied with showing his comedy to be an innovation. Despite the growing interest in Italian comedy at the French court and the highly successful performance of *La Calandra* — as well as Catherine's commissioning of *L'Eugène* itself — Jodelle opens his prologue by claiming that comedy is unappreciated: he claims that the genre 'à tous ne plai[t] pas' [does not please anyone] (*L'Eugène*, p. 3, 'Prologue', l. 2). Here he is likely acknowledging the idea that while attention was increasingly being paid to comedy at the court, few writers outside this context had considered comedy to be worthwhile entertainment. He is, then, emphasising his originality in bringing comedy to the stage and in recognising the enjoyment which comedy could provide. Jodelle's subsequent verses again give prominence to his innovation in writing comedy in French:

> Voyant aussi que ce genre d'escrire
> Des yeux François si long temps se retire,
> Sans que quelqu'un ait encore esprouvé
> Ce que tant bon jadis on a trouvé,
> [Cet autheur] a bien voulu dépendre ceste peine,
> Pour vous donner sa Comedie Eugene. (*L'Eugène*, ll. 25–30).

> [Seeing also that this genre of writing | Has long been removed from French eyes, | Without anyone having yet experienced | The excellence which was formerly found, [This writer] wanted greatly to go to lengths | To give you his comedy *Eugène*.]

Here Jodelle again stresses the ingenuity of his endeavour to create comic theatre, while at the same time asserting the excellence of the ancients and the mediocrity of contemporary drama. Yet, although his is the first original comedy to be written in French, Jodelle must have been aware of previous French translations of Terence: even if he was unfamiliar with Estienne's work, he surely knew of the *Therence en françois*, which was still popular and had been printed in several editions by the mid-century.[32] It is, of course, also likely that he was aware of the Italian comic performances which took place at the court, following the success of *La Calandra*. Classical comedy had, through translation and performance, already been brought to life in France, and the absence of references in Jodelle's prologue to any previous work again suggests that he wanted to be known as a pioneer of comic drama, and the first to recognise the genre's literary worth.

Of course, other theoreticians had already prescribed appropriate models for imitation in the reinvention of comic theatre: Estienne argues for the importance of imitating the ancients and the Italians, and Du Bellay alludes to the usefulness of these same models. However, while Jodelle, too, comments on the excellence of the ancients, he also claims that he takes no inspiration from them:

> L'invention n'est point d'un vieil Menandre,
> Rien d'estranger on ne vous fait entendre,
> Le style est nostre, et chacun personnage
> Se dit aussi estre de ce langage. (*L'Eugène*, p. 4, 'Prologue', ll. 32–40)

> [The argument is not that of an old Menander, | You will witness nothing foreign here, | The style is ours, and every character | Can be said to be from this language too.]

Synecdochically referring to the ancients as 'Menandre', the Greek playwright who influenced Terence, Jodelle asserts that there are no classical elements in his own comedy, and that the argument, style, and characters are entirely French.[33] Jodelle, then, at once claims that he has restored comedy to its former, ancient excellence, and that he has taken no inspiration from the classical writers themselves. Jodelle's insistence that 'rien d'estranger' can be found in his work may also be a reference to Italian comedy, especially given the Italian presence at the French court and his request from the Italian queen to write *L'Eugène*. It is possible that he wanted to draw attention away from Italian sources, both to avoid direct comparison with Italian plays, and to give more prominence to his own innovation in writing drama. Clearly, Jodelle's statement that he has reinvented classical greatness — but with no reliance on the classics — is paradoxical; yet it constitutes a further attempt to emphasise the originality of his own work.

In the subsequent lines of the prologue, Jodelle outlines his method for restoring this excellence to drama, and the outcomes of the approach he has taken:

> Mais retraçant la voye des plus vieux
> [...]
> Cestuy-ci donne à la France courage
> De plus en plus ozer bien d'advantage,
> Bien que souvent en ceste Comedie
> Chaque personne ait la voix plus hardie,
> Plus grave aussi qu'on ne permettroit pas,
> Si l'on suyvoit le Latin pas à pas.
> <div align="right">(<i>L'Eugène</i>, p. 4, 'Prologue', ll. 43–46)</div>

[But by retracing the path of the ancients | [...] | This gives France the courage | To dare ever for more, | Although often in this comedy | Each person has a bolder voice, | And a more serious one than would have been possible | If it had followed Latin step for step.]

We saw in Chapter 1 that the encouragement of emulation, and not imitation, of one's sources was prevalent in contemporary rhetorical debate, where Estienne advised writers to employ Italian prose and not classical verse in reinventing drama. Here Jodelle uses the *via* topos — which had been employed in discussions of imitation by writers from Lucretius to Poliziano — as a means of proving that his own work has surpassed the ancients. As Colin Burrow has shown, this topos 'implied that an imitator could follow a predecessor without slavishly replicating an earlier text, and might wander off from the public road into a landscape of the fancy which lay beyond its borders'.[34] Jodelle's own 'landscape of the fancy' is the creation of an original comedy in French, and in deviating from the well-known track, rather than following the ancients *pas à pas*, he has managed not just to recreate drama in contemporary France, but even to enhance and improve comic theatre itself.[35] The voices of Jodelle's characters, he claims, are bolder and more serious than those of their classical counterparts: by rejecting slavish imitation of the Roman writers, he has elevated the status of comedy, allowing it to be considered a worthier literary genre from a humanist perspective.[36] Still, by describing that he has followed the path of the ancients, he contradicts for a second time his previous remark that there is nothing classical or 'foreign' in his comedy. Again, Jodelle is seeking to showcase his own innovation, though his argument for originality is paradoxical.

Similarly, a number of features mentioned in Jodelle's prologue indicate that when writing his comedy, he was very keenly aware of the precedent set not only by the ancient model, but also more recently by the Italians. Firstly, he refers to classical stage design:

> Quant au théâtre, encore qu'il ne soit
> En demy-rond, comme on le compassoit
> Et qu'on ne l'ait ordonné de la sorte
> Que l'on faisoit, il faut qu'on le supporte.
> <div align="right">(<i>L'Eugène</i>, p. 4, 'Prologue', ll. 62–66)</div>

[As for the theatre, even though it is not | In a half-round, as it used to be structured | And that it has not been arranged in the way | That it used to be, we must put up with it.]

Although we cannot say for certain that the Italians had constructed a half-round theatre in France, there is evidence to suggest that Serlio's 'Grand Ferrare' contained a purpose-built room for entertainments, particularly plays. The extravagant theatre space constructed for *La Calandra* was, as we have seen, also noted as a particularly memorable aspect of the Lyons performance. Jodelle was no doubt aware of these impressive theatre spaces; it is also possible that he had read Serlio's *Terzo libro*, if not Estienne's own work on theatre, which contained the only previous reference in French to a 'demy rond' except for Pieter Coecke van Aelst's 1550 translation of Serlio (*Les Abusez*, p. 3).[37] Having recently returned from Italy, it may also be that Jodelle had seen first-hand one of these half-round theatres during his travels. In any case, his awareness of this theatre structure, as well as his request for the audience to tolerate the absence of it for his own comedy, indicates his concern that his play may not surpass his classical and Italian predecessors; indeed, he is mindful that it may not even equal their performances. Secondly, Jodelle refers to his use of the interval in his comedy:

> Veu que l'exquis de ce vieil ornement
> Ore se voüe aux Princes seulement:
> Mesme le son qui les actes separe,
> Comme je croy, vous eust semblé barbare.
> (*L'Eugène*, p. 4, 'Prologue', ll. 67–70)

[Seeing as the charm of this ancient ornament | Has before been aimed only at princes, | Even the sound which separates the acts | To you, I think, will seem barbarous.]

While no music or words for these intervals survive, this feature was clearly included as part of the performance, as well as the division of the comedy into acts. This constitutes another innovation for French theatre: despite Estienne's praise of the feature a decade earlier, *L'Eugène* is the first original play to include intervals, and the first comedy with intervals in France to be performed in the more public space of a university, and not to an exclusive courtly audience, as *La Calandra* had been. Yet, his warning to the spectators that they may initially find the feature displeasing may not only be directed at his university audience: the grand majority of the Hôtel de Reims spectators would have been absent from the Lyons performance. Jodelle's reference to the interval is a further nod to the classical influence which he had previously denied. It may also allude to the Italian model: *barbare* is an Italianised adjective, and during these years was swiftly becoming synonymous in France with the Italians themselves, as a derogatory reference to their foreign and unaccustomed behaviour at the court.[38] Again, in striving to emphasise his own innovation and denying ancient or foreign influence, Jodelle confirms his reliance on these very models. Additionally, his portrayal of the Italians in a subtly unflattering light hints yet again at Jodelle's insecurity that his comedy may not equal theirs.

   Although he no doubt takes inspiration from classical and Italian models, Jodelle also bases *L'Eugène* on medieval drama, despite his protests to the contrary. In the 1800s, Louis Petit de Julleville went so far as to define *L'Eugène* as a 'véritable farce, mais prolongée, divisée en actes et en scènes' [truly a farce, though longer and divided into acts and scenes], which is a fair assessment of the play;[39] more recently Mazouer, too, observes Jodelle's reliance on the farce for his plotline and characterisation.[40] The comedy is not written in the prose form which had been praised by Estienne and which was highly fashionable in Italy; instead it is composed in the octosyllabic form conventional of farce. The denouement of the play — in which the town's abbot reaches a deal with the husband of his beloved that both may continue to sleep with her — is obscene, which is not unusual for a classical comedy;[41] however, it is also highly cynical and hardly resolutory, as was typical of the farce model.[42] Again, Jodelle's theory is at odds with his practice: while he rejects the ancient, foreign, and medieval models, his play is a melting pot of all three sources. It is possible that his haste in writing the play contributed to his reliance on the familiar farce model: he spent very little time writing L'Eugène, as his friend Charles de La Mothe tells us in his collection of Jodelle's works: 'La plus longue et difficile Tragedie ou Comedie, ne l'a jamais occupé à la composer et escrire plus de dix matinees: mesme la Comedie d'Eugene fut faite en quatre traittes' [The longest and most difficult tragedy or comedy never took him more than ten mornings to compose and to write: even the comedy of L'Eugène was ready within four short sittings].[43] It may be that Jodelle had rushed the play in a bid to impress the queen, who had commissioned it, though had little time to develop his comedy sufficiently away from the medieval sources he would have known well.

   While Jodelle's prologue at once denies and reveals his models, it also provides an insight into his reasons for making the case for his innovation and originality. For instance, once again he criticises medieval comedy, metonymising farce as 'sabots' (the wooden shoes worn by its actors):

> Mais dites-moy, que recueillerez-vous,
> Quels vers, quel ris, quel honneur, et quels mots,
> S'on ne voyoit ici que des sabots?
>   (L'Eugène, p. 2, 'Prologue', ll. 57–60)

[But tell me, what would be gained, | What verses, what laughter, what honour, and what words, | If you only saw wooden shoes here?]

Here he asserts that a farce writer would never gain honour or recognition. Although in practice Jodelle himself does not move far from the farce model, his implication is that he deserves to be celebrated and remembered for his new and original comedy. Clearly Jodelle aimed to be known as France's first writer of humanist drama, and he seeks repeatedly to prove his innovation and his move away from previous sources in order to be worthy of this status. Perhaps this is also partly why he wrote his tragedy (Cléopâtre captive) extremely quickly, as La Mothe mentions. Jean Vauquelin de la Fresnaye (1536–1608) notes that Jodelle was not the first to plan on writing tragedy; he was only the first to complete it. The idea had originally belonged to Jean-Antoine de Baïf:

> Jodelle [...] fist voir sa Cleopatre,
> En France des premiers au Tragique theatre,
> Encor que de Baïf, un si brave argument
> Entre nous eust esté choisi premierement.[44]

[Jodelle [...] had performed his Cleopatra, | The first in France of tragic theatre, | Even if Baïf had been the first among us | To choose such a noble argument.]

It is possible that Jodelle had hurried to complete his plays in his eagerness to be remembered as the first dramatic writer in France.

Yet it may also be that Jodelle sought to gain wider renown. Returning to his subtle denigration of the Italians in his prologue, this is a technique which he employs also throughout the play. He draws on a number of Italian words with the precise aim of creating insults: when one character behaves in a cowardly fashion, for instance, he is referred to as 'Messer Coyon'. This nickname employs the Italian title 'Messer', as well as coining a term from the Italian *coglioni* [testicles], to denote a foolish and cowardly person (*L'Eugène*, p. 16, 1.3.413). The latter had been used just once before in French, in a variation (*coyonnerie*) in Le Maçon's translation of Boccaccio.[45] While Jodelle's insults are subtle, they are early instances of the Franco-Italian cultural rivalry which was to characterise French comedy in later decades, as we shall see in Part III: indeed, the technique of turning Italian words against the Italians themselves was to become common (and even recommended) practice. It was at this time that the Italian presence at the French court began to be resented by native poets, who often saw the work of their Tuscan counterparts favoured by Catherine and others.[46] Concurrently, French humanists were widely concerned that they were latecomers in literary history, and that the Italians had completed much of the work which remained from the ancient writers: some scholars have referred to this unease as a crisis — or, more recently, a critique — of 'exemplarity'.[47] Dually linked to this critique of exemplarity and this resentment of Italian models at the French court was an attempt not only to imitate, but also to surpass, Italian sources.[48] For example, Antoine de Saint-Denis, who was completing a set of French stories based on the *Decameron* during these years, boasted of having vastly improved on the work of Boccaccio in his *Comptes du monde adventureux* [Tales of the Adventurous World]:

> Cest autheur hardy a premier en la France
> Imité le discours des comptes de Florence,
> Et en les imitant a vaincu le Boccace
> Et devance ses pas suivant mesmes sa trace.[49]

[This bold author was the first in France | To imitate the speech of the Florentine tales, | And in imitating them has conquered Boccaccio | And overtaken his steps while only following his path.]

In a bid to claim the short story genre as French, Saint-Denis uses the same *via* topos as Jodelle when discussing his sources: he has overtaken his models by retracing their path. It is possible that Jodelle, too, aimed to show French comedy to be superior to its Italian counterpart, both by denying foreign influences and by using his play subtly to mock the Italians. Indeed, by 1556 Jodelle was openly anti-Italian: he ridiculed the Italians' 'vices vilains' [evil vices] and 'cœurs effeminez' [effeminate hearts];[50] he also criticised their competitiveness, as well as their attempts to prove themselves to be superior court poets:

> Mais que diray-je de leur race,
> Qui encore aujourd'huy pourchasse
> De se faire nommer de nous
> Le peuple le mieux né de tous?[51]

[But what shall I say about their race, | Which is still today competing | To have themselves named by us | As the best-born people of all?]

Jodelle's prefatory materials to *L'Eugène* suggest that this play was an early attempt not only to escape the overshadowing precedent set by ancient and Italian playwrights, but to himself become an exemplar of comic theatre. This notion of cultural rivalry, which manifested itself in various ways through drama in later decades, will be returned to and examined in greater detail in Part III.

Jodelle largely succeeded in his aim to be recognised as France's first playwright. As Pasquier recalls, at the Hôtel de Reims *L'Eugène* met with 'un grand applaudissement de toute la compagnie' [great applause from the entire audience], and the windows of the Collège de Boncourt were 'tapissées d'une infinité de personnages d'honneur, et la cour si pleine d'escoliers que les portes du collège en regorgeaient' [lined with an infinity of honourable people, and the yard so full of students that the college doors were bursting].[52] Pasquier is unequivocal in his praise of Jodelle as the first French dramatic writer: 'Quand à la Comedie et Tragedie, nous en devons le premier plant à Estienne Jodelle' [As for comedy and tragedy, it was Estienne Jodelle who laid the first foundations];[53] welcoming Jodelle into the Pléiade, Ronsard also points to Jodelle's innovation:

> Jodelle heureusement sonna
> D'une vois humble et d'une vois hardie
> La Comedie, avec la Tragedie,
> Et d'un ton double, ore bas, ore haut,
> Remplit premier le François échafaut.[54]

[Jodelle happily announced | With one humble and one bold voice | Comedy, with tragedy, | And in a double tone, now low, now high, | Was the first to fill the French stage.]

Yet it would be wrong to state that *L'Eugène* single-handedly established comedy as a respected genre in France.[55] The previous chapters have shown that French and Italian theoreticians, translators, patrons, and organisers had contributed to proving the worthiness of comedy as a genre of humanist literature; Jodelle, too, was inspired by Italian performances and commissioned by an Italian patron to write his comedy. *L'Eugène* forms part of the back-and-forward narrative of attempts to reinvent comic theatre, providing the first example that comedy could be written and brought to life in French, as well as demonstrating the entertainment value of comic theatre. This comedy can, then, be described as a transitional play: while it reproduces in some ways the medieval farce, it also shows classical and neoclassical drama to be stage-worthy, and incorporates features recommended by earlier theoreticians which were to become customary in French theatre. We shall see in Part III that over the next decade this comedy helped to smooth the way for other writers, who managed more successfully to move away from immediate literary ancestors. *L'Eugène* also set an important precedent for theatre outside the court. As explored in the Introduction, no French writers in the sixteenth century made a living as comic dramatists, and the majority of comedies were composed by lawyers and doctors with a *collège* education: some of these writers (such as Jacques Grévin and Rémy Belleau) were directly inspired by *L'Eugène*, having themselves possibly acted in the Boncourt performance. This live experience had clearly been memorable to them, since Jodelle's dramatic writings appeared only twenty years after the performances in a posthumous volume of his works.[56] Ultimately, then, this play managed more effectively than the treatises of writers such as Estienne and Du Bellay to convince French humanists of the value of comic theatre, and although Jodelle did not eclipse the achievements of the ancients or Italians — who remained important models throughout the century — he both broadened access to comedy and showed it to be successful entertainment, securing a new and more widespread respect for the genre in France.

An Unintentional Farce: Jodelle's *Masquarades* (1558)

Unlike the Italian performances in France, *L'Eugène* received little to no funding: it did not comprise specially-made sets, staging, or costumes, and the actors were members of the court or else students of the Collège de Boncourt (in his tragedy, Jodelle himself insisted on playing the title role of Cleopatra). The performance also took place as a one-off event, rather than to celebrate a special occasion or festival as the Italian comedies had. Yet following the 1552 performances, Jodelle became increasingly well-known at Fontainebleau, and was a favourite of Henri II. The most successful organisers of comedy at the court were also gradually disappearing: Alamanni, who had contributed to the performances of *La Calandra*, *I Lucidi*, and *La Flora*, died in 1556; Ippolito had also moved back to Italy in 1550 to pursue his (ultimately unsuccessful) dream of becoming pope.[57] By 1558, when a series of festivities had hurriedly to be organised to mark the return of Henri II to Paris following the victorious Siege of Calais, Jodelle was the most obvious choice to write and put together these elaborate entertainments. With just three days to go before Henri's return, the Conseil de Paris sent Jodelle a generous payment to fund the celebrations, which were due to take place on 17 February in the Hôtel de Ville, a building which was also owned by the court. Jodelle had initially planned to 'faire et composer une comedie ou poesye' [compose and stage a comedy or poem]:[58] however, he decided instead to write an array of Latin *icones*, praising figures such as Catherine de' Medici and Marguerite de France; he also organised a series of Italian-style masquerades. This performance was highly ambitious, and comprised a procession of the Argonauts, along with a specially built Argo; a number of monologues from illustrious classical figures such as Minerva; and a parade by Mnemosyne, the Greek goddess of memory. Although this was not a comedy, it is the first major performance designed for celebration at the court entrusted to a French writer. For this reason, and because it was closely based on Italian precedents, it is worth briefly exploring these masquerades as a final case study in this chapter.

Few scholars have commented on these masquerades, and fewer still have noted that the performance went badly wrong.[59] The event did not start well: the weather was terrible, and the Conseil accounts note that the king, queen, dauphin, and Marguerite de France were forced to take a coach and arrived wet through; we are also told that 'l'artillerye [...] faisoit si grand bruyt que les haquenées qui menoient lad.coche eurent peur et cuyderent faire choir le Roy en descendant d'icelle' [the artillery made such a noise that the horses pulling the aforementioned coach were frightened, and made the King fall on his way out].[60] However, it is clear from contemporary accounts of the masquerades, as well as from Jodelle's aforementioned *Recueil*, that the situation went from bad to worse after the masquerades started. Jodelle himself was devastated at the quality of the performance: 'Ni ma raison ni les raisons de tous mes amis ne m'ont persuadé qu'à grand peine que ce desastre fust peu de chose' [It took a lot for my own reasoning, as well as the reasoning of all of my friends, to convince me that this disaster was not the be-all and end-all] (*Recueil*, p. 121); the Conseil, too, was so displeased with the performance that they insisted Jodelle return the money they had given him for it.[61] The failure of the performance was apparently caused by four separate aspects of the masquerades, which Jodelle himself identifies in his *Recueil*.

Firstly, in the style of the Italian performances at the court, as well as of *La Calandra*, Jodelle had planned to incorporate in the masquerades a series of lavish costumes. As the Conseil notes, Jodelle spent a large sum on materials to make these: 'Fut achepté grande quantité de draps de soye et de canetille d'or pour faire les accoustremens' [A great quantity of silk and golden cannetille was bought to make the costumes].[62] To provide just one example, the most impressive of these costumes was intended to be three children representing cherubs, naked and complete with elaborate wings, accompanying the entourage of Mnemosyne; they should have carried baskets containing diadems of laurels, palms, and ivy to gift each member of the nobility (*Recueil*, p. 123). It is likely that the wreaths, a motif which had already been included in *La Calandra* to signify literary accomplishment, were intended also to represent Jodelle's own achievement in creating masquerades in French. Yet to Jodelle's dismay, the children arrived for the performance fully clothed and wearing less than convincing costumes, ruining the desired effect: 'Au lieu d'enfans nuds, les Parisiens mirent de leurs enfans vestus et bien peu desguisés' [Instead of naked children, the Parisians had their children clothed and very poorly dressed-up]; additionally, they had left insufficient time to complete the diadems and could not find natural leaves (*Recueil*, p. 123). Instead, as Jodelle explains, the diadems had to be put together 'de toutes les sortes' [with all kinds of things] (*Recueil*, p. 123). He blames the failure of the costumes on the Parisians, who could not bring to life his artistic vision and who had instead 'mequaniquement mesnagé les habits' [put together the costumes perfunctorily] (*Recueil*, p. 117).

The second feature which Jodelle had planned to incorporate was an impressive theatre space. As the Conseil accounts indicate, the masquerades took place after a feast;[63] the tables, then, had to be removed, while the spectators were to be sat where Jodelle had planned:

> Quant à la salle on m'avoit asseuré que [...] les tables des deus costés s'abbatroient, et que le Roy avecques sa compaignie tenant tout ce hault qu'on avoit fait plancheyer pour eus, tout le reste se rangeroit des deus costés devers le hault, tellement que la moitié Presque de la salle me demeureroit tout vuide [...] estant là comme dedans un theatre. (*Recueil*, pp. 118–19)

> [As for the room, I had been assured that [...] the tables on both sides would be put down, and that the king and his retinue would occupy the raised space that had been laid for them, and that the others would be sat at the sides of the room, sloping towards the raised space: this would leave almost half of the room empty for me [...] being there as though in a theatre.]

This sloping layout recalls the classical 'demy rond' that Jodelle had aimed to incorporate for *L'Eugène*. In spite of the short time he was given to create such a space, Jodelle clearly wanted to provide as impressive and authentic an experience as possible: he had hoped that the spectators would feel as though they were in a theatre ('comme dedans un theatre'). Additionally, in the same way as the organisers of *La Calandra* had created an elaborately decorated room, Jodelle commissioned a certain 'Baptiste excellent peintre' [excellent painter Baptiste] to paint the panels in the hall (*Recueil*, p. 92): as argued by Georges Wildenstein, and subsequently by Graham and McAllister-Johnson, this is probably the artist Baptiste Pellerin (*c.* 1530–75).[64] Jodelle's most detailed description is of a painting of Janus, which decorated a panel next to the king, and held a key in his right hand (*Recueil*, p. 88). Jodelle explains that this god, after which the month January is named, was chosen to depict the fortuitousness of the beginning of that year: 'J'avois voulu montrer par ceste peinture, combien le mois de Janvier nous a esté favorable' [I had wanted to show by this painting how favourable the month of January was to us]; however, he must also have chosen the figure of Janus to please the king, since this was one of Henri's preferred motifs at Fontainebleau (*Recueil*, p. 88). Henri was proud, for example, of the bronze bust of Janus which had been sculpted by the Bolognese court poet Francesco Primaticcio (1504–70), who had resided at Fontainebleau since 1532 and was a close ally of Jodelle (figure 4.1).[65]

As well as taking inspiration from an Italian artist for the motifs, it is possible that Jodelle imitated Serlio in his set design. Although Serlio himself had died in Lyons four years prior to these masquerades, his work was still widely read; as we have seen, it is possible that Jodelle, too, had read Serlio's work on theatre. Jodelle tells us very little about his ideas for this set: he mentions only that his design included 'rochers' [rocks] (*Recueil*, p. 117). Yet the only known set which included rocks (*sassi*) is Serlio's pastoral set (figure 4.2).[66]

While he may have intended for his set to resemble that of Serlio, which is in any case simpler than the other comic and tragic sets, Jodelle was again unable to bring to fruition his arrangements. Far too little space was left for the performance area, and the actors were barely distinguishable: they were 'troublés [...] perdus dedans ceste multitude, et parlans jusques contre la face du Roy' [flustered [...] lost in the crowd, and speaking right in the king's face] (*Recueil*, pp. 118–19). The Conseil notes that the room was so crowded that the performance was unable take place: 'Il y avoit si grande confusion et presse en la Grande Salle, qu'ilz ne sceurent achever

FIG. 4.1. Francesco Primaticcio, *Double Head*, bronze, *c.* 1543.
J. Paul Getty Museum, Los Angeles. Digital image courtesy of the Getty's
Open Content Program.

leur jeu' [There was such a crush and confusion in the Grande Salle that they were unable to finish their play].[67] As for the rocks he had asked the Parisians to paint for his set, his instructions were apparently misheard, and they painted *clochers* [bell-towers] instead of *rochers*: 'Voir qu'on m'avoit fait au lieu des rochers des clochers [...] que peut-on penser que je devinse?' [Seeing as they made bell-towers instead of rocks for me [...] what on earth did they think I had planned?] (*Recueil*, p. 117). Enea Balmas has posited that this final complaint may be hyperbolic; yet even if it is, this description helps us to gauge the level of Jodelle's disappointment with the result of his masquerades, as well as his frustration with the Parisians hired to help him.[68]

Thirdly, it appears as though Jodelle had planned to hire professional actors for the performance, though ran out of time to find any: 'Comment bon Dieu eussé-je cherché de bons acteurs, veu que les trois jours que j'avois d'espace se fussent coulés à les chercher?' [How in the name of the good Lord was I meant to acquire good actors, seeing as the entire three days I had were spent trying to find them?] (*Recueil*, p. 117). Jodelle himself was forced to play the part of Jason, seeing as his actor did not turn up; he also had to ask 'cinq ou six gentils hommes miens amis' [five or six of my gentleman friends] to play the part of Argonauts, who were 'muets' [dumb], since they did not know their lines (*Recueil*, p. 118). Jodelle was even unhappy with his own performance, admitting that he was more focused on keeping his temper: 'Qui doute que recitant moymesme avecques les autres, je ne peusse de beaucoup les soulager, si le desordre et l'extreme colere ne m'eussent fait du tout perdre?' [Who on earth thinks me able to help improve the others just by acting with them, when chaos and extreme anger were threatening to tip me over the edge?] (*Recueil*, p. 118). Finally, while no music for the performance survives, we can infer that the masquerades were written in the Italian style, since the rhyme scheme of the lyrics is based very closely on their Italian counterparts (*Recueil*, p. 103, n. 86). Jodelle makes just one reference to the music in his *Recueil*: 'Dès le commencement par la faute d'une musique se naistre une rizée' [From the start of the performance, when a wrong note sounded, laughter started to brew] (*Recueil*, p. 121). Clearly the music, too, was poorly executed, and despite being based on a successful Italian model, failed to impress the spectators.

It is no coincidence that each of the masquerades' most prominent features — the costumes, staging, actors, and music — were the features that had been singled out for especial praise by the spectators of *La Calandra*. As we have seen, Jodelle was by this time openly hostile towards the Italian presence at the court, and disliked their competitivity. Yet Jodelle's own masquerades were, like *L'Eugène*, imitated from — and indeed intended to equal — the Italian tradition. The masquerade too was an Italian innovation, being imported into France by Ippolito, who had organised a number of these performances at Fontainebleau. As Adeline Lionetto has noted, the masquerade was also a particularly fitting choice for this occasion, which took place in the middle of the carnival season, which was regularly celebrated with masquerades in Italy.[69] Jodelle was an ambitious poet, and no doubt hoped to derive personal benefit from these masquerades as much as he had aimed to impress the king. In writing of his despair at the performance, he hints at the recognition

FIG. 4.2. 'Scena satirica', in Sebastiano Serlio, *Le premier livre d'Architecture et le second livre de Perspective de Sebastien Serlio Bolognois, mis en langue françoise, par Jehan Martin* (Paris: Jean Barbé, 1545), fol. 70^v. Bibliothèque numérique de l'INHA, Bibliothèque de l'Institut National d'Histoire de l'Art, collections Jacques Doucet, NUM 4 RES 1476.

that he had aimed to earn by them, 'driven mad' as he was by 'l'ignorance que sembloient avoir ces Parisiens de ce qui leur pouvoit apporter honneur' [the ignorance that these Parisians seem to have of that which could have brought them honour] (*Recueil*, p. 116). In referring to the potential honour in this performance, it is clear that he had intended to use theatre once again to enhance French literature and culture, as well as to elevate his own renown and recognition as an innovative dramatist, as he had with *L'Eugène*. Although these masquerades were based on the Italian model, in another parallel with *L'Eugène*, Jodelle was evidently affected by the overshadowing precedent that the Italians had set. He speaks of his concern at the start of the account at the 'expectation qu'on avoit de moy' [expectation that everyone had of me] (*Recueil*, p. 117); he also describes the quality of previous performances, which may have diminished the impact of his own: when explaining how he was forced to act in the play, for example, he recalls other, more talented performers the king had seen: 'Qui est celui qui ignore combien de plus grands que moy se sont mis en France sur le theatre devant sa mesme Majesté?' [Who on earth could forget how many actors, far better than I, had taken to the French stage in front of his same Majesty?] (*Recueil*, p. 118). It is possible that Jodelle was intimidated by the Italian performers which were regularly hosted at the French court, and was aware of his own poor acting in comparison.

Despite aiming to produce his own ambitious, Italianate performance at the court, rivalling the traditions which had dominated and thereby gaining more recognition for himself, Jodelle was unable to ensure the success of any part of his masquerades. It may be that the masquerades failed because Jodelle was too ambitious in his planning. In true humanist style, he prided himself on his mastery of every field:

> Je suis dedans Paris encor que j'en sois loing,
>   Où je desseine, et taille, et charpente et massonne,
> Je brode, je pourtray, je coupe, je façonne,
> Je cizele, je grave, émaillant, et dorant,
> Je griffonne, je peins, dorant et colorant,
> Je tapisse, j'assieds, je festonne et decore,
> Je musique, je sonne, et poëtise encore.[70]

[I am in Paris even when I am far from it, | Where I draw, sculpt, craft and build, | I embroider, sketch, I trim, I mould, | I chisel, I carve, with enamel and gold; | I scribble, I paint, with gold and colours, | I upholster, I fix, I festoon and decorate, | I compose music, I play it, and write poetry too.]

He may have sought to plan so many aspects of the masquerade that he could not properly manage any of them, especially given the short time he was given. Cooper has also suggested that it may have been too great a challenge for Jodelle to present as a conquering hero Henri, who had suffered a long series of setbacks throughout the decade, such as the defeats in Siena in 1555 and at Saint-Quentin in 1557.[71] Additionally, we have seen that Jodelle was quick to blame the masquerades' failure on the incompetence of the Parisians, who apparently lacked his artistic vision. He claims that this was common knowledge: 'Chacun sçait que la main de mes ouvriers ne peut suivre l'abondance de mes executions' [Everyone knows that the hands of my workers could not follow the abundance of my designs] (*Recueil*, p. 88). Yet it may also be that they were unwilling to help Jodelle. Although he was popular with the king, he was disliked by many others at the court: Pierre de L'Estoile, for example, described Jodelle as 'le poëte le plus vilain et lascif de tous' [the nastiest and most lecherous poet of all].[72] While each of these factors — overambition, a tight schedule, a difficult subject, ineptitude, and deliberate unhelpfulness — no doubt contributed to the failure of these masquerades, it may also be that Jodelle lacked the skills and experience of the Italians. Their designers, musicians, and actors were well used to putting together such events, often at short notice; masquerades were also regular events as part of carnival celebrations, and organisers and performers knew what to expect. No doubt the *Recueil* itself was intended to offset the failure of Jodelle's play: as Michèle Clément has argued, he sets out his plans as a means of showing his ambition and innovation, even if they could not be fully realised in the performance itself.[73] Yet Jodelle never fully recovered from the failure of his masquerades. He was given a last opportunity to write a celebratory play, after being invited by the Cardinal of Lorraine to compose a comedy for the 1559 double royal marriage of the king's daughter Élisabeth to Philip II of Spain, and Marguerite de France to Emmanuel-Philibert, the Duke of Savoy. Evidence suggests that this comedy was very nearly ready, since a new, possibly Italianate, stage had been constructed for the performance: a note in the margin of Gabriello Simeoni's 1561 *L'Epitalamio* indicates that 'sur un mode nouveau [un] Théâtre [fut] érigé a Paris pour représenter des comédies' [in the new mode [a] theatre [was] constructed in Paris to stage these comedies].[74] However, the king's sudden and violent death in a jousting accident prevented any celebrations from taking place, and no text of this comedy survives. Jodelle never regained favour at the court: there are few records of his activity throughout the 1560s, and he died in poverty in 1573.

The performances which took place at the court in the 1550s reveal several key features of mid-century comedy in France. Italian comedy was increasingly popular, and the organisers of these plays were skilled at demonstrating their own native talent. The comedies were left in the original Italian language, performed by Italian troupes, and set in highly recognisable Italian cities. The material that was performed was also varied — comedies were selected that had been inspired by Plautus, and not just the well-known Terence — and put into practice features such as the prose style, specially designed costumes, and trained actors. Although these features had each been recommended by Estienne in the 1540s, it was the Italians who first brought them to life with *La Calandra*, and continued the tradition at the court throughout the 1550s. It is likely that these comedies had been organised by the Florentine network at Fontainebleau, led by Alamanni, who provided a major diplomatic link with Italy, was well connected with Italian dramatic writers, and interested in comic theatre himself. Alamanni or other royal patrons may have funded these performances, which required at the very least costumes and paid actors; additionally, there is evidence that the performances were tailored to suit the king and queen, and it is possible that the organisers hoped to secure financial reward, especially in the wake of the lucrative *La Calandra*. What is also clear is that comedy was beginning to form part of festival and celebration culture in France, as it had in Italy. This was to set a precedent for the next two decades in France, when comedy played an important part in courtly carnivals, weddings, and baptisms.

Although Jodelle was the first French author to turn his hand to comedy in 1552, it was at the request of the Italian Catherine. *L'Eugène* was a turning point in that it was the first comedy in French to incorporate an original plot, as well as innovations such as intervals and act divisions. It was also instrumental in introducing comic theatre to audiences outside the context of the court. Clearly, Jodelle viewed *L'Eugène* as an opportunity to be recognised as France's first dramatist, and his prologue is focused firstly on emphasising his innovation, and secondly on diminishing the influence of classical and Italian sources. Yet, in describing how he has simultaneously rejected, followed, and improved on his predecessors — possibly in an attempt to eclipse the work of Italian rivals — he provides evidence of his reliance on them. Conversely, he also fails to move away from medieval sources, which he criticises, and many aspects of his play are reminiscent of the farce model. Given his imitation of medieval drama, as well as the important framework for comic theatre set out by theoreticians and translators in the previous decade, we should not overstate Jodelle's achievement, nor take too literally his claims to innovation. His success with *L'Eugène* no doubt contributed to his selection as the organiser of Henri II's triumphant return to Paris in 1558, however, which he viewed as a further opportunity to gain recognition as a writer of plays. Yet in basing the ambitious masquerades he wrote for this occasion on the Italian tradition, including the imitation of its four features of costumes, staging, actors, and music, Jodelle clearly took on too much responsibility, and was incapable of ensuring the performance's success. It may also be that he lacked the experience to bring together such a major performance, while the Italians were well versed in quickly bringing to fruition plays of a similar scale.

Although Jodelle's plans for an elaborate performance failed, the French approach to Italian and comic plays had undergone a shift during the 1550s. Classical theatre was increasingly treated with respect by humanists, and Jodelle had shown with *L'Eugène* that a reinvented style could at once impress and entertain. Part III will examine how comedy started to thrive outside royal circles, college students having been convinced of the viability of theatre as a humanist genre. We will also continue to assess the complex relationship of French writers with their Italian counterparts, which began to be characterised far more by rivalry than by reverence. This chapter has explored how Jodelle's awareness of the precedent set by Italian playwrights, as well as his bid to overshadow them and to earn recognition for himself, helped to bring comic theatre to life on the French stage. Consequently, his comedy is subtly marked with anti-Italian insults, as well as an endeavour to mask his sources. Yet, as we shall see in the next two chapters, French writers in the 1560s became increasingly skilled at composing Italianate comedy. They were, as a result, able to transform their work into a far more overt weapon, taking to a new level Jodelle's attempts to resist and to rival Italian culture.

Notes to Chapter 4

1. Other comedies performed at the court during this period can be found in Lebègue, 'Tableau de la comédie française de la Renaissance', pp. 282–83.
2. Estienne Jodelle, *L'Eugène: édition critique avec introduction, notes et glossaire*, ed. by Michael Freeman (Exeter: Exeter University Press, 1987) (hereafter referenced in main text as *L'Eugène*).
3. Estienne Pasquier, *Des recherches de la France*, 10 vols (Paris: L. Sonnius, 1617), VI, [s.n.] (Chapter vii).
4. See Victor Graham, Jodelle's *Eugène, ou La Rencontre* Again', *Renaissance News*, 14.3 (1961), 161–64.
5. Estienne Jodelle, *Le Recueil des inscriptions, 1558: A Literary and Iconographical Exegesis*, ed. by Victor Graham and William McAllister-Johnson (Toronto: University of Toronto Press, 1972) (hereafter referenced in main text as *Recueil*).
6. Lucien Romier, *Les Origines politiques des guerres de religion*, 2 vols (Paris: Perrin, 1913), I, 5, n. 1.

7. Reproduced in *Il bibliofilo*, ed. by Carlo Lozzi, 11 vols (Bologna: Società tipografica già compositori, 1884), VI, 85.

8. See Raymond Lebègue, 'La Comédie italienne en France au XVIe siècle', *Revue de Littérature Comparée*, 24 (1950), 5–24 (p. 17).

9. For more information on this wedding performance, see Artemis Preschl, *Shakespeare and Commedia dell'Arte: Play by Play* (Abingdon: Routledge, 2017), p. 8.

10. Alamanni and Buonamico had both been members of the Accademia degli Infiammati [Academy of the Inflamed], a literary academy active in Padua throughout the 1540s. For more information on Buonamico and Firenzuola, see Agnolo Firenzuola, *Opere*, ed. by Adriano Seroni (Florence: Sansoni, 1971), p. 627.

11. Agnolo Firenzuola, *I Lucidi, commedia*, ed. by Lodovico Domenichi (Florence: I Giunti, 1552), [s.n.] (prefatory letter 'Al magnifico e suo molto onorato messer Aldighieri della Casa').

12. Giuseppe Parini, *Versi e prose di Giuseppe Parini*, ed. by Giuseppe Giusti (Florence: Felice le Monnier, 1846), p. 460. For more information on Firenzuola's prose, see Agnolo Firenzuola and Giovanni Battista Gelli, *Tesoretto della lingua toscana*, ed. by Nicola Giosafatte Biagioli (Paris: G. Didot, 1822), pp. 8–10 ('Preface').

13. See Appendix III for a full synopsis of *I Lucidi*.

14. Candiard, 'Roman Comedy in Early Modern Italy and France', p. 327.

15. Giovanni Cappello, 'Relazione del Clarissimo Messer Giovanni Cappello, ambasciator in Francia nell'anno 1554', in *Relations des ambassadeurs vénitiens sur les affaires de France au xvie siècle*, ed. by Niccolò Tommaseo, 2 vols (Paris: Imprimerie Royale, 1838), II, 366–85 (p. 372).

16. See Luigi Alamanni, *La Flora, in versi e prose di Luigi Alamanni, edizione ordinata e raffrontata sui codici per cura di Pietro Raffaelli, con un discorso intorno all'Alamanni e al suo secolo*, ed. by Pietro Raffaelli, 2 vols (Firenze: Le Monnier, 1859), II, 321–403 (further references are to this edition).

17. Ibid., I, 2.

18. A summary of the plot can be found in Appendix III.

19. Henri Hauvette, *Un exilé florentin à la cour de France au XVIe siècle* (Paris: Hachette & Cie, 1903), p. 152.

20. Alamanni, *La Flora*, I, 24. Cited in Hauvette, *Un exilé florentin à la cour de France au XVIe siècle*, p. 350.

21. Bernardo Buoninsegni's letter is reproduced in *Miscellanea storica senese*, 4.12 (1896), 201. Cited in Hauvette, *Un exilé florentin à la cour de France au XVIe siècle*, p. 145.

22. Alamanni, *La Flora*, I, 2.

23. Ibid.

24. See Andrea Gareffi, *La scrittura e la festa: teatro, festa e letterature nella Firenze del Rinascimento* (Bologna: Il Mulino, 1991), p. 101. It is not, as Lebègue has claimed, solely 'imitée des pièces de Térence' [imitated from Terence's plays]. 'Tableau de la comédie française de la Renaissance', p. 302.

25. Alamanni, *La Flora*, I, 2.

26. For more information on Alamanni's increased responsibilities, see Hauvette, *Un exilé florentin à la cour de France au XVIe siècle*, pp. 144–45.

27. This letter is reproduced in *Catalogo della libreria Capponi o sia de' libri italiani del fù marchese Alessandro Gregorio Capponi*, ed. by Alessandro Pompeo Barti and Domenico Giorgi (Rome: Bernabò e Lazzarini, 1747), p. 10. This reading of the *Electra* was examined in Chapter 3.

28. *Il bibliofilo*, ed. by Lozzi, VI, 85.

29. See the prefatory letter of the 1556 edition of *La Flora*, 'Al molto Mag. et nobilissimo M. Filippo Salviati, Andrea Lori': 'Questo Carnoval passato [...] mostra una Comedia di Luigi Alamanni' [This past carnival [...] a comedy by Luigi Alamanni was performed]. Alamanni, *La Flora, con gl'intermedii di A. Lori* (Florence: Lorenzo Torrentino, 1556).

30. *Cléopâtre captive* met with a warm reception from the king, who gifted Jodelle five hundred *écus*. Pasquier, *Des recherches de la France*, VI, [s.n.] (Chapter vii).

31. Noirot, 'French Humanist Comedy in Search of an Audience', p. 88.

32. Translations of Terence in this period are discussed throughout Lawton, *Contribution à l'histoire de l'humanisme en France*.

33. The patriotism in these lines by Jodelle has also been noted in Tilde Sankovitch, *Jodelle et la création du masque: étude structurale et normative de L'Eugène* (York, SC: French Literature Publications, 1979), p. 15.

34. Colin Burrow, *Imitating Authors: Plato to Futurity* (Oxford: Oxford University Press, 2019), p. 359.

35. Boccaccio, too, had outlined how he liked to follow the path, but not the exact footsteps, of his predecessors. This famous letter from the *Familiares* is analysed in Pigman, 'Versions of Imitation in the Renaissance', p. 21.

36. Emmanuel Buron has also contended that this prologue aimed to enhance the worthiness of comedy from the spectators' viewpoint. '"Comique" et "propriété" dans la préface de l'"Amoureux repos" de Guillaume des Autelz', in *Le Léxique métalitteraire français (XVIe-XVIIe siècles)*, ed. by Michel Jourde and Jean-Charles Monferran (Geneva: Droz, 2006), pp. 67–87 (p. 85).

37. Pieter Coecke van Aelst had printed his French translation in Antwerp, which had probably not yet made its way to Paris. Sebastiano Serlio, *Des antiquités, le troisième livre translaté d'italien en français*, trans. by Pieter Coecke van Aelst (Antwerp: P. Coecke, 1550). For more information on this translation, see Magali Vène, *Bibliographia Serliana: catalogue des éditions imprimées des livres du traité d'architecture de Sebastiano Serlio (1537–1681)* (Paris: Picard, 2007), pp. 75–76.

38. On the use of the term *barbare* during these years to refer to the Italians, see Marina Marietti, *Quêtes d'une identité collective chez les Italiens de la Renaissance* (Paris: Université de la Sorbonne Nouvelle, 1990), p. 80.

39. Louis Petit de Julleville, *Le Théâtre en France: histoire de la littérature dramatique depuis ses origines jusqu'à nos jours* (Paris: A. Colin, 1921), p. 85.

40. Mazouer, *Le Théâtre français de la Renaissance*, p. 341.

41. A fuller plot summary can be found in Appendix III.

42. Madeleine Lazard has also commented on 'le cynisme du dénouement' [the cynicism of the dénouement] in her *Le Théâtre en France au XVIe siècle* (Paris: Presses universitaires de France, 1980), p. 178. Further examples of *L'Eugène*'s parallel with the farce can be found in David Bradby, 'France: The 16th Century', in *The Cambridge Guide to Theatre*, ed. by Martin Banham (Cambridge: Cambridge University Press, 2000), pp. 385–86 (p. 386), and Jeffery, *French Renaissance Comedy*, p. 100.

43. Jodelle, *Œuvres et meslanges poétiques*, ed. by Charles de La Mothe (Paris: Mamert Patisson, 1574), p. 12.

44. Jean Vauquelin de la Fresnaye, *Art poétique*, ed. by Georges Pellissier, 2 vols (Paris: Garnier, 1885), II, 119 (ll. 1035–38).

45. See Huguet, *Dictionnaire de la langue française du seizième siècle*, II, 621.

46. This resentment has been well documented by a number of scholars, such as Smith in *The Anti-courtier Trend in Sixteenth-century French Literature*, Thomas Greene in *The Light in Troy: Imitation and Discovery in Renaissance Poetry* (New Haven, CT: Yale University Press, 1982), and Balsamo in *Les Rencontres des muses*.

47. On the crisis of 'exemplarity', see primarily François Rigolot, 'The Renaissance Crisis of Exemplarity', *Journal of the History of Ideas*, 54.4 (1998), 557–63. Peter Burke has argued that given that 'exemplarity' was also widely accepted during this period, 'critique' is a more appropriate description: see his 'Exemplarity and Anti-exemplarity in Early Modern Europe', in *The Western Time of Ancient History: Historiographical Encounters with the Greek and Roman Pasts*, ed. by Alexandra Lianeri (Cambridge: Cambridge University Press, 2011), pp. 48–59.

48. Henri Chamard even argued that the Pléiade was formed during these years primarily as a means of competing with Italian writers. Chamard, *Histoire de la Pléiade*, 4 vols (Paris: Didier, 1961–64), I, 167. Also cited in MacPhail, *The Voyage to Rome in French Renaissance Literature*, p. 34.

49. Antoine de Saint-Denis, *Comptes du monde adventureux* (Paris: Estienne Groulleau, 1555), pp. 13–14 (prefatory sonnet).

50. Estienne Jodelle, 'Estienne Jodelle au peuple français', in *Œuvres complètes*, ed. by Enea Balmas, 2 vols (Paris: Gallimard, 1965), II, 113–21 (p. 114).

51. Ibid., pp. 114–15. More information about Jodelle's rivalry with the Italians in this poem can be found in Richard Cooper, 'Mario Equicola et la France', in *Parcours et rencontres: mélanges de*

langue, d'histoire et de littérature française offerts à Enea Balmas, ed. by Paolo Carile, Giovanni Dotoli, and Anna Maria Raugei, 2 vols (Paris: Klincksieck, 1993), I, 167–82 (p. 167).

52. Pasquier, *Des recherches de la France*, VI, [s.n.] (Chapter vii).
53. Ibid., VII, [s.n.] (Chapter vi).
54. Pierre de Ronsard, 'À Jean de La Péruse, poète', in *Œuvres complètes*, V, 262.
55. See claims made by scholars such as: Donald Perret, *Old Comedy in the French Renaissance (1576–1620)* (Geneva: Droz, 1992), p. 15; and Philip Koch, 'French Drama in the Seventeenth Century', in *Comedy: A Geographic and Historical Guide*, ed. by Maurice Charney, 2 vols (Westport: Praeger Publishers, 2005), II, 331–49 (p. 333).
56. See Jodelle, *Œuvres et meslanges poétiques*, ed. by La Mothe, pp. 188–292.
57. Ippolito's movements are vividly explored in Giulia Vidori, 'Negotiating Power in Sixteenth-century Italy: Ippolito II d'Este between Rome, France, and Ferrara' (unpublished doctoral thesis, University of Oxford, 2018).
58. *Les Registres des délibérations du Bureau de la Ville de Paris (1552–1558)*, ed. by François Bonnardot and others, 21 vols (Paris, Imprimerie Nationale, 1888), IV, 522.
59. Smith, for example, points out that there was just a 'technical hitch' in the production. *The Anti-courtier Trend in Sixteenth-century French Literature*, p. 111.
60. *Les Registres des délibérations du Bureau de la Ville de Paris*, ed. by Bonnardot and others, p. 523.
61. Adeline Lionetto, 'Splendeurs et misères de la ville de Paris dans le *Recueil des inscriptions, devis et masquarades* de Jodelle', *Seizième siècle*, 9 (2013), 81–93 (p. 83).
62. *Les Registres des délibérations du Bureau de la Ville de Paris*, ed. by Bonnardot and others, p. 522.
63. Ibid., p. 523.
64. Georges Wildenstein, 'La Collection de tableaux d'un amateur de Ronsard', *Gazette de Beaux-Arts*, 6.51 (1958), 5, n. 2; Jodelle, *Le Recueil des inscriptions, 1558*, p. 92, n. 71.
65. Jodelle even dedicated a sonnet to Madame de Primadis, printed posthumously in the edited collection, *Œuvres et meslanges poétiques*, ed. by La Mothe, p. 106. For more information on Jodelle's relationship with the Primaticcio family, see John Hall, 'Primaticcio and Court Festivals', *Bulletin of the John Rylands University Library of Manchester*, 58.2 (1976), 353–77 (pp. 374–75).
66. Serlio, *Il secondo libro*, fol. 70^v.
67. *Les Registres des délibérations du Bureau de la Ville de Paris*, ed. by Bonnardot and others, p. 522.
68. See Enea Balmas, *Un poeta francese del Rinascimento: Estienne Jodelle. La sua vita, il suo tempo* (Florence: Olschki, 1962), pp. 369–72.
69. Adeline Lionetto, '"Je me fis quasi de tous métiers": Etienne Jodelle et la promotion de la figure du poète panepistemon', *Anamorfose: Revista de Estudios Modernos*, 4.1 (2018), 1–18 (p. 8).
70. Estienne Jodelle, 'Epithalame de Madame Marguerite', in *Œuvres complètes*, ed. by Balmas, I, 176. Also cited in *Recueil*, p. 7. A fuller discussion of this poem can be found in David Ledbetter, *Harpsichord and Lute Music in 17th-century France* (Basingstoke: Palgrave Macmillan, 1987), pp. 15–16.
71. See Cooper, 'The Theme of War in Renaissance Entries', pp. 25–26.
72. Pierre de L'Estoile, *Mémoires pour servir à l'histoire de France depuis 1515 jusqu'en 1574*, in *Mémoires-journaux, 1574–1611*, ed. by Alphonse Lemerre, 12 vols (Paris: Tallandier, 1982), XII, 386–87.
73. Michèle Clément, 'Jodelle ou la fête de papier', in *La Fête au XVIe siècle*, ed. by Marie Viallon-Schoneveld (Saint-Étienne: Université de Saint-Étienne, 2003), pp. 159–70.
74. Gabriello Simeoni, *L'Epitalamio*, in *Description de la Limagne d'Auvergne*, ed. by Toussaint Renucci (Paris: Didier, 1944), p. 17. Richard Cooper has also commented on this stage in his 'Gabriele Simeoni visionario', in *Cinquecento visionario tra Italia e Francia*, ed. by Nerina Clerici (Florence: Olschki, 1992), pp. 279–97.

PART III

The Politics of Comedy in Renaissance France (1561–1580)

CHAPTER 5

Resistance and Rivalry:
Anti-Italianism in the
Comedy of Jacques Grévin

'Nostre France est trop abbreuvee
De vostre feinte controuvee
Et deceptive intention.'

[Our France is thoroughly sick
Of your crafty lies
And deceptive intents.]
(Jacques Grévin, *Les Esbahis*, 1561)

Efforts by playwrights to undermine the Italian presence in France swiftly intensified in the 1560s. The relationship between France and Italy was growing increasingly hostile, and as French dramatists grew more seasoned, they began to experiment with new methods of using drama as nationalist propaganda. In the years following Jodelle's understated attempts to overshadow the Italian comic precedent, anti-Italian sentiment began to occupy a central position in both plot and characterisation. Part III of this book shifts the main focus from performance to politics, examining the portrait of Italy painted by French comedy from 1560 to 1580. Using a range of case studies, both chapters ask how originally Italianate comedy was used by French writers as a weapon against the Italians themselves, both to resist the influx into France of Italian literature and language and to rival the perceived cultural dominance of Italy in Europe. Comic theatre has not previously been used as a means of documenting anti-Italian sentiment in France; yet, the various audio and visual devices employed by writers enabled comic drama to function as a very particular kind of propaganda. This analysis will help to provide a fresh perspective on the largely unstable relationship between France and Italy during these decades, as well as an innovative framework for interpreting how this relationship was articulated and navigated. Additionally, these final two chapters break new ground in tracing the emergence of comic theatre in sixteenth-century France, further identifying the complex ways in which comedy was both understood and utilised.

   This chapter focuses on the theatrical work of one writer, Jacques Grévin. An extremely versatile figure, Grévin was on the one hand a celebrated doctor, employed as personal physician to Marguerite de France; on the other, he was a well-known poet and member of the Pléiade, who worked closely with writers such as Pierre de La Ramée (*c.* 1515–72), Ronsard, and Du Bellay. Despite his talent and renown, Grévin's career was far from straightforward: he was a prominent Huguenot, and was exiled to England for a period in the 1560s on account of his beliefs. He was the first writer after Jodelle to compose original humanist drama in French: he wrote three comedies, *La Trésorière* [The Treasurer's Wife] (1558), *Les Esbahis* [Taken by Surprise] (1561), and *La Maubertine* [The Lady from Place Maubert] (1558), the last of which is now lost.[1] *La Maubertine* seems to have been censured on religious grounds: Grévin describes 'la *Maubertine* [...] que j'avoye bien deliberé de donner, si elle ne m'eust este desrobée' [*La Maubertine* [...] which I had strongly considered having performed, had they not taken it from me].[2] Like Jodelle, Grévin also composed tragic theatre, completing his play *César* in 1561.[3] Grévin's curiosity in humanist drama may partly be accounted for by his relationship with Charles Estienne, whom Grévin had desperately wanted to impress. As noted in Chapter 1, Grévin was at one point engaged to Estienne's accomplished daughter Nicole, herself a well-known writer and the object of Grévin's affections for several years.[4] The marriage never took place; in 1561, Nicole married Jean Liebault, a doctor from Dijon.

This chapter begins with a brief examination of anti-Italianism in *La Trésorière*; however, the main subject of discussion will be Grévin's second extant comedy, *Les Esbahis*, in which Grévin realises more fully both his dramatic skills and comedy's potential as propaganda. In *Les Esbahis*, Grévin uses a number of techniques to convince readers and spectators of the ability of French culture both to resist and to rival its Italian counterpart; he also discusses his motives for writing theatre in the 'Brief discours pour l'intelligence de ce theatre' [Brief Discourse for the Comprehension of this Theatre], and the prefatory letter 'Au Lecteur' [To the Reader]. As further evidence of his approach to comedy and to his Italian models, this chapter will examine a unique copy of the first edition of Grévin's *Le theatre*, which belonged to the author himself and which contains annotations and revisions, dating from 1567, in his own hand.[5] It is likely that Grévin started to revise his comedies with a view to producing an updated edition; however, this edition never went to press. Grévin's health had always been fragile, and he died in Turin at the age of thirty-two, midway through his edits.[6] Grévin's revisions to his 'Brief discours pour l'intelligence de ce theatre' are particularly important, and have never before been assessed.

La Trésorière (1558)

Interest in classical and Italian comedy continued to rise throughout the 1550s and 1560s. Although he may not even have been aware of Jodelle's *L'Eugène*, Jacques Peletier commented in his 1555 literary treatise that the comedies of Terence were by then 'antre les meins de chacun' [in everybody's hands];[7] Peletier's treatise also shows that by the mid-1550s, comic theatre was largely accepted in France as a viable mode of humanist production, particularly in comparison with his 1541 translation of Horace's *Ars poetica*, which shows no interest in comic theatre and actively dissuades writers from imitating certain aspects of classical tragedy.[8] As with the 1548 performance of *La Calandra* and the subsequent courtly productions examined in Chapter 4, many comedies continued to be supported by the Italian presence in France. For the 1559 double marriage of the king's daughter Élisabeth to Philip II of Spain and of Marguerite de France to Emmanuel-Philibert, the Duke of Savoy (mentioned in the previous chapter), Marcantonio Sidonio, Ercole II d'Este's favourite *buffone* [fool] was commissioned to stage a comedy, for which he brought Italian actors from Lyons; the performance was scheduled to take place at the Hôtel de Guise, and the stage designer was the Bolognese Primaticcio, who had inspired Jodelle's representation of Janus as part of the failed 1558 masquerades.[9] Although this performance — like Jodelle's opportunity to redeem himself with a comedy for this occasion — would have been prevented by the king's death, Sidonio was in any case murdered by one of the actors during one of the final rehearsals, as a letter from 7 July 1559 shows:

> Questa notte passata è stato amazzato Marc'Antonio [...] ove egli si era rettirato con de suoi recitanti à dare ordine alla comedia che dovea fare recitare alla mason di Guisa, et dicono essere stato amazzato di 38 ferrite da uno de detti recitanti.[10]

> [Last night Marc'Antonio was murdered [...] where he had retired with his actors to give a bit of shape to the comedy which would have been performed at the Hôtel de Guise, and it is said that he was killed with thirty-eight wounds, from one of the actors.]

Hybrid comic threatrical genres, again inspired by the Italian model, were also growing increasingly popular. *La Belle Genièvre*, a dramatisation of the story of Ginevra from Ariosto's *Orlando furioso*, was the first tragi-comedy to be staged in France: this performance was commissioned by Catherine de' Medici and took place at Fontainebleau as part of the 1564 carnival festivities.[11]

Given that the performance of a comedy was becoming an increasingly popular component of celebrations, it is no surprise that the up-and-coming Grévin was commissioned by Henri II to compose a comedy for the wedding of his daughter Claude in January 1559. The performance was in the end cancelled due to 'quelques empeschemens différée' [various obstacles];[12] it may well be that the comedy could not fit into the tight schedule of the wedding celebrations. *La Trésorière* was instead brought to life a month later in a low-key performance at the Collège de Beauvais, the author's alma mater.[13] Prior to studying at Beauvais, Grévin had spent a period at the Collège de Boncourt, where it is possible that — as a thirteen-year-old scholar — he had either seen or played a role in Jodelle's *L'Eugène*.[14] It also seems likely that it was during his time at Boncourt that Grévin developed his interest in humanist tragedy: his tutor Marc Antoine Muret had composed the aforementioned Latin tragedy *Julius Caesar*, and Grévin followed suit in 1561 with a reworking in French of this same story.[15] Grévin's presence at (or participation in) the performance of *L'Eugène* would also account for the many similarities between *L'Eugène* and

La Trésorière in language and plotline, noted by Émile Chasles and Gustave Attinger.[16] Yet, as we will see, there are also parallels between *L'Eugène* and *La Trésorière* in the subtle anti-Italian attitudes demonstrated in the plays, although the techniques used to communicate these attitudes are different.

Firstly, Grévin seeks to conceal various models. Like Jodelle, Grévin denies any influence from medieval French theatre:

> N'attendez donc en ce Théâtre
> Ne farce, ne moralité:
> Mais seulement l'antiquité.[17]

[Don't therefore expect in this play | A farce, or morality; | But only antiquity].

Although *La Trésorière* relies heavily on *L'Eugène* — which was in turn inspired by the farce — it is true that Grévin makes greater efforts to move away from medieval drama. While he does not leave the farce behind completely, his assertions that he has rejected native predecessors have a more solid foundation than Jodelle's similar claims.[18] However, whereas Jodelle also denied using as a foundation classical sources ('L'invention n'est point d'un vieil Menandre', *L'Eugène*, p. 4, 'Prologue', l. 32), Grévin instead advises his reader to anticipate a wholly ancient play, composed in the vernacular. Unlike Jodelle, Grévin is proud to voice his use of the classical models, and he alerts the readers and spectators to his aim to reinvent ancient drama with *La Trésorière*. We may, then, expect for Grévin also to identify his Italian sources. As well as being based on classical comedy, *La Trésorière* takes inspiration from a number of Italian paradigms, which have been explored in detail by Barbara Bowen; yet, Grévin makes no mention of Italian models in his prefatory materials.[19] Again, this contrasts sharply with Jodelle's prologue, which had openly denied any reliance on foreign sources ('Rien d'estranger on ne vous fait entendre', *L'Eugène*, p. 4, 'Prologue', l. 33). Although both playwrights use different techniques, Grévin's aim may also have been to conceal his Italian sources, giving the impression that he himself had reinvented classical comedy, without having recourse to any other mediators. As we saw in Chapter 4, Jodelle's denial of his classical and Italian sources actually draws more attention to them; perhaps Grévin decided to dispense altogether with references to Italian models in order to avoid this very risk.

Grévin's other demonstration of anti-Italianism in *La Trésorière* also differs from the strategy used by Jodelle, though, again, their aims may have been similar. While Jodelle's choice of linguistic borrowings from the Italians — always of negative or derogatory terms, such as *Messer* and *coyon* — is clearly intended to communicate some element of superiority over the Italian culture, Grévin's omission of Italian lexis from *La Trésorière* has a similar effect. As we have seen, Italian was extremely popular at the French court during these years, and the employment of Italian lexis in humanist French writings was becoming almost customary. It may be, then, that Grévin deliberately avoided using Italian terminology in a bid to break away from Italian culture; Lapeyre, too, has observed 'la réticence de Grévin [à la langue italienne] et son propos délibéré de céder le moins possible à cette invasion' [the unwillingness of Grévin [to use the Italian language] and his deliberate attempt to yield as little as possible to this invasion].[20] While Jodelle employed a range of terms intended to make the Italian language appear foolish, Grévin draws attention away from Italian altogether. By promoting the use of French above all foreign influences, Grévin makes a nationalist statement, showing the current reliance on Italian in France to be nothing more than a trend. It is also possible that he again aimed to minimise the appearance of his dependence on Italian language or literature, thereby helping to establish France — and not Italy — as a forerunner of comic theatre. In the same way, the comedy is set 'non loing de la place Maubert' [not far from the Place Maubert];[21] Grévin also reveals that the character of the Protenotaire is a member of the Collège de Beauvais:

> Vray est que le Protenotaire
> Principal de tout' ceste affaire
> Est de nostre université.[22]

[It is true that the Protenotaire | The leader of this whole affair | Is of our university.]

By situating *La Trésorière* unmistakeably in Paris, also indicating that some characters will be identifiable to spectators, Grévin emphasises the play's French nature, as well as its creation by a French writer.

While Grévin does not use *La Trésorière* directly to criticise Italian culture, his omission of references to Italian models, avoidance of Italian terms, and efforts to accentuate the French aspects of his play are all subtle indications of anti-Italian sentiment. Although Grévin does not employ the same techniques as Jodelle to denigrate the Italians, the aims of both playwrights — to present comic theatre as a French genre, and to minimise the appearance of the presence of Italian culture in France — seem to have been the same. *La Trésorière*, then, can be said to mark the start of Grévin's venture to use theatre as a polemical weapon, testing the waters for the far more overt attack on Italian culture that he was to craft two years later with *Les Esbahis*.

Les Esbahis (1561)

By 1561, the tension between Catholics and Protestants in France was swiftly escalating. Religious and political hostilities were intensified by the rise of iconoclasm, and were again aggravated by the accidental death in 1559 of Henri II, followed by the sudden demise eighteen months later of the sixteen-year-old François II. The 1561 Colloquy of Poissy did little to alleviate tensions, which peaked with the massacre of Vassy on 1 March 1562. As Bruce Hayes has shown, it is perhaps unsurprising that theatre at this time started to be employed with persuasive or polemical ends in mind.[23] Many of these plays are hybrid, fusing classically-inspired comedy with medieval forms such as the *sermon joyeux* and the farce: examples include Conrad Badius's *Comedie du pape malade* [Comedy of the Mad Pope] (1561) and Jacques Bienvenu's *Comédie du monde malade et mal pensé* [Comedy of the Mad and Ill-conceived World] (1568);[24] Rémy Belleau's attempt at recreating a comedy in the Terentian style, *La Reconnue* [The Recognised Lady] (1562), also seeks to show the virtue of the Protestant faith through the figure of its wholesome heroine.[25] At the court, too, theatre was judged to be a useful distraction from chaos and unrest, as well as a means of encouraging the pacification of rival factions.[26] The aforementioned *La Belle Genièvre*, for instance, depicts the happiness of two parties allied after a series of obstacles; Ronsard's pastoral dialogues acted at the same carnival (entitled simply *Bergeries*) were also intended to narrow the Catholic-Protestant divide, portraying the peaceful lives of shepherds called 'Navarin' and 'Guisin', clearly reflecting the names of the major opposing factions.[27]

Following the deaths of her husband and son, Catherine de' Medici became Regent Queen-Mother, overseeing the reign of her ten-year-old son, Charles IX; Catherine's new authority brought with it a further increased presence of Italian culture at the French court. As well as holding substantial political sway, Catherine patronised Italian artists, writers, and performers; scholars such as Balsamo and Thomas Hope have shown that during these years, Italian became the fashionable language with which to communicate with other courtiers at Fontainebleau, and lexical borrowings from Italian in French also became increasingly prevalent.[28] While comedy started to be used as propaganda in the Wars of Religion, playwrights also began to exploit the genre's potential to make a nationalist statement. As we have seen, this is the case in Jodelle's *L'Eugène* and Grévin's *La Trésorière*; however, by the time that Grévin came to write his *Les Esbahis* in 1561, he was both skilled at composing Italianate comedy and convinced of the need for a bolder intervention in the influx of Italian culture into France.

Les Esbahis was performed in February 1561, again at the Collège de Beauvais, and almost a year later broke new ground with its circulation among the wider public in the first ever printed edition of an original French comedy.[29] Grévin was by this stage a well-known writer: Ronsard claimed in a prefatory poem to this first edition that Grévin's work outshone that of the other, ageing members of the Pléiade: 'Tu nous as surmontez, qui sommes jà grisons' [You have surpassed us, we who are already going grey].[30] Very little, however, is known about the 1561 performance: it is possible that Grévin's controversial behaviour and position during the Wars of Religion affected his popularity. Around a year earlier, his comedy *La Maubertine* was most likely censured; at the same time, Grévin's printer Martin L'Homme was hanged as a heretic and Grévin himself was exiled to England on account of his Protestantism.[31] Although it is probable that Grévin was present when *Les Esbahis* was staged (he was certainly back in France by June 1561, when he defended his PhD thesis in medicine), Grévin was still in England just a month prior to this performance, which is when he dedicated to Elizabeth I his poem 'Le Chant du cygne', which discusses the dangers presented by the inevitable civil wars in France.[32]

Resistance to the Catholics in *Les Esbahis*

Many Protestants were instinctively opposed to the Italians, and some of the most famous anti-Italian propagandists in sixteenth-century France — for example, Innocent Gentillet and Henri Estienne — were also prominent Huguenots. One anonymous Protestant pamphlet urged the king to ban the Italians from France altogether; others openly blamed Catherine de' Medici and her Italian supporters for the continuing violence of the wars.[33] Gentillet, for instance, was one of many to point out the manipulative and deceitful tactics used by the Italians — or else by French citizens who try to imitate the Italians — to control French politics: 'Depuis on s'est gouverné a l'Italienne ou à la Florentine, c'est à dire en suyvant les enseignemens de Machiavel florentin [...] ne sont-ce pas Machiavelistes, Italiens ou Italianisez, qui manient les seaux de la France?' [Since we have been ruled in the Italian or Florentine style, that is to say, by following the teachings of the Florentine Machiavelli [...] is it not the Machiavellians, Italians or Italianised, who govern the seals in France?].[34] Grévin, too, was hostile towards the Italians. Catherine Douël Dell'Agnola has pointed out Grévin's particular contempt for Catherine de' Medici: he scorned as cowardly her various endeavours to avoid civil war and to safeguard the throne for her sons, such as making sporadic Protestant alliances and appointing as Chancellor Michel de l'Hôpital, who straddled both Catholicism and Protestantism.[35] Grévin also condemned in his 1561 poetry collection *La Gélodacrye* the artificial and untrustworthy display of Catholicism by the Italians at the French court. He claimed, for instance, that the Italians — and particularly the Italian clergy — sought to hide their vice under a veil of feigned piety: they apparently made it their mission to 'faire tousjours grand'chere et s'addonner aux vices' [make merry always and give themselves over to vice].[36] Linked to this mistrust was Grévin's resentment that many French bishoprics were being handed over to the Italian clergy, who had arrived at the court in far greater numbers since Catherine became regent.

Grévin claimed in the 'Avant-Jeu' to *La Trésorière* that his comic theatrical writings would not 'mesler la religion | Dans le subject des choses feinctes' [mix religion | In with themes of craftiness];[37] the Parlement had also passed decrees in 1541 and 1548 setting limits on Christian mystery play performances and banning altogether the *mystères de la passion*. Noirot has claimed that *Les Esbahis* 'deliberately eschewed religious topics', possibly as a result of these decrees; yet, this play does have a distinct anti-Catholic slant.[38] The majority of its characters comment on the Catholics' indecent behaviour: even the Gentilhomme, one of the most minor characters, remarks that Agnès must be 'quelque demourant de chanoine' [the leftovers of some canon] (*Les Esbahis*, III.2.1231); he also uses monasticism as an analogy to explain that prostitution could no longer be secret, since so many people were involved in the process:

> Mais qui desormais vouldra rire
> Et demener vie joyeuse
> Avecq une religieuse
> Du bas mestier, il fault devant

> En advertir tout le couvant
> Qui ne les vault prendre à la chaude. (III.2.1136–41)

[But who these days would want to laugh | And to fool around | With Sister Smut, | When first you must | Inform the whole convent | If you don't want to find them all against you?]

Many other slurs in the play centre on the supposed duplicitousness of Catholics. The Advocat, for instance, tells of his experience with women who have dressed up as monks in order to be smuggled into a monastery for the monks' sexual pleasure:

> L'habit d'un moine
> Ya aussi grande efficace:
> Soit en habillant une grace
> Pour ainsi plus secretement
> La faire entrer dans le couvant. (III.4.1390–94)

[A monk's habit | Is also extremely useful | For dressing up a young woman | To help her enter more secretly | Into a monastery.]

Although Grévin has pledged to keep religion separate from his comedy, he does use *Les Esbahis* to underscore the perceived deceitful and lewd behaviour of the Catholics, thereby pushing his own Protestant agenda.

It is likely that in criticising the Catholics, Grévin is also vicariously mocking the Italians. The Italian Pantaleoné — discussed in detail in the next section — is the most corrupt of all the characters. While the Italians in France were identified increasingly with the Catholics, Grévin takes every opportunity to emphasise Pantaleoné's immorality. He is always inebriated and extremely lascivious in his interactions with women; the native French characters repeatedly accuse him of a range of vices, including sodomy. Even the servant Julien, infuriated at Pantaleoné's poor French, refers to him as such: 'Je vous feray parler François | Encor' que soyez bougrino' [I'll make you speak French | Even if you are a bugger] (V.1.2123–24). This was a stereotypical insult directed at the Italians at this time, and sodomy was even dubbed 'le vice italien' [the Italian vice]. The French were no doubt aware that prominent artists such as Leonardo da Vinci, Michaelangelo, and of course Giovanni Antonio Bazzi (better known as 'Il Sodoma') had been accused of sodomy — they may also have been aware of the high number of arrests for sodomy in Italy[39] — and these allegations were often used as a means of communicating scorn for Italian Catholicism.[40] Pantaleoné is accused of a number of other vices which are then extended to the Italians as a whole. For instance, after Agnès is abandoned by Pantaleoné, the bawd Claude expresses relief that Agnès is finally safe from the clutches of the 'jalous Italiens' [jealous Italians] (III.2.1286). With the character of Pantaleoné, Grévin draws further attention to the Italians' hypocrisy and insincerity, alerting spectators to their use of Catholicism as a mask for immorality.

Italian Cultural Resistance in *Les Esbahis*: Artifice

Some of these elements of anti-Italianism in *Les Esbahis* are clearly imitated from Italian literature. The allusion to women dressing in habits in order to enter monasteries illicitly, for instance, is taken from Boccaccio's *Decameron*, which recounts several similar stories.[41] As in *La Trésorière*, numerous features of *Les Esbahis* are also imitated from the Italian comic model: Attinger and Enzo Bottasso have pointed out Grévin's close reliance on the themes typical of Italian comedy;[42] others have drawn more specific parallels between *Les Esbahis* and Estienne's translation of *Gl'ingannati* which, given Grévin's attachment to Nicole Estienne, is hardly surprising.[43] Yet the most recognisable feature of Italian comedy imitated by Grévin is again one which he transforms into an anti-Italian statement. The braggart soldier was a well-known device used by Italian dramatists to mock the Spaniards, particularly following the sackings of Prato in 1512 and Rome in 1527.[44] As we saw in Chapter 1, Estienne omitted altogether from his translation of *Gl'ingannati* the character of the Spanish braggart Giglio, averting the problems of presenting in his play an offensive and xenophobic caricature. By contrast, Grévin takes the Spanish soldier of Italian comedy and transforms him into an Italian one, whom he places at the very centre of the comedy's action. Grévin's Pantaleoné — a failed soldier and expatriate Italian in France — is a vehicle for exploring two of Grévin's specific prejudices against Italian culture, and as such is a targeted attack against the presence of the Italians at the French court.

The first prejudice embodied by the character of Pantaleoné is the perceived artificial and hypocritical behaviour of Italians at the courts in France. In a way that builds on Grévin's depiction of the Catholics as untrustworthy, Pantaleoné serves both to show Italian courtiers to be insincere and duplicitous and to mock French courtiers who imitate Italian mannerisms. Grévin was well known for such criticisms in his poetry, which also used humour to express animosity towards the Italians:[45] many poems in the aforementioned *La Gélodacrye* (literally 'laughter and tears') parody the affected and dishonest attitudes shown by the Italians in France and encouraged by writers such as Machiavelli and Castiglione.[46] As Gentillet tells us in his *Anti-Machiavel*, Machiavelli's principles reached the height of their popularity in France at the same time as *Les Esbahis* was written; the artful and ornate Italian style of speaking, promoted by Castiglione, was also highly fashionable at the French courts.[47] This mode of speech, dubbed the *messeresque* due to the vogue of referring to other courtiers as *Messer*, was so popular — and indeed, so widely thought to be an excellent means of disguising one's true thoughts or feelings — that the phrase *dissimuler comme un Italien* [dissimulate like an Italian] become almost proverbial at this time.[48] This heightened appreciation in France for the *messeresque* no doubt accounts for Grévin's exaggerated and unforgiving depiction of Pantaleoné.

In the Italian representation of the Spanish braggart, the Spanish techniques of pursuing women are frequent sources for parody. In Piccolomini's *L'amor costante* (1536), for instance, Capitan Francisco Marrada repeatedly kisses the servant Agnoletta's hand in the Spanish fashion: this gesture, no doubt, would have been performed by the Italian actor in an overly stylized and affected manner, showing

Spanish cajolery to be foolish and absurd.[49] In the same way, Grévin holds up to ridicule Italian modes of seduction — especially those which predominated at the courts — which involved, primarily, a reliance on poetry and music. Although the Provençal troubadour tradition had originated in France, where noble women such as Eleanor of Aquitaine had supported practices such as singing and poetry recitation to catch the attention of one's beloved at the court, by the 1500s these conventions had long died out.[50] Yet in Italy a reliance on such practices still prospered: Castiglione, for example, advises the courtier that music and poetry can be a highly fulfilling means of attracting one's beloved: 'Chi intende nella dolcezza della musica per altra causa, che per questa? Chi a compor versi, almen nella lingua vulgare, se non per esprimere quegli affetti che dalle donne sono causati?' [Who employs the sweetness of music for another cause than this? Who composes poetry, at least in their own language, if not to express the fondnesses caused by women?].[51] Pantaleoné is the embodiment of the gallant Italian courtier, using music and poetry throughout the comedy to pursue the naive protagonist Magdalêne. For instance, Pantaleoné makes his grand entrance in the play by placing himself underneath Magdalêne's window in the style of the Italian courtly serenade;[52] there he plays the lute, while singing some of Ariosto's best-known and most passionate verses:

> Per rihaver l'ingegno mio m'è aviso
> Che non bisogna che per l'aria io poggi
> Nel cerchio de la Luna, o in Paradiso;
> Che 'l mio non credo che tanto alto alloggi.
> Ne' bei vostri occhi e nel sereno viso,
> Nel sen d'avorio e alabastrini poggi
> Se na va errando; et io con questo labbia
> Lo corrò, se vi par ch'io la rihabbia.   (II.3.831–58)

[To regain my wits I believe | That I need not rise through the air | To the circle of the moon, nor to heaven; | For I do not believe that my own wits reside so high. | In your beautiful eyes and serene face, | In your bosom of ivory and breasts of alabaster | They wander; and myself with these lips | Will reclaim them, if you believe that I deserve them.]

These lines from canto XXXV of the *Orlando furioso* describe Ariosto's own lack of sanity in love; the poet compares himself with the main protagonist Orlando, already in the grips of his terrifying *furia*. In much the same way as the Italian playing the Spanish soldier could take advantage of a kissing gesture to mock the Spanish culture, a French actor playing Pantaleoné would be able to deliver these lines in an exaggerated manner, showing the Italian modes of seduction to be overblown and contrived. Clearly, Grévin has chosen this extract from Ariosto as one which he already considers to be excessively performative and affected. As well as using gestures and vocal effects to parody the delivery of Italian courtly love poetry, the actor would also be able to take advantage of the music's comic potential, again holding up to ridicule the artificiality of the Italian pursuit of women. The ability to sing while at the same time playing the lute was so commended by Castiglione as a virtue of the courtier that Thomas Hoby included it as part of the summarising rules of his English translation of the *Cortegiano* (Rule 43: 'to play upon the Lute, and singe to it with the ditty'), printed the same year in which *Les Esbahis* was written.[53] Yet, as indicated by a disparaging comment from Antoine earlier in the comedy that Pantaleoné's lute is 'mal acordé' [poorly tuned] (1.3.402), we can imagine that the instrument is broken down and unpleasant to hear; no doubt the actor playing Pantaleoné would also sing as tunelessly as possible, adding to the offensiveness of his song and showing the audience how aggravating it would be to be on the receiving end of such a serenade. Again, Grévin is mocking the Castiglionian convention of trying to seduce one's beloved with music and poetry; not only is it excessive and artificial, but often the delivery is crude and flawed.

Grévin's parodying of the affectedness of these Italian conventions is linked to his criticism of another mode of behaviour he has witnessed at the French court: *sprezzatura*. Although a notoriously difficult word to translate, *sprezzatura* can be understood as a kind of 'studied carelessness' or 'nonchalance'; the term was given a new meaning by Castiglione, who described a concealment of effort when seeking to impress one's superiors and to obtain support at the court.[54] The practice of *sprezzatura*, which allows the courtier to appear naturally poised and accomplished, was exploited by ambitious courtiers in Italy and also in France. Grévin was not the only writer to object to the practice of *sprezzatura* at the French court: Du Bellay, for instance, in his poem 'Contre les Pétrarquistes' [Against the Petrarchists], uses the example of Petrarch's poetry to criticise the language used by the Italians in pursuit of their beloved, which is presented as forthright and sincere but which is actually adulatory and duplicitous, concealing the speaker's true nature:

> J'ay oublié l'art de petrarquizer,
> Je veulx d'Amour franchement deviser,
> Sans vous flater, et sans me déguiser.[55]

[I have forgotten the art of Petrarchising, | I want to approach love frankly, | Without flattering you, and without disguising myself.]

In *Les Esbahis*, Pantaleoné is inept at the practice of *sprezzatura*: although his efforts to seduce Magdalêne are clearly intended to appear uncontrived, his out-of-tune lute and (no doubt) poor singing voice, paired with his choice of overly effusive verses, instead show the performativity of his actions. Throughout the play Pantaleoné employs different techniques to make his love appear natural and unaffected: for instance, when Magdalêne ignores his serenades towards the end of the comedy, Pantaleoné instead addresses his lute:

> Sus mon mignon, qu'on amolisse,
> Avec ton honeste service,
> Et une plus qu'humble priere,
> La cruauté de ceste fiere. (v.1.2069–72)

[Come on, my treasure, | With your honest service | And more than humble imploration, | Soften the cruelty of this honoured lady.]

Although feigning a mournful order to his lute, Pantaleoné's intention is clearly to attract Magdalêne's attention and to arouse admiration for him. Of course, she never expresses an interest in Pantaleoné, who meets only with scornful remarks from the servant Julien. Pantaleoné's attempt at combining music and poetry with the artful *sprezzatura* is worse than futile: it shows him to be calculating and makes him a subject of ridicule to the other characters and, in turn, to the spectators and readers.

Despite Pantaleoné's efforts to seduce Magdalêne — which are in themselves presented as deceitful and artificial — he cannot and should not be trusted. In the same way as Piccolomini had very carefully depicted his Spanish soldier as a womanizer, Pantaleoné tries his luck with women throughout the play, though at the same time declares his love for Magdalêne.[56] It also transpires that prior to the comedy's action, Pantaleoné had taken the married Agnès to Italy to be his lover, possibly against her will.[57] The native French characters often take the opportunity not only to mock Pantaleoné's artifice, but also to emphasise that they will not be deceived by it. Julien claims that he does not even have to speak to an Italian to know that they are untrustworthy:

> Vous n'avez gueres que la bave,
> Je le scay bien, je vous cognoy,
> Vous regardant quand je vous voy. (v.1.2097–99)

[You're just a windbag, | I know it well, I know your sort, | I know it just to look at you.]

As well as boasting that he can recognise Italian deceit as soon as he sees it, Julien also asserts that a Frenchman would never be misled by Italian flattery:

> Jamais, jamais la faincte voix
> N'eust pouvoir envers un François.
> Il ne vault point tant de gambades,
> Tant de chansons, ny tant d'aubades. (v.1.2095–98)

[Never, never could your deceitful talk | Have power over a Frenchman. | He will have none of your frolicking, | Your songs, nor your serenades.]

The reader or spectator is in turn reminded that they, too, should be wary of Italian artifice.[58] Additionally, while Grévin is using Pantaleoné to parody Italian rhetoric and to warn the spectator or reader against being duped by it, this scene is also a comment on the clarity of the French literary style in comparison with its ornate Italian counterpart. Many French humanists were proud of their frank and direct style, which they often promoted using wordplay: the term *franchement* [frankly] in Du Bellay's aforementioned poem, for instance, draws parallels with the word *France*, showing this style to be part of their national culture.[59] By contrast, Grévin judged the Italian style to prioritise aesthetics while concealing meaning. As well as using Pantaleoné to mock this style, Grévin outlines in his 'Brief discours' that in his own theatre he has tried to '[ensuyre] la nayveté de nostre vulgaire et les communes manieres de parler' [follow the naturalness of our native language and the common ways of speaking], and has avoided a verbose and ornate rhetoric which he considered only able to 'espouvanter les petits enfans' [scare small children].[60] French writings are shown not only to be more trustworthy, but also to be superior to those of Italian poets.

Italian Cultural Resistance in *Les Esbahis*: Cowardice

A second prejudice against the Italians, which is again explored through the character of Pantaleoné, is that of cowardice. It was around this time, when the Wars of Religion were becoming increasingly violent, that the reputation in France of the Italians as incompetent and cowardly soldiers began to intensify. Gentillet claimed that Italian captains were 'couards, lasches et pusillanimes, qui descouragent plustost leurs soldats qu'ils ne leur donnent à combattre' [lazy and spineless cowards, who discourage their soldiers more than they spur them on to fight];[61] In 1565 Henri Estienne (the nephew of Charles Estienne) warned French writers against using Italian militaristic terms, in case future readers were mistakenly to think that the Italians were superior in battle: 'Car d'ici peu d'ans, qui sera celuy qui ne pensera que la France ait appris l'art de la guerre en l'eschole de l'Italie quand il verra qu'elle usera des termes Italiens?' [For not long from now, who will think that France learned the art of war from the Italians, when they see that we make use of Italian terms?].[62] Grévin, too, poured scorn on the Italians in France too busy with courtly society to focus on military endeavours: in *La Gélodacrye* he refuses to call the Italians 'Romains', with the historical connotations of this term of great warriorship, instead referring to them ironically as 'leurs bons successeurs, les braves Courtisans' [their good successors, the brave courtiers].[63] He also persuades (the as yet unidentifiable) Beaumais against a trip to Italy, where one learns not only how to deceive but also how to be a coward:

> On dit qu'en Itale un François se desguise:
> Aussi tu pourros bien en feignant deviser,
> Ainsi comme un Prothé me faire desguiser,
> Tant un Italien finement poltronisé.[64]

[It is said that in Italy a Frenchman disguises himself: | In the same way you would learn to sweet talk, | Changing at will like some sort of Proteus, | Like one of those fine Italian cowards.]

It has gone unnoticed by scholars that Pantaleoné, too, is used by Grévin to deride the Italians' perceived cowardice, and many do not even point out that Pantaleoné is a failed soldier.[65] Yet in almost every scene in which he appears, Pantaleoné boasts of his military prowess: 'Moy qui pour une cannonade | Jamais ne me suis estonné' [Not even cannonfire | Can take me by surprise'] (v.1.2107–08); despite being dismissed from the military, he is also dressed in full soldier's gear, and proudly sports 'sa cappe et sa tocque' [his cape and his hat] (III.3.356–57). Although Pantaleoné's name has sometimes been singled out as insignificant,[66] it is possible that he is named after Captain Pantaléon, a figure well known to certain early modern readers: in the year before *Les Esbahis* was written, he escaped from a shipwreck when travelling from the Indies to Portugal.[67]

As with Pantaleoné's serenades, this overblown caricature of a cowardly soldier would no doubt be emphasised by the actor. We can imagine that the performer, dressed in an extravagant costume (though one which, like his lute, might be past its best), could swagger, use a booming voice, or employ arrogant facial expressions.

This behaviour in itself would evoke laughter in the audience, holding Pantaleoné up as a subject of ridicule; yet, his bragging and hyperbolic actions are made even more comical by their juxtaposition with his responses to events. Clearly, Grévin has been influenced by figures such as the eponymous protagonist in the fifteenth-century monologue *Le Franc-archer de Bagnolet*, who boasts of his countless military successes and then collapses in terror, having mistaken trees for cavalrymen,[68] and also Piccolomini's Capitan Francisco, who brags that his victories have gained him fame in Africa and Italy, but who subsequently flees from a street brawl.[69] For instance, when Pantaleoné describes at length his own military triumphs and threatens the servant Julien, then Julien challenges Pantaleoné in return, Pantaleoné apologises and pretends that he mistook Julien for someone else:

JULIEN	Sçavez vous bien que cest mastin,
	Fantosme du mont Aventin,[70]
	Sepulchre à punaise, pendart,
	Demourant de tout le cagnart,
	Si vous ne me parlez plus doux
	Je vous assommeray de coups.
	[...]
PANTALEONÉ	Non non, messer Juliano,
	Je pensoy que ce fust un autre,
	Car quant à moy je suis tout vostre,
	Et ne voudroy rien attenter
	Qui fust pour vous mescontenter. (v.1.2114–28)

[JULIEN   Do you even know what you're all about, | Ghost of the Aventine Hill, | You horrible fleabag, you good-for-nothing, | No better than a beggar's leftovers. | If you don't speak to me more nicely | I'll knock your block off.
PANTALEONÉ   No, no, messer Juliano, | I thought you were someone else, | I for one am your faithful servant, | I would never try anything | Which might displease you.]

Despite Pantaleoné's many tales of fearlessness and victory, he does not dare to confront even the family servant, who speaks to him with scorn and disregard; instead, Pantaleoné again uses artifice to evade a difficult situation.

Certainly, as well as caricaturing the Italians as cowardly, Grévin is warning the French against being deceived by the appearance that the Italians falsely present: although their dress and actions may be ostentatious, they are in reality no match for their French counterparts in courage and heroism. In the same way as Julien emphasises that a Frenchman would never be duped by Italian flattery, there are reminders throughout the comedy that none of the characters is taken in by Pantaleoné's bravado; in turn, the reader or spectator recalls that they too should be cautious when admiring Italian military accomplishments. In our very first meeting in the play with Pantaleoné, for instance, we are told by Julien as an aside to expect empty bragging and boasting:

Vous le verrez tantost vanter,
Tantost elever ses beaux faicts,

> Et conter ceux qu'il a deffaicts
> A la prise d'un poulaillier,
> Et comme il sçait bien batailler
> Quand il fault romper un huys ouvert
> Ou bien un paste descouvert
> Pour y plonger ses mains dedans. (II.3.806–13)

[You'll see him bragging everywhere, | Boasting of his fantastic feats, | Counting those he vanquished | When he conquered a chicken coop, | And how he bravely battles | When he has to break down an open door | Or into a meat pie | To plunge his hands in it.]

A number of characters also employ Italianised language to further mock Pantaleoné's bragging. When the Advocat asks whether or not Julien has seen Pantaleoné, he is met with the scornful reply: 'Qui, ce forfante? [...] Je l'en incaque, ce coion' [Who, that braggart? I don't give a stuff about that show-off] (III.3.1350–52); Pantaleoné is also referred to on several occasions as 'Messer Coioni' [Mr Big-Balls] (II.3.785). Julien employs the technique of macaronic Italian to claim that Pantaleoné impresses only himself:

> Prime de la caze Frenese,
> Grand escuyer de sa maison
> Quand il est seul. (V.1.2102–04)

[The best of the Frenzy casa, | Foremost swordsman of his house | When he is alone.]

This Italianised language reinforces the idea of cowardice as an Italian trait: this is an idea to which we shall return in the next section. Yet it also allows Grévin to mock the distinguished Farnese family, who were celebrated in Italy for their military careers. By Gallicising their name to 'Frenese', meaning 'frantic' or 'frenzied', Grévin shows that it is not just Pantaleoné who is worthy of ridicule by the French: even the most prominent Italian soldiers should be shown contempt.[71] Additionally, by giving many of these insults to Julien, Grévin indicates that French citizens of all social classes should feel welcome to mock and to deride Italian culture. While Pantaleoné is used as a means of caricaturing Italian artifice and cowardice, the reactions to him of the native characters help to show that Italians are far from welcome in France, as well as to alert readers and spectators to the dangers of trusting the Italians or taking at face value their accomplishments.

Italian Cultural Rivalry in *Les Esbahis*

As Eric MacPhail has noted, French writers considered Italian literature to be dually 'an inspiring model and a dangerous rival'.[72] We have seen, however, that French writers at this time were eager not just to imitate the works of their Italian counterparts, but to surpass them: Jodelle's attempts in the early and mid-1550s to eclipse the theatre of Italian playwrights are examples of this. Italy's status as more of a literary and linguistic rival than a model comes into sharper focus in the 1560s and 1570s, with the publication of works such as Ronsard's epic poem *La Franciade*, which intended to show that France could excel in any literary genre;[73] other works, such as Henri Estienne's manifesto *De la precellence du langage françois* [On the eminence of the French language] (1579),[74] set out to prove that French was the best language in Europe, and that while Italian was the inheritor of Latin, France had more in common with the allegedly superior Greek.[75] The increasingly explicit aim of many French humanists was to demonstrate that their language and writings surpassed those of other European cultures, with the greatest rival being Italy.[76]

While Grévin's *Les Esbahis* attempts to resist the influx into France of Italian culture, singling out for particular criticism Italian artifice and cowardice, this comedy also seeks to rival Italian culture, thereby showing France to be a forerunner of European literature and language. We have already witnessed comic theatre as a means of subtly rivalling Italian culture: Jodelle, for instance, masked his Italian models with the possible intention of competing with them; he also employed Italian lexis in order to hold the Italians themselves up to ridicule. While Grévin also concealed his Italian influences in *La Trésorière*, he took a different approach to Jodelle by avoiding Italian lexis altogether, in what may have been a bid to further draw attention away from Italian sources. Although some of these techniques have been employed in previous comedies, others are unprecedented, and even pave the way for advice provided by later French humanists on the possibility of overshadowing Italian culture. A close look in this section at Grévin's own, previously unseen annotations to his 'Brief discours pour l'intelligence de ce theatre' will also allow us a fresh perspective on the methods employed to attempt to rival earlier models.

Italian Cultural Rivalry in *Les Esbahis*: Literature

Following the precedents of Jodelle's *L'Eugène* and his own *La Trésorière*, in *Les Esbahis* Grévin also seeks to draw attention away from Italian literature. No doubt with the intention of again masking his reliance on Italian models, Grévin's attempt to shift the focus from Italian literature is more rigorous than that which we have witnessed in previous comedies. His methods for shifting the focus are threefold: firstly, he makes no mention of Italian sources in his prefatory material. Despite Pinvert's assertion that since Grévin so clearly despised the Italians, he would not have imitated any Italian sources, we have seen that Grévin relies heavily on writers such as Piccolomini, as well as on Estienne's translation of *Gl'ingannati*.[77] Clearly, Grévin is proud of both classical and contemporary French models, and he praises Jodelle's first attempt at writing comedy, while acknowledging that Jodelle took inspiration from the ancients: 'Je sçay bien qu'Estienne Jodelle [...] les a tirées des Grecs et Latins pour les remplanter en France' [I know very well that Estienne Jodelle [...] took them from the Greek and Latin writers, to transplant them into France].[78] Yet Grévin acknowledges no Italian influence, either in his own work or in Jodelle's comedy. Secondly, Grévin gives *Les Esbahis* a very specific location. In the same way as he set *La Trésorière* near the precise 'place Maubert', the action of *Les Esbahis* takes place only a few feet away, still in the university quarter, at the Carrefour Saint-Séverin (figure 5.1):

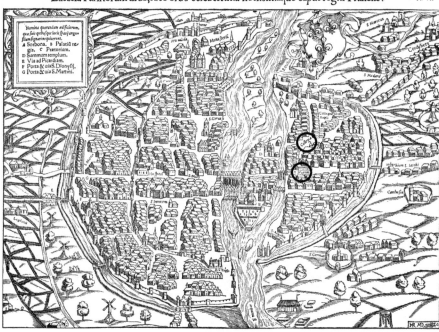

PARIS EN 1530

Fac-similé du Plan de Sébastien Munster

FIG. 5.1. Sebastian Münster's map of Paris. I have circled the Place Maubert of *La Trésorière* ('Collegia') and the Carrefour Saint-Séverin of *Les Esbahis*. Sebastian Münster, *Cosmographia* (Basle: Heinrich Petti, 1550), pp. 88–89. Reproduced with the permission of the David Rumsey Map Collection, David Rumsey Map Center, Stanford Libraries.

By again setting his comedy in a highly recognisable location, Grévin draws attention away from the play's Italian influences; additionally, the proximity of the Carrefour Saint-Séverin to the setting of *La Trésorière* helps to interconnect the two plays, encouraging the reader or spectator to recall Grévin's own corpus of work, rather than a comedy which is set elsewhere. Finally, Grévin shifts the focus from the Italian comic model by deliberately confusing the reader or spectator. As well as being the name of a famous captain, 'Pantaleoné' is clearly a reference to 'Pantalone', a stock character in the *commedia dell'arte*, a genre which was admired throughout the French courts during these years, as we saw in Chapter 4. As Douël Dell'Agnola has observed, Grévin's choice of name for Pantaleoné is an attempt to 'affaiblir les types comiques' [weaken stock types]: since Pantalone of the *commedia dell'arte* is the figure of the parsimonious merchant, and not of the braggart soldier, Grévin's Pantaleoné recalls nothing of this stock type.[79] While Grévin's other techniques draw attention away from his Italian models, this method helps to undermine Italian comedy by putting it into disarray, overwriting well-known characters and disrupting what they had come to represent.

As well as shifting attention from his Italian models, Grévin is keen to emphasise his own innovation. Although he does acknowledge his debt to Jodelle in his prefatory material, he also claims that true humanist theatre is non-existent in France: 'Je diray ceci sans arrogance, que je suis encores à voir Tragedies et Comedies Françoises' [I say this without arrogance: I am yet to see tragedies and comedies in French].[80] While he recognises that Jodelle did imitate ancient playwrights ('Je sçay bien qu'Estienne Jodelle […] les a tirées des Grecs et Latins pour les remplanter en France'), Grévin is clearly aware that Jodelle's comedy was also based on the farce model.[81] Although Grévin himself did not fully move away from the farce with *Les Esbahis* — most notably, he still uses the octosyllabic form typical of medieval drama — his comment indicates that he considers his own play the first to be worthy of the title of *comédie*. Grévin aims to set the standard for drama in France, proving to his audience and readership that *Les Esbahis* is a prototype for comedy.

Grévin's 1567 annotations to his 'Brief discours pour l'intelligence de ce theatre' provide further evidence that he intends for his own plays to become models for imitation. Although the edits he makes are not numerous, they all suggest that he believes his own play to have surpassed native French work, as well as foreign and ancient drama. His first edit to the 'Brief discours' completely removes all references to Muret, who had, as we saw, taught him at Boncourt and largely inspired Grévin's tragedy *César*. In the printed edition, Grévin denies basing *César* on Muret's Latin tragedy, although he does acknowledge that Muret was his mentor, and is thereby responsible for the most impressive parts of his theatre:

> Mais revenons à nostre Tragedie de Jules Cesar, laquelle nous avons mise en avant en nostre langue, non que je l'aye empruntee, estimants que je l'eusse prise du Latin de Marc Anthoine de Muret: car là ou elles seront confrontées, on trouvera la verité. Je ne veux pourtant nier que s'il se trouve quelque traict digne d'estre loué, qu'il ne soit de Muret, lequel a esté mon precepteur quelque temps es lettres humaines, et auquel je donne le meilleur, comme l'ayant appris de luy.[82]

> [But let us return to our tragedy of Julius Caesar, which I have put forward in our language. Some think that I borrowed it, relying on the Latin version by Marc Antoine Muret; yet, when both plays are compared, they will see the truth of the matter. However, I do not want to deny that if some praiseworthy trait is found in my play, that it is not Muret's own, for he was my mentor in language and literature for some time, and I think most highly of him, having learnt from him.]

In the annotated copy in the Museum Plantin-Moretus, Grévin crosses out all references to Muret, and instead inserts an explanation that he had imitated only the aforementioned 'Latins': 'A leur imitation donques j'ay faist ceste […] Tragedie de Jules Cesar' [In their imitation, therefore, I wrote this tragedy of Julius Caesar] (p. 3). Before crossing out altogether the passage pertaining to Muret, it is also evident from Grévin's annotations that he was intending to replace 'lequel a esté mon precepteur' [he was my mentor] with 'j'ay ouy a esté mon precepteur' [I've heard it said that he was my mentor] (see figures 5.2 and 5.3).

When he completed his print edition in 1561, Grévin freely described how Muret

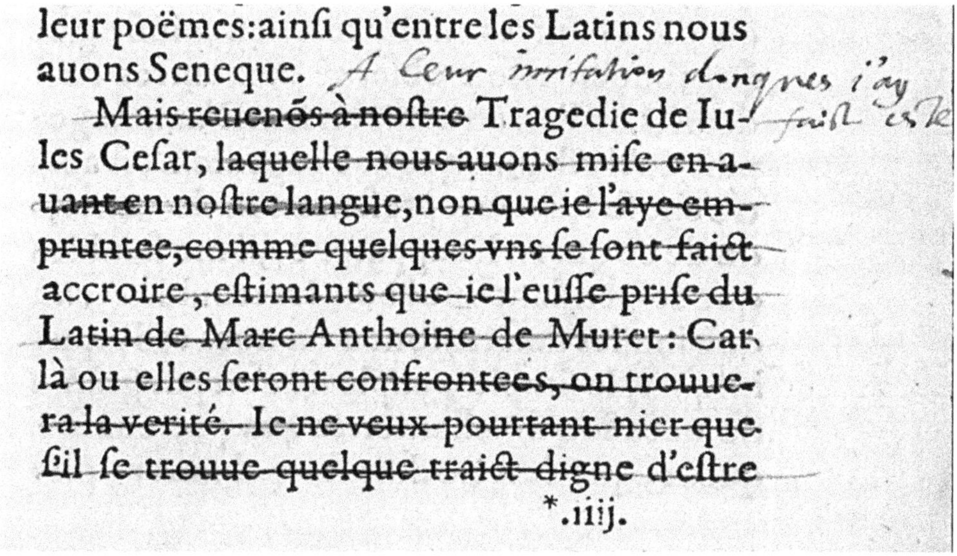

leur poëmes:ainſi qu'entre les Latins nous auons Seneque. ~~A~~ *A Ceur innitation dongres i'ay faiſt esſe*
~~Mais reuenôs à noſtre~~ Tragedie de Iu~~-~~ les Ceſar, ~~laquelle nous auons miſe en a-uant en noſtre langue, non que ie l'aye em-pruntee, comme quelques vns ſe ſont faiſt accroire, eſtimants que ie l'euſſe priſe du Latin de Marc Anthoine de Muret: Car là ou elles ſeront confrontees, on trouue-ra la verité. Ie ne veux pourtant nier que ſil ſe trouue quelque traiſt digne~~ d'eſtre
*.iiij.

FIG. 5.2. Jacques Grévin, 'Brief discours pour l'intelligence de ce theatre', in *Le theatre de Jaques Grevin* (Paris: Vincent Sertenas, 1562), p. 3. Museum Plantin-Moretus, R. 19. 34.

DISCOVRS *ſont* *i'ay ouy* ~~loué, qu'il ne ſoit de Muret, lequel a eſté mon precepteur quelque temps es lettres humaines, & auquel ie donne le meilleur, comme l'ayant appris de luy.~~ *en laquelle*

FIG. 5.3. Jacques Grévin, 'Brief discours pour l'intelligence de ce theatre', in *Le theatre de Jaques Grevin* (Paris: Vincent Sertenas, 1562), p. 4. Museum Plantin-Moretus, R. 19. 34.

guided him in theatre: six years later, Grévin does not only claim that Muret's mentorship is mere hearsay, but subsequently decides that it would be best to avoid any references to Muret. Clearly, Grévin intended to draw the reader's attention away from any possible native intermediary between himself and the ancients: his aim is to create the impression that in writing his tragedy, his only sources were the Roman playwrights. This further suggests that Grévin's own theatre should be the model for later French playwrights, setting the standard as the first examples of humanist drama in French. This is of course untrue: although Grévin is dismissive of Jodelle's comedy, he does not even mention Jodelle's tragedy *Cléopâtre captive*, which Jodelle had written in the classical and Italian style almost a decade previously. Nor does he mention the work of Estienne, whose own approach to classical and Italian models is quite contrary to that of Grévin.

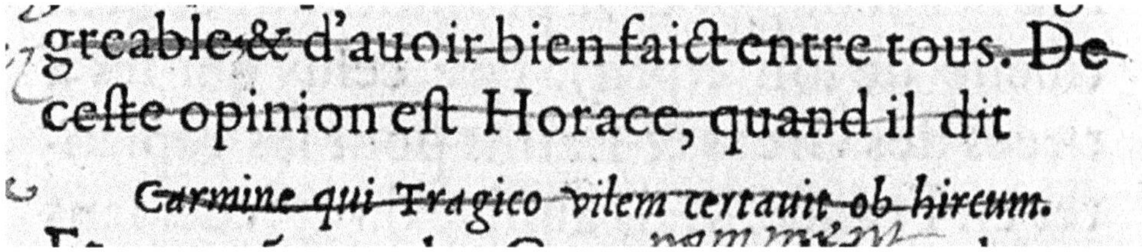
greable & d'auoir bien faict entre tous. De
ceste opinion est Horace, quand il dit
Carmine qui Tragico vilem certauit ob hircum.

FIG. 5.4. Jacques Grévin, 'Brief discours pour l'intelligence de ce theatre', in *Le theatre de Jaques Grevin*, (Paris: Vincent Sertenas, 1562), p. 2. Museum Plantin-Moretus, R. 19. 34.

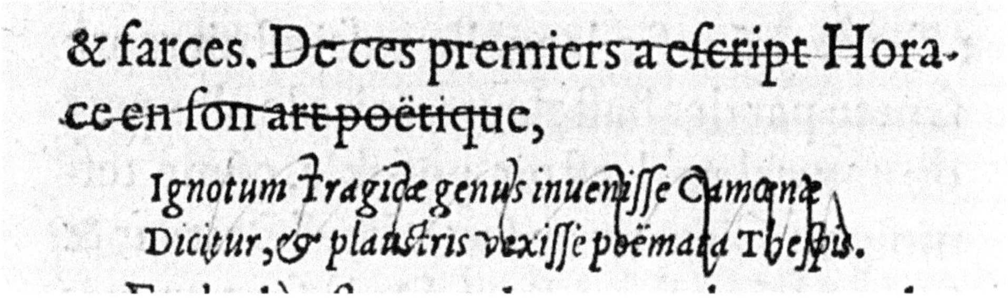
& farces. De ces premiers a escript Hora-
ce en son art poëtique,
Ignotum Tragicæ genus inuenisse Camenæ
Dicitur, & plaustris vexisse poëmata Thespis.

FIG. 5.5. Jacques Grévin, 'Brief discours pour l'intelligence de ce theatre', in *Le theatre de Jaques Grevin*, (Paris: Vincent Sertenas, 1562), p. 8. Museum Plantin-Moretus, R. 19. 34.

Although Grévin does recognise his debt to 'Les Latins', thereby asserting his reliance on classical playwrights, his second set of edits again indicates that he is keen to emphasise his originality in writing theatre. It is possible that Grévin considered his printed edition to have too great a focus on ancient exemplars, which drew attention away from his own efforts to inaugurate tragedy and comedy in France. He thereby crosses out a number of allusions to classical writers: most notably, he removes each of Horace's dicta regarding tragedy and comedy. He crosses through, for instance, Horace's description of the first poet winning the prize of a goat for his tragedy; he also removes Horace's comments on the poet and actor Thespis creating a new style of tragedy (see figures 5.4 and 5.5):

It is possible that Grévin judged a discussion of Horace's *Ars poetica* to be unnecessary, given Peletier's 1541 translation and subsequent 1555 updating of this treatise, which were increasingly popular throughout the 1560s; yet, it is more likely that he intended for the 'Brief discours' to have more of a focus on his own theatre.[83] Grévin's aim to take ownership of his theatre, diverting attention from classical and contemporary sources, is also clear from the final significant edit to his prefatory material. He describes how comedy is the mirror of life: 'Comme disoit Andronique, la Comedie est le mirouer de la vie journaliere. Ceste seule cause m'a esmeu d'avantage à mettre celles cy [les Comedies] en avant, en la composition desquelles j'ay plustost ensuyvi la nayveté de nostre vulgaire' [As Andronicus said, comedy is the mirror of daily life. This very cause was the true instigator for me to put these [comedies] forward, following in their composition the naturalness of our native language].[84] These lines indicate that Grévin has most certainly read and assimilated Peletier's reworking of Horace, since Peletier also discusses the

Horatian notion of comedy as mirror of daily life, though he, like Grévin, cites Livius Andronicus as his source: 'La Comedie à etè dite par Live Andronique, le premier Ecriteur de Comedies Latines, le miroer de la vie' [Comedy has been said by Livius Andronicus, the first writer of Latin Comedies, to be the mirror of life].[85] Since the Andronicus source was (and remains) missing, Peletier's reference to this alternative source is scholarly ostentation, as I have shown elsewhere;[86] Grévin has thereby relied not only on Horace but also on Peletier. Although Grévin does not remove the mirror reference in his 1567 edits, he does replace the more ambiguous 'celles cy' [these] with the possessive 'les miennes' [mine] (see figure 5.6):

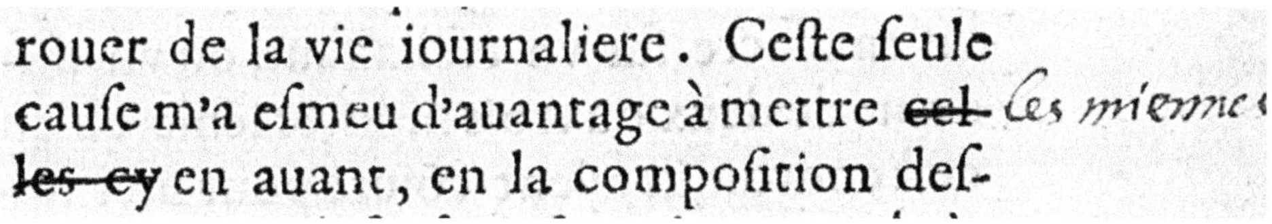

rouer de la vie iournaliere. Ceſte ſeule
cauſe m'a eſmeu d'auantage à mettre ~~cel~~ Ces miennes
~~les ey~~ en auant, en la compoſition deſ-

FIG. 5.6. Jacques Grévin, 'Brief discours pour l'intelligence de ce theatre', in *Le theatre de Jaques Grevin*, (Paris: Vincent Sertenas, 1562), p. 5. Museum Plantin-Moretus, R. 19. 34.

Grévin's specification that these comedies are his own ('les miennes') strikes a different tone to his more imprecise description of the comedies six years previously. Again, Grévin intends to draw attention to his own work, taking the focus away from ancient and other contemporary theatre and amplifying his own achievement.

Moving away from Grévin's handwritten revisions, a closing comment to his brief letter 'Au Lecteur' which precedes his plays again reinforces the notion that he intended for his own comedies to be exemplars for future playwrights to follow. Setting out his hope for his plays, he writes: 'Celles cy pourront suffire pour monstrer le chemin à ceux qui viendront apres nous' [These will be enough to show the path to those who come after me].[87] Like Jodelle, Grévin is employing the *via* topos as a means of discussing exemplarity: yet, while Jodelle used this metaphor to describe his reliance on the ancients ('retraçant la voye des plus vieux' [retracing the path of the ancients], *L'Eugène*, p. 4, 'Prologue', l. 43), Grévin is asserting that his own comedies will be the path for later writers. Here we can draw on the classical tripartite analysis of the *via* topos set out by Pigman: following a literary model; catching up with it; and finally surpassing it.[88] Whereas Jodelle aimed to follow the path in order to catch up with ancient exemplars, Grévin describes having overtaken all other models — both classical and contemporary — on that path, and himself as the guide to a foremost model for theatre. Here Grévin puts out of the picture classical sources, his immediate French predecessors, and also the Italian models, which he himself has imitated. He aims for his own theatre to be the source for imitation for later writers; however, he also intends for French theatre itself to be a paradigm. Especially given that he was writing this letter to accompany the printed edition of his comedies — achieving a level of mobility and accessibility which previous French theatre had not — it is possible that he hoped for this edition to influence also writers from other cultures, eclipsing not only ancient drama but also the widely-known Italian accomplishments.

Italian Cultural Rivalry in *Les Esbahis*: Language

Grévin, in his *La Trésorière*, avoided altogether Italian lexis with two aims in mind: firstly, to draw attention away from his Italian models, thereby helping to establish comic drama as a French genre; and secondly, to show that the popularity of the Italian language in France was nothing more than a passing trend. *Les Esbahis*, too, is used to fulfil similar aims, though the techniques Grévin employs are again entirely different from methods he has used previously.[89] We explored in Chapter 4 Jodelle's employment of the term 'Messer Coyon' to mock Italian courtly greetings; we also saw that Grévin uses the term 'Messer Coioni' in *Les Esbahis* to parody the overblown and ornate *messeresque*. Yet Grévin makes use not just of this Italianism, but of a broad range of terms coined from the Italian. We examined earlier the variety of insults used against Pantaleoné, such as 'forfante' ('coward', from the Italian of the same word, III.3.1350); he is also called a 'ruffien' (from the Italian *ruffiano*, v.4.2392), and the term *poltronisque* ('cowardly', from the Italian *poltrone*, v.4.2062), which is used to describe his serenades, is adjectivized to form a hapax. Crucially, each term which has been coined in French from the Italian is used to describe a negative concept, usually to denote either cowardice or criminality: Grévin's choice of Italian lexis, then, reflects what he perceives to be Italian characteristics. This technique pre-empts one of Henri Estienne's best-known pieces of advice, set out in his 1578 *Deux dialogues du nouveau langage françois italianizé* [Two Dialogues on the New Italianised French Language]: that Italian words should only be employed in French to denote words that relate to Italian idiosyncrasies, which must in themselves be foolish or immoral. Estienne gives as an example *ciarlatano*, explaining that because the Italians are charlatans themselves, it is permissible to render this term into *charlatan* in French.[90] Grévin, too, presents Italian lexis as useful only in criticism of the Italians themselves: his use of Italian, then, is a dual attack on both Italian language and culture.

As well as showing the Italian language to be useful only for a defamatory purpose, Grévin seeks to emphasise that Italian is unwelcome in France: he does this in three different ways. Firstly, when a French character speaks no Italian, they wear it like a badge of honour: the servant Julien, for instance, smugly claims: 'Je suis Julien, | Qui n'enten mot d'italien' [I am Julien | Who understands not one word of Italian] (v.1.2120–21). The ability to speak Italian in this play is shameful, rather than praiseworthy. Secondly, Grévin shows the invasion of Italian to be unwelcome by making Pantaleoné what Enrico Malato defines as a 'personaggio storpialingue' [a character who mixes up his languages].[91] Pantaleoné's language is a blend of French and Italian, a perfect example of the *jergonnage* which Henri Estienne was to criticise a decade later in his *Deux dialogues*.[92] This is a technique which had previously been exploited by Italian playwrights to mock the Spanish language; Piccolomini's Capitan Francisco, for example, speaks macaronic Italian mixed with Spanish, to the great annoyance of the Italian characters: 'Y por la lengua se puede conocer; que me ha quedado la habla toscana assi bien come se fuesse nascido en medio de Sena' [And it can be recognised from my accent that I have maintained the Tuscan accent such that it is like I was born in the middle of the Sena].[93] Using this same technique with Pantaleoné, the presence of Italian in his attempts to speak French is shown to be highly infuriating to the French characters. For instance, Pantaleoné repeatedly confuses *despetto* with *dépit* [despite]: 'En despetto de ce vieil pere [...] Despetto du pere felon' [Despetto this old father [...] Despetto this unfaithful father] (II.3.775–79); this enrages Julien so much that he yells back at Pantaleoné in imitation of his own macaronic language:

> Forfanti, Coioni, Poltroni,
> Li compagnoni di Toni,[94]
> Le mal San Lazaro te vingue
> Et le mau de terre te tingue! (II.3,839–42)

> [Forfanti, Coioni, Poltroni, | The companioni of Toni, | The San Lazaro disease vingue you | And the evils of the earth tingue you!]

As with Pantaleoné's affectedness, the actor performing this role no doubt used a heavy and exaggerated Italian accent, making the audience laugh but also emphasising Pantaleoné's disparity with the native French characters. Grévin further distances Pantaleoné from the others by contrasting his macaronic French with a highly traditional language form used by the native characters: as Lapeyre has pointed out, the French protagonists all retain the inflection of the diphthong *oye* as '[wa]', whereas in the 1560s the Italianised pronunciation of '[e]' was fashionable.[95] The collective reaction to Pantaleoné illustrates the unwelcomeness of the Italian language in France, emphasising that it is worthy of scorn and ridicule; however, the distortedness of his language also provides a written and oral example of the perceived corruption to French which the prevalence of Italian at the courts could cause. Pantaleoné's macaronic French, then, also functions as a warning to spectators and readers to resist the current infiltration of the Italian language into their own.

Thirdly, Grévin uses a speech by the Gentilhomme to show the unwelcomeness in France of the Italian language. This speech, addressed to Pantaleoné, is delivered in the closing scene of *Les Esbahis*, a scene in which problems encountered during a play are usually resolved, leaving characters — and also readers and spectators — satisfied and content. Yet the Gentilhomme's speech is bitter and resentful, attacking at once Italian language and culture:

> Pensez vous nous rendre estonnez
> Par une langue deceptive
> Comme si la nostre captive
> Ne pouvoit respondre un seul mot?
> Pensez vous le François si sot,
> Qu'il n'egalle bien en parole
> Toute l'apparente frivolle
> De vostre langue effœminee,
> Qui comme une espesse fumee
> Nous donnant au commencement
> Un effroyable estonnement,
> A la parfin s'esvanoüit
> Avecque le vent qui la suit?

> Nostre France est trop abbreuvee
> De vostre feinte controuvee
> Et deceptive intention.   (v.4.2339–55)

[Do you think that you amaze us | With a deceptive language, | As if our own captive language | Cannot reply with even a word? | Do you think French so foolish | That its words cannot outdo | All of the deceit and frivolity | Of your effeminate language, | Which, like a puff of smoke, | Gave us a terrific fright | At the beginning, | In the end will disappear | With the wind that blows it? | Our France has had enough | Of your crafty lies | And deceptive intents.]

Here Grévin promotes a number of interrelated ideas about the Italian language. The first is that the Italian language is inferior to French: the emphasis that French will 'egalle *bien*' [*well* equal] (v.4.2444, my emphasis) its Italian counterpart clearly suggests that French does not just equal, but surpasses, the Italian language. Connected to this is a second idea: that the prevalence of Italian in France is nothing but a passing trend. The Gentilhomme does acknowledge that the French were initially impressed at the Italian language: 'Nous donnant au commencement | Un effroyable estonnement' [Gave us a terrific fright | At the beginning] (v.4.2448–49); yet, he outlines that French is by no means 'captive' (v.4.2441) to Italian. He uses the analogy of smoke blowing away with the wind to show that the French admiration for Italian will quickly pass when another fashion comes along: 'A la parfin s'esvanoüit | Avec le vent qui la suit' [In the end will disappear | With the wind that blows it] (v.4.2451–52. According to the Gentilhomme, the popularity in France of Italian is neither impactful nor long-lasting: it is appreciated only because people enjoy following trends, which are by definition ever-changing. Grévin's acknowledgement of the fleeting acclaim for Italian in France again pre-empts Estienne's *Deux dialogues*, which put forward this same idea while contemptuously referring to those who follow fashionable languages as 'pindarizans'.[96]

   This comparison of Italian to smoke also hints at a third idea about the Italian language: not only is Italian ephemeral and easily overcome, but it is shallow and capricious. This image is reinforced by the range of adjectives which are used to describe Italian, such as 'deceptive' (v.4.2440) and 'frivolle' (v.4.2445), which each point to its untrustworthiness and superficiality. Given that the concept of effeminacy was, at this time, often associated with vanity and fickleness, the description of Italian as 'effœminee' (v.4.2446) also implies that the language is heavily ornamented so as to conceal its lack of depth.[97] Repeating for a second time the term *déceptive*, the Gentilhomme emphasises at the end of his speech the perceived artifice of Italian:

> Nostre France est trop abbreuvee
> De vostre feinte controuvee
> Et deceptive intention.   (v.4.2339–55)

[Our France has had enough | Of your crafty lies | And deceptive intents.]

As well as criticising the *messeresque*, again showing the Italian language to be deceptively artful and ornate, the inference is that French is superior: not only is the Gentilhomme's native language trustworthy and unaffected, it is robust enough to withstand the whims of fashion. The Gentilhomme is also unequivocal that Italian — and the Italians — are no longer welcome in France, an idea which is reinforced when, shortly following this speech, the French characters physically chase Pantaleoné from the stage. These final lines of the speech, combined with the action of chasing away the Italian expatriate, form an important closing comment from Grévin: he leaves the spectators and readers wondering about the possibility of a space occupied only by French language and culture, freed from what he has presented as an at once irritating and dangerous presence. While the Italians themselves are shown to be unwelcome, the native French characters play a vital role in making this obvious to Pantaleoné and, finally, in forcing his exit; Grévin closes the play by reminding readers and spectators that they, too, can play their part in resisting the infiltration into France of Italian language and culture.

Grévin's efforts to transform Italianate comedy into anti-Italian propaganda provide new perspectives not just on the status of French theatre in the 1560s, but also on the ways in which writers explored the turbulent relationship between France and Italy in this period. It is possible to recognise in *La Trésorière* Grévin's resentment of the influence in France of Italian literature and language, and although this was a sentiment also expressed by Jodelle in his *L'Eugène*, Grévin takes a different approach in his comedy. He subtly conceals the Italian influence, as well as heightening the perception of comedy as a French genre; he also resists the influx into France of the increasingly fashionable Italian language. By the time Grévin came to write *Les Esbahis* three years later, a number of key cultural shifts had taken place: firstly, comic theatre was more widely accepted as a useful political and polemical tool; and secondly, anti-Italian attitudes were ever more prominent and pervasive. Both shifts can be explained in part by the tensions and uncertainty caused by the Wars of Religion, as well as by the unexpected deaths in quick succession of two monarchs, which greatly enhanced the power of Catherine de' Medici. The increased prominence of comedy as propaganda and of anti-Italian sentiment in France, combined with Grévin's own improved skill and confidence in writing theatre, equipped him to turn his understated hostilities in *La Trésorière* into an intense and unmistakeable attack on Italian language and culture in *Les Esbahis*.

Les Esbahis is the first example of theatre which makes an overtly anti-Italianist statement, and comments on a range of features associated with the Italians during these years while at the same time seeking both to resist and to rival Italian culture. This play offers us a clearer picture of the resentment experienced by French citizens towards the Italians at this time, as well as broadening our understanding of the range of techniques used by comic playwrights to convey a highly political message. Also clear is that many of these techniques pre-empt the advice set out a decade later by well-known polemicists such as Henri Estienne and Gentillet. Yet, there is no evidence that *Les Esbahis* was impactful as propaganda: there are no records of Italian responses to the play, although there was sufficient demand for a second edition to be printed a year after it was first circulated, and the comedy may have been performed again in 1578, the year in which Estienne's *Deux dialogues* was printed.[98] Nonetheless, *Les Esbahis* testifies to a reversal in the way that the Italians were presented as part of comic theatre in France. Just twenty years previously, Estienne had omitted the controversial Spanish soldier of Italian comedy, Grévin remodels him into an Italian parody; Estienne had proudly set out his Italian sources, Grévin uses a variety of techniques to conceal them; Estienne had encouraged writers to imitate Italian comedy, Grévin seeks to establish himself as the model for imitation. Admiration for the Italians had turned into antagonism, which was to intensify as France's political and religious strife persisted. As we shall see in the final Chapter 6, while Grévin's anti-Italianist comedy may not have evoked a direct response from the Italians, it did set a precedent for future French playwrights, who not only followed Grévin's model of comedy as propaganda, but also expanded on his example.

Notes to Chapter 5

1. Both *La Trésorière* and *Les Esbahis* were printed as part of the collection *Le theatre de Jaques Grevin de Cler-mont en Beauvaisis, à tres illustre et treshaulte princesse ladame Claude de France, Duchesse de Lorraine. Ensemble, la seconde partie de L'Olimpe & de la Gelodacrye* (Paris: Vincent Sertenas and Guillaume Barbé, 1562).

2. Jacques Grévin, *La Trésorière, Les Esbahis*, ed. by Élisabeth Lapeyre (Paris: Librairie Honoré Champion, 1980), p. 40 ('Au Lecteur'). All references to *Les Esbahis* and *La Trésorière* are taken from this edition, hereafter referred to as *Comédies* (but note that quotations from *Les Esbahis* are provided without reference to a particular edition). Pinvert has suggested that *La Maubertine* is simply another name for *La Trésorière*, but given that Grévin provides distinct plot synopses for each play and also laments the censuring of *La Maubertine*, it is unlikely that they are the same comedy. Pinvert, *Jacques Grévin*, p. 172.

3. Jacques Grévin, *César*, trans. by Jeffrey Foster (Paris: Nizet, 1974).

4. Nicole Estienne's most famous work is *Les misères de la femme mariée, où se peuvent voir les peines et tourmens qu'elle reçoit durant sa vie* [The Miseries of the Married Woman, Detailing the Sufferings and Torments which She Undergoes in Life] (Paris: Pierre Menier, [n.d]), in which she speaks out against domestic violence and inequality in marriage. Grévin completed his 1560 poetry collection, *L'Olimpe*, in Nicole's honour, identifying her with the anagram 'sien en election' [his by choice]. Jacques Grévin, *L'Olimpe de Jacques Grévin, ensemble les autres œuvres poëtiques dudict auteur* (Paris: Robert Estienne, 1560), p. 40.

5. Jacques Grévin, *Le theatre* (Paris: Vincent Sertenas, 1562), Museum Plantin-Moretus, R 19. 34. Dirk Imhof and Nico De Brabander — the curators of the Plantin-Moretus Museum, where Grévin's personal copy of his plays is held — have kindly made possible my examination. Lapeyre's edition of this play documents some other edits Grévin made to his plays in this copy, though omits any discussion of its prefatory materials.

6. Turin was at this time part of the independent Duchy of Savoy.

7. Peletier, *L'art poëtique départi en deux livres*, p. 70.

8. For more information, see Rayfield, 'The Poetics of Comedy in Jacques Peletier du Mans's *Art poëtique* (1555)'.

9. For more information on this comedy, see Sergio Monaldini, 'Visioni del comico', *Maske und Kothurn*, 50.3 (2005), 45–64.

10. Giulio Alvarotto to the Duke of Ferrara, 'Ambasciatori Francia', busta 35, Archivio di stato Modena. Also cited in Monaldini, 'Visioni del comico', p. 49.

11. Both Brantôme and Pierre Dan describe this play as a 'comédie': Brantôme, *Œuvres complètes*, , III, 370; Pierre Dan, *Le Trésor des Merveilles de la Maison Royale de Fontainebleau* (Paris: Sébastien Cramoisy, 1642), p. 242. Paul Laumonier convincingly showed this play to be a tragi-comedy: see *Ronsard, poète lyrique: étude historique et littéraire* (Paris: Hachette, 1932), esp. p. 220.

12. Grévin, *Le theatre*, p. 47.

13. Jacques Grévin, *Théâtre complet et poésies choisies de Jacques Grévin*, ed. by Lucien Pinvert (Paris: Garnier Frères, 1922), p. 5.
14. Opinions are divided on whether Grévin studied at Beauvais, Boncourt, or both. It is probable that the latter is true: for arguments on both sides, see Marcel Raymond, *L'Influence de Ronsard sur la poésie française* (Geneva: Droz, 1965), p. 286; Henri Chamard, 'Le Collège de Boncourt et les origines du théâtre classique', in *Mélanges offerts à M. Abel Lefranc*, ed. by Lavaud, pp. 246–60 (p. 251, n. 1); Grévin, *Théâtre complet et poésies choisies*, ed. by Pinvert, p. 6.
15. For more information on Muret's tragedy, see Patrick Kragelund, *Roman Historical Drama: The Octavia in Antiquity and Beyond* (Oxford: Oxford University Press, 2016), pp. 408–09.
16. See Chasles, *La Comédie en France au seizième siècle*, p. 37; Gustave Attinger, *L'Esprit de la commedia dell'arte dans le théâtre français* (Paris: Librairie Théâtrale, 1950), p. 93.
17. Grévin, *La Trésorière*, in *Comédies*, p. 5 ('Prologue', ll. 60–63).
18. As Jean-Claude Ternaux has pointed out, *La Trésorière* does retain some aspects typical of the farce. Professions in the play, for instance, often dictate a character's personality: the *trésorier* himself is avaricious, a vice with which such a profession was often associated. See Jean-Claude Ternaux, 'La Comédie humaniste et la farce: *La Trésorière* de Grévin', *Seizième Siècle*, 6 (2010), 77–93 (p. 81).
19. Barbara Bowen has demonstrated, for instance, how the plot makes use of Ariosto's *I suppositi*: see *Les Caractéristiques essentielles de la farce française et leur survivance dans les années 1550–1620* (Urbana: University of Illinois Press, 1964), p. 107. Lapeyre has also examined Grévin's reliance on prototypes in the *commedia dell'arte* for his own characters. See her 'Introduction', in Grévin, *Comédies*, , p. 38.
20. Lapeyre, 'Introduction', in Grévin, *Comédies*, p. 51.
21. Grévin, *La Trésorière*, in *Comédies*, p. 6 ('Prologue', l. 74).
22. Ibid. (ll. 75–78).
23. Bruce Hayes, *Hostile Humor in Renaissance France* (Newark: University of Delaware Press, 2020).
24. Conrad Badius, *Comedie du pape malade et tirant à la fin* ([Paris(?)]: [n.pub.], 1561); Jacques Bienvenu, *Comedie du monde malade et mal pensé* ([Paris(?)]: [n.pub.], 1568). Though these plays are described as *comédies*, they can more accurately be described as belonging to the farce or *sermon joyeux* tradition, comprising a series of monologues and little structure. See *La Comédie à l'époque d'Henri II et de Charles IX*, ed. by Rosalba Guerini, 1.7 (1995), 283.
25. Rémy Belleau, *Les œuvres poétiques de Remy Belleau, redigees en deux Tomes* (Paris: Mamert Patisson, 1578), II, 110–53. See Rémy Belleau, *La Reconnue*, ed. by Jean Braybrook (Geneva: Droz, 1989); Jean Braybrook, *Rémy Belleau et l'art de guérir* (Berlin: De Gruyter, 2013).
26. Catherine de' Medici was highly aware of the importance of distracting her subjects in civil war, writing in a letter to Charles IX in 1563 that 'il [faut] deux choses pour vivre en repos avec les François et qu'ils aimassent leur Roy: les tenir joyeux, et occuper à quelque exercice' [two things are necessary to ensure that one lives in peace with one's subjects and that they love their King: keep them happy, and keep them busy with something]. *Lettres de Catherine de Médicis,* ed. by Hector Ferrière-Percy, 11 vols (Paris, Imprimerie Nationale, 1880–97), II, 92.
27. Frances Yates, *The French Academies of the Sixteenth Century* (Paris: Kraus, 1973), p. 252. This performance — as well as its political resonances — are discussed throughout Scott and Sturm-Maddox, *Performance, Poetry and Politics on the Queen's Day*.
28. Balsamo, 'L'Italianisme lyonnais et l'illustration de la langue française', p. 222; Thomas Hope, *Lexical Borrowing in the Romance Languages: A Critical Study of Italianisms in French and Gallicisms in Italian from 1100 to 1900* (Oxford: Basil Blackwell, 1971). See also Bartina Wind, *Les Mots italiens introduits en français au XVIe siècle* (Deventer: Æ. E. Kluwer, 1926).
29. Grévin, *Le theatre*, pp. 113–219.
30. Ibid., fol. A3^r ('Élégie de Pierre de Ronsard à Jacques Grévin').
31. *La Comédie à l'époque d'Henri II et de Charles IX*, ed. by Catherine Douël Dell'Agnola, 1.7 (1995), 5.
32. Ibid., p. 73: as Douël Dell'Agnola points out, Grévin would not in any case have returned to France before December 1560, when Catherine de' Medici freed the Prince of Condé, who was at the forefront of the 1560 Amboise Conspiracy.

33. Precisely, 'defendre aux Italiens l'accès dans notre Pays' [prevent the Italians from entering our country]. [Anon.], *Traité de la grande prudence et subtilité des Italiens* ([n.p.: n.pub., n.d]). Only an English translation of this treatise survives: *A Discovery of the great subtilitie and wonderful wisedome of the Italians* (London: John Wolfe, 1591). For more information on this pamphlet, see Heller, *Anti-Italianism in Sixteenth-century France*, p. 209.

34. Innocent Gentillet, *Discours sur les moyens de bien gouverner: contre Nicolas Machiavel Florentin*, ed. by Charles Edward Rathé (Geneva: Droz, 1968), p. 38 (hereafter referred to as *Anti-Machiavel*). Although Catherine is certainly one of the figures to whom Gentillet refers, it is possible that he is also alluding to René de Birague, Keeper of the Seals in France and close ally of Catherine and Charles IX.

35. *La Comédie à l'époque d'Henri II et de Charles IX*, ed. by Douël Dell'Agnola, pp. 73–82 ('Introduction to *Les Esbahis*'); Scott and Sturm-Maddox, *Performance, Poetry and Politics on the Queen's Day*, p. 14.

36. Jacques Grévin, *La Gélodacrye et les vingt-quatre sonnets romains*, ed. by Michèle Clément (Saint-Étienne: Université Saint-Étienne, 2001), p. 40 (book 1, sonnet 21, l. 11).

37. Grévin, *La Trésorière*, in *Comédies*, p. 47 ('Avant-Jeu', ll. 6–7).

38. Noirot, 'French Humanist Comedy in Search of an Audience', p. 87.

39. This number was probably due to efficient law enforcement which, by the late 1400s, saw two-thirds of Florentine men officially charged with sodomy by the age of forty. See Michael Rocke, 'Gender and Sexual Culture in Renaissance Italy', in *Gender and Society in Renaissance Italy*, ed. by Judith Brown and Robert Charles Davis (London: Routledge, 1998), pp. 150–70 (p. 166).

40. Du Bellay, for instance, criticised the relationship of the late Pope Julius III with Innocenzo del Monte, who had been made a cardinal for no apparent reason: Du Bellay calls Innocenzo 'un Ganymede avoir le rouge sur la teste' [Ganymede with red on his head]. Du Bellay, *The Regrets*, ed. by Helgerson, p. 157 (sonnet 105). For a more detailed discussion of the French view of Italian homosexuality during these years, see Melanie Hawthorne, ' "Comment peut-on être homosexuel?": Multinational (In)Corporation and the Frenchness of Salomé', in *Perennial Decay: On the Aesthetics and Politics of Decadence*, ed. by Liz Constable, Dennis Denisoff, and Matthew Potolsky (Philadephia: University of Pennsylvania Press, 1999), pp. 159–82 (pp. 164–65).

41. In the fourth tale of the first day, for example, a monk smuggles a beautiful woman into his monastery and is spotted by an abbot, who does not sanction the monk, but lusts after the woman too. See Boccaccio, *Decameron*, ed. by Elena Ceva Valla and Mario Marti (Milan: Rizzoli, 1974), pp. 47–51.

42. Attinger, *L'Esprit de la commedia dell'arte dans le théâtre français*, p. 93; Enzo Bottasso, 'Le commedie dell'Ariosto nel teatro francese', *Giornale storico della letteratura italiana*, 128 (1951), 41–80 (p. 44).

43. See Max Kawczyński, 'Über das Verhältnis des Lustspiels *Les Contens* von Odet de Turnèbe zu *Les Esbahis* de Jacques Grévin und beider zu den Italienern', in *Festschrift zum VIII: Allgemeinen deutschen Neuphilologentage in Wien Pfingsten*, ed. by Jakob Schipper (Leipzig: Wilhelm Braumüller, 1898), pp. 239–50, (p. 250), cited in Lapeyre, 'Introduction', in Grévin, *Comédies*, pp. 31–32.

44. This character was first used as part of Roman theatre. See Daniel Boughner, 'The Braggart in Italian Renaissance Comedy', *Proceedings of the Modern Language Association*, 58.1 (1943), 42–83 (pp. 48–49).

45. Smith, for example, has argued that mockery of Italians at the courts is Grévin's 'field of speciality' in his poetry. See *The Anti-courtier Trend in Sixteenth-century French Literature*, p. 117.

46. See also MacPhail, *The Voyage to Rome in French Renaissance Literature*, pp. 115–16.

47. Gentillet commented in 1576 that 'les livres de Machiavel sont depuis quinze ans ença aussi familiers et ordinaires ès mains des Courtisans' [the books of Machiavelli have been for fifteen years very familiar and customary to the courtiers]. Gentillet, *Anti-Machiavel*, p. 39. See Antonio d'Andrea, 'The Political and Ideological Context of Innocent Gentillet's *Anti-Machiavel*', *Renaissance Quarterly*, 23.4 (1970), 397–411 (p. 397, n. 1).

48. This phrase was used, for example, by Jacques Yver throughout *Le Printemps d'Yver* (Paris: J. Ruelle, 1572). See Sozzi, *Rome n'est plus Rome*, pp. 23–24.

49. This gesture is discussed further in Boughner, 'The Braggart in Italian Renaissance Comedy', p. 51.

50. Joan Kelly, 'Did Women Have a Renaissance?', in *The Italian Renaissance*, ed. by Harold Bloom (New York: Chelsea House, 2004), pp. 151–76 (esp. p. 160).

51. Castiglione, *Il libro del Cortegiano*, p. 277. More information on music as forming an integral part of the 'performance-driven world of the courtier' can be found in Blake Wilson, *Singing to the Lyre in Renaissance Italy: Memory, Performance, and Oral Poetry* (Cambridge: Cambridge University Press, 2020), p. 293.

52. The Italian style of serenade is the subject of discussion throughout Katritzky, *The Art of 'Commedia'*.

53. Baldassare Castiglione, *The Book of the Courtyer*, ed. by Virginia Cox, trans. by Thomas Hoby (London: Dent, 1994), p. 369.

54. Bruce Dickey, 'Ornamentation in Sixteenth-century Music', in *A Performer's Guide to Renaissance Music*, ed. by Jeffery T. Kite-Powell (Bloomington: Indiana University Press, 2007), pp. 300–25 (p. 301). Eugenia Paulicelli also opts not to translate *sprezzatura* throughout her *Writing Fashion in Early Modern Italy: From Sprezzatura to Satire* (Farnham: Ashgate, 2014), given the many meanings of the term in different contexts throughout Castiglione's guidebook.

55. Du Bellay, 'Contre les Pétrarquistes', in *Œuvres complètes*, p. 257. For more information on this poem, see Bernard Weinberg, 'Du Bellay's "Contre les Pétrarquistes"', *L'Esprit Créateur*, 12 (1972), 159–77.

56. 'FRANCISCO: Quiero bien á otra persona del mundo si no alla señora Anioletta. AGNOLETTA: Credete ch'io non sappia che voi avete altre pratiche che le mie?' [FRANCISCO: *(heavy Spanish accent)* I cannot love any person in the world other than my lady Anioletta. AGNOLETTA: You really think I believe you to be faithful to me and me alone?] (Piccolomini, *L'amor costante*, I.12).

57. Dora Rigo Bienaimé has also noted that despite playing the 'amante sospiroso [...] in sostanza rimane un essere infido, sciocco, vile, infingardo' [sighing lover [...] Pantaleoné is nothing but an unfaithful, foolish, mean, and lazy figure]. Dora Rigo Bienaimé, *Grévin: poeta satirico, e altri saggi sulla poesia del cinquecento francese* (Pisa: Giardini, 1967), p. 129.

58. For more information on comedy as persuasion in the Renaissance, see Rayfield, 'Rewriting Laughter in Early Modern Europe', pp. 75–76.

59. Du Bellay had already made the French frankness a subject of his 1558 *Regrets*.

60. Grévin, *Le theatre*, p. 5 ('Brief discours pour l'intelligence de ce theatre').

61. Gentillet, *Anti-Machiavel*, p. 303.

62. Henri Estienne, *Traicté de la conformité du langage françois avec le grec*, ed. by Léon Feugère (Geneva: Slatkine, 1853), p. 24.

63. Grévin, *La Gélodacrye*, p. 41 (book I, sonnet 22, l. 9).

64. Ibid., p. 35 (book I, sonnet 13, ll. 11–14).

65. See for example Giacomo Cavallucci, *Odet de Turnèbe* (Naples: Raffaele Pironti, 1942), p. 80.

66. For instance in Teresa Jaroszewska, 'Un capitan italien en costume espagnol', in *Les Mots et les choses du théâtre: France, Italie, Espagne, XVIᵉ–XVIIᵉ siècles* (Geneva: Droz, 2017), pp. 211–26 (p. 223).

67. Captain Pantaléon's adventure was told, for instance, in Pierre du Jarric, *Histoire des choses plus memorables advenues tant ez Indes Orientales*, 3 vols (Bordeaux: Millanges, 1610–14), I, 399. Unfortunately, his story seems to have now been forgotten, and his name was last mentioned in Archibald Duncan, *Mariner's Chronicle* (New Haven, CT: George Gorton, 1834), p. 392.

68. A fuller explanation of this monologue can be found in Georges Gassies, *Anthologie du théâtre français du Moyen Âge: théâtre comique: jeux et farces des XIIIᵉ, XVᵉ et XVIᵉ siècles*, 2 vols (Paris: Delgrave, 1925), II, 25–138.

69. For more information see Boughner, 'The Braggart in Italian Renaissance Comedy', p. 51.

70. The Aventine Hill in Rome is another reference to Italians as the cowardly and unworthy successors of the valiant Romans.

71. For variants on the term *frenese* see Huguet, *Dictionnaire de la langue française du seizième siècle*, IV, 205.

72. MacPhail, *The Voyage to Rome in French Renaissance Literature*, p. 34.

73. This poem was never completed, and only four out of the intended twenty-four books went to print. Paul Cohen, 'In Search of the Trojan Origins of French: The Uses of History in the

Elevation of the Vernacular in Early Modern France', in *Fantasies of Troy: Classical Tales and the Social Imaginary in Medieval and Early Modern Europe*, ed. by Alan Shepard and Stephen David Powell (Toronto: Centre for Reformation and Renaissance Studies, 2005), pp. 63–80 (p. 71).

74. For a comprehensive survey of this manifesto, see Charles Baldwin, *Renaissance Literary Theory and Practice: Classicism in the Rhetoric and Poetic of Italy, France and England, 1400–1600* (Gloucester: P. Smith, 1959), pp. 34–36.

75. Philip Ford, 'What Does "Renaissance" Mean?', in *Cambridge History of French Literature*, ed. by William Burgwinkle, Nicholas Hammond, and Emma Wilson (Cambridge: Cambridge University Press, 2011), pp. 180–87 (p. 185).

76. The attempts of French writers to assert their superiority over Italian culture is the subject of much of MacPhail, *The Voyage to Rome in French Renaissance Literature*.

77. '[À cause de son] dégoût et l'horreur de l'italianisme [...] l'auteur ne demanderait pas un modèle à l'Italie' [Because of his disgust and horror for Italianism [...] the author would not use an Italian model]. Grévin, *Théâtre complet et poésies choisies*, ed. by Pinvert, p. 182.

78. Grévin, *Le theatre*, p. 1 ('Brief discours pour l'intelligence de ce theatre').

79. *La Comédie à l'époque d'Henri II et de Charles IX*, ed. by Douël Dell'Agnola, p. 82 ('Introduction to *Les Esbahis*').

80. Grévin, *Le theatre*, p. 1 ('Brief discours pour l'intelligence de ce theatre').

81. Ibid.

82. Ibid., pp. 3–4.

83. Peletier's rewriting of the *Ars poetica* for a contemporary readership is the subject of Rayfield, 'The Poetics of Comedy in Jacques Peletier du Mans's *Art poëtique* (1555)', which includes the first translation into English of Peletier's chapter on theatre.

84. Grévin, *Le theatre*, p. 5 ('Brief discours pour l'intelligence de ce theatre').

85. Peletier, *Art poëtique*, p. 70.

86. Rayfield, 'The Poetics of Comedy in Jacques Peletier du Mans's *Art poëtique* (1555)', 49.

87. Grévin, *Le theatre*, p. 48 ('Au Lecteur').

88. Pigman, 'Versions of Imitation in the Renaissance', pp. 25–26.

89. Although he goes into little detail, Édouard Bourciez also comments on the opposition to the Italian language in this comedy: 'Nous pouvons voir quelle revanche prenait déjà l'esprit français contre l'invasion du langage étranger' [We can observe what stand the French language was already taking against the invasion of the foreign language]. Édouard Bourciez, *Les Mœurs polies et la littérature de cour sous Henri II* (Paris: Hachette, 1866), p. 293.

90. Henri Estienne, *Deux dialogues du nouveau langage françois italianizé et autrement desguizé, principalement entre les courtisans de ce temps*, ed. by Pauline Smith (Geneva: Slatkine, 1980), p. 93.

91. Enrico Malato, *Storia della letteratura italiana: la letteratura italiana fuori d'Italia*, 14 vols (Rome: Salerno, 2002), XII, 310.

92. See Estienne, *Deux dialogues du nouveau langage françois italianizé*, p. 44 (prefatory poem 'Remonstrance aux autres courtisans, amateurs du françois italianizé et autrement desguisé' [Remonstrance to the other courtiers, amateurs of the Italianised and otherwise disguised French], l. 3).

93. Piccolomini, *L'amor costante*, p. 340 (II.1).

94. 'Toni' refers to Saint Antoine, whose companion is a pig; the 'mal San Lazaro' is leprosy. See Grévin, *Les Esbahis*, in *Comédies*, p. 130, nn. 840–41.

95. They rhyme: for instance, *monnoye* with *proye*. See Lapeyre, 'Introduction', in Grévin, *Comédies*, p. 51.

96. See Estienne, *Deux dialogues du nouveau langage françois italianizé*, p. 44 ('Remonstrance aux autres courtisans', l. 2).

97. For an account of the relationship between effeminacy and vanity in the early modern period, see Mario DiGangi, ' "Male Deformities": Narcissus and the Reformation of Courtly Manners in *Cynthia's Revels*', in *Ovid and the Renaissance Body*, ed. by Goran Stanivukovic (Toronto: University of Toronto Press, 2001), pp. 94–110. More information on Renaissance approaches to effeminacy can be found in *Masculinities and Femininities in the Middle Ages and Renaissance*, ed. by Frederick Kiefer (Turnhout: Brepols, 2009).

98. Jules Haraszti explored this possibility in his article 'La Comédie française de la Renaissance et la scène', *Revue d'histoire littéraire de la France*, 16 (1909), 285–301.

CHAPTER 6

Comedy as Propaganda:
Pierre de Larivey and Odet de Turnèbe

Vous le recognoistrez à ses grandes moustaches noires,
retroussées en dents de sanglier.

[You'll know him from his huge black moustache,
all twisted up like a boar's tusks.]

(Odet de Turnèbe, *Les Contens*, 1580)

Religious tensions in France continued to escalate throughout the 1560s and 1570s. They were intensified by the shattering 1572 St Bartholomew's Day Massacre, in which around ten thousand were killed, and heightened still with the 1574 accession of Henri III, the fourth king on the French throne in a period of just fifteen years.[1] These tensions coincided with a rise in objections to Italian culture in France: while Protestants had largely already been opposed to the presence of the Italians, whom they associated with Catholicism, these major events did nothing to alleviate hostilities. Anti-Catholic, and anti-Italian, sentiments were also aggravated by the increasing power and influence of Catherine de' Medici, who by the early 1570s sided openly with the Catholics. Many were convinced that Catherine herself was responsible for the Massacre, following a rumour that the (failed) assassination attempt on Huguenot leader Gaspard de Coligny — which had partly precipitated the event — had been ordered by Catherine as a weak and underhand peace-making attempt. By 1575, Venetian ambassador Giovanni Michele remarked on the widespread animosity in France towards Catherine: 'Elle est accusé de tous les malheurs qui ont désolé ce royaume. Étrangère et italienne, jusqu'ici elle était peu aimée; à présent elle est haïe' [She is accused of every misery which has devastated this kingdom. Foreign and Italian, she has been little loved until now; at present she is hated].[2]

Leaving aside the anti-Italian sentiments of the Protestants, a criticism brought more generally against the Italians in France during this period was of their commercial dominance. Some held the Italians responsible for France's debts of millions of francs: it was well known that many nobles in the first half of the century had been ruined by the campaigns in Italy; others had run into debt more recently, unable to keep up with the lavish lifestyle enjoyed by Italians at the French court.[3] Between 1560 and 1580 no fewer than ten edicts had to be passed in France, banning sumptuous clothing and putting restrictions on the amount of money that could be spent on them.[4] Italian goods were extremely popular: by the end of the 1560s in Lyons, for instance, Italian goods represented over two-thirds of sales;[5] weapons, perfumes, cloths, and even occasional theatrical props or costumes proved to be marketable.[6] Italian banks founded in France earlier in the century were increasingly successful, and by 1573 Antoine du Verdier, *conseiller du roi* in Lyons, condemned the Italian banks set up during the reign of François I as '[une] invention très dommageable ne tendant qu'à la totale ruine des hommes' [a most damaging invention, leading only to men's total ruin].[7] The extra taxes imposed in 1569 were widely blamed on the Italians, who seemed themselves to benefit from them,[8] and by 1571 the Italians accounted for twenty-five per cent of France's taxed wealth, despite constituting only five per cent of the taxed population.[9]

Yet, despite hostility towards Catherine, as well as resentment of the Italians' commercial success, Italian literature and culture still thrived at the court, being promoted by those most in power. When Charles IX gained autonomy from Catherine, he continued to support Italian literature and arts: he generously patronised, for instance, the Franco-Florentine academies that had formerly been associated with his mother.[10] Henri III also capitalised fully on his Medicean heritage: he learnt fluent Italian under Jacopo Corbinelli, witnessed various plays in Venice and Mantua during his 1574–75 tour of Italy, and collected a broad range of books in Italian for his personal library.[11] In the early 1570s, humanist and writer Jacques Yver acknowledged that everyone at court was expected to know the short stories of Boccaccio: 'C'est une honte entre les filles bien nourries et entre ces mieux apprins courtisans de les ignorer' [It is an embarrassment for well-bred ladies and for learned courtiers not to know them].[12] It was at this time that historian Jean-Papire Masson was also compiling his lengthy *Vitae trium Hetruriae Procerum*, a work extolling the Tuscan masters Dante, Petrarch, and Boccaccio;[13] Gabriel Pannonius, too, was putting together his *Petit Vocabulaire en langue françoise et italienne* [Little Vocabulary in the French and Italian Languages], which was intended to help courtiers learn the most fashionable phrases.[14]

The prevalence of Italian culture at the courts in the 1570s did not go unchallenged; more widespread hostilities towards Catherine de' Medici and towards the commercial pre-eminence of the Italians in France were also voiced. These hostilities were embodied in the form of events: two months before the St Bartholomew's Day Massacre, for example, French citizens rioted against Italians in Lyons, with the Italians accused of killing children to sell their blood for secret uses to Catherine de' Medici.[15] Other attacks were made in French writings: among the most prominent were Protestant works such as Gentillet's 1576 *Anti-Machiavel* and Henri Estienne's 1578 *Deux dialogues du nouveau language françois italianizé*. As we saw, Grévin had pre-empted some of Gentillet's and Estienne's ideas in his 1561 *Les Esbahis*, helping to show comic theatre to be a viable weapon for mocking and showing to be unwelcome in France Italian literature and culture. Stricter laws started to be put in place regarding propaganda, and the 1579 Édit de Blois, for instance, banned performances of controversial comedies 'sous peine de prison et punition corporelle' [under pain of prison and corporal punishment].[16] In this final chapter, we continue the focus on the politics of comic theatre, examining the anti-Italian attitudes present in French comedy as the 1570s drew to a close. While writers still relied on the Italian model, they experimented with a range of techniques which allowed them to present Italy under a new light, developing in canny ways theatre as a form of nationalist — and anti-Italian — propaganda. An analysis of comedy as propaganda at this later stage in the century offers us a new angle on the shifting status of comic theatre, as well as on the position at this time of Franco-Italian relations, through the dual lens of cultural resistance and rivalry. The first, shorter case study in this chapter is *Les Six Premières Comédies facecieuses* [The First Six Facetious Comedies] (1579), a collection of six humanist comic plays in French by Pierre de Larivey (1549–1619).[17] Larivey, an unswerving Catholic, never voiced concerns about the presence of the Italians in France, and in fact claimed to admire them; yet, the prefatory material to his comedies clearly indicates some element of resistance to and rivalry with the Italian cultural influence. The main case study in this chapter is *Les Contens* [The Happy Ones] (1580), a comedy written by the Protestant Odet de Turnèbe for the Advent festivities shortly before his premature death.[18] Like Grévin, Turnèbe uses his play both to resist and to rival Italian literature and culture; *Les Contens*, however, points to a series of new concerns about the Italians at this stage of the century, as well as a shift in attitudes towards them, which has not previously been documented.

Pierre de Larivey's *Les Six Premières Comédies facecieuses* (1579)

The small number of comedies written in the late 1560s and early 1570s might be explained by the increasing preoccupations and dangers of the civil wars; there was a reduced literary production across many genres during these years, and Mazouer is right to assert that 'la production comique ne reprend qu'à la fin des années 1570' [comic production does not resume until the end of the 1570s].[19] Still, there was little dispute at this stage that comic theatre was a viable humanist genre, capable of elevating the French literary canon. The Italian model also remained popular: the few comedies printed during this period were each inspired by Italian sources, such as La Taille's *Le Négromant* [The Necromancer] (1574), a translation of Ariosto's 1509 comedy *Il negromante*. At the courts, Catherine continued to patronise comedy: a 1571 poem by Baïf, written to apprise Charles IX of the activities of his literary academy in his absence, describes a comedy he was writing at Catherine's request:

> Je di que j'essayoy [...]
> [...] la basse Comedie
> D'un parler simple et nét
> [...]
> Terence, auteur Romain, que j'imite aujourd'huy
> Et, comme il suit Menandre, en ma langue j'ensuy;
> Ce que j'ay fait m'étant commandé de le faire
> Afin de contenter la Royne vostre mere.[20]

[I am trying out [...] | [...] low Comedy | In a clear and simple style | [...] | Terence, a Roman author, who I imitate today | And, as he followed Menander, in my language I follow him; | This is what I have been doing, being commanded so | To please the queen, your mother.]

French writers were also returning from their Italian travels with copies of Italian plays: Montaigne, for example, arrived back in France in 1580 with 'un paquet d'onze comedies' [a pack of eleven comedies].[21]

Given the continued interest in Italian comedy, it is perhaps unsurprising that Larivey turned his mind to writing *Les Six Premières Comédies facecieuses*, especially given his own interest in Italian literature and culture. Larivey spent much of his life working in Paris as secretary to the *conseiller du roi* Monsieur de Pardessus, before retiring to Troyes where he was appointed canon of the church of Saint-Estienne.[22] Along with writers such as Pierre Tamisier (1541–91) and Claude Binet (*c.* 1553–1600), Larivey formed part of the Parisian circle of what has been termed retrospectively the 'Français italianisants' [Italianizing Frenchmen], who all promoted the importance of Italian literature in France;[23] Larivey himself also completed translations into French of the short stories of Straparola and the philosophies of Firenzuola and Piccolomini.[24] Evidence suggests that Larivey himself was of Italian heritage, possibly belonging to the Giunti, a family of Florentine printers.[25] It may be that Larivey, or his ancestors, had directly gallicized their name: *Giunti* means 'the arrived', just like the French *L'Arrivee*, as it was sometimes written during his lifetime. As well as admiring Italian literature and himself coming from an Italian background, Larivey's Catholicism must also have encouraged a certain sympathy towards the presence of the Italians in France, whose most important figures were supporting the Catholic cause.[26] Yet, there are numerous indications in Larivey's 1579 collection of comedies that he had a more complex relationship with Italian sources than has previously been thought. Despite his self-professed admiration for Italian literature, in his prefatory materials Larivey makes use of a number of techniques deliberately aimed at undermining his models' achievements and at keeping the focus on his own.

Larivey's techniques for minimising the achievements of his models were so effective that it was almost three hundred years before anyone recognised his plays as translations of original Italian texts.[27] *Le Lacquais* is based on *Il ragazzo* by Lodovico Dolce; *La Veuve* on *La vedova* by Niccolò Buonaparte; *Les Esprits* on *L'aridosia* by Lorenzino de Medici; *Le Morfondu* on *La gelosia* by Antonfrancesco Grazzini; *Les Jaloux* on *I gelosi* by Vincenzo Gabbiani; and *Les Escolliers* on *La zecca* by Girolamo Razzi. Certainly, Larivey makes a number of adaptations to these Italian plays, which have been traced in some more recent studies. For instance, he gallicizes the names of people and places, erases references to Italian politics and history, and removes several of the longer Italian monologues;[28] he also replaces allusions to Italian literary figures: for example, instead of praise of Pietro Bembo in *Il ragazzo*, we find references to Ronsard and Baïf.[29] Additionally, Larivey cuts the number of scenes and some of the more minor characters, changes which have been documented in detail by Anne Rogé.[30] Despite shortening each play, however,

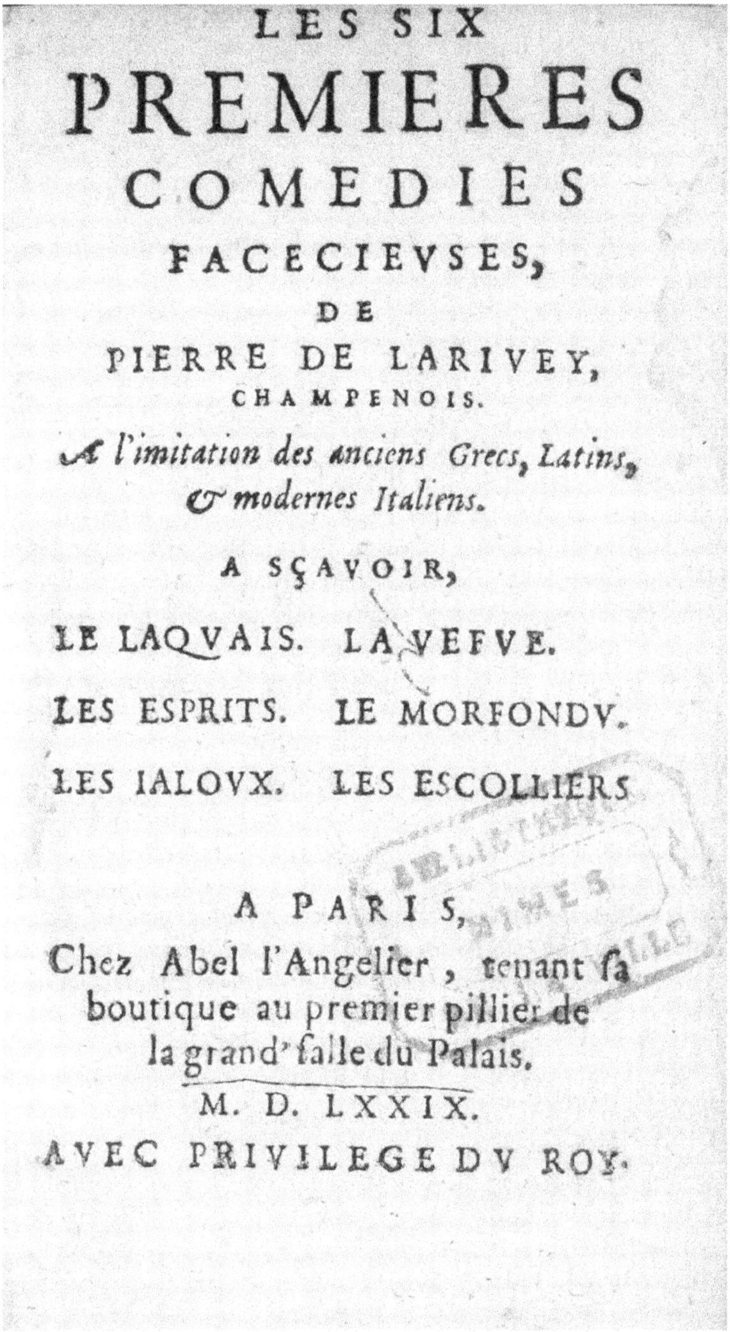
LES SIX
PREMIERES
COMEDIES
FACECIEVSES,
DE
PIERRE DE LARIVEY,
CHAMPENOIS.
A l'imitation des anciens Grecs, Latins, & modernes Italiens.
A SÇAVOIR,
LE LAQVAIS. LA VEFVE.
LES ESPRITS. LE MORFONDV.
LES IALOVX. LES ESCOLLIERS
A PARIS,
Chez Abel l'Angelier, tenant sa boutique au premier pillier de la grand' salle du Palais.
M. D. LXXIX.
AVEC PRIVILEGE DV ROY.

FIG. 6.1. Pierre de Larivey, *Les six premieres comedies facecieuses de Pierre de Larivey Champenois, à l'imitation des anciens Grecs, Latins et modernes Italiens* (Paris: Abel l'Angelier, 1579), title-page. BnF, Bibliothèque Carré d'art / Nîmes, 8344_68_01.

no plot modifications are made, and the majority of dialogue that Larivey retains is a faithful translation of the Italian original. Scholars such as Michael Freeman have acknowledged Larivey's reluctance to admit that his plays are so closely based on Italian models, also asking whether he gallicizes names and places so as to misdirect readers away from their plays' Italian sources; yet, it has gone largely unnoticed that Larivey uses his prefatory materials also to direct attention away from Italian models.[31]

As we have already seen, Jodelle and Grévin sought to minimise the appearance of their reliance on the Italians either by denying Italian influence, or by avoiding references to Italian models altogether. Larivey, on the other hand, acknowledges very openly his reliance on Italian sources. On the title-page of his collection, he advertises the comedies as written 'à l'imitation des anciens Grecs, Latins et modernes Italiens' [in imitation of the Ancient Greeks, Romans, and Modern Italians] (see figure 6.1).

In his prefatory letter to François d'Amboise, who was himself later to write comic plays, Larivey claims to have been inspired by 'Laurens de Medicis [...] François Grassin, Vincent Gabian, Jherosme Razzi, Nicolas Bonapart, Loyse Dolce, et autres'. Here he identifies each of the writers that he has translated. Yet, Larivey also nods to his inspiration by 'autres', such as 'le Cardinal Bibbiene, le Piccolomini, et l'Aretin, tous les plus excellens de leur siècle' [Cardinal Bibbiena, Piccolomini, and Aretino, all the most excellent [dramatists] of their century].[32] While Larivey does comment on his Italian sources, then, he also draws attention to the wrong models, implying that he has imitated comedies such as Bibbiena's *La Calandra* or Aretino's *Il marescalco*. In this way, as well as drawing attention to the wrong sources, he also leads his reader to the false conclusion that he has imitated creatively a range of Italian dramatists to devise his own, original comedies. In addition, his description on the title-page of his plays as imitations of ancient and modern plays strengthens this deliberate illusion that he has created new material. Again, he draws attention to the wrong models — he has used Italian sources, rather than classical comedies — and the term *imitation*, rather than *traduction*, implies that he has worked more creatively, drawing on a range of sources when writing each play. At the same time, Larivey praises the innovation of previous translators into French of classical and Italian plays: 'Je sçay qu'assez de bons ouvriers, et qui méritent beaucoup pour la promptitude de leur esprit, en ont traduict quelques unes' [I know of several hard workers, whose swiftness of spirit is praiseworthy indeed, who have translated some [comedies]].[33] Yet in his praise, he wholly separates his own work from the work of these translators, implying that his comedies belong to a different, more original category. Each of these components goes some way towards convincing the reader that Larivey has relied on Italian models far more loosely than a comparison of his plays with their Italian model would indicate.

In the same way, although Larivey mentions a range of Italian sources in his prefatory letter, he does not refer to them again in his collection. Instead, in the prefaces to individual comedies, he focuses on his alleged use of classical models, giving the impression that he has sidestepped the 'modernes Italiens' and has himself adapted ancient comedy into new and original work. In the preface to *Les Esprits*, for instance, Larivey states that '[il] a faict ceste Comedie à l'imitation et de Plaute et de Terence ensemble' [he has completed this comedy imitating a combination of Plautus and Terence].[34] Although it is true that Lorenzino de' Medici wrote *L'aridosia* in imitation of both of these classical sources, *Les Esprits*, in turn, is for the most part a translation of *L'aridosia*. By signposting Lorenzino's models, rather than declaring his own use of Lorenzino's play, Larivey again creates the impression that he has creatively transplanted the work of the ancients into an original comedy. Larivey uses his prefatory material to enhance the reader's sense of his originality in one final way: he nods repeatedly to a crisis of exemplarity. For example, again in his preface to *Les Esprits*, he describes his regret that the ancients have created such great work, leaving little left to be done: 'Il nous est impossible pouvoir parfaitement faire ou dire aucune chose, sinon ce qui a esté dict ou faict par eux [nos devanciers]' [It is impossible for us to do or to say anything perfectly, other than what they [our ancestors] have already done].[35] Again, Larivey turns the focus away from the Italian source of his play, insinuating that he himself has struggled to create original work when faced with the overwhelming precedent of the ancients. In reality, it was Lorenzino who moulded the drama of ancient models into a modern and original comedy, and Larivey who translated into French this Italian work.

Larivey's selection of comedies to translate is again suggestive of his aims to conceal his Italian sources and to make his own work appear more original. There are other comedies which must have been more of an instinctive choice: *La Calandra*, for instance, was well known in France and had not yet been translated into French; the playwright Bibbiena was also singled out for praise in Larivey's prefatory letter. Yet, Larivey decided to translate an array of far more obscure comedies. It is true, as Yvonne Bellenger has pointed out, that Larivey's ancestors, the Giunti, had printed most of these plays; however, it is difficult to believe that he did not have access to many more, especially given his familiarity with Bibbiena, Piccolomini, and Aretino.[36] Patrizia De Capitani Bertrand has also rightly suggested that Larivey intended to introduce new plays which would contain elements 'susceptibles d'enrichir la scène française' [likely to enrich the French stage].[37] As with his translations of Italian short stories and philosophy, there is no doubt that Larivey aimed to elevate his national literature with this particular work, and to expand the corpus of plays available in French. At the same time, however, he could have chosen plays which he knew to have been successful in Italian, rather than selecting comedies which were largely obscure; it is also curious that he seeks to conceal his sources, rather than very clearly setting them out, as is the case with each of his other Italian translations.[38] In 1611, Larivey added to his collection by adding another three translations of comedies: *La gostanza* [The Constant Lady] by Girolamo Razzi, *Il fedele* [The Faithful One] by Luigi Pasqualigo, and *Gl'inganni* [The Tricks] by Niccolò Secchi. Again, these plays were presented as original comedies, with no reference made to their status as translated texts; they were also obscure and so unlikely to be recognised as translations by Larivey's readership (and indeed were not recognised as such until the nineteenth century).[39]

Although the comedies that Larivey chooses to translate were little known, Lorenzino, Grazzini, and Dolce were more prominent figures than the other three authors. It is notable that while Larivey modifies the titles of the works by more notable figures, he translates far more closely the titles of comedies by minor authors: *I gelosi* [The Jealous Ones] by Gabbiani, for example, is translated as *Les Jaloux*. It is possible that Larivey took greater care to conceal his reliance on more easily identifiable figures. In the same way, Larivey does not match his translations of comedies by more prominent figures with their original Italian prefaces. While it is true that Larivey weaves into the prefaces much of his own material — such as his nods to false classical models — he also inserts lengthy sections translated from Italian prefaces, which do not match the comedy that they introduced in their original language. For instance, although *Les Esprits* is imitated from Medici's *L'aridosia*, Larivey bases much of its preface on that of Ercole Bentivoglio's *I fantasmi* [The Ghosts] (1545), also, presumably, taking his title of *Les Esprits* from Bentivoglio's play.[40]

While, as we have seen, Larivey does not count himself among previous French translators of comedy — helping to create the illusion that his own works are not translations, but imitations — he also asserts his status as the first to be writing original plays in French. In his prefatory letter, he claims that 'j'en jette les premiers fondemens' [I am laying the first foundations [for comedy]]; he also states that: 'Puis-je dire cecy sans arrogance, que je n'en au encores veu de Françoises, j'enten qui ayent esté representees, comme advenues en France' [I say this without arrogance, that I have not yet seen any French [comedies] — I mean any that have been performed — come to be in France].[41] If Larivey did not know that Jodelle's *L'Eugène* (by now also printed in Paris) had been performed, he was surely aware of the performances of Grévin's two comedies, which had been printed in numerous editions since 1561, with another possible performance taking place the year before Larivey's comedies were printed.[42] Additionally, Larivey's assertion that he knows of no previous comedies, along with the denial of his arrogance, is lifted directly from Grévin's similar statement in his own preface to *Les Esbahis*: 'Je diray ceci sans arrogance, que je suis encores à voir Tragedies et Comedies Françoises'.[43] Evidently, Larivey was aware of previous French comedies, but again intended to aggrandize his own accomplishments by strengthening the illusion that he was a precursor.

Still, it is his Italian models which he seeks most cunningly to conceal. While his attitude towards Italian sources is not openly antagonistic, his attempts to draw attention away from the texts on which he has closely relied — thereby heightening the sense of his originality, and centring the focus on his own achievements — clearly point to some element of rivalry with his models. As we have seen, Jodelle and Grévin had similar motives when writing their plays; however, Larivey uses a wholly different set of techniques to achieve his end. Previous playwrights had either avoided mentioning or denied their reliance on their Italian models; Larivey, on the other hand, does declare his use of Italian sources. Yet, he draws attention to the wrong ones — such as Bibbiena, Piccolomini, and Aretino — and presents his work in his letter, prefaces, and title-page as creative imitations of ancient and

Italian materials. In addition, he protests about the difficulty of creating original work; he also chooses more obscure comedies to translate, and changes the names of plays by more prominent figures. Larivey's Italian models, then, are hidden in plain sight. By gaining renown with his translations of these little-known plays, it is likely that he hoped himself to be recognised as a comic model, not just in France but elsewhere. As he states in his preface to *Le Lacquais*, he wrote these comedies 'affin de n'[en] aller plus chercher ailleurs' [so that they would not have to be sought out elsewhere].[44] Indeed, if his collection were to provide the basis for comic writing not just in France, but across Europe, it would be to the detriment of the Italian models which were the foundation of this very collection.

Odet de Turnèbe's *Les Contens* (1580)

While Larivey did convince readers for several centuries that his plays were original, he did not achieve his aim of inspiring fellow writers to imitate his comedies. As we shall see in the Afterword, there was a hiatus in the production of comic theatre after 1580, with the exception of very few plays. Additionally, despite Larivey's claims to be the first writer to have his comedies staged — as well as his friend Guillaume Chasble's praise that with his comedies, 'il tient les écoutans penduz à sa parole' [he kept the audience hanging on every word][45] — there is also no way of knowing whether performances of his comedies actually took place.[46] This is also the case with *Les Contens*, a comedy written in the winter of 1580 by Odet de Turnèbe, a young lawyer, magistrate, and the first president of the Cour des Monnaies. It is possible that a performance took place in these legal circles as part of the 1581 Epiphany celebrations: there are numerous references to events which took place just prior to this, as well as to a cold month of January.[47] No references to this possible performance survive, however, and six months later, Turnèbe died from a 'fièvre chaude' [hot fever] — most likely the plague — at the age of twenty-eight.[48] *Les Contens* was printed posthumously by his friend Pierre de Ravel in 1584, who spotted it by chance at a relative's house in Paris.[49] This was the first original comedy in French to be printed on its own, and not as part of a collection.[50]

While we know little of the play's reception, *Les Contens* provides us with an important insight into Turnèbe's anti-Italianism, and into contemporary attitudes towards the Italians more generally. There is scant evidence in Turnèbe's non-theatrical writings to suggest that he opposed the presence in France of the Italians; indeed, at a young age he travelled to Italy for his studies, and also wrote sonnets in fluent Italian for the humanist salon hosted by the 'dames des Roches', Catherine des Roches and her mother Madeleine.[51] Yet Turnèbe was also a Huguenot, who were increasingly averse to the Italians and to Italian culture during this period. Turnèbe's father Adrien, one of France's foremost Greek scholars, was also known for his hostility towards the Italians towards the end of his life. Attempts were made posthumously to prove that Adrien too was a Protestant, though debate is still divided; whether or not this was the case, he made public his scorn towards secular aspects of Italian culture.[52] Like Grévin, Adrien mocked their attitudes at court, singling out for criticism their duplicity, boasting, and sense of cultural superiority. As part of his *De nova captandae utilitatis e literis ratione: epistola ad Leoquernum* [Concerning the New Method of Reaping Profit from Writings: Letter to Leoquernus], for instance, he provides the would-be French poet with ironic advice:

> Si le rusé marchant est menteur asseuré,
> Et s'il sçait pallier d'un fard bien coloré
> Mille bourdes qu'il a en France rapportées
> [...]
> Si, vanteur, il sçait bien son art authoriser,
> Louer les estrangers, les François mespriser;
> Si des lettres l'honneur à luy seul il reserve
> Et desdaigne en crachant la françoise Minerve
> [...]
> Bref, d'un Italien tu auras le pelaige.[53]

[If the deceitful merchant is an assured liar, | And if he knows how to prettily cover up | The thousand fibs he has brought to France | [...] | If, braggart, he knows how to manipulate his art | To praise foreigners, and to disdain Frenchmen; | If he reserves honourable titles only for himself | And scornfully spits in the face of the French Minerva | [...] | Well, you'll fool everyone that you are Italian.]

Like his father, Odet de Turnèbe objects to the Italians' deceit and bragging; yet, as we shall see, he uses his comedy also to raise a range of criticisms absent from Adrien's work.

The plot-line of *Les Contens* is, as Norman Spector has shown, closely based on that of Grévin's *Les Esbahis*, which Turnèbe must have had to hand when writing his own play.[54] Additionally, Turnèbe takes as a model Terence, translating a number of lines from his Roman comedies.[55] Yet, like Jodelle, Grévin, and Larivey, Turnèbe also takes inspiration from the Italians. We will see that Turnèbe utilises some material from Piccolomini's comedy; he also bases some elements of the dialogue on Bibbiena's *La Calandra* and Girolamo Parabosco's *I contenti*.[56] He even takes the title of *Les Contens* from this latter play, which led scholars to believe for several hundred years that they were the same play.[57] While he imitates Italian comedy, he still uses the material as a weapon against Italian culture; he also takes inspiration from Grévin's Italian braggart soldier as a means of deriding the presence of the Italians in France. However, although both Grévin and Turnèbe have the same motives in mind, Turnèbe's soldier, Rodomont, is characterised in an entirely different way: whereas Pantaleoné in *Les Esbahis* is an Italian expatriate in France, Turnèbe's Rodomont is a French soldier eager to model his own behaviour on that of the Italians. This figure of the desperate would-be Italian reveals a number of anti-Italian sentiments which cannot be found in Grévin's comedy; Rodomont also provides a new angle on the ways in which French attitudes towards the Italians in France had undergone a shift since the early 1560s.

Italian Cultural Resistance in *Les Contens*: Chivalry

Unlike his father, Odet de Turnèbe was not active at the French court; however, he had a clear picture of the Italian influence there, which he had probably picked up from Adrien. Evidently, Turnèbe *fils* was also familiar with a range of anti-Italian works, such as the *Deux dialogues* by Estienne, who had been an admiring student of Turnèbe's father at the Collège royal, or des trois langues, as the Collège de France was variously known in his lifetime.[58] As we have seen, many of these texts outlined that Italians seemed to have taken over the court, as in Estienne's complaint: 'Pour quarante ou cinquante Italiens qu'on y voyoit autresfois, maintenant on y voit une petite Italie' [Before you might see forty or fifty Italians [at the court]; now it is a mini Italy];[59] Gentillet also blamed the prevalence of Italian culture at the court for the increased disloyalty and deceit of French courtiers: 'Plusieurs François Italianisez [sont] perfides et desloyaux, ayans apris de l'estre par la doctrine de Machiavel' [A number of Italianized Frenchmen are perfidious and disloyal, and have learned how to be so through Machiavelli's doctrine].[60] While Grévin had already alluded to Italian artifice and deceit at court, parodying the outdated Italian reliance on the troubadour tradition of seducing women through music and poetry, Turnèbe mocks this same trait in *Les Contens* as a dependence on medieval chivalry and honour. Ostentatious displays of valour are used by Rodomont, the would-be Italian character, as a means of attracting women; this behaviour had been popularised in France not only by the Italian courtiers, who considered themselves 'direct descendants' of the medieval knight, but also by the importation of and appreciation for texts such as Ariosto's *Orlando furioso*.[61] Estienne too had singled out this trait for mockery in his *Deux dialogues*, criticising the 'courtisan nouveau [qui] s'estime un bien grand cavalier | Voire entre les grands singulier' [new courtier [who] considers himself a great knight | Towering even over the greats].[62]

Rodomont embodies the Italianate courtier who 's'estime un bien grand cavalier' [considers himself a great knight], and is convinced that his shows of honour and bravery will win the love of Geneviefve. He claims that being in love will inspire him even to outdo the plights of the most famous lovers of chivalric literature:

> J'avois tousjours jusques ici pensé que tout ce que l'on lit dans [...] *Roland le Furieux* et autres Romans, fussent choses controuvées à plaisir [...]. Mais maintenant que j'esprouve en moy-mesmes, quelles sont les passions qu'une beauté cruelle peut donner, je ne m'estonne plus des armes que ces anciens preux faisoient: et me semble encores qu'il s'y portoient assez laschement. (pp. 301–02, II.4)

> [I had always thought that everything one reads in the [...] *Orlando Furioso* and in other books was just made up for the reader's pleasure [...]. But now that I myself am experiencing the passions that a cruel beauty can inflict, I am no longer surprised at the feats accomplished by the old gallant knights, and it actually seems to me that they were a bit slack in their endeavours.]

Rodomont thus pledges that to win the graces of Geneviefve he would 'tuer dix ou douze mille hommes d'armes, ou [...] prendre quelque ville impregnable' [kill ten or twelve thousand soldiers, or [...] take under siege some impregnable city]

(p. 276, 1.3); even in the epilogue, after which his shows of valiance have failed to seduce Geneviefve, he still attempts to charm the female spectators with boasts of his horsemanship: 'Et là vous pourrez cognoistre avec quelle dexterité je manie un cheval, à courbettes, au galop, à bons, à ruades, et luy donne carriere' [Just watch with what dexterity I control a horse, with a courbette, a gallop, a leap, a kick, commanding the arena] (p. 363, v.6). Rodomont has difficulty even in discussing love without using militaristic terms. He can only describe his feelings, for example, with metaphors of war: Geneviefve's expressions are '[des] coups de canon qui battent en flanc dans les bastions de mon ame' [cannonfires which flatten the bastions of my soul] (p. 275, 1.3). Rodomont's idea of love is inextricably linked with his behaviour and expressions as 'un grand cavalier'.

Although Estienne and others scorned this figure of the Italianate 'grand cavalier', the chivalric romance was also falling out of favour as the Wars of Religion grew in intensity. Michel Simonin has shown how the popularity of this genre decreased as the realities of war juxtaposed with the feats completed by imagined heroes; Turnèbe, as a Protestant, would have been particularly sceptical regarding this valorous approach to courtship made fashionable again by the Italians.[63] It is unsurprising, then, that Rodomont's attempted chivalry and grand deeds meet with no success: just as Pantaleoné fails to impress Magdalêne with his Italian serenading in *Les Esbahis*, Geneviefve is horrified by Rodomont's attempts to win her over with his boasts of military feats. Even Rodomont's valet, Nivelet, is mortified by the foreign and outdated techniques his master uses to try to seduce Geneviefve. Again turning Italian comedy into a weapon to make an anti-Italian statement, Turnèbe imitates a joke from Piccolomini's 1544 comedy *Alessandro*.[64] In Piccolomini's play, the Italian Capitan Malagigi continually spurns his servant's advice, instead dismissing it with a 'si vede ben che tu non sei prattico nelle Guerre' [obviously you know nothing about the art of war].[65] In *Les Contens*, when Nivelet urges Rodomont to adopt an approach to women more suited to the French, Rodomont rejects his advice, since Nivelet is not a soldier:

> NIVELET Monsieur les filles de Paris ne se plaisent point à ouir parler de meurtres et carnages. Elles veulent qu'on les entretienne de petits propos joyeux [...] elles vous fuyent, comme une mauvaise beste, tant vous leurs faites pœur.
> RODOMONT Je cognois à tes propos, que tu n'as gueres bien retenu ce que je t'ay monstré touchant le fait de la guerre. Car si tu eusses pris plaisir au mestier des armes, tu ne parlerois de la sorte que tu fais, et te dis bien plus que tu trouverois [...] le son des trompettes, fifres et tambours, plus harmonieux que celuy des violons, luths et espinettes. (pp. 276–77, 1.3)

> [NIVELET Sir, the women of Paris take no pleasure in hearing about murder and carnage. They want to be entertained with charming little remarks. They run away from you as though you were a wild beast — that's how scared they are of you.
> RODOMONT I can tell just from listening to you that you haven't at all taken in what I've told you about war. If you actually took pleasure in warfare, you wouldn't be talking the way you are, and I'm telling you that you'd find [...] the sounds of trumpets, fifes and drums more harmonious than those of violins, lutes, and spinets.]

While Nivelet's advice, as well as Rodomont's undaunted protests, emphasise the foolishness of trying to seduce women using the Italian chivalric approach, this dialogue also comments on Italian excess. Rodomont's reference to the 'luth' reminds readers that music and poetry, too, are useless in attracting women, possibly also harking back to the failure of Grévin's Pantaleoné to seduce Magdalêne with his lute. While the Italian approach to love is exaggerated and contrived — relying on overblown music and poetry, or else on hyperbolic claims to chivalry — French women prefer a direct and straightforward approach, with only some 'petits propos joyeux'. As in *Les Esbahis*, Turnèbe promotes an unembellished and inartificial rhetoric, reminding the reader of the long-standing pride in the links between 'frankness' and France.

Italian Cultural Resistance in *Les Contens*: Cowardice

While Turnèbe parodies Rodomont's attempts at chivalry and boasts of military success, it is also emphasised throughout that such bragging is unfounded. As we saw in Chapter 5, the Italians were accused of cowardice throughout the various paroxysms of the Wars of Religion, and their reputation for such behaviour continued to peak throughout the 1570s. Henri Estienne, in his 'Remonstrance aux autres courtisans', sets out a long diatribe against Italian cowardice, claiming that the Italians had been useless in warfare since the classical era and that the French could only rely on themselves for military success:

> On est venu à nouvelles leçons,
> Que les François aux François ont apprises,
> Et bravement en usage ils ont mises.[66]

[We have learned some new lessons, | That Frenchmen have taught to Frenchmen, | And we have bravely put them to use.]

In the same way as Grévin characterised Pantaleoné as a 'poltron courtesan', Rodomont too is a coward.[67] As well as boasting to Geneviefve, he recounts false tales of his soldierly prowess to every other character. He even introduces himself to the spectator and reader by describing at length the ways in which he has fought: 'En camp clos, armé, desarmé, à la pique, à l'espee et cappe, à l'espee et dague, à la hache, et à l'espee à deux mains' [In a camp, armed, disarmed, with a pike, with a sword and cape, with a sword and dagger, with an axe, and with a sword in each hand] (p. 275, I.3). His claims throughout the play grow increasingly exaggerated, to the point where he describes how warriors beg him to test their armour, since no weapon could possibly be as strong as Rodomont himself:

> Aussitost que quelque Capitaine veut acheter un corps de cuirasse [...] il me prie de luy faire compagnie, pour esprouver ses armes: et si elles sont si bien trempées qu'elles puissent resister à un coup de poing deschargé de toute ma force sans estre faucées, alors il les achète, s'asseurant bien qu'il n'y a mousquet qui les puisse enfoncer. (pp. 331–32, IV.2)

[As soon as some captain or another wants to buy a suit of armour [...] they beg me to go with them to try it out, and if the armour is so hardy that it can

> withstand a full-force blow from my fist, then the captain buys it, in the safe
> knowledge that no musket out there can possibly pierce it.]

In reality, Rodomont's actions are far from those of a daring warrior. When he is arrested for debt he is led meekly away 'comme une mariée' [like a bride] (p. 314, III.2); at one point Rodomont is even forced to leave the stage, since he is cold and misses his fire (p. 281, 1.4). To draw further attention to his cowardice, Turnèbe also uses irony, with Rodomont boasting of his modesty while at the same time inventing ever greater feats: 'Je ne suis homme qui prenne plaisir de me vanter: mais si ma rapière pouvoit parler, elle diroit choses qui vous feroient faire le signe de la croix' [I am not a man who delights in boasting, but if my sword could talk, it would tell you things that would make you cross yourself] (p. 332, IV.2). In the same way, the very name of Rodomont is ironic, since it is based on Orlando's boastful — though wholly fearless — enemy Rodomonte in Ariosto's *Orlando furioso*. Again, Turnèbe is taking an Italian source and using it to mock the Italians, turning the courageous figure of Rodomonte into a cowardly soldier. In this way, Turnèbe is also reinforcing the newly coined term *rodomontade* as meaning 'bragging', emphasising the boastful rather than the valiant traits of Ariosto's Italian character.[68] Turnèbe's Rodomont, then, is a warning against the foolishness of attempting to imitate Italian culture in France, and a reminder that the empty bragging of the Italians is not a characteristic to be replicated.

Although Grévin indicates that Pantaleoné is wearing a soldier's cape and hat, capitalising on the visual elements of comedy to emphasise his cowardice, Turnèbe is even more artful in using these elements for such an effect. The servant Antoine is scornful of the fact that Rodomont owns only a 'vieil harnois tout descloué, et quelque meschante haridelle qu'encores possible il doit' [an old and raggedy suit of armour, and some old nag that he is still paying off] (p. 279, 1.4); in other scenes Rodomont is dressed in a 'habit de velour, lequel il porte autant meschant que bon' [velvet suit, which has long seen better days] (p. 274, 1.2). In the same way as Pantaleoné's lute was old and untuned, while such elaborate clothes indicate that Rodomont is desperate to impress others with his appearance, further proving himself to be great soldier, in their dilapidated condition they are far from fooling even the servant character. As well as giving Rodomont overblown, though tattered, clothing, Turnèbe has equipped Rodomont with an excessive moustache: he shows off '[des] grandes moustaches noires, retroussées en dents de sanglier' [a huge black moustache, all twisted up like a boar's tusks] (p. 311, III.1). A moustache was not only regarded as an indication of masculinity but was also a feature typical of great soldiers, often parodied in the *commedia dell'arte* (figure 6.2).

Henri Estienne, too, had recently mocked the fashion in France for growing a moustache, and many others associated it with the Italians: the French word *moustache* even derived from the Italian *mostaccio*.[69] Since Rodomont's only skills are in boasting, and he is shown to be cowardly wherever possible, this outward symbol of masculinity and military success only emphasises his artificiality. In addition to his costume, Turnèbe creates a caricature of the cowardly Italian soldier through Rodomont's gestures, including lines which the actor could exploit for comic effect:

FIG. 6.2. A reimagining of a 1577 'Capitan Spavento', illustrated by the French writer and
artist Maurice Sand, in which the 'Capitan' draws special attention to his moustache,
in Maurice Sand, *Masques et bouffons: comédie italienne*, 2 vols (Paris: Michel Lévy Frères,
1860), I, 174. Facsimile of a copy held in the British Library, 11795.g.14.

'Mettant bravement la main à ma flamberge, je les ay receus d'une telle façon, que d'une imbroncade que j'ay ruee au milieu de la pance du premier, je l'ay jetté tout plat dans le ruisseau' [Bravely putting my hand on my sword, I took them in an impressive fashion: with an *imbroccata* I plunged it right in the stomach of the first soldier, with such force that I threw him straight into the river] (p. 330, IV.2). The actor could accompany his boasting with overblown gestures, which are again at odds with Rodomont's behaviour in the play, further emphasising his cowardice. Additionally, such exaggerated gestures were associated with the Italians in France during these years, and writers had started to express their irritation that some French citizens were imitating these actions. Estienne, for example, despaired of the French courtiers whose gestures replicated this Italian style: 'Je me suis avisé de vous demander si les François n'italianizoyent point quant aux gestes aussi' [I am minded to ask you whether the French are Italianising themselves even in their gestures].[70] Rodomont's artificial and contrived boastings, appearance, and actions impress nobody; again, this character is used by Turnèbe as a means of showing to be foolish French attempts to imitate Italian behaviour.

Resistance to the Catholics in *Les Contens*

As we saw in Chapter 5, Grévin used *Les Esbahis* as anti-Catholic propaganda, seeking to show the Italians' alleged faith to be a convenient mode of masking their corrupt ends with a semblance of piety. Some scholars have claimed that *Les Contens* contains no anti-clericalism; however, this is untrue.[71] Certainly, the anti-Catholic sentiments in the play are less palpable, which may be accounted for by the increased dangers presented to the Protestants in France: still, while religious reference are scarcer in *Les Contens*, the play does function as a work of anti-Catholic — and, by extension, anti-Italian — rhetoric. We can identify some more or less innocuous insults: the character Louyse, for example, taunts the lengthy Dominican style of preaching: 'Que le sermon m'a ennuié ceste matinee: jamais je n'ay pensé voir l'heure que ce Jacobin sortiroit de chaire' [The sermon bored me to tears this morning: I never thought I'd see the day when that Jacobin left the pulpit] (p. 293, II.2). Additionally, in the same way as Grévin ensures that the Italian Pantaleoné is the most immoral of all the characters, Rodomont is also scorned for his corrupt actions. As well as being untrustworthy, presenting a false appearance, he is both squandering and unkind. While spending all of his money 'aux dez, aux Bordeaux et aux cabarets' [on gambling, brothels, and public houses] (p. 284, I.6), for instance, he leaves his valet Nivelet without adequate clothing: Nivelet complains of 'ces vieux escarpins tous descousus qu'il me donne, apres les avoir portez un an ou deux, [qui] ne me peuvent gueres bien remparer la plante des pieds contre le froid et les boues' [the thin old shoes which he gives me, half falling apart after he has worn them for a year or two, which barely protect the soles of my feet from the cold and the mud] (p. 284, I.2). The other characters refer to Rodomont throughout the play as a 'pendart' [someone who should be hanged]; Basile also remarks that if Geneviefve marries Rodomont, 'elle pourroit bien dire que son douaire seroit assigné sur un gibet: car je pense que ce beau traine-gaine n'a point de plus certain heritage' [she might as well cede her dowry to the gallows, for that is most certainly the fate of that old lout] (p. 279, I.4). Like Grévin, by transforming his would-be Italian figure into the play's most immoral character, Turnèbe is alluding to the hypocrisy of the Italians in France, who were strongly associated with devout Catholicism.

Turnèbe also points out the hypocrisy inherent to a number of specifically Catholic practices, showing how they are employed for transgressive purposes. He demonstrates that organised worship is a subterfuge for immorality: Basile, for instance, is able illicitly to visit Geneviefve's bedroom while her mother is at church; the character Alix, too, spends her holiday working as a prostitute while telling her husband that she is on a pilgrimage (p. 328, IV.1). Confession is used to persuade Geneviefve to commit sexual acts with her next-door neighbour, as the cunning Françoise solemnly advises that her confessor has taught that 'il fault aymer son prochain comme soy mesme' [you must love your neighbour like yourself] (p. 288, I.7); sermons, too, are used to justify corrupt ends, and are employed by Françoise to prove her wisdom and to convince Geneviefve to have sex with Basile: 'Mesme j'ay ouy prescher cest advent dernier, que le diable est fin, pour ce qu'il est vieil' [As I heard preached in a sermon last Advent, the devil is shrewd, for his is old] (p. 287, I.7). The eavesdropping Nivelet repeats to the audience how easy it is to 'faire son profit des sermons' [use sermons for one's profit] (p. 287, I.7), adding that Françoise must have been taught her own scheming ways: 'Je croy que ceste vieille sempiternelle a esté à l'eschole de quelque frere frapart' [I'm sure that this loose-lipped old witch must have been schooled by some merry friar] (p. 286, I.7). While this play contains fewer anti-Catholic references than *Les Esbahis*, many insults are unmistakeable; Turnèbe's attempts to undermine the Catholic faith in this comedy also help to explain his strongly anti-Italian position.

Reactions to Rodomont

We examined in Chapter 5 the contempt of the native French characters towards Pantaleoné in *Les Esbahis*: they show him to be unwelcome at each opportunity, deliver a violent invective against him, and finally force his exit from the stage. As well as mocking Pantaleoné's artifice, the French characters also emphasise that they are too canny to be misled by Italian deceit, in turn reminding the readers and spectators to be wary of such trickery and contrivance. Given that the presence of the Italians in France was no less contested by the late 1570s, and that elements such as their behaviour at court, their purported cowardice, and their identification with Catholicism were meeting with ever more explicit aversion, we might expect the characters in *Les Contens* to show the same contempt for Rodomont as is shown towards Pantaleoné. Certainly, the characters are clear from Act I that they will not be deceived by Rodomont's contrivance and pretence: they refer to him as a 'beau Capitaine de trois cuittes' [gimcrack Captain] (p. 279, I.4) and an 'happelourde' [bigmouth bogus] (p. 279, I.4).[72] Yet, their other reactions to Rodomont are different in tone from reactions to Pantaleoné in *Les Esbahis*. There are no diatribes against him and no inferences that his behaviour is unwelcome in France; rather, he is the subject of ridicule, and never a direct subject: insults are made stealthily, or in a way in which he does not understand. Rodomont is not only unsuccessful in his bid to replicate supposedly Italian, artificial behaviour: dissimulations are turned against him, and he is himself shown to be the dupe.

Turnèbe employs a number of techniques to turn dissimulations against Rodomont, each without his knowledge. Firstly, hyperbole is used to show the foolishness of Rodomont's attempts at chivalry. For instance, Alfonse's reply to Rodomont's eventual refusal to marry Geneviefve is not meant to be taken literally: 'C'est bien loing de soustenir leur honneur [...] ainsi que faisoient les anciens chevaliers de la table ronde' [This is a far cry from sheltering ladies' honour [...] as the old knights of the round table used to do] (p. 358, v.5). While the other characters — as well as the audience — would take to be tongue-in-cheek Alfonse's comment, Rodomont takes the criticism at face value, and is extremely offended at this apparent slight to his honour. Rodomont's hurt reaction only intensifies the humour for onlookers, showing to be even more ridiculous the exaggeratedness of his chivalrous behaviour. A second technique used to mock Rodomont is irony. Eustache, for example, responds sarcastically to each of Rodomont's false tales of valour: 'Je n'avois encores esté desjeuné de telles prouesses, et ne les croyois pas facilement, si un autre me les racontoit, Dieu me le veuille pardoner' [I have never heard such exploits, and would not easily believe them if I heard them from anyone else's lips, may God forgive me] (p. 332, IV.2). Although Eustache's irony would make the audience laugh, Rodomont takes this sarcasm at face value, and his smug reaction and obliviousness to such insults again shows his behaviour to be ridiculous. Finally, Turnèbe uses asides to enhance the sense that the audience is participating in jokes about Rodomont: when Eustache dismisses Rodomont's boasts, for example, delivering the aside 'je vous en croy sans jurer, mais non pas demain' [I won't believe your stories anytime soon], he repeats it to Rodomont as 'un chascun doit bien craindre vostre main' [Any man would fear such a hand] (p. 333, IV.2). Rather than questioning Eustache's response, Rodomont is satisfied at the others' apparent terror of him: again, the characters and the audience are party to a joke about Rodomont, from which he is himself excluded. Whereas in *Les Esbahis* Pantaleoné is a direct target of attack by the other characters, much of the ridicule of Rodomont takes place without his knowledge, and Rodomont's ignorance in itself heightens the humour. Rodomont is presented more as an unthreatening source of amusement than as an entity to be forced out of France. While Grévin showed the Italians themselves to be unwelcome in France, Turnèbe uses a different approach: he parodies the 'François italianisants' at the courts, showing that imitation of Italian behaviour is practised only by those who are too foolish to realise how ridiculous it is. The audience and readers are also invited to join in the mockery of such behaviour, and are in turn encouraged to avoid such behaviour themselves.

A final deterrent against the imitation of Italian behaviour in France is the way in which money is presented. As we have seen, the commercial success of the

Italians was causing widespread resentment in France at this time. As a would-be Italian, Rodomont is clearly attempting to give the impression of affluence: he dresses himself up in velvet and armour, and also hires Nivelet as his valet. Yet, his clothes are run-down and he never has money to pay Nivelet, who complains that Rodomont '[n'a] jamais assemblé cent escus en une bourse' [has never put a hundred écus in one purse] (p. 284, 1.6). Indeed, the whole of Paris seems to know about Rodomont's inability to save money: 'Quand on veut parler d'un homme liberal, voire plustost prodigue, on n'use plus d'autre comparaison, sinon que l'on dit, il ressemble au Capitaine Rodomont' [When a description is needed of a liberal — nay, prodigal — man, the only comparison needed is with Captain Rodomont] (p. 284, 1.6); at the end of the play, Rodomont is also jailed for debt. Turnèbe is indicating that, despite the famous wealth of the Italians, imitation of Italian behaviour will not make one rich; in this play, in fact, it is those who avoid Italian behaviour who are most prosperous. Basile, for instance, is often praised for his resourcefulness: 'Vrayement je ne m'estonne pas si le Seigneur Basile est en grace, puis il a le bruit d'estre riche, et de ne faire folles dispenses' [Truly, I am not surprised that Seigneur Basile is in favour, since he is rumoured to be rich, and to avoid crazy spending] (p. 284, 1.6). The French merchant Thomas also cheats Rodomont himself out of money, selling Rodomont's goods for twice their value (p. 327, IV.I).[73] Again, the French characters are entirely unthreatened by Rodomont, and manage even to turn his false appearance back on him. Ultimately, Turnèbe is demonstrating how the imitation of Italian behaviour in France serves no purpose, and may even be counterproductive: Rodomont has gained nothing from his would-be Italianisms, and while the other characters treat him as a source of amusement, they also take advantage of his foolish behaviour. As an example that there are no financial benefits to imitating Italian culture in France — and indeed, that these actions leave one open both to ridicule and to double-dealing — Rodomont serves as a final dissuasion to the audience and readers from such behaviour, also illustrating the advantages of embracing their own French culture.

Italian Cultural Rivalry in Les Contens: Literature

Grévin used Les Esbahis as a vehicle for drawing attention away from Italian culture, thereby establishing his own comedy as a forerunner of the genre; we examined his revisions to an intended new edition of the play, which both removed references to precedents and emphasised his own innovation. Despite making use of Italian sources for Les Contens — we examined his employment of Piccolomini, Bibbiena, and Parabosco, for instance — Turnèbe, too, endeavours to prove his originality in writing this play, while at the same time minimising the appearance of any Italian influence. Like Grévin, Turnèbe ultimately intends to establish himself as a model for later playwrights, while showing the superiority of French writing to its Italian counterpart. To fulfil these aims Turnèbe uses a number of techniques which are similar to those used by Grévin and Jodelle; however, he takes them to a new level, expanding on them to convey more forcefully his message.

Scholars such as Eugène Lintilhac acknowledged many years ago that this comedy is 'très française' [very French]; yet, no criticism has set out how Turnèbe achieves this effect.[74] We saw in Chapter 5 that Grévin sought to draw attention away from the play's Italian models — and to its French location — by giving Les Esbahis a highly recognisable setting: the Carrefour Saint-Séverin. This setting also linked to the location of his other comedy, La Trésorière, centring the emphasis on Grévin's own corpus of work, and thus on France. Turnèbe, too, sets his comedy in locations which would have been well known to his spectators and readers, thereby focusing attention on the French context of this play.[75] However, whereas Grévin refers only to the Carrefour Saint-Séverin, Turnèbe names a wide range of locations. Antoine, for instance, provides a lengthy description of his trip around Paris, where he has been running to try to find Françoise: 'Apres j'ay passé par les blancs manteaux, les Billettes, Sainte Croix, et m'en suis venu à Saint Merry, Saint Jacques, Saint Eustache, Saint Germain, et autres Eglises et lieux de devotion' [After this, I passed by [Notre-Dame-des-]Blancs Manteaux, the [Cloître des] Billettes, Sainte-Croix, and then I came to Saint Merry, Saint Jacques, Saint Eustache, Saint Germain, and other churches and places of devotion] (p. 346, v.1). Here Turnèbe goes to even greater lengths than Grévin to ensure that his comedy is unmistakeably Parisian; additionally, in Antoine's description of his trip there is also an inside joke for his Parisian audience. The churches he visits are at opposite ends of the city, meaning that he took a route which was unnecessarily convoluted (figure 6.3).[76] This joke — which is made for the benefit of the play's Parisian spectators or readers, excluding any other audiences — both helps to emphasise the French context of Turnèbe's play and to draw attention away from its Italian influences.

Another way in which Turnèbe ensures that his play is 'très française' is to refer to contemporary, real-life situations, which only his Parisian readers or spectators would understand. For instance, after having discovered that Basile has taken her daughter's virginity, Louyse exclaims: 'Dois-je envoyer querir le commissaire? Si je le mets en justice un chascun se rira de moy, et qui plus est, on me jouera aux pois pillez et à la bazoche' [Should I send for the sergeant? If I bring him to justice everyone will laugh at me, and what's more, they'll put me in a comedy on the stage] (p. 321, III.7). Evidently, Louyse and her dilemma are already being portrayed in comedy: it is likely, then, that Turnèbe is referring ironically to a real-life event which the spectators or readers would recognise. Like the elaborate route through Paris taken by Antoine, this inside joke helps to centre attention on the French context of the play, at the same time minimising the appearance of Italian influences.

As we saw in Chapter 5, Grévin deliberately avoided all references to Italian literature in his paratextual materials, with the aim of redirecting the focus away from his reliance on Italian models. In the same way, Turnèbe in Les Contens makes no mention of Italian sources in his prologue, instead concentrating on flattering potential women spectators or readers, praising their 'esprit vif' [lively spirit] and 'capacité d'entendement' [reasoning skills] (p. 267, 'Prologue'). Yet, another paratextual source offers a sharper insight into Turnèbe's relationship with his models: this is a sonnet, included as a postscript in the posthumous edition printed

Lutetia Parisiorum urbs, toto orbe celeberrima notissimaque caput regni Franciæ.   Pl. VII

FIG. 6.3. I have edited Sebastian Münster's map of Paris (previously seen in Chapter 5) to show the needlessly complicated route of the churches visited by Antoine in his attempt to locate Françoise, in Sebastian Münster, *Cosmographia* (Basle: Heinrich Petti, 1550), pp. 88–89. Reproduced with the permission of the David Rumsey Map Collection, David Rumsey Map Center, Stanford Libraries.

by Turnèbe's friend Ravel:

> Resjouy-toy Paris œil unique de France,
> Un de tes citoyens monte sur l'eschafaut
> Du Theatre François, à qui point il ne chaut
> De ceder la couronne au Comique Terence
> [...]
> Nous trouverons enfin que de Tournebu vault
> Trop plus que l'Africain, et que son eloquence.
> Terence ne faisoit luy seul son beau Latin,
> Deux grands seigneurs romains avoient part au butin
> [...]
> Il n'est ainsi du nostre, ains il a ce Bonheur
> Qu'il n'a second ny tiers qui partisse l'honneur,
> N'ayant pour compagnons Scipion ne Lelie. (p. 365, 'Sonnet')

[Rejoice, Paris, the only eye of France, | One of your citizens has ascended the stage | Of the French theatre, one to whom nobody has thought | Of granting the crown of comic Terence | [...] | We would in the end find that Turnèbe is worth | Far more than the African and his eloquence. | Terence did not create his beautiful Latin alone, | Two great Roman masters took a share in these spoils | [...] | This is not the case with our writer, who thus has the fortune | Of sharing the honour with no second or third author, | Having no Scipio or Laelius for his companions.]

Despite being the only instance of a postscript in sixteenth-century French comedy, it has been commented on by few scholars. It is possible that this sonnet was written in the third-person by Turnèbe; however, it is more likely that it was composed by his friend Ravel, specifically for inclusion in the first, posthumous edition. In either case, it is evident that the author sought to make the case for Turnèbe as the first original French playwright. We saw in Chapters 4 and 5 that both Jodelle and Grévin attempted to prove their innovation, Jodelle maintaining that he borrowed neither from ancient nor contemporary drama and Grévin glossing over all references to other playwrights in his 1567 amendments. Here Turnèbe, or indeed Ravel, bypasses all modern writers of comedy, while at the same time dismissing and devaluing the achievements of the ancients.

This sonnet firstly presents Turnèbe as a forerunner of comedy in France by inviting Paris to rejoice in the fact that Turnèbe has ascended 'l'eschafaut | Du Theatre François'. By calling readers to celebrate this accomplishment, the insinuation is that Turnèbe's work is unprecedented, and that citizens of Paris have been impatient for this overdue triumph. Given that Turnèbe almost certainly had to hand Grévin's play when composing *Les Contens*, and that Ravel must surely have known of the works of Grévin and Larivey — indeed, the wording of this claim also indicates that he knew of Jodelle's comedy — this invitation is clearly an attempt to aggrandize Turnèbe's achievement, in a bid to present him retrospectively to readers as the first original French playwright.[77] Additionally, this sonnet attempts not only to show that Turnèbe is the first in France to create original comedy, but also that he is the first to reinvent classical comic theatre: the writer laments that nobody has considered turning over to Turnèbe Terence's crown — presumably, the laurel wreath used to indicate literary accomplishment — in recognition of his status as a comic writer ('à qui point il ne chaut | De ceder la couronne au Comique Terence'). Turnèbe is presented as the only contemporary writer deserving of the accolades afforded to Terence, and the only worthy reinventor of classical comedy. There is no nod to the Italians as intermediaries between ancient and contemporary, nor is there any mention of the extensive use made by Turnèbe of Italian sources. Indeed, it is again even through an Italian genre, the sonnet, that the Italians' own achievements are diminished.[78]

The second half of the sonnet further draws attention away from Italian comic models, and also from contemporary French predecessors, with a description of how Turnèbe has worked alone, taking no support or guidance from other sources. It is at this point that the writer of the sonnet suggests that Turnèbe is deserving of even greater recognition than Terence, since Terence was assisted in writing his comedies: 'Deux grands seigneurs romains avoient part au butin'. These 'deux seigneurs' denote 'Scipion [et] Lelie', considered by authors such as Donatus, Cicero, and Quintilian to have collaborated with Terence on his comedies, in spite of

Terence's protests to the contrary in the prologue to *Adelphoe* (160 BCE). This same accusation had been reignited by Montaigne in the first book of the *Essais*, printed several months before Turnèbe wrote his play.[79] While Jodelle had denied the influences of his classical ancestors, and Grévin had omitted references to ancient sources, in this sonnet Terence's achievements are openly dismissed, and are used as a means of aggrandizing Turnèbe's work. Given Turnèbe's reliance on both classical and contemporary sources, his innovation is clearly overstated; however, this sonnet provides yet further evidence that dramatists in this period were keen to claim comic theatre not only for themselves, but for France. While this poem puts forward a more forceful case than the ways in which Jodelle and Grévin explore their relationships with their models, it constitutes yet another attempt to escape from the overshadowing tradition of the ancients and the Italians, using the printing of this play as a means of making a name for French writers.

Italian Cultural Rivalry in *Les Contens*: Language

It is finally worth exploring Turnèbe's attempts to show the superiority of the French language to Italian. He uses several techniques in order to achieve this aim, the first of which resembles Grévin's bid to prove that French surpasses the Italian language, but which Turnèbe again takes to a new extreme. We saw in Chapter 5 that Grévin, pre-empting the advice of Henri Estienne, employed only Italian lexis which relates to either foolish or immoral concepts — such as *forfante* or *ruffien* — reflecting the characteristics which he considered to be typically Italian. Turnèbe replicates this same technique, employing only Italian terms which denote negative concepts. Many of these are absent from *Les Esbahis*: Turnèbe is the first comic writer to use, for instance, 'bravade' (p. 355, v.4) from *bravado*, and 'chiourme' (p. 333, IV.2) from *ciurma* [riffraff]. Again, being that terms denoting negative concepts are the only words gallicised from the Italian, the impression is given that the Italians are associated with the characteristics they denote. Yet, unlike Grévin, Turnèbe is so eager to draw attention to these characteristics that he sometimes gallicises words which entirely lose their meaning in translation. For instance, Florindo Cerreta has observed that Turnèbe transposes Bibbiena's term 'barbafiorito' [flowery-beard] directly into 'barbefleurie'.[80] The unusual term 'barbafiorito', however, is only used in *La Calandra* because the character Ruffo continually mixes it up with *ermafrodito* [hermaphrodite], with which it rhymes. When Louyse then mistakenly uses 'barbefleurie' in *Les Contens*, the joke is anticlimactic because *barbefleurie* sounds little like *hermafrodites*.[81] Although Turnèbe seeks to show to be ridiculous the Italian language and culture by gallicising Italian terms, his choices are sometimes so specialized that some would not have the intended humorous impact; indeed, it is doubtful that they would even be understood by the audience or readers.

   Although Estienne promoted the technique of using only Italian words which indicated foolish concepts, we saw that he advised against using any Italian militaristic terms, in case future readers assumed that the Italians were superior to the French in warfare. Turnèbe disregards this recommendation in *Les Contens* and instead employs a proliferation of Italian terminology related to warfare and the military. Each of these terms, which appear throughout, are used by the would-be Italian Rodomont: we see for instance the term 'bastion' (p. 275, I.3) from *bastione*, and 'embuche' (p. 342, IV.5) from *imboscata* [ambush].[82] As though to draw further attention to the fact that each of these terms derives from the Italian, Turnèbe also incorporates into the play words such as 'imbroncade' (p. 330, IV.2) a hapax borrowed from *imbroccata* [thrust], and 'lancepessade' (p. 331, IV.2) from *lanciaspezzata* [lance corporal], which later in the century became *anspessade*. These terms are so specialized that it is likely that Turnèbe coined them himself.[83] While Turnèbe takes the opposite action to what Estienne recommends in the *Deux dialogues*, the proliferation, length, and precision of these terms are again aimed at proving to be ridiculous the Italian language and culture. Since they are each pronounced by Rodomont, who pairs them with his bragging, overblown costumes and gestures, and a series of cowardly actions, these long and ornate terms are shown to be empty and meaningless. Again, the Italian culture — as well as its language — is shown to be artificial and untrustworthy: Turnèbe seeks to demonstrate that while it may be flamboyant, there is little of substance beneath its surface.

As a counterpoint to the supposed showiness of the Italian language, and reflecting Grévin's reinforcement of the emblematic 'frankness' of French, Turnèbe uses a noticeably straightforward and unaffected style throughout his comedy, emphasised by a frequent use of idioms.[84] This style was striking even to near contemporaries: Charles Maupas, in his 1626 edition of the comedy, renamed *Les Desguisez* [Those in Disguise] for reasons unknown, praises Turnèbe's forthright and unadorned style, pointing out to the reader that the play might even be useful in allowing the reader to pick up various colloquialisms: 'Tissue de plusieurs beaux traicts et façons de parler de nostre langue [*Les Contens* enseigne] quelques formules de parler et Compliments François'[85] [Formed from numerous excellent remarks and modes of expression from our language [*Les Contens* teaches] several French turns of phrase and ways of speaking].[86] Turnèbe's straightforward style and natural flow of speech in his comedy is emphasised by his use of prose, and made even more distinct in comparison to writers such as Jodelle, who had in their plays employed the medieval verse form.[87] This prose style is, of course, imitated from the Italians: again, Turnèbe is using Italian sources as a means not only of creating his own comedy but also of showing to be superior the natural and unaffected French language. By juxtaposing his straightforward French style with ornate Italian terminology, Turnèbe demonstrates to spectators and readers that fashionable Italianate rhetoric and turns of phrase should be dismissed in favour of their frank, native style.

While scholars have long noted that anti-Italian sentiments were circulated in this period in literary forms such as the dialogue (e.g. Estienne's *Deux dialogues*) and the political treatise (e.g. Gentillet's *Anti-Machiavel*), the recently revived genre of comic theatre was also employed as a means of denigrating not only the Italians, but also the presence of Italian language and culture in France. Writers turned to comic theatre as a practice capable of elevating the cultural, political, and literary status of France, as well as of resisting and rivalling the commanding influence of the Italian peninsula. Yet, the Italians themselves had been a key intermediary between classical and contemporary in the emergence in France of comic drama; in this way, French writers were effectively turning an Italian genre against the Italians themselves. Since the reinvention of comedy in France, writers were increasingly creative and ambitious in the ways in which they transformed drama into an anti-Italian weapon, although no evidence suggests that the comedies either of Grévin or Turnèbe functioned successfully as impactful propaganda. As in the case of *Les Esbahis*, there are no indications of an Italian response to *Les Contens*, though the play was sufficiently well known for it to be reprinted again in Maupas's 1626 edition.

Despite the anti-Italianism inherent to the play, the French characters react to Rodomont in a way in which we might not expect. Although the characters in *Les Esbahis* treat Pantaleoné with contempt, in *Les Contens* Rodomont is mocked surreptitiously, while the protagonists show that they are entirely unthreatened by him. The influence of the Italians in France was still pervasive during these years, and although Turnèbe himself was not directly involved in courtly life, it is evident that he knew of and resented the bids of his compatriots to imitate the Italian expatriates. Yet, he uses a different strategy to Grévin: by showing that Rodomont is indirectly mocked, rather than openly driven out, Turnèbe urges the French courtier against the ignorance of imitating Italian culture. The range of techniques implemented in this comedy, which both adapt and expand on the nationalist propaganda of previous playwrights — as well as on the drama of the Italian playwrights themselves — is testament to the fact that French writers by this stage were far more adept at working with comic theatre and with their sources: clearly, dramatists were sufficiently skilled so as to turn humanist comedy to political ends, not only imitating Italian theatre but manipulating it at will to tell a new story. The analysis of these new stories in Part III has helped to provide a different perspective not only on the resistance to the presence of Italian culture in France, but also on the aspirations of French writers to rival Italian culture on a national and international scale. Since interest in comedy was revived in France forty years previously, admiration for the Italians had turned into antagonism; Italian drama, too, was transformed from a paragon to be replicated into a parody of the Italians themselves. Through the enmity and ingenuity of their French successors, the Italians — over four decades of ambition, imitation, and experimentation — were at this point the subjects of their own jokes.

Notes to Chapter 6

1. This figure is only an estimate: for the difficulty of producing exact numbers of deaths in the Massacre, see Harry Leonard, 'The Huguenots and the Bartholomew's Massacre', in *The Huguenots: History and Memory in Transnational Context: Essays in Honour of Walter C. Utt*, ed. by David J. B. Trim (Leiden: Brill, 2011), pp. 43–67 (p. 43).

2. Niccolò Tommaseo, *Relations des ambassadeurs vénitiens sur les affaires du France au XVIe siècle*, 2 vols (Paris: Imprimerie Royale, 1838), I, 243. Also cited in Smith, *The Anti-courtier Trend in Sixteenth-century French Literature*, p. 155.

3. For more detail on France's debts during these years, see Frederic Baumgartner, *Henri II: King of France 1547–1559* (Durham, NC: Duke University Press, 1988), p. 247.

4. These restrictions are documented in François-Jacques Chasles, *Dictionaire universel, chronologique, et historique, de justice, police, et finances*, 3 vols (Paris: Claude Robustel, 1725), II, 368.

5. Gascon, *Grand commerce et vie urbaine au XVIe siècle*, I, 108–09.

6. Listed at the time as 'accoustrements pour faire momeries' [garb for putting on plays]. These lists are reproduced in Marc Brésard, *Les Foires de Lyon aux quinzième et seizième siècles* (Paris: École de Chartes, 1914), p. 195.

7. Antoine du Verdier, *Prosopographie* (Lyons: Antoine Gryphe, 1573), p. 491.

8. For more information on these taxes see Smith, *The Anti-courtier Trend in Sixteenth-century French Literature*, p. 155.

9. Ibid., p. 206; Balsamo, 'L'Italianisme lyonnais et l'illustration de la langue française', p. 212.

10. For more information, see Yates, *The French Academies of the Sixteenth Century*, p. 2.

11. Jacqueline Boucher, *La Cour de Henri III* (Rennes: Ouest-France, 1986), p. 27.

12. Yver, *Le Printemps d'Yver*, [s.n.] ('Lettre au favorable et bienveillant lecteur').

13. Jean-Papire Masson, *Vitae trium hetruriae procerum Dantis, Petrarchae, Boccacii* (Paris: Denis du Pré, 1587).

14. Gabriel Pannonius, *Petit vocabulaire en langue françoise et italienne* (Lyons: Roger de Brey, 1578). See Jean Balsamo, Vito Castiglione Minischetti, and Giovanni Dotoli, *Les Traductions de l'italien en français au XVIe siècle* (Fasano: Schena, 2009), p. 329.

15. Heller, *Anti-Italianism in Sixteenth-century France*, pp. 80–81.

16. See Gustave Lanson, 'Études sur les origines de la tragédie classique en France: comment s'est opérée la substitution de la tragédie aux mystères et moralités', *Revue d'Histoire littéraire de la France*, 2 (1903), 177–231 (p. 205).

17. All Larivey references are from Pierre de Larivey, *Théâtre complet: Les six premieres comedies facecieuses (Le Laquais, La Veuve, Les Esprits)* (Paris: Classiques Garnier, 2011–18).

18. All references to *Les Contens* are from Charles Mazouer's edition, in *La Comédie à l'époque d'Henri III (1580–1589)*, ed. by Mazouer, 2.8 (2017), 229–366. Though Turnèbe never openly declared himself a Protestant, his Huguenot views are clearly exemplified throughout his 'Sonets sur les ruines de Luzignan par Odet de Tournebu', printed posthumously in Catherine des Roches, *La Puce de Madame des Roches* (Paris: Abel L'Angelier, 1582), pp. 71^v–74^v.

19. *La Comédie à l'époque d'Henri III*, ed. by Mazouer, p. 238.

20. Jean-Antoine de Baïf, *Poésies choisies*, ed. by Louis Becq de Fouquières (Paris: Charpentier, 1874), p. 52. This poem was most likely written in 1571, since it also refers to the story of the king quelling the sound of growling dogs, an analogy of the issues faced by the Academy during that year. For more information, see Yates, *The French Academies of the Sixteenth Century*, p. 61, n. 1.

21. Michel de Montaigne, *Journal de voyage en Italie*, ed. by Maurice Rat (Paris: Garnier, 1955), p. 192.

22. Madeleine Lazard and Luigia Zilli, 'Introduction', in Pierre de Larivey, *Le Lacquais*, ed. by Madeleine Lazard and Luigia Zilli (Paris: Nizet, 1987), p. 9.

23. A fuller description of the 'Français italianisants' in the group can be found in Jean Balsamo, 'Larivey traducteur de *L'Institution Morale*', in *Pierre de Larivey, Champenois: chanoine, traducteur, auteur de comédies et astrologue (1541–1619)*, ed. by Yvonne Bellenger (Paris: Klincksieck, 1993), pp. 73–81 (pp. 77–78).

24. Giovanni Francesco Straparola, *Les facecieuses nuictz de Straparole*, trans. by Pierre de Larivey (Paris: Abel L'Angelier, 1576); Agnolo Firenzuola, *Deux livres de filosofie fabuleuse de M. A. Firenzuola*, trans. by Pierre de Larivey (Lyons: Benoist Rigaud, 1579); Alessandro Piccolomini, *La philosophie et institution morale d'Alexandre Piccolomini*, trans. by Pierre de Larivey (Paris: Abel L'Angelier, 1581).

25. The earliest reference to Larivey's ancestry is by eighteenth-century scholar Pierre-Jean Grosley, who describes Larivey as an 'ayeul de la famille des Giunti de Florence, ayant passé en France [et qui] avoit pris le nom de l'Arrivé qui rend le Giunto Italien' [descendant of the Florentine Giunti family, having travelled through France and [who] took the name of L'Arrivé, the equivalent of the Italian Giunto]. Grosley, *Mémoires historiques et critiques pour l'histoire de Troyes*, 2 vols (Paris: Veuve Duchesne, 1774), II, 419. Louis Morin suggests that the Giunti family may have been present in France since the thirteenth century: Morin, *Les Trois Pierre de Larivey: biographie et bibliographie* (Troyes: J.-L. Paton, 1937), pp. 5–11.

26. Larivey was clearly content with the contemporaneous massacre of the Protestants, maligning those who complained about the era and claiming that 'c'est un grand pêché que tels personages vivent [...] il n'y eût jamais temps plus plaisant, ny plus heureuse vie que celle du jourd'huy' [it is a great shame that such people are still alive [...] there has never been a more pleasant time, nor a happier life than that of today]. Larivey, *Les six premieres comedies*, p,. 59, II ('Prologue' to *Le Lacquais*).

27. See Michael Freeman, 'Une source inconnue des *Esprits* de Pierre de Larivey', *Bibliothèque d'Humanisme et Renaissance*, 41 (1979), 137–45 (p. 137).

28. Pietro Toldo, 'La Comédie française de la Renaissance', *Revue d'histoire littéraire de la France*, 7 (1898), 554–603 (pp. 593–94).

29. Anne Rogé, 'Traductions de théâtre ou trahison théâtrale: l'imitation renaissante comme appropriation culturelle', *Carnets*, 14 (2018), 1–13 (p. 7).

30. Ibid., p. 5.

31. See for example Michael Freeman, 'Introduction', in Pierre de Larivey, *Les Esprits*, ed. by Michael Freeman (Exeter: University of Exeter Press, 1978), p. 12.

32. Larivey, *Les six premieres comedies*, pp. 37–38, II ('Epistre à Monsieur d'Amboise, Avocat en Parlement').

33. Ibid., p. 39, II.

34. Ibid., p, 380, II ('Preface' to *Les Esprits*).

35. Ibid.

36. Yvonne Bellenger, 'Avant-propos', in *Pierre de Larivey, Champenois*, pp. 7–11 (p. 8).

37. De Capitani Bertrand, *Du spectaculaire à l'intime*, p. 248.

38. In his other translations he even advertises the Italian writers in each title: *Les facecieuses nuictz de Straparole*, *Deux livres de filosofie fabuleuse de m. A. Firenzuola*, and *La philosophie et institution morale d'Alexandre Piccolomini*.

39. Guy Degen has commented on Larivey's 'ruse' with these choices in his 'Une leçon du théâtre', in *Pierre de Larivey, Champenois*, ed. by Bellenger, pp. 15–39 (p. 16).

40. See Freeman, 'Une source inconnue des *Esprits* de Pierre de Larivey'.

41. Larivey, *Les six premieres comedies*, p. 39, II ('Epistre à Monsieur d'Amboise, Avocat en Parlement').

42. On the likelihood of this performance, see Haraszti, 'La Comédie française de la Renaissance'.

43. Grévin, *Le theatre*, p. 1 ('Brief discours pour l'intelligence de ce theatre').

44. Larivey, *Les six premieres comedies*, p. 59, II ('Preface' to *Le Lacquais*).

45. Piccolomini, *La philosophie et institution morale*, [s.n.] (liminary sonnet).

46. Madeleine Lazard discusses the likelihood of these performances throughout 'Le Dessein de Larivey et son public', in *Pierre de Larivey, Champenois*, ed. by Bellenger, pp. 49–60.

47. Rodomont, for instance, mentions a Flanders expedition, boasting that 'Je ne crandrois d'affronter le camp du Roy d'Espagne' [It would be nothing to me to assail the King of Spain's camp] (p. 276, 1.3). This refers to the preparations for battle against the Spanish King Philip II, which took place in the final weeks of 1580. See Odet de Turnèbe, *Les Contens*, ed. by Robert Aulotte (Paris: Sedes, 1985), p. 45. References to the month of January include Girard's claim that 'pour un mois de janvier il fait merveilleusement vilain' [it is horribly cold for the month of January] (p. 335, IV.4).

48. For details of his death, see *Bibliothèque françoise de la Croix du Maine et de Du Verdier*, ed. by Jean Antoine Rigoley de Juvigny, 6 vols (Paris: Michel Lambert, 1772), II, 203.

49. 'Me trouvant au logis de quelques miens parens de par-de là, je rencontray en ma voye une comedie escrite à la main, dont Odet de Tournebu, qui est allé de vie à trespas n'a pas longtemps, estoit auteur' [Finding myself at the house of some relatives across the way, I came across a handwritten comedy, the author of which was Odet de Turnèbe, who left this life not long ago]. Pierre de Ravel, 'Lettre à Monsieur du Sault', in Odet de Turnèbe, *Les Contens: Comedie nouvelle en prose Françoise*, ed. by Pierre de Ravel (Paris: Felix le Mangnier, 1584), p. 2. This manuscript has never been found.

50. Romain Weber, 'Les Neapolitaines de François d'Amboise, deux textes pour le prix d'un: comédie et histoire comique combinées', *Cahiers de recherches médiévales et humanistes*, 32 (2016), 221–35 (p. 221).

51. For more information on Turnèbe's writings as part of this salon, see Anne Larsen, 'Chastity and the Mother-daughter Bond: Odet de Turnèbe's Response to Catherine des Roches', in *Renaissance Women Writers: French Texts/American Contexts*, ed. by Anne Larsen and Collette Winn (Detroit, MI: Wayne State University Press, 1994), pp. 172–88.

52. See Geneviève Demerson, *Polémiques autour de la mort de Turnèbe* (Clermont-Ferrand: Centre de Recherches sur la Réforme et la Contre-Réforme, 1975); John Lewis, *Adrien Turnèbe, 1512–1565: A Humanist Observed* (Geneva: Droz, 1998), pp. 295–315.

53. Adrien de Turnèbe, *De nova captandae utilitatis e literatis ratione: epistola ad Leoquernum* (Paris: Veuve P. Attignant, 1559), fol. 2^r. French translation by Joachim Du Bellay in Du Bellay, *La Monomachie de David et de Goliath, ensemble plusieurs autres œuvres poétiques*, ed. by Ernesta Caldarini (Geneva: Droz, 1981), p. 145 (ll. 37–68). More information on this poem can be found in Smith, *The Anti-courtier Trend in Sixteenth-century French Literature*, p. 121.

54. Spector provides a lengthy appendix of possible borrowings in his edition: Odet de Turnèbe, *Les Contens*, ed. by Norman Spector (Paris: Marcel Didier, 1961), pp. 145–68.

55. See Lawton, *Contribution à l'histoire de l'humanisme en France*, pp. 141–43.

56. Turnèbe's reliance on *La Calandra* is discussed in Florindo Cerreta, 'A Case of Homophonic Word-play in Turnèbe's *Les Contens*', *Italica*, 41.4 (1964), 434–37.

57. La Croix du Maine and Du Verdier, *Bibliothèques françoises*, IV, 56.

58. See Louis Clément, *Henri Estienne et son œuvre française* (Geneva: Slatkine, 1967), p. 185.

59. Estienne, *Deux dialogues du nouveau langage françois italianizé*, p. 397.

60. Gentillet, *Anti-Machiavel*, p. 41.

61. Aldo Scaglione has discussed the Italian perception of the medieval knight in his *Knights at Court: Courtliness, Chivalry and Courtesy from Ottonian Germany to the Italian Renaissance* (Berkeley: University of California Press, 1991), p. 230. More information on the reception of Ariosto in France can also be found in Cioranescu, *L'Arioste en France*.

62. Estienne, *Deux dialogues du nouveau langage françois italianizé*, p. 45 ('Remonstrance aux autres courtisans', ll. 25–30).

63. Michel Simonin, 'La Disgrâce d'Amadis', *Studi Francesi*, 28 (1984), 1–35.

64. Alessandro Piccolomini, *Comedia intitolata Alessandro* (Rome: Girolama Cartolari, 1545).

65. Alessandro Piccolomini, *L'Alessandro*, ed. by Florindo Cerretta (Siena: La Galluzza, 1966), p. 185 (I. 4). See Spector, 'Appendix', in Turnèbe, *Les Contens*, ed. by Spector, p. 146.

66. Estienne, *Deux dialogues du nouveau langage françois italianizé*, p. 58 ('Remonstrance aux autres courtisans', ll. 206–08).

67. Grévin, *La Gélodacrye*, p. 34 (book 1, sonnet 12, ll. 1–2).

68. Huguet, *Dictionnaire de la langue française du seizième siècle*, VI, 616.

69. For Estienne's criticism of the French fashion for moustaches, see *Deux dialogues du nouveau langage françois italianizé*, pp. 190–91.

70. Ibid., p. 322.

71. See for example Donald Beecher, 'Introduction', in Odet de Turnèbe, *Satisfaction all Around*, ed. and trans. by Donald Beecher (Ottawa: Carleton University Renaissance Center, 1979), p. 21.

72. It is possible that Turnèbe is imitating 'trois cuittes' from Rabelais: see *Pantagruel*, in *Œuvres complètes*, pp. 209–335 (p. 329). Huguet defines 'trois cuittes' as 'ayant subi trois cuissons' [having undergone three rounds of cooking], and 'happelourde' as 'fausse pierre précieuse' [fake precious stone]. See *Dictionnaire de la langue française du seizième siècle*, II, 677, and IV, 438.

73. This may be a borrowing from Estienne's 1566 *Apologie pour Hérodote*, in which Estienne describes the 'marchands qui prestent de la merchandise, au lieu d'argent, contans cependant la merchandise pour deux fois autant qu'elle vaut' [merchants who lend merchandise instead of money, yet lend this merchandise for twice its actual worth]. Henri Estienne, *Apologie pour Hérodote*, ed. by Paul Ristelhuber, 2 vols (Paris: Lisieux, 1879), I, 182. Noted in Spector, 'Appendix', in Turnèbe, *Les Contens*, ed. by Spector, p. 161.

74. Eugène Lintilhac, *Histoire générale du théâtre en France*, 5 vols (Paris: Flammarion, 1904–10), II, 377.

75. Mazouer also discusses the highly detailed picture of Parisian life created by Turnèbe in this comedy. See *Le Théâtre français de la Renaissance*, p. 322.

76. Odet de Turnèbe, *Satisfaction all Around*, p. 101.

77. Ronsard, as we saw in Chapter 5, described Jodelle's feat of writing comedy thus: '[Jodelle] remplit premier le François échafaut' [Jodelle was the first to fill the French stage]. Ronsard, 'À Jean de La Péruse, poète'.

78. In the same way, Du Bellay also used to denigrate the Italians throughout his *Les Regrets*.

79. Michel de Montaigne, *Essais*, ed. by Alexandre Micha, 3 vols (Paris: Garnier Flammarion, 1979), I, 301.

80. Florindo Cerreta, 'A Case of Homophonic Word-play in Turnèbe's *Les Contens*', *Italica*, 41.4 (1964), 434–37.

81. Ibid., p. 436.

82. A fuller list can be found in Spector, 'Introduction', in Turnèbe, *Les Contens*, ed. by Spector, pp. 31–34.

83. See 'imbroncade' and 'lancepessade' in Huguet, *Dictionnaire de la langue française du seizième siècle*, IV, 555, 766.

84. For instance: 'Quand on parle du loup on en voit la queuë' [Speak of the devil] (p. 308, II.7); 'Il n'est pire eau que celle qui dort' [Still waters run deep] (p. 321, III.7).

85. Maupas uses *compliment* with its pre-seventeenth-century significations, meaning both 'to complete' and 'to express respectfully'. See Huguet, *Dictionnaire de la langue française du seizième siècle*, II, 393.

86. Charles Maupas, 'À tous seigneurs et gentils-hommes estrangers, amateurs de la langue Françoise', in Odet de Turnèbe, *Les Desguisez*, ed. by Charles Maupas (Blois: G. Collas, 1626), pp. 1–2.

87. This difference has been remarked upon by numerous scholars: Charles Mazouer, for example, criticised Jodelle's 'vers toujours un peu abrupt et compliqué' [ever abrupt and complicated rhymes] in comparison to Turnèbe's natural prose style. *La Comédie à l'époque d'Henri III*, ed. by Mazouer, pp. 231–61 (p. 237, 'Introduction to *Les Contens*').

AFTERWORD

> — Avez-vous leu ceste farce [de *Pathelin*] de bout en bout? Car desja tantost
> vous en avez fait mention.
> — Ouy, mais il y a longtemps. Toutesfois il me souvient encore de plusieurs
> bons mots, voire de maints bons et beaux traicts, et de la bonne disposition
> conjoincte avec l'invention gentille; tellement qu'il me semble que je luy fay
> grand tort en l'appelant une farce, et qu'elle merite bien le nom de comedie.

> ['Have you read from cover to cover this farce [of *Pathelin*]? For you have
> already mentioned it numerous times.'
> 'Yes, but a long time ago. Nonetheless, I still recall its clever remarks and its
> many wonderful witticisms; I also recall its excellent *dispositio* combined with
> impressive *inventio*, so much so that it seems to me that calling it a 'farce' does
> it a great disservice, and that it wholly deserves the name of "comedy"'.]

> (Henri Estienne, in *Deux dialogues du nouveau langage françois italianizé*, 1578)

Some of this book's key findings can be summarised by — and also help to clarify
— this comment from Estienne's *Deux dialogues*, a work completed towards the end
of the period in question. Firstly, it is evident that by the late 1570s a distinction was
being drawn between comedy and farce, and that certain qualities were expected in
a play before it was judged to be a true *comédie*. According to Estienne, these qualities
included a play's wit, as well as clever *dispositio* and *inventio*: it is the success of these
elements in *Pathelin* that, he claims, should shift its classification from 'farce' to
'comedie'. Yet, though Estienne acknowledges the difference in these classifications,
the boundaries between them are still evidently blurred. The *Deux dialogues* at once
recognises the emergence of humanist comedy in France and argues that medieval
comedy had pre-empted the requirements for such drama: no story is told of a
transition from one to the other, and despite setting out the new qualities which
were expected of a comedy, Estienne suggests that medieval writers had known
these all along. With this suggestion, Estienne dismisses the significance of the
Italian model: despite the confinement of the genre mainly to courts and college,
the influence on French writers of Italian playwrights, patrons, and performers was
key to the division between farce and comedy which Estienne describes. No doubt
Estienne's own anti-Italianism was partly responsible for this dismissal, and it is this
antagonism which characterises French comedy itself towards the end of the period
in question. Although French comedians made use of the Italian model in a bid to
enhance their native literature and culture, they also used it as an innovative means
of undermining the Italians themselves. Estienne's comment, then, indicates both
the complexity of the emergence of comedy in France in this period, and also the

hostile state of Franco-Italian relations, on which comedy itself can provide new perspectives.

Forty years before the *Deux dialogues* was completed, it was Estienne's own uncle, Charles Estienne, who had first promoted the importance of the Italian model in reinventing classical comedy, and who had explicitly rejected native medieval drama as falling short of the humanist ideal. His endeavours to prove that comic theatre deserved a place within the literary canon were either unconvincing to or unnoticed by his peers, and the superficial interest shown in comedy by mid-century writers such as Du Bellay and Mesmes did little to persuade others of the humanist value of drama. Indeed, writers such as Sébillet were wholly averse to the notion of reviving classical comedy, instead urging the continuation of medieval styles such as the farce. The Italian performance of *La Calandra* in 1548 was a major event in the history of comic theatre in France, convincing its noble spectators that the genre could both impress and entertain; the series of Italian comedies patronised at court in the wake of *La Calandra* also inspired French writers to turn their hand to the genre. Yet, we witness a certain degree of resentment for the Italian models even in Jodelle's first attempt at composing his own comedy. Over the next two decades, the influx of Italian culture into the French court was a cause of ever greater animosity towards the Italians; additionally, the literary success of the Italians was increasingly concerning to many French humanists, who were eager to establish France as the arbiter of European culture but found themselves to be latecomers. As writers grew more familiar with Italianate comedy in France, they began to experiment with techniques for turning the genre against the Italians themselves, using their plays both to resist and to compete against the influence of Italian culture. Despite the continued popularity of the farce, by 1580 the humanist value of comedy was largely undisputed, and the genre was used not just as a means of enriching French literature but also as a political weapon against the rival Italians, both to enhance France's standing in European culture and to emphasise that the presence of the Italians in France was wholly unwelcome.

The emergence in France of comedy continued to be complex even in the decades following the period under discussion in this book. Evidently, for the next several years there continued to be a market in France for Italian comedy: in 1582 the exiled Italian friar Giordano Bruno had printed in Paris his Italian comedy *Il candelaio* [The Candle-Bearer], and although it is unlikely to have been performed, it met with sufficient success for a second edition to be printed later that same year.[1] In 1584 François d'Amboise, the writer to whom Larivey had addressed the prefatory letter of his *Comédies*, printed his own comedy, entitled *Les Neapolitaines* [The Neapolitans].[2] As the title would suggest, this play is based on Italian sources; however, d'Amboise used this comedy to instead target the Spanish, the braggart Dom Dieghos caricaturing various facets of Spanish culture. Yet, while Italianate comedy continued to be appreciated in certain circles, the medieval farce style still prevailed. Even as Henri Estienne called in 1578 for *Pathelin* to be given the title of *comédie*, this same play was performed at a festival at Saint-Maixent.[3] At the same time, and in spite of the efforts of Charles Estienne forty years previously to prove that comic theatre was not solely a language-learning tool, comedy started to be printed again with a didactic slant. In 1578, for instance, the schoolmaster Gérard de Vivre wrote and had printed a comedy for his students, entitled *La Fidélité nuptiale* [Marital Fidelity], in which he asserts that comedy is the best way of teaching languages: 'Il n'y a moyen plus facile, ny plus profitable à la jeunesse (qui desirent de bien profiter en quelque langue que ce soit) que l'exercice d'apprendre, et jouer quelquefois des Comedies' [There is no easier nor more profitable way for young people (who wish to benefit from whichever language) than the exercise of learning and sometimes of performing comedies].[4] As we saw in Chapter 2, in 1585 Mesmes's *I suppositi* was also reprinted by Hierosme de Marnef 'pour l'utilité de ceux qui desirent sçavoir la langue Italienne' [to assist those who wish to learn the Italian language].

Enthusiasm for comedy diminished further in the 1590s. This coincides with the death in 1589 of Catherine de' Medici, one of France's greatest patrons of comedy, and the accession eight months later of Henri IV. The new king, who was largely focused on political and religious affairs, paid little attention to the genre. He confesses to having fallen asleep during comedy, and relates in a letter to the Marquess of Verneuil that he was too distracted to focus on a later performance. 'J'ay ouy une fort belle comédie, mais je pensois plus en vous qu'en elle' [I had acted for me a very good comedy, but I thought of you rather than of the play].[5] Although Henri IV had little interest in humanist comedy, his admiration of farce was well known. It was reported that farce could make him laugh 'jusqu'aux larmes' [until he cried]; performances of the farce, then, took precedence for many years at court.[6] Between the late 1580s and the 1620s, a few performances of comedies took place at the Hôtel de Bourgogne and in the provinces; playwrights such as Alexandre Hardy also met with some success, as did the 1611 collection by Larivey. With the exception of these plays, however, few details about comedy in this period survive; indeed, by the time that Pierre Corneille wrote his first comedy *Mélite* in 1625, he complained of having no precedents to follow: 'Je n'avais pour guide qu'un peu de sens commun avec les exemples de feu Hardy' [My only guide was the little common sense in the examples provided to me by the late Hardy].[7]

This book has not argued that the reinvention of comedy in France was a success, nor has it claimed that innovators such as Charles Estienne achieved their aims for comic theatre. Neither has this book sought to prove that comedy was popular with the general public throughout the sixteenth century, nor that the medieval farce was left behind in favour of humanist comic theatre. Instead, it has brought out in clearer detail than before the forward-and-backward movement of comedy in France, challenging the long-standing position that sixteenth-century writers neatly prepared a path for their better-known successors. Additionally, this book has provided evidence for the crucial role of Italian patrons, playwrights, and performers in bringing comedy to France; it has also shown that as well as setting an example, the Italian model invited the competition of French writers. Analysis of the rivalry which consequently manifested itself in French comedy has been able to offer new perspectives on the Franco-Italian relationship, and on the religious, political, and cultural tensions which characterised it. It is an injustice to these comedies to judge them solely on their literary value, on whether they are 'good' or 'bad', and to dismiss their work in favour of the more polished drama of Corneille or Molière. The controversies which frustrated the emergence of comic theatre in France, as well as the creative reworkings of comedy as a polemical weapon, point to the value of these plays not just in a literary sense but also in a historical one. One may still say that there is nothing funny about comedy and, especially, that there is nothing funny about sixteenth-century French comedy. Yet, in this case, comedy's most valuable contribution is the richness of insights it provides into the world which shaped it, and which in return it sought to shape.

Notes to the Afterword

1. Giordano Bruno, *Il candelaio* (Paris: Guillaume Julian, 1582); Andrews, *Scripts and Scenarios*, p. 243.
2. François d'Amboise, *Les Neapolitaines* (Paris: Abel L'Angelier, 1584).
3. See Lanson, 'Études sur les origines de la tragédie classique en France', p. 205.
4. Gérard de Vivre, *Comédie de la fidelité nuptiale* (Paris: Nicolas Bonfons, 1578), p. 1 ('Aux Lecteurs').
5. Henri IV de Bourbon, *Recueil des lettres missives de Henri IV*, ed. by Jules Berger de Xivrey, Joseph Guadet, 12 vols (Paris: Imprimerie Royale, 1843–1876), VII, 12. Cited in Lanson, 'Études sur les origines de la tragédie classique en France', p. 220.
6. Pierre de L'Estoile, *Mémoires et registre-journal de Henri III, Henri IV et de Louis XIII*, ed. by Jean-François Michaud and Jean-Joseph-François Poujoulat, 2 vols (Paris: Champollion-Figeac, 1847), II, 413.
7. Pierre Corneille, *Œuvres complètes*, ed. by Georges Couton, 2 vols (Paris: Gallimard, 1980), I, 5 ('Examen de Mélite').

BIBLIOGRAPHY

Manuscripts

'Ambasciatori Francia', Archivio di Stato di Modena

CONEGRANI, GIORGIO, 'Descrittione dell'entrate delle Maestadi del Re et Regina in Lione', 4 October 1548, Archivio di stato Mantua, Archivio Gonzaga, Serie E, busta 641

DANDINO, HIERONIMO, and MICHELE DELLA TORRA, 'Dandino e della Torre au Cardinal Farnese', BAV, 14.092

ESTIENNE, CHARLES, 'Livre des jeux et theatres antiques', BAV, *Reg. Lat.* 1697 <https://digi.vatlib.it/view/mss_Reg.lat.1697> (last accessed 27 July 2021)

Primary Sources

ACCADEMIA DEGLI INTRONATI, *Comedie à la maniere des anciens, et de pareille matiere, intitulée Les Abusez. Composée premierement en langue Tuscane, par les professeurs de l'academie Senoise, nommez Intronati, et depuis traduicte en nostre langaige Françoys, par Charles Estienne*, trans. by Charles Estienne (Paris: Denis Janot for Pierre Roffet, 1540)

——*Comedie à la maniere des anciens, et de pareille matiere, intitulée Les Abusez*, trans. by Charles Estienne (Paris: Estienne Groulleau, 1549)

ALAMANNI, LUIGI, *La Flora, comedia, con gl'intermedii di A. Lori* (Florence: Lorenzo Torrentino, 1556)

——*La Flora, in versi e prose di Luigi Alamanni, edizione ordinata e raffrontata sui codici per cura di Pietro Raffaelli, con un discorso intorno all'Alamanni e al suo secolo*, ed. by Pietro Raffaelli, 2 vols (Firenze: Le Monnier, 1859)

ALBERTI, LEON BATTISTA, *L'architettura* [*De re aedificatoria*], ed. by Giovanni Orlandi and Paolo Portoghesi, 2 vols (Milan: Il Polifilo, 1966)

——*On the Art of Building in Ten Books*, trans. and ed. by Joseph Rykwert, Neil Leach, and Robert Tavernor (Cambridge, MA: MIT Press, 1988)

AMBOISE, FRANÇOIS D', *Les Neapolitaines* (Paris: Abel L'Angelier, 1584)

ANEAU, BARTHÉLEMY, *Quintil Horatien*, in Joachim Du Bellay, *La Deffence, et illustration de la langue françoyse*, ed. by Jean-Charles Monferran (Geneva: Droz, 2001)

ANON., *A Discovery of the great subtilitie and wonderful wisedome of the Italians* (London: John Wolfe, 1591)

——*Facezie, motti, buffonerie et burle del Piovano Arlotto* (Florence: I Giunti, 1565)

——*La Farce de Maistre Pierre Pathelin* (Lyons: Guillaume le Roy, 1485)

——*Le grand triumphe faict à l'entrée du Treschrestien et tousiours victorieux Monarche, Henry second de ce nom, Roy de France, en sa noble ville et cite de Lyon. Et de la Royne Catherine son espouse* (Paris: B. de Gourmont, 1548)

——*Le Nouveau Pathelin* (Paris: Jean Saint-Denis, 1530)

——*Le Testament de Pathelin* (Paris: Denys Janot, [n.d.])

ARETINO, PIETRO, *Teatro*, ed. by Giovanna Rabitti, Carmine Boccia, and Enrico Garavelli, 2 vols (Rome: Salerno, 2010)

ARIOSTO, LODOVICO, *Comedie tres elegante en laquelle sont contenues les amours recreatives d'Erostrate fils de Philogone de Catania en Sicile et de la belle Polymneste fille de Damon bourgeois d'Avignon*, trans. by Jacques Bourgeois (Paris: Guillaume de Marnef, 1545)

——*La comedie des supposez de M. Louys Arioste, en italien et françoys*, trans. by Jean-Pierre de Mesmes (Paris: Estienne Groulleau, 1552)

——*La comedie des supposez de M. Louys Arioste, italien et françois. Pour l'utilité de ceux qui desirent sçavoir la langue italienne*, trans. by Jean-Pierre de Mesmes (Paris: Hierosme de Marnef, 1585)

——*Orlando furioso*, ed. by Marcello Turchi and Edoardo Sanguineti, 2 vols (Milan: Aldo Garzanti, 1974)

AUTELZ, GUILLAUME DES, *Replique de Guillaume des Autelz, aux Furieuses Defenses de Louis Meigret* (Lyons: Jean de Tournes, 1551)

BADIUS, CONRAD, *Comedie du pape malade et tirant à la fin* ([Paris(?)]: [n.pub.], 1561)

BAÏF, JEAN-ANTOINE DE, *Le Brave, comedie de Jan Antoine de Baif, jouee devant le Roy en l'hostel de Guise à Paris le XXVIII de janvier M. D. LXVII* (Paris: Robert Estienne, 1567)

Œuvres complètes, ed. by Malcolm Quainton and Elizabeth Vinestock, 3 vols (Paris: Champion, 2017)

——*Poésies choisies*, ed. by Louis Becq de Fouquières (Paris: Charpentier, 1874)

BALMAS, ENEA, and OTHERS, eds, *Théâtre français de la Renaissance*, 3 series, 21 vols (Florence: Olschki, 1986–2018)

BELLEAU, RÉMY, *Les œuvres poétiques de Remy Belleau, redigees en deux Tomes*, 2 vols (Paris: Mamert Patisson, 1578)

——*La Reconnue*, ed. by Jean Braybrook (Geneva: Droz, 1989)

BIBBIENA, BERNARDO DOVIZI DA, *La Calandra: commedia elegantissima per Messer Bernardo Dovizi da Bibbiena, testo critico annotato a cura di Giorgio Padoan* (Padua: Antenore, 1985)

BIENVENU, JACQUES, *Comedie du monde malade et mal pensé* ([Paris(?)]: [n.pub.], 1568)

BLOEMENDAL, JAN, 'Tyrant or Stoic Hero? Marc-Antoine Muret's *Julius Caesar*', in *Recreating Ancient History: Episodes from the Greek and Roman Past in the Arts and Literature of the Early Modern Period*, ed. by Karl Enenkel and others (Leiden: Brill, 2001), pp. 303–19

BOCCACCIO, GIOVANNI, *Le Decameron de Messire Jehan Bocace Florentin, nouvellement traduict d'Italien en Francoys par Maistre Anthoine le Macon conseiller du Roy et tresorier de l'extraordinaire des guerres*, trans. by Antoine Le Maçon (Paris: Estienne Roffet, 1545)

——*Decameron*, ed. by Elena Ceva Valla and Mario Marti (Milan: Rizzoli, 1974)

BONNARDOT, FRANÇOIS, and OTHERS, eds, *Registres des délibérations du Bureau de la Ville de Paris (1552–1558)*, 21 vols (Paris: Imprimerie Nationale, 1888)

BOURBON, HENRI IV, DE, *Recueil des Lettres missives de Henri IV*, ed. by Jules Berger de Xivrey and Joseph Guadet, 12 vols (Paris: Imprimerie Royale, 1843–76)

BRANTÔME, PIERRE DE BOURDEILLE SEIGNEUR DE, *Œuvres complètes*, ed. by Ludovic Lalanne, 12 vols (Paris: Jules Renouard, 1864–82)

——*Vies des dames illustres françoises et etrangères*, ed. by Louis Moland (Paris: Garnier, 1868)

BRUNO, GIORDANO, *Il candelaio* (Paris: Guillaume Julian, 1582)

CAPPELLO, GIOVANNI, 'Relazione del Clarissimo Messer Giovanni Cappello, ambasciator in Francia nell'anno 1554', in *Relations des ambassadeurs vénitiens sur les affaires de France au xvie siècle*, ed. by Niccolò Tommaseo, 2 vols (Paris: Imprimerie Royale, 1838), II, 366–85

CASTIGLIONE, BALDASSARE, *Il libro del Cortegiano*, ed. by Giulio Preti (Turin: Einaudi, 1965)

——*The Book of the Courtyer*, ed. by Virginia Cox, trans. by Thomas Hoby (London: Dent, 1994)

CHAPPUYS, CLAUDE, *Discours de la Court: présenté au Roy par M. Claude Chappuys, son libraire et Valet de Chambre ordinaire* (Paris: André Roffet, 1543)

CICERO, *De finibus bonorum et malorum libri quinque, cum brevibus annotationibus Petri Joanis Olivarii Valentini* (Paris: Simon de Colines, 1537)

——*De oratore*, ed. by Harris Rackham, trans. by Edward William Sutton (Cambridge, MA: Harvard University Press, 2014)

——*Epistulae ad Atticum*, ed. by David Roy Shackleton Bailey (Stuttgart: Teubner, 1987)

——*Epistolae familiares. Tertia editio*, ed. by Robert Estienne (Paris: Robert Estienne, 1532)

——*Epistulae ad familiares*, ed. by David Roy Shackleton Bailey (Cambridge: Cambridge University Press, 1977)

CORNEILLE, PIERRE DE, *Œuvres complètes*, ed. by Georges Couton, 2 vols (Paris: Gallimard, 1980)

DAN, PIERRE, *Le Trésor des Merveilles de la Maison Royale de Fontainebleau* (Paris: Sébastien Cramoisy, 1642)

DOLCE, LODOVICO, *Fabritia* (Venice: Gabriel Giolito, 1560)

——*Il ragazzo* (Venice: Niccolò Zoppino, 1541)

DOLET, ETIENNE, *La maniere de bien traduire d'une langue en autre* (Lyons: Estienne Dolet, 1540)

DU BELLAY, JEAN, *Defense pour le roy treschrestien contre les calomnies de Jacques Omphalius* (Paris: Charles Estienne, 1554)

DU BELLAY, JOACHIM, *La Deffence et illustration de la langue françoyse*, ed. by Henri Chamard, 2nd edn (Paris: Didier, 1966)

——*La Monomachie de David et de Goliath, ensemble plusieurs autres œuvres poétiques*, ed. by Ernesta Caldarini (Geneva: Droz, 1981)

——*Œuvres complètes*, ed. by Richard Cooper and others, 2 vols (Paris: Honoré Champion, 2003)

——*The Regrets, with the Antiquities of Rome, Three Latin Elegies, and The Defense and Enrichment of the French Language,* trans. and ed. by Richard Helgerson (Philadelphia: University of Pennsylvania Press, 2006)

DU JARRIC, PIERRE, *Histoire des choses plus memorables advenues tant ez Indes Orientales*, 3 vols (Bordeaux: Millanges, 1610–14)

DU VERDIER, ANTOINE, *Prosopographie* (Lyons: Antoine Gryphe, 1573)

DUNCAN, ARCHIBALD, *Mariner's Chronicle* (New Haven, CT: George Gorton, 1834)

ERASMUS, *Il Ciceroniano*, ed. by Angiolo Gambara (Brescia: La Scuola, 1965)

——*Opus epistolarum Des. Erasmi Roterodami*, ed. by Percy Stafford Allen and others, 12 vols (Oxford: Clarendon Press, 1906–2002)

——*The Correspondence of Erasmus*, trans. by R. A. B. Mynors and D. F. S. Thomson, 16 vols (Toronto: University of Toronto Press, 1974)

ESTIENNE, CHARLES, *L'Agriculture et maison rustique*, ed. by Jean Liebault (Paris: Jaques Du Puys, 1564)

——*De dissectione partium corporis humani libri tres* (Paris: Simon de Colines, 1545)

ESTIENNE, HENRI, *Apologie pour Hérodote*, ed. by Paul Ristelhuber, 2 vols (Paris: Lisieux, 1879)

——*Deux dialogues du nouveau langage françois italianizé et autrement desguizé, principalement entre les courtisans de ce temps*, ed. by Pauline Smith (Geneva: Slatkine, 1980)

——*Traicté de la conformité du langage françois avec le grec*, ed. by Léon Feugère (Geneva: Slatkine, 1853)

ESTIENNE, NICOLE, *Les misères de la femme mariée, où se peuvent voir les peines et tourmens qu'elle reçoit durant sa vie* (Paris: Pierre Menier, [n.d])

ESTIENNE, ROBERT, *Dictionarium, seu latinae linguae thesaurus*, 2 vols (Paris: R. Stephanus, 1531)

FIRENZUOLA, AGNOLO, *Deux livres de filosofie fabuleuse de M. A. Firenzuola*, trans. by Pierre de Larivey (Lyons: Benoist Rigaud, 1579)

——*I Lucidi, comedia*, ed. by Lodovico Domenichi (Florence: I Giunti, 1552)

——*Opere*, ed. by Adriano Seroni (Florence: Sansoni, 1971)

FIRENZUOLA, AGNOLO, and GIOVANNI BATTISTA GELLI, *Tesoretto della lingua toscana*, ed. by Nicola Giosafatte Biagioli (Paris: G. Didot, 1822)

FREGOSO, BATTISTA, *Contramours: L'Anteros ou Contramour*, trans. by Thomas Sébillet (Paris: Martin le Jeune, 1581)

GASSIES, GEORGES, *Anthologie du théâtre français du Moyen Âge: théâtre comique: jeux et farces des XIIIe, XVe et XVIe siècles*, 2 vols (Paris: Delgrave, 1925)

GENTILLET, INNOCENT, *Discours sur les moyens de bien gouverner: contre Nicolas Machiavel Florentin*, ed. by Charles Edward Rathé (Geneva: Droz, 1968)

GILLES, NICOLAS, *Le second volume des Croniques et annales de France* (Paris: R. Anvil for J. de Roigny, 16 Aug. 1549)

GIRALDI CINZIO, GIOVANNI BATTISTA, *Discorso intorno al comporre delle commedie e delle tragedie*, ed. by Giulio Antimaco (Milan: Daelli, 1864)

GRÉVIN, JACQUES, *César*, trans. by Jeffrey Foster (Paris: Nizet, 1974)

—— *La Gélodacrye et les vingt-quatre sonnets romains*, ed. by Michèle Clément (Saint-Étienne: Université Saint-Étienne, 2001)

—— *L'Olimpe de Jacques Grévin, ensemble les autres œuvres poëtiques dudict auteur* (Paris: Robert Estienne, 1560)

—— *Le theatre de Jaques Grevin de Cler-mont en Beauvaisis, à tres illustre et treshaulte princesse ladame Claude de France, Duchesse de Lorraine. Ensemble, la seconde partie de L'Olimpe & de la Gelodacrye* (Paris: Vincent Sertenas and Guillaume Barbé, 1562)

—— *Théâtre complet et poésies choisies*, ed. by Lucian Pinvert (Paris: Garnier Frères, 1922)

—— *La Trésorière, Les Esbahis*, ed. by Élisabeth Lapeyre (Paris: Librairie Honoré Champion, 1980)

GROSLEY, PIERRE-JEAN, *Mémoires historiques et critiques pour l'histoire de Troyes*, 2 vols (Paris: Veuve Duchesne, 1774)

HORACE, *L'Art poétique d'Horace*, trans. by Jacques Peletier du Mans ([Paris(?)]: [n.pub.], 1541)

—— *L'Art poétique d'Horace traduit en vers françois par Jacques II Peletier du Mans* (Paris: Michel de Vascosan, 1545)

JODELLE, ESTIENNE, *L'Eugène: édition critique avec introduction, notes et glossaire*, ed. by Michael Freeman (Exeter: University of Exeter Press, 1987)

—— *Œuvres complètes*, ed. by Enea Balmas, 2 vols (Paris: Gallimard, 1965)

—— *Œuvres et meslanges poétiques*, ed. by Charles de La Mothe (Paris: Mamert Patisson, 1574)

—— *Le Recueil des inscriptions, 1558: A Literary and Iconographical Exegesis*, ed. by Victor Graham and William McAllister-Johnson (Toronto: University of Toronto Press, 1972)

KOOPMANS, JELLE, ed., *Recueil des sermons joyeux* (Geneva: Droz, 1988)

L'ESTOILE, PIERRE DE, *Mémoires-journaux, 1574–1611*, ed. by Alphonse Lemerre, 12 vols (Paris: Tallandier, 1982)

—— *Mémoires et registre-journal de Henri III, Henri IV et de Louis XIII*, ed. by Jean-François Michaud and Jean-Joseph-François Poujoulat, 2 vols (Paris: Champollion-Figeac, 1847)

LABORDE, LÉON DE, *Les Comptes des bastiments du roi*, 2 vols (Paris: Libraire de la Société, 1880)

LA CROIX DU MAINE, FRANÇOIS GRUDÉ DE, and ANTOINE DU VERDIER, *Bibliothèque françoise de la Croix du Maine et de Du Verdier*, ed. by Jean Antoine Rigoley de Juvigny, 6 vols (Paris: Michel Lambert, 1772)

LANDO, ORTENSIO, *Paradoxes, ce sont propos contre le commune opinion*, trans. by Charles Estienne (Paris: Charles Estienne, 1553)

LARIVEY, PIERRE DE, *Les Esprits*, ed. by Michael Freeman (Exeter: University of Exeter Press, 1978)

—— *Le Lacquais*, ed. by Madeleine Lazard and Luigia Zilli (Paris: Nizet, 1987)

—— *Les six premieres comedies facecieuses de Pierre de Larivey Champenois, à l'imitation des anciens Grecs, Latins et modernes Italiens* (Paris: Abel l'Angelier, 1579)

——— *Théâtre complet: Les six premieres Comedies facecieuses (Le Laquais, La Vefve, Les Esprits)*, ed. by Luigia Zilli (Paris: Classiques Garnier, 2011)

LA TAILLE, JEAN DE, *La Famine, ou les gabeonites, tragedie prise de la Bible et suivant celle de Saül, ensemble plusieurs autres oeuvres poëtiques de Jehan de La Taille de Bondaroy* (Paris: Frédéric Morel, 1573)

———*Les Corrivaus*, ed. by Denis Drysdall (Paris: Marcel Didier, 1974)

LEMAIRE DE BELGES, JEAN, *La Concorde des deux langages* (Paris: Droz, 1947)

LESTOCQUOY, JAN, ed., *Correspondance des nonces en France: Dandino, Della Torre et Trivulto (1546–1551)* (Paris: E. de Boccard, 1966)

MACHIAVELLI, NICCOLÒ, *La Mandragola, Clizia*, ed. by Ezio Raimondi and Gian Mario Anselmi (Milan: Mursia, 1984)

———*Le Prince de Nicolas Machiavelle secretaire et citoien de Florence Traduit d'Italien en Françoys par Guillaume Cappel*, trans. by Guillaume Cappel (Paris: Charles Estienne, 1553)

MAGNY, OLIVIER DE, *Hymne sur la naissance de Madame Marguerite de France, fille du roy Henri II, en l'an 1553, par Olivier de Magny, avec quelques lyriques de luy* (Paris: Abel L'Angelier, 1553)

MARGUERITE D'ANGOULÊME, QUEEN OF NAVARRE, *Heptaméron*, ed. by Simone de Reyff (Paris: Garnier Flammarion, 1982)

———*Lettres de Marguerite d'Angoulême, sœur de François I, reine de Navarre*, ed. by Jules Renouard, 2 vols (Paris: Jules Renouard, 1841)

———*Œuvres complètes*, ed. by Nicole Cazauran, Geneviève Hasenohr, and Olivier Millet, 4 vols (Paris: Champion, 2002)

MAROT, CLÉMENT, *Œuvres de Clément Marot*, ed. by Alfred Philibert-Soupé, 2 vols (Lyons: Louis Perrin, 1869)

MASSON, JEAN-PAPIRE, *Vitae trium hetruriae procerum Dantis, Petrarchae, Boccacii, ad Paschelem serenissimum Venetorum Ducem* (Paris: Denis du Pré, 1587)

MEDICI, CATHERINE DE', *Lettres de Catherine de Médicis*, ed. by Hector Ferrière-Percy, 11 vols (Paris: Imprimerie Nationale 1880–97)

MESMES, JEAN-PIERRE DE, *La Grammaire italienne, composée en Françoys* (Paris: Gilles Corrozet, 1548)

MONTAIGNE, MICHEL DE, *Essais*, ed. by Alexandre Micha, 3 vols (Paris: Garnier Flammarion, 1979)

———*Journal de voyage en Italie*, ed. by Maurice Rat (Paris: Garnier, 1955)

MÜNSTER, SEBASTIAN, *Cosmographia* (Basle: Heinrich Petti, 1550)

NYROP, KRISTOFFER, and ÉMILE PICOT, eds, *Nouveau recueil des farces françaises des XVe et XVIe siècles* (Paris: Damascène Morgand et Charles Fatout, 1880)

OMPHALIUS, JACOBUS, *De elocutionis imitatione ac apparatu* (Paris: Simon de Colines, 1537)

PANNONIUS, GABRIEL, *Petit vocabulaire en langue françoise et italienne* (Lyons: Roger de Brey, 1578)

PASQUIER, ESTIENNE, *Des recherches de la France*, 10 vols (Paris: L. Sonnius, 1617)

PELETIER DU MANS, JACQUES, *L'art poétique départi en deux livres* (Lyons: Jean de Tournes, 1555)

PETRARCA, FRANCESCO, *Il Petrarca*, ed. by Antonio Brucioli (Lyons: Guillaume Rouillé, 1550)

PICCOLOMINI, ALESSANDRO, *L'amor costante, comedia del Stordito Intronato, composta per la venuta dell'Imperatore in Siena l'anno del XXXVI* (Venice: Andrea Arrivabene, 1540)

———*L'amor costante*, in *Commedie del Cinquecento*, ed. by Nino Borsellino, 2 vols (Milan: Feltrinelli, 1962), I

———*Comedia intitolata Alessandro* (Rome: Girolama Cartolari, 1545)

———*L'Alessandro*, ed. by Florindo Cerretta (Siena: La Galluzza, 1966)

——*La philosophie et institution morale d'Alexandre Piccolomini*, trans. by Pierre de Larivey (Paris: Abel L'Angelier, 1581)

POSTEL, GUILLAUME DE, *De orbis terrae concordia*, 2 vols (Paris: Gromors, 1544)

RABELAIS, FRANÇOIS, *Œuvres complètes*, ed. by Mireille Huchon (Paris: Gallimard, 1994)

RIDOLFI, LUCANTONIO, *Ragionamento havuto in Lione da Claudio de Herbere, Gentil'huomo Franceze, et da Alessandro degli Uberti, Gentil'huomo fiorentino, sopra alcuni luoghi del cento novelle del Boccaccio* (Lyons: Guillaume Rouillé, 1557)

ROCHES, CATHERINE DES, *La Puce de Madame des Roches* (Paris: Abel L'Angelier, 1582)

RONSARD, PIERRE DE, *Œuvres complètes*, ed. by Paul Laumonier, Raymond Lebègue, and Isidore Silver, 18 vols (Paris: Hachette, 1914–75)

RUBYS, CLAUDE DE, *Histoire veritable de la ville de Lyon, contenant ce, qui a esté obmis par maistres Symphorien Champier & autres, auec vn sommaire recueil de l'administration politicque de ladicte ville. Ensemble vn petit discours de la maison illustre des Medicis de Florence* (Lyons: Bonaventure Nugo, 1604)

SAINT-DENIS, ANTOINE DE, *Comptes du Monde Adventureux* (Paris: Estienne Groulleau, 1555)

SCÈVE, MAURICE, *The Entry of Henri II into Lyon: September 1548*, ed. by Richard Cooper (Tempe: Medieval and Renaissance Texts and Studies, 1997)

——*La magnificence de la superbe et triumphante entree de la noble et antique Cité de Lyon faicte au Treschrestien Roy de France Henry deuxiesme de ce nom, et à la royne Catherine son Espouse le XXIII. de Septembre M.D.XLVIII* (Lyons: Guillaume Rouillé, 1549)

——*La magnifica et triumphale entrata del christianiss. re di Francia Henrico secondo, Colla particulare descritione della Comedia che fece recitare in Lione la Natione Fiorentina a richiesta di sua Maestà Christianissima*, trans. by Francesco Mazzei (Lyons: Guillaume Rouillé, 1549)

SÉBILLET, THOMAS, *Art poétique*, ed. by Félix Gaiffe (Paris: Droz, 1932)

——*Art poétique françois*, ed. by Francis Goyet (Paris: Nizet, 1988)

SERLIO, SEBASTIANO, *Des antiquités, le troisième livre translaté d'italien en français*, trans. by Pieter Coecke van Aelst (Antwerp: P. Coecke, 1550)

——*Il terzo libro di Sabastiano serlio Bolognese, nel qual si figurano, e descrivono le antiquità di Roma, e le altre che sono in Italia, e fuori d'Italia* (Venice: Francesco Marcolini, 1544)

——*Le premier livre d'Architecture et le second livre de Perspective de Sebastien Serlio Bolognois, mis en langue françoise, par Jehan Martin* (Paris: Jean Barbé, 1545)

——*Sebastiano Serlio on Domestic Architecture: Different Dwellings from the Meanest Hovel to the Most Ornate Palace: The Sixteenth-century Manuscript of Book VI in the Avery Library of Columbia University*, trans. and ed. by Myra Nan Rosenfeld (New York: Architectural History Foundation, 1978)

SIMEONI, GABRIELLO, *L'Epitalamio*, in *Description de la Limagne d'Auvergne*, ed. by Toussaint Renucci (Paris: Didier, 1944), p. 17

SOPHOCLES, *Tragedie de Sophocles, intitulée Electra*, trans. by Lazare de Baïf (Paris: Estienne Rosset, 1537)

STRAPAROLA, GIOVANNI FRANCESCO, *Les facecieuses nuictz de Straparole*, trans. by Pierre de Larivey (Paris: Abel L'Angelier, 1576)

TERENCE, *Comoediae sex, tum ex Donati commentariis*, ed. by Robert Estienne (Paris: Robert Estienne, 1529)

——*Ex Terentii comoediis colloquendi Formulae ceu Flosculi* (Paris: Chrestien Wechel, 1533)

——*Ex Terentii comoediis optimae, copiosissimae atque certissimae loquendi formulae* (Paris: Chrestien Wechel, 1530)

——*P. Terentii Afri comici Andria*, ed. by Charles Estienne (Paris: Simon de Colines and François Estienne, 1541)

——*Premiere comedie de Terence, intitulée L'Andrie, nouvellement traduicte de Latin en François, en faveur des bons espritz, studieux des antiques recreations*, trans. by Charles Estienne (Paris: André Roffet, 1542)

——— *Premiere comedie de Terence, intitulée L'Andrie, nouvellement traduicte de Latin en François, en faveur des bons espritz, studieux des antiques recreations*, trans. by Charles Estienne (Paris: Estienne Groulleau, 1552)

——— *Terentii Comoediae sex, a Guidone Juvenale explanatae, et a Jodoco Badio, cum annotationibus suis, recognitae*, ed. by Jodocus Badius Ascensius and Guido Juvenalis (Lyons: Johannes Trechsel, 1493)

——— *Therence en françois* (Paris: Antoine Vérard, [n.d.])

TISSIER, ANDRÉ, ed., *Recueil des farces (1450–1550)*, 13 vols (Geneva: Droz, 1986–2000)

TOMMASEO, NICCOLÒ, ed., *Relations des ambassadeurs vénitiens sur les affaires de France au xvie siècle*, 2 vols (Paris: Imprimerie Royale, 1838)

TURNÈBE, ADRIEN DE, *De nova captandae utilitatis e literis ratione: epistola ad Leoquernum* (Paris: Veuve P. Attignant, 1559)

TURNÈBE, ODET DE, *Les Contens: Comedie nouvelle en prose Françoise*, ed. by Pierre de Ravel (Paris: Felix le Mangnier, 1584)

——— *Les Contens*, ed. by Norman Spector (Paris: Marcel Didier, 1961)

——— *Les Contens d'Odet de Turnèbe*, ed. by Robert Aulotte (Paris: Sedes, 1985)

——— *Satisfaction all Around*, ed. and trans. by Donald Beecher (Ottawa: Carleton University Renaissance Center, 1979)

——— *Les Desguisez*, ed. by Charles Maupas (Blois: G. Collas, 1626)

VASARI, GIORGIO, *Le opere di Giorgio Vasari*, ed. by Gaetano Milanesi, 9 vols (Florence: G. C. Sansoni, Editore, 1878)

——— *Le vite de' più eccellenti pittori, scultori ed architetti*, ed. by Fernandino Ranalli, 2 vols (Florence: Batelli, 1848)

VAUQUELIN DE LA FRESNAYE, JEAN, *Art poétique*, ed. by Georges Pellissier, 2 vols (Paris: Garnier, 1885)

VITRUVIUS, *On Architecture*, trans. by Frank Granger, 2 vols (Cambridge, MA: Harvard University Press, 2014)

VIVRE, GÉRARD DE, *Comédie de la fidelité nuptiale* (Paris: Nicolas Bonfons, 1578)

YVER, JACQUES, *Le Printemps d'Yver* (Paris: J. Ruelle, 1572)

Secondary Texts

ACIDINI LUCHINAT, CRISTINA, *The Medici, Michelangelo, and the Art of Late Renaissance Florence* (New Haven, CT: Yale University Press, 2002)

AHMED, EHSAN, *The Law and the Song: Hebraic, Christian and Pagan Revivals in Sixteenth-century France* (Birmingham, AL: Summa, 1997)

ALLEN BROWN, PAMELA, 'The Traveling Diva and Generic Innovation', *Renaissance Drama*, 44.2 (2016), 249–67

ANDREWS, RICHARD, *Scripts and Scenarios: The Performance of Comedy in Renaissance Italy* (Cambridge: Cambridge University Press, 1993)

ATTINGER, GUSTAVE, *L'Esprit de la commedia dell'arte dans le théâtre français* (Paris: Librairie Théâtrale, 1950)

BAKER, PATRICK, *Italian Renaissance Humanism in the Mirror* (Cambridge: Cambridge University Press, 2015)

BALDWIN, CHARLES, *Renaissance Literary Theory and Practice: Classicism in the Rhetoric and Poetic of Italy, France and England, 1400–1600* (Gloucester: P. Smith, 1959)

BALMAS, ENEA, *Un poeta francese del Rinascimento: Estienne Jodelle. La sua vita, il suo tempo* (Florence: Olschki, 1962)

BALSAMO, JEAN, 'L'Italianisme lyonnais et l'illustration de la langue française', in *Lyon et l'illustration de la langue française à la Renaissance*, ed. by Bernard Colombat and Gérard Defaux (Lyons: ENS, 2003), pp. 211–29

——'Larivey traducteur de *L'Institution Morale*', in *Pierre de Larivey, Champenois: chanoine, traducteur, auteur de comédies et astrologue (1541–1619)*, ed. by Yvonne Bellenger (Paris: Klincksieck, 1993), pp. 73–81

——*Les Rencontres des muses: italianisme et anti-italianisme dans les lettres françaises de la fin du XVI*e *siècle* (Geneva: Slatkine, 1992)

BALSAMO, JEAN, VITO CASTIGLIONE MINISCHETTI, and GIOVANNI DOTOLI, *Les Traductions de l'italien en français au XVI*e *siècle* (Fasano: Schena, 2009)

BANHAM, MARTIN, ed., *The Cambridge Guide to Theatre* (Cambridge: Cambridge University Press, 2000)

BARISH, JONAS, 'The Problem of Closet Drama in the Italian Renaissance', *Italica*, 71.1 (1994), 4–30

BASCHET, ARMAND, *Les Comédiens italiens à la cour de France sous Charles IX, Henri III, Henri IV et Louis XIII: d'après les lettres royales, la correspondance originale des comédiens, les registres de la trésorerie de l'épargne et autres documents* (Paris: Plon, 1882)

BASTIN-HAMMOU, MALIKA, 'Teaching Greek with Aristophanes in the French Renaissance, 1528–1549', in *Receptions of Hellenism in Early Modern Europe*, ed. by Natasha Constantinidou and Han Lamers (Leiden: Brill, 2019), pp. 72–93

BAUMGARTNER, FREDERIC, *Henri II: King of France 1547–1559* (Durham, NC: Duke University Press, 1988)

BEAM, SARA, *Laughing Matters: Farce and the Making of Absolutism in France* (New York: Cornell University Press, 2007)

BELLENGER, YVONNE, ed., *Pierre de Larivey, Champenois: chanoine, traducteur, auteur de comédies et astrologue (1541–1619)* (Paris: Klincksieck, 1993)

BERZAL DE DIOS, JAVIER, *Visual Experiences in Cinquecento Theatrical Spaces* (Toronto: University of Toronto Press, 2019)

BINGEN, NICOLE, 'Sources et filiations de la *Grammaire italienne* de Jean-Pierre de Mesmes', *Bibliothèque d'Humanisme et Renaissance*, 46.3 (1984), 633–38

BIVILLE, FRÉDÉRIQUE, EMMANUEL PLANTADE, and DANIEL VALLAT, eds, '*Les vers du plus nul des poètes': nouvelles recherches sur les Priapées: actes de la journée d'étude organisée le 7 novembre 2005 à l'Université Lumière-Lyon II* (Lyons: Maison de l'Orient et de la Méditerranée, 2008)

BIZER, MARC, *La Poésie au miroir: imitation et conscience de soi dans la poésie latine de la Pléiade* (Paris: Honoré Champion, 1995)

——'Qui a païs n'a que faire de "patrie": Joachim Du Bellay's Resistance to a French Identity', *Romanic Review*, 91.4 (2000), 375–95

BLACK, DAISY, 'Theatre and Performance', in *The Routledge History of Women in Early Modern Europe*, ed. by Amanda Capern (Abingdon: Routledge, 2019), pp. 357–85

BLACK, ROBERT, *Humanism and Education in Medieval and Renaissance Italy: Tradition and Innovation in Latin Schools from the Twelfth to the Fifteenth Century* (Cambridge: Cambridge University Press, 2001)

BORZA, ÉLIE, 'Catalogue des travaux inédits d'humanistes consacrés à Sophocle, jusqu'en 1600', *Humanistica Lovaniensia: Journal of Neo-Latin Studies*, 52 (2003), 196–216

BOUCHER, JACQUELINE, *La Cour de Henri III* (Rennes: Ouest-France, 1986)

BOUDOU, BÉNÉDICTE, JUDIT KECSKEMÉTI, and MARTINE FURNO, eds, *La France des humanistes: Robert et Charles Estienne: des imprimeurs pédagogues* (Turnhout: Brepols, 2009)

BOURCIEZ, ÉDOUARD, *Les Mœurs polies et la littérature de cour sous Henri II* (Paris: Hachette, 1866)

BOTTASSO, ENZO, 'Le commedie dell'Ariosto nel teatro francese', *Giornale storico della letteratura italiana*, 128 (1951), 41–80

BOUGHNER, DANIEL, 'The Braggart in Italian Renaissance Comedy', *Proceedings of the Modern Language Association*, 58.1 (1943), 42–83

BOWEN, BARBARA, *Les Caractéristiques essentielles de la farce française et leur survivance dans les années 1550–1620* (Urbana: University of Illinois Press, 1964)

BRADBY, DAVID, 'France: The 16th Century', in *The Cambridge Guide to Theatre*, ed. by Martin Banham (Cambridge: Cambridge University Press, 2000), pp. 385–86

BRAYBROOK, JEAN, *Rémy Belleau et l'art de guérir* (Berlin: De Gruyter, 2013)

BRERETON, GEOFFREY, *French Comic Drama: From the Sixteenth to the Eighteenth Century* (London: Methuen, 1977)

BRÉSARD, MARC, *Les Foires de Lyon aux quinzième et seizième siècles* (Paris: École de Chartes, 1914)

BRYCE, JUDITH, 'The Theatrical Activities of Palla di Lorenzo Strozzi in Lyon in the 1540s', in *Theatre of the English and Italian Renaissance*, ed. by Ronnie Mulryne, Margaret Shewring (New York: St Martin's Press, 1991), pp. 55–72

BULLARD, MELISSA MERIAM, *Filippo Strozzi and the Medici: Favour and Finance in Sixteenth-century Florence and Rome* (Cambridge: Cambridge University Press, 1980)

BUONINSEGNI, BERNARDO, [LETTER], *Miscellanea storica senese*, 4.12 (1896), 201

BURON, EMMANUEL, '"Comique" et "propriété" dans la préface de l'"Amoureux repos" de Guillaume des Autelz', in *Le Léxique métalitteraire français (XVIe-XVIIe siècles)*, ed. by Michel Jourde and Jean-Charles Monferran (Geneva: Droz, 2006), pp. 67–87

BURKE, PETER, 'Exemplarity and Anti-exemplarity in Early Modern Europe', in *The Western Time of Ancient History: Historiographical Encounters with the Greek and Roman Pasts*, ed. by Alexandra Lianeri (Cambridge: Cambridge University Press, 2011), pp. 48–59

BURROW, COLIN, *Imitating Authors: Plato to Futurity* (Oxford: Oxford University Press, 2019)

CANDIARD, CÉLINE, 'Roman Comedy in Early Modern Italy and France', in *The Cambridge Companion to Roman Comedy*, ed. by Martin Dinter (Cambridge: Cambridge University Press, 2019), pp. 325–38

CARLSON, MARVIN, *Theories of the Theatre: A Historical and Critical Survey, from the Greeks to the Present* (New York: Cornell University Press, 1993)

CAVALLUCCI, GIACOMO, *Odet de Turnèbe* (Naples: Raffaele Pironti, 1942)

CAVE, TERENCE, *The Cornucopian Text: Problems of Writing in the French Renaissance* (Oxford: Clarendon Press, 1979)

CERRETA, FLORINDO, 'A Case of Homophonic Word-play in Turnèbe's *Les Contens*', *Italica*, 41.4 (1964), 434–37

——'A French Translation of *Gl'Ingannati*: Charles Estienne's *Les Abusez*', *Italica*, 54.1 (1977), 12–34

CHAMARD, HENRI, 'Le Collège de Boncourt et les origines du théâtre classique', in *Mélanges offerts à M. Abel Lefranc par ses élèves et ses amis*, ed. by Jacques Lavaud (Paris: Droz, 1936), pp. 246–60

——*Histoire de la Pléiade*, 4 vols (Paris: Didier, 1961–64)

CHARTIER, ROGER, 'Stratégies éditoriales et lectures populaires, 1530–1660', in *Histoire de l'édition française,* ed. by Henri-Jean Martin and Robert Chartier, 4 vols (Paris: Promodis, 1982–86), I, 584–603

CHASLES, ÉMILE, *La Comédie en France au seizième siècle* (Geneva: Slatkine Reprints, 1969)

CHASLES, FRANÇOIS-JACQUES, *Dictionaire universel, chronologique, et historique, de justice, police, et finances*, 3 vols (Paris: Claude Robustel, 1725)

CIORANESCU, ALEXANDRE, *L'Arioste en France: des origines à la fin du xviiiè siècle* (Paris: Presses modernes, 1938)

CLÉMENT, LOUIS, *Henri Estienne et son œuvre française* (Geneva: Slatkine, 1967)

CLÉMENT, MICHÈLE, 'Jodelle ou la fête de papier', in *La Fête au XVIe siècle*, ed. by Marie Viallon-Schoneveld (Saint-Étienne: Université de Saint-Étienne, 2003), pp. 159–70

CLOULAS, IVAN, *Henri II* (Paris: Fayard, 1985)

COCKRAM, SARAH, *Isabella d'Este and Francesco Gonzaga: Power Sharing at the Italian Renaissance Court* (London: Routledge, 2016)

COHEN, PAUL, 'In Search of the Trojan Origins of French: The Uses of History in the Elevation of the Vernacular in Early Modern France', in *Fantasies of Troy: Classical Tales and the Social Imaginary in Medieval and Early Modern Europe*, ed. by Alan Shepard and Stephen David Powell (Toronto: Centre for Reformation and Renaissance Studies, 2005), pp. 63–80

COLLETET, GUILLAUME, *Vie de Jean-Pierre de Mesmes* (Paris: M. Ph. Tamizey de Larroque, 1878)

COOPER, RICHARD, 'Le Cercle de Lucantonio Ridolfi', in *L'Émergence littéraire des femmes à Lyon à la Renaissance: 1520–1560*, ed. by Michèle Clément and Janine Incardona (Saint-Étienne: Université de Saint-Étienne, 2008), pp. 29–50

—— 'Court Festival and Triumphal Entries under Henri II', in *Court Festivals of the European Renaissance: Art, Politics and Performance*, ed. by Elizabeth Goldring and Ronnie Mulryne (Abingdon: Routledge, 2002), pp. 51–75

—— 'Gabriele Simeoni visionario', in *Cinquecento visionario tra Italia e Francia*, ed. by Nerina Clerici (Florence: Olschki, 1992) pp. 279–97

—— 'Le Juge comme personnage littéraire à la Renaissance', in *L'Intime du droit à la Renaissance*, ed. by Max Engammare and Alexandre Vanautgaerden (Geneva: Droz, 2014), pp. 451–77

—— 'Mario Equicola et la France', in *Parcours et rencontres: mélanges de langue, d'histoire et de littérature française offerts à Enea Balmas*, ed. by Paolo Carile, Giovanni Dotoli, and Anna Maria Raugei, 2 vols (Paris: Klincksieck, 1993), I, 167–82

—— 'Scève, Serlio et la Fête', in *Maurice Scève: le poète en quête d'un langage*, ed. by Vân Dung Le Flanchec, Michèle Clément, and Anne-Pascale Pouey-Mounou (Paris: Classiques Garnier, 2020), pp. 339–53

—— 'The Theme of War in Renaissance Entries', in *Ceremonial Entries in Early Modern Europe: The Iconography of Power*, ed. by Maria Ines Aliverti, Ronnie Mulryne, and Anna Maria Testaverde (Farnham: Ashgate, 2015), pp. 15–46

CORNILLIAT, FRANÇOIS, 'From "Defense and Illustration" to "Dishonor and Bastardization": Joachim Du Bellay on Language and Poetry', *Modern Language Notes*, 130.4 (2015), 730–56

COTTRELL, ROBERT, 'Allegories of Desire in Lemaire's *Concorde des deux langages*', *French Forum*, 23.1 (1998), 261–300

CUMMINGS, ANTONY, *The Maecenas and the Madrigalist: Patrons, Performers and the Origins of the Italian Madrigal* (Philadelphia: American Philosophical Society, 2004)

D'AMICO, JACK, 'Drama and the Court in *La Calandra*', *Theatre Journal*, 43.1 (1991), 93–106

D'ANDREA, ANTONIO, 'The Political and Ideological Context of Innocent Gentillet's *Anti-Machiavel*', *Renaissance Quarterly*, 23.4 (1970), 397–411

DE CAPITANI BERTRAND, PATRIZIA, *Du spectaculaire à l'intime: un siècle de commedia erudita en Italie et en France* (Paris: Champion, 2005)

DEGEN, GUY, 'Une leçon du théâtre', in *Pierre de Larivey, Champenois: chanoine, traducteur, auteur de comédies et astrologue (1541–1619)*, ed. by Yvonne Bellenger (Paris: Klincksieck, 1993), pp. 15–39

DELCOURT, MARIE, *La Tradition des comiques anciens en France avant Molière* (Liège: Faculté de Philosophie et Lettres, 1934)

DEMERSON, GENEVIÈVE, *Polémiques autour de la mort de Turnèbe* (Clermont-Ferrand: Centre de Recherches sur la Réforme et la Contre-Réforme, 1975)

DI MARIA, SALVATORE, *The Italian Tragedy in the Renaissance: Cultural Realities and Theatrical Innovations* (Lewisburg, PA: Bucknell University Press, 2002)

—— *The Poetics of Imitation in the Italian Theatre of the Renaissance* (Toronto: University of Toronto Press, 2013)

DICKEY, BRUCE, 'Ornamentation in Sixteenth-century Music', in *A Performer's Guide to Renaissance Music*, ed. by Jeffery T. Kite-Powell (Bloomington: Indiana University Press, 2007), pp. 300–25

DIGANGI, MARIO, '"Male Deformities": Narcissus and the Reformation of Courtly Manners in *Cynthia's Revels*', in *Ovid and the Renaissance Body*, ed. by Goran Stanivukovic (Toronto: University of Toronto Press, 2001), pp. 94–110

EVDOKIMOVA, LUDMILLA, 'La Traduction en vers des comédies de Térence dans l'édition d'Antoine Vérard: le choix du style et du destinataire', in *'Pour acquerir honneur et pris': mélanges de moyen français offerts à Giuseppe Di Stefano*, ed. by Maria Colombo Timelli and Claudio Galderisi (Montreal: Ceres, 2004), pp. 111–21

ESPINER-SCOTT, JANET, 'Note sur le cercle de Henri de Mesmes et sur son influence', in *Mélanges offerts à M. Abel Lefranc par ses élèves et ses amis*, ed. by Jacques Lavaud (Paris: Droz, 1936), pp. 354–58

EYRES, PATRICK, 'British Naumachias: The Performance of Trial and Memorial', in *Performance and Appropriation: Profane Rituals in Gardens and Landscapes*, ed. by Michel Conan (Washington, DC: Dumbarton Oaks Research Library and Collection, 2007), pp. 171–94

FERGUSON, MARGARET, 'The Exile's Defense: Du Bellay's *La deffence et illustration de la langue françoyse*', *PMLA*, 93.2 (1978), 275–89

—— *Trials of Desire: Renaissance Defenses of Poetry* (New Haven, CT: Yale University Press, 1983)

FINOTTI, FABIO, 'Perspective and Stage Design, Fiction and Reality in the Italian Renaissance Theater of the Fifteenth Century', *Renaissance Drama*, 36 (2010), 21–42

FINZI-CONTINI CALABRESI, BIANCA, '"Bawdy Doubles": Pietro Aretino's *Commedie* (1588) and the Appearance of English Drama', *Renaissance Drama*, 36 (2010), 207–35

FONTES-BARATTO, ANNA, 'Les Fêtes à Urbin en 1513 et *La Calandra* de Bernardo Dovizi da Bibbiena', in *Les Écrivains et le pouvoir en Italie à l'époque de la Renaissance*, ed. by André Rochon (Paris: Université de la Sorbonne Nouvelle, 1974), pp. 69–75

FORD, PHILIP, *The Judgement of Palaemon: The Contest between Neo-Latin and Vernacular Poetry in Renaissance France* (Boston: Brill, 2013)

—— 'What Does "Renaissance" Mean?', in *Cambridge History of French Literature*, ed. by William Burgwinkle, Nicholas Hammond, and Emma Wilson (Cambridge: Cambridge University Press, 2011), pp. 180–87

FORD, PHILIP, and INGRID DE SMET, eds, *Eros et Priapus: érotisme et obscenité dans la littérature néo-latine* (Geneva: Droz, 1997)

FORSYTH, ELLIOTT, 'Discussion: French Renaissance Tragedy and its Critics: A Reply to Donald Stone, Jr', *Renaissance Drama*, 2 (1969), 207–22

FREEMAN, MICHAEL, 'Une source inconnue des *Esprits* de Pierre de Larivey', *BHR*, 41 (1979), 137–45

GAREFFI, ANDREA, *La scrittura e la festa: teatro, festa e letterature nella Firenze del Rinascimento* (Bologna: Il Mulino, 1991)

GASCON, RICHARD, *Grand commerce et vie urbaine au XVIe siècle: Lyon et ses marchands*, 2 vols (Paris: Mouton, 1971)

GENETTE, GÉRARD, *Seuils* (Paris: Seuil, 1987)

GRAHAM, VICTOR, 'Jodelle's *Eugène*, ou *La Rencontre* Again', *Renaissance News*, 14.3 (1961), 161–64

GREENE, THOMAS, *The Light in Troy: Imitation and Discovery in Renaissance Poetry* (New Haven, CT: Yale University Press, 1982)

GUIGUE, GEORGES, *La Magnificence de la superbe et triumphante entree de la noble et antique cité de Lyon* (Lyons: Société des Bibliophiles Lyonnais, 1927)

HALL, JOHN, 'Primaticcio and Court Festivals', *Bulletin of the John Rylands University Library of Manchester*, 58.2 (1976), 353–77

HARASZTI, JULES, 'La Comédie française de la Renaissance et la scène', *Revue d'histoire littéraire de la France*, 14 (1909), 285–301

HAUVETTE, HENRI, *Un exilé florentin à la cour de France au XVIe siècle* (Paris: Hachette & Cie, 1903)

HAWTHORNE, MELANIE, '"Comment peut-on être homosexuel?": Multinational (In)Corporation and the Frenchness of Salomé', in *Perennial Decay: On the Aesthetics and Politics of Decadence*, ed. by Liz Constable, Dennis Denisoff, and Matthew Potolsky (Philadephia: University of Pennsylvania Press, 1999), pp. 159–82

HAYES, BRUCE, *Hostile Humor in Renaissance France* (Newark: University of Delaware Press, 2020)

HELLER, HENRY, *Anti-Italianism in Sixteenth-century France* (Toronto: University of Toronto Press, 2003)

HENKE, ROBERT, 'Border-crossing in the Commedia dell'Arte', in *Transnational Exchange in Early Modern Theater*, ed. by Robert Henke and Eric Nicholson (Aldershot: Ashgate, 2008), pp. 19–34

HOBHOUSE, PENELOPE, and PATRICK TAYLOR, eds, *The Gardens of Europe* (London: George Philip & Son, 1990)

HOPE, THOMAS, *Lexical Borrowing in the Romance Languages: A Critical Study of Italianisms in French and Gallicisms in Italian from 1100 to 1900* (Oxford: Basil Blackwell, 1971)

HOWARTH, WILLIAM, ed., *French Theatre in the Neo-classical Era, 1550–1789* (Cambridge: Cambridge University Press, 1997)

HUGUET, EDMOND, *Dictionnaire de la langue française du seizième siècle*, 7 vols (Paris: Didier, 1925–67)

JAROSZEWSKA, TERESA, 'Un capitan italien en costume espagnol', in *Les Mots et les choses du théâtre: France, Italie, Espagne, XVIe–XVIIe siècles* (Geneva: Droz, 2017), pp. 211–26

JEFFERY, BRIAN, *French Renaissance Comedy, 1552–1630* (Oxford: Clarendon Press, 1969)

JENSEN, KRISTIAN, 'The Humanist Reform of Latin and Latin Teaching', in *The Cambridge Companion to Renaissance Humanism*, ed. by Jill Kraye (Cambridge: Cambridge University Press, 1998), pp. 63–81

JOHNSON, ALFRED FORBES, *Sixteenth-century French Printing* (London: E. Benn, 1928)

JOHNSON, EUGENE, *Inventing the Opera House: Theater Architecture in Renaissance and Baroque Italy* (Cambridge: Cambridge University Press, 2018)

—— 'The Theater at Lyon of 1548: A Reconstruction and Attribution', *Artibus et Historiae*, 35.69 (2014), 173–202

JONDORF, GILLIAN, *French Renaissance Tragedy: The Dramatic Word* (Cambridge: Cambridge University Press, 1990)

KAMMERER, ELSA, 'Une sainte femme desirée: le *Magdalon de la Madalena* de Jean de Vauzelles', in *L'Émergence littéraire des femmes à Lyon à la Renaissance: 1520–1560*, ed. by Michèle Clément and Janine Incardona (Saint-Étienne: Publications de l'Université de Saint-Étienne, 2008), pp. 69–88

KATRITZKY, PEG, *The Art of 'Commedia': A Study in the 'Commedia Dell'Arte' 1560–1620 with Special Reference to the Visual Records* (Amsterdam: Rodopi, 2006)

KAWCZYŃSKI, MAX, 'Über das Verhältnis des Lustspiels *Les Contens* von Odet de Turnèbe zu *Les Esbahis* de Jacques Grévin und beider zu den Italienern', in *Festschrift zum VIII: Allgemeinen deutschen Neuphilologentage in Wien Pfingsten*, ed. by Jakob Schipper (Leipzig: Wilhelm Braumüller, 1898), pp. 239–50

KELLY, JOAN, 'Did Women Have a Renaissance?', in *The Italian Renaissance*, ed. by Harold Bloom (New York: Chelsea House, 2004), pp. 151–76

KENNY, NEIL, *Born to Write: Literary Families and Social Hierarchy in Early Modern France* (Oxford: Oxford University Press, 2020)

KENT, DALE, *The Rise of the Medici: Faction in Florence, 1426–1432* (Oxford: Oxford University Press, 1978)

KIEFER, FREDERIC, ed., *Masculinities and Femininities in the Middle Ages and Renaissance* (Turnhout: Brepols, 2009)

KNECHT, ROBERT, *Francis I* (Cambridge: Cambridge University Press, 1984)

KNIGHT, ALAN, *Aspects of Genre in Late Medieval French Drama* (Manchester: Manchester University Press, 1983)

KOCH, PHILIP, 'French Drama in the Seventeenth Century', in *Comedy: A Geographic and Historical Guide*, ed. by Maurice Charney, 2 vols (Westport: Praeger Publishers, 2005), II, 331–49

KRAGELUND, PATRICK, *Roman Historical Drama: The Octavia in Antiquity and Beyond* (Oxford: Oxford University Press, 2016)

LANGER, ULLRICH, and JAN MIERNOWSKI, eds, *Anteros: actes du colloque de Madison* (Orléans: Paradigme, 1994)

LANSON, GUSTAVE, 'Études sur les origines de la tragédie classique en France: comment s'est opérée la substitution de la tragédie aux mystères et moralités', *Revue d'Histoire littéraire de la France*, 2 (1903), 177–231

LARSEN, ANNE, 'Chastity and the Mother-daughter Bond: Odet de Turnèbe's Response to Catherine des Roches', in *Renaissance Women Writers: French Texts/American Contexts*, ed. by Anne Larsen and Collette Winn (Detroit, MI: Wayne State University Press, 1994), pp. 172–88

LAU, ERICH, *Charles Estienne: Biographie und Bibliographie* (Leipzig: Vertheim Bechstein, 1930)

LAUMONIER, PAUL, *Ronsard, poète lyrique: étude historique et littéraire* (Paris: Hachette, 1932)

LAWRENSON, THOMAS, *The French Stage in the XVIIth Century: A Study in the Advent of the Italian Order* (New York: AMS Press, 1986)

LAWTON, HAROLD, *Contribution à l'histoire de l'humanisme en France: Térence en France au XVI siècle, éditions et traductions* (Geneva: Slatkine, 1970)

——— *French Renaissance Dramatic Theory* (Manchester: Manchester University Press, 1949)

LAZARD, MADELEINE, 'Le Dessein de Larivey et son public', in *Pierre de Larivey, Champenois: chanoine, traducteur, auteur de comédies et astrologue (1541–1619)*, ed. by Yvonne Bellenger (Paris: Klincksieck, 1993), pp. 49–60

——— *Le Théâtre en France au XVIe siècle* (Paris: Presses universitaires de France, 1980)

LEWICKA, HELENA, ed., *Le Comique verbal en France au XVIe siècle: actes du colloque organisé par l'Institut d'Études Romanes et le Centre de Civilisation Française de l'Université de Varsovie, avril 1975* (Warsaw: Warsaw University Press, 1981)

LEBÈGUE, RAYMOND, 'La Comédie italienne en France au XVIe siècle', *Revue de Littérature Comparée*, 24 (1950), 5–24

——— 'Tableau de la comédie française de la Renaissance', *BHR*, 8 (1946), 278–344

——— *La Tragédie française de la Renaissance* (Brussels: Office de Publicité, 1954)

LEDBETTER, DAVID, *Harpsichord and Lute Music in 17th-century France* (Basingstoke: Palgrave Macmillan, 1987)

LEES-JEFFRIES, HESTER, 'Pictures, Places, and Spaces: Sidney, Wroth, Wilton House and the *Songe de Poliphile*', in *Renaissance Paratexts*, ed. by Helen Smith and Louise Wilson (Cambridge: Cambridge University Press, 2011), pp. 185–203

LENIENT, CHARLES, *La Satire en France au Moyen âge* (Paris: Hachette, 1893)

LEONARD, HARRY, 'The Huguenots and the Bartholomew's Massacre', in *The Huguenots: History and Memory in Transnational Context: Essays in Honour of Walter C. Utt*, ed. by David J. B. Trim (Leiden: Brill, 2011), pp. 43–67

LEVILLAIN, PHILIPPE, ed., *The Papacy: An Encyclopaedia*, 3 vols (London: Routledge, 2002)

LEWIS, JOHN, *Adrien Turnèbe, 1512–1565: A Humanist Observed* (Geneva: Droz, 1998)

LINTILHAC, EUGÈNE, *Histoire générale du théâtre en France*, 5 vols (Paris: Flammarion, 1904–10)

LIONETTO, ADELINE, ' "Je me fis quasi de tous métiers": Etienne Jodelle et la promotion de la figure du poète panepistemon', *Anamorfose: Revista de Estudos Modernos*, 4.1 (2018), 1–18

——'Splendeurs et misères de la ville de Paris dans le *Recueil des inscriptions, devis et masquarades* de Jodelle', *Seizième siècle*, 9 (2013), 81–93

LOZZI, CARLO, ed., *Il bibliofilo*, 11 vols (Bologna: Società tipografica già compositori, 1884)

McFARLANE, IAN, *The Entry of Henri II into Paris, 16 June 1549* (Binghamton, NY: Medieval and Renaissance Texts and Studies, 1982)

McGOWAN, MARGARET, 'Lyon: A Centre for Water Celebrations', in *Waterborne Pageants and Festivities in the Renaissance: Essays in Honour of J. R. Mulryne*, ed. by Margaret Shewring (Oxford: Taylor & Francis, 2016), pp. 37–50

——*The Vision of Rome in Late Renaissance France* (New Haven, CT, & London: Yale University Press, 2000)

McLAUGHLIN, MARTIN, *Literary Imitation in the Italian Renaissance: The Theory and Practice of Literary Imitation in Italy from Dante to Bembo* (Oxford: Clarendon Press, 1995)

——'The Recovery of Terence in Renaissance Italy: From Alberti to Machiavelli', in *The Reinvention of Theatre in Sixteenth-century Europe: Traditions, Texts and Performance*, ed. by Tom Earle and Catarina Fouto (Oxford: Legenda, 2015), pp. 115–39

MacPHAIL, ERIC, *The Voyage to Rome in French Renaissance Literature* (Saratoga, CA: Anma Libri, 1990)

McPHERSON, DAVID, 'Roman Comedy in Renaissance Education: The Moral Question', *The Sixteenth Century Journal*, 12.1 (1981) 19–30

MALATO, ENRICO, *Storia della letteratura italiana: la letteratura italiana fuori d'Italia*, 18 vols (Rome: Salerno, 2005)

MANETTI, GIANNOZZO, *Vite di Dante, Petrarca e Boccaccio*, ed. by Angelo Solerti (Milan: Vallardi, 1904)

MARIETTI, MARINA, *Quêtes d'une identité collective chez les Italiens de la Renaissance* (Paris: Université de la Sorbonne Nouvelle, 1990)

MARTINEZ, RONALD, 'Etruria Triumphant in Rome: Fables of Medici Rule and Bibbiena's *Calandra*', *Renaissance Drama*, 36 (2010), 69–98

——'Spectacle', in *The Cambridge Companion to the Italian Renaissance*, ed. by Michael Wyatt (Cambridge: Cambridge University Press, 2014), pp. 239–59

MAZOUER, CHARLES, *Le Théâtre français de la Renaissance* (Paris: Champion, 2002)

MEERE, MICHAEL, ed., *French Renaissance and Baroque Drama: Text, Performance, Theory* (Newark: University of Delaware Press, 2015)

MEERE, MICHAEL, and CAROLINE GATES, 'Farce, Community, and the Performativity of Violence in Rabelais's *Quart Livre*: The Chiquanous Episode', in *French Renaissance and Baroque Drama: Text, Performance, Theory*, ed. by Michael Meere (Newark: University of Delaware Press, 2015), pp. 39–62

MELEHY, HASSAN, *The Poetics of Literary Transfer in Early Modern France and England* (Abingdon: Routledge, 2016)

MELZI, ROBERT, '*Gl'Ingannati* and its French Renaissance Translation', *Kentucky Foreign Language Quarterly*, 12.3 (1965), 180–90

MICHELET, JULES, *Histoire de France*, 17 vols (Paris: Chamerot, 1855)

MILNER-DAVIES, JESSICA, 'Farce', in *Encyclopedia of Humor Studies*, ed. by Salvatore Attardo, 2 vols (London & New York: SAGE Publications, 2014), I, 233–36

MILSTEIN, JOANNA, *The Gondi: Family Strategy and Survival in Early Modern France* (Abingdon: Routledge, 2018)

MITCHELL, BONNER, 'Circumstance and Setting in the Earliest Italian Productions of Comedy', *Renaissance Drama*, 4 (1971), 185–97

—— 'Firenze illustrissima: l'immagine della patria negli apparati delle Nationi fiorentine per le feste di Lione del 1548 e di Anversa del 1549', in *Firenze e la Toscana dei Medici nell'Europa del '500: Relazioni artistiche; il linguaggio architettonico*, ed. by Giancarlo Garfagnini, 3 vols (Florence: L. S. Olschki, 1983), III, 995–1004

—— 'Les Intermèdes au service de l'état', in *Les Fêtes de la Renaissance*, ed. by Jean Jacquot and Elie Konigson, 3 vols (Paris: Centre national de la recherche scientifique, 1956), III, 117–31

MONALDINI, SERGIO, 'Visioni del Comico', *Maske und Kothurn*, 50.3 (2005), 45–64

MONFERRAN, JEAN-CHARLES, *L'Amour des amours* (Paris: Société des Textes Français Modernes, 1996)

MORIN, LOUIS, *Les Trois Pierre de Larivey: biographie et bibliographie* (Troyes: J.-L. Paton, 1937)

NAGELSMIT, EELCO, 'Visualizing Vitruvius: Stylistic Pluralism in Serlio's Sixth Book on Architecture', in *The Transformation of Expression in the Early Modern Arts*, ed. by Joost Keizer and Todd Richardson (Leiden: Brill, 2012), pp. 339–72

NAGLER, ALOIS MARIA, *Theatre Festivals of the Medici, 1539–1637* (New Haven, CT: Yale University Press, 1964)

NAVARRETE, IGNACIO, 'Strategies of Appropriation in Speroni and Du Bellay', *Comparative Literature*, 41.2 (1989), 141–54

NOIROT, CORINNE, 'French Humanist Comedy in Search of an Audience: The Case of Jean de la Taille', in *French Renaissance and Baroque Drama: Text, Performance, Theory*, ed. by Michael Meere (Newark: University of Delaware Press, 2015), pp. 83–100

NORTON, GLYN, *The Ideology and Language of Translation in Renaissance France and their Humanist Antecedents* (Geneva: Droz, 1984)

—— 'Theories of Prose Fiction in Sixteenth-century France', in *Cambridge History of Literary Criticism*, ed. by Glyn Norton, 9 vols (Cambridge: Cambridge University Press, 1999), III, 305–13

—— 'Translation Theory in Renaissance France: The Poetic Controversy', *Renaissance and Reformation*, 11 (1975), 30–45

NORTON, GLYN, and MARGA COTTINO-JONES, 'Theories of Prose Fiction and Poetics in Italy: novella and romanzo', in *Cambridge History of Literary Criticism*, ed. by Glyn Norton, 9 vols (Cambridge: Cambridge University Press, 1999), III, 322–38

OMONT, HENRI, *Anciens inventaires et catalogues de la Bibliothèque nationale* (Paris: E. Leroux, 1908)

PACIFICI, VINCENZO, *Ippolito II d'Este, Cardinale di Ferrara: da documenti originali inediti* (Tivoli: Società Storia e d'Arte, 1984)

PANAYOTAKIS, COSTAS, *Decimus Laberius: The Fragments* (Cambridge: Cambridge University Press, 2010)

PARINI, GIUSEPPE, *Versi e prose di Giuseppe Parini*, ed. by Giuseppe Giusti (Florence: Felice le Monnier, 1846)

PATER, WALTER, *The Renaissance* (New York: The Modern Library, 1934)

PAULICELLI, EUGENIA, *Writing Fashion in Early Modern Italy: From Sprezzatura to Satire* (Farnham: Ashgate, 2014)

PERRET, DONALD, *Old Comedy in the French Renaissance (1576–1620)* (Geneva: Droz, 1992)

PETIT DE JULLEVILLE, LOUIS, *Le Théâtre en France: histoire de la littérature dramatique depuis ses origines jusqu'à nos jours* (Paris: A. Colin, 1921)

PICOT, ÉMILE, *Des Français qui ont écrit en italien au XVI⁰ siècle* (Paris: E. Bouillon, 1902)

—— *Les Français italianisants au XVI⁰ siècle*, 2 vols (Paris: Champion, 1906)

PICOT, ÉMILE, ed., *Recueil général des sotties*, 3 vols (Paris: Firmin Didot, 1902–12)

PIGMAN, GEORGE, 'Versions of Imitation in the Renaissance', *Renaissance Quarterly*, 33.1 (1980), 1–32

PINVERT, LUCIEN, *Jacques Grévin (1538–1570): sa vie, ses écrits, ses amis, étude biographique et littéraire* (Paris: A. Fontemoing, 1899)

POGUE, SAMUEL, *Jacques Moderne: Music Printer of the Sixteenth Century* (Geneva: Droz, 1969)

POMPEO BARTI, ALESSANDRO, and DOMENICO GIORGI, eds, *Catalogo della libreria Capponi o sia de' libri italiani del fù marchese Alessandro Gregorio Capponi* (Rome: Bernabò e Lazzarini, 1747)

PRESCHL, ARTEMIS, *Shakespeare and Commedia dell'Arte: Play by Play* (Abingdon: Routledge, 2017)

QUAINTON, MALCOLM, 'The Mysterious Case of the Missing Source Edition of Jean-Antoine de Baïf's *Le Brave*', in *Court and Humour in the French Renaissance: Essays in Honour of Professor Pauline Smith*, ed. by Sarah Alyn Stacey (Oxford: Peter Lang, 2009), pp. 127–46

RAYFIELD, LUCY, 'The Poetics of Comedy in Jacques Peletier du Mans's *Art poëtique* (1555)', *Classical Receptions Journal*, 13.1 (2021), 31–48

—— 'Rewriting Laughter in Early Modern Europe', in *The Palgrave Handbook of Humour, History, and Methodology*, ed. by Hannah Burrows and Daniel Derrin (London: Palgrave Macmillan, 2021), pp. 71–91

RAYMOND, MARCEL, *L'Influence de Ronsard sur la poésie française* (Geneva: Droz, 1965)

REVARD, STELLA PURCE, *Pindar and the Renaissance Hymn-ode, 1450–1700* (Tempe: Arizona Centre for Medieval and Renaissance Studies, 2001)

RIGO BIENAIMÉ, DORA, *Grévin: poeta satirico, e altri saggi sulla poesia del cinquecento francese* (Pisa: Giardini, 1967)

RIGOLOT, FRANÇOIS, 'The Renaissance Crisis of Exemplarity', *Journal of the History of Ideas*, 54.4 (1998), 557–63

ROCKE, MICHAEL, 'Gender and Sexual Culture in Renaissance Italy', in *Gender and Society in Renaissance Italy*, ed. by Judith Brown and Robert Charles Davis (London: Routledge, 1998), pp. 150–70

ROGÉ, ANNE, 'Traductions de théâtre ou trahison théâtrale: l'imitation renaissante comme appropriation culturelle', *Carnets*, 14 (2018), 1–13

ROMIER, LUCIEN, *Les Origines politiques des guerres de religion*, 2 vols (Paris: Perrin, 1913)

—— *Le Royaume de Catherine de Médicis: la France à la veille des guerres de religion*, 2 vols (Paris: Perrin, 1922)

SAND, MAURICE, *Masques et bouffons: comédie italienne*, 2 vols (Paris: Michel Lévy Frères, 1860)

SANKOVITCH, TILDE, *Jodelle et la création du masque: étude structurale et normative de L'Eugène* (York, SC: French Literature Publications, 1979)

SCAGLIONE, ALDO, *Knights at Court: Courtliness, Chivalry and Courtesy from Ottonian Germany to the Italian Renaissance* (Berkeley: University of California Press, 1991)

SCHEPPER, SUSANNA DE, '"For the Common Good and for the National Interest": Paratexts in English Translations of Navigational Works', in *Renaissance Cultural Crossroads: Translation, Print and Culture in Britain, 1473–1640*, ed. by Sara Barker and Brenda Hosington (Leiden: Brill, 2013), pp. 185–208

SCHWARTE, LUDGER, 'Anatomical Theatre as Experimental Space', in *Collection, Laboratory, Theatre: Scenes of Knowledge in the Seventeenth Century*, ed. by Jan Lazardzig, Helmar Schramm, and Ludger Schwarte, 2 vols (Berlin: Walter de Gruyter, 2005), I, 75–103

SCOTT, VIRGINIA, *Women on the Stage in Early Modern France: 1540–1750* (Cambridge: Cambridge University Press, 2010)

SCOTT, VIRGINIA, and SARA STURM-MADDOX, *Performance, Poetry and Politics on the Queen's Day: Catherine de Médicis and Pierre de Ronsard at Fontainebleau* (London: Routledge, 2007)

SHEARMAN, JOHN, *Mannerism* (London: Pelican, 1967)

SIMONIN, MICHEL, 'La Disgrâce d'Amadis', *Studi Francesi*, 28 (1984), 1–35

SMITH, HELEN, and LOUISE WILSON, eds, *Renaissance Paratexts* (Cambridge: Cambridge University Press, 2014)

SMITH, PAULINE, *The Anti-courtier Trend in Sixteenth-century French Literature* (Geneva: Droz, 1966)

SOZZI, LIONELLO, *Boccaccio in Francia nel cinquecento* (Geneva: Slatkine Reprints, 1999)

—— *Rome n'est plus Rome: la polémique anti-italienne et autres essais sur la Renaissance; suivis de 'La dignité de l'homme'* (Paris: Champion, 2002)

STAMATAKIS, CHRIS, *Sir Thomas Wyatt and the Rhetoric of Writing: 'Turning the Word'* (Oxford: Oxford University Press, 2012)

STEWART, PAMELA, 'A Play on Doubles: The *Calandra*', *Modern Language Studies*, 14.1 (1984), 22–32

STONE, DONALD, 'An Approach to French Renaissance Drama', *Renaissance Drama*, 9 (1966), 279–89

—— *French Humanist Tragedy: A Re-assessment* (Manchester: Manchester University Press, 1974)

STRONG, ROY, *Art and Power: Renaissance Festivals, 1450–1650* (Berkeley: University of California Press, 1984)

STRUBEL, ARMAND, *Le Théâtre au Moyen Âge: naissance d'une littérature dramatique* (Rosny-sous-Bois: Bréal, 2003)

TERNAUX, JEAN-CLAUDE, 'La Comédie humaniste et la farce: *La Trésorière* de Grévin', *Seizième Siècle*, 6 (2010), 77–93

TERRUSI, LEONARDO, 'La *Philadelphia* di Lelio Manfredi: una commedia italiana del primo Cinquecento nella biblioteca del re di Francia', in *Letteratura italiana, letterature europee*, ed. by Guido Baldassari and Silvana Tamiozzo (Rome: Bulzoni, 2002), pp. 333–39

THIEBAUT, DOMINIQUE, 'Un artiste florentin au service de du Cardinal de Tournon: Giovanni Capassini', in *Kunst des Cinquecento in der Toskana*, ed. by Monika Cämmerer (Munich: Bruchmann, 1992), pp. 176–85

TILLEY, ARTHUR, *The Literature of the French Renaissance*, 2 vols (Cambridge: Cambridge University Press, 1904)

TOLDO, PIETRO, 'La Comédie française de la Renaissance', *Revue d'histoire littéraire de la France*, 5 (1898), 554–603

TYLUS, JANE, 'Women at the Windows: *Commedia dell'Arte* and Theatrical Practice in Early Modern Italy', *Theatre Journal*, 49.3 (1997), 323–42

TUBBS, SHANE, and OTHERS, eds, *History of Anatomy: An International Perspective* (New York: John Wiley & Sons, 2019)

VÈNE, MAGALI, *Bibliographia Serliana: catalogue des éditions imprimées des livres du traité d'architecture de Sebastiano Serlio (1537–1681)* (Paris: Picard, 2007)

VILLEY, PIERRE, *Les Sources italiennes de la 'Deffence et illustration de la langue françoise'* (Paris: Champion, 1908)

VIDORI, GIULIA, 'Negotiating Power in Sixteenth-century Italy: Ippolito II d'Este between Rome, France, and Ferrara' (unpublished doctoral thesis, University of Oxford, 2018)

WARNER, LYNDAN, *The Ideas of Man and Woman in Renaissance France: Print, Rhetoric, and Law* (Farnham: Ashgate, 2011)

WEBER, ROMAIN, 'Les Neapolitaines de François d'Amboise, deux textes pour le prix d'un: comédie et histoire comique combinées', *Cahiers de recherches médiévales et humanistes*, 32 (2016), 221–35

WEINBERG, BERNARD, 'Charles Estienne and Jean de la Taille', *Modern Language Notes*, 61.4 (1946), 262–65

—— *Critical Prefaces of the French Renaissance* (Evanston, IL: Northwestern University Press, 1950)

—— 'Du Bellay's "Contre les Pétrarquistes"', *L'Esprit Créateur*, 12 (1972), 159–77

WILDENSTEIN, GEORGES, 'La Collection de tableaux d'un amateur de Ronsard', *Gazette de Beaux-Arts*, 6.51 (1958)

WILEY, WILLIAM, *Early Public Theatre in France* (Cambridge, MA: Harvard University Press, 1960)

WILSON, BLAKE, *Singing to the Lyre in Renaissance Italy: Memory, Performance, and Oral Poetry* (Cambridge: Cambridge University Press, 2020)

WIND, BARTINA, *Les Mots italiens introduits en français au XVIe siècle* (Deventer: Æ. E. Kluwer, 1926)

WOODS-MARSDEN, JOANNA, 'Portrait of the Lady, 1430–1520', in *Virtue and Beauty: Leonardo's 'Ginevra de' Benci' and Renaissance Portraits of Women*, ed. by David Alan Brown (Washington, DC: National Gallery of Art, 2001), pp. 62–87

WORTH-STYLIANOU, VALERIE, 'Reading Monolingual and Bilingual Editions of Translations in Renaissance France', in *Translation and the Transmission of Culture between 1300 and 1600*, ed. by Jeanette Beer and Kenneth Lloyd-Jones (Kalamazoo, MI: Kalamazoo Press, 1995), pp. 331–58

—— '*Translatio* and Translation in the Renaissance: From Italy to France', in *Cambridge History of Literary Criticism*, ed. by Glyn Norton, 9 vols (Cambridge: Cambridge University Press, 1999), III, 127–35

YATES, FRANCES, *The French Academies of the Sixteenth Century* (Paris: Kraus, 1973)

ZORZI, ELVIRA GARBERO, 'Court Spectacle', in *Italian Renaissance Courts*, ed. by Sergio Bertelli, Franco Cardini, and Elvira Garbero Zorzi (London: Sidgwick & Jackson, 1986), pp. 127–89

APPENDIX I

Jean-Pierre de Mesmes's Prefatory Letters (1552)

1. Transcription

Le Traducteur au Seigneur Henry de Mesmes Jureconsultes

Cousin, en revisitant ces jours passez les vieilles compositions de ma premiere jeunesse, je trouvay (sans y penser) la presente traduction, dont le subject, non moins honeste que delectable, m'a esmeu la mettre en Lumiere avec sa source Italienne, pour donner plus de contentement aux curieux espritz et à vous plus de passetemps, mesme quant serez ennuyé de l'estude de la tetrique Jurisprudence qui demande (comme j'ay tousjours ouy dire) l'homme tout à soy: toutesfois, Cousin, si vous me croyez ne la croyez point: ains par intervales desrobez vous de sa veue et vous allez promener au mont de Parnase avec les Muses mignardes et par especial avec les Italiques, lesquelles vous sont familiers et privées, voire autant ou plus que les Grecques et Latines.

Aux Lecteurs

Vous pourrez trouver (amys Lecteurs) au commencement et à la fin de quelques pages de ceste Comedie, le François ne correspondre pas mot pour mot à l'Italien, ce qui ne vous doit retarder: car le Traducteur ne n'est voulu tant assubiettir ny contraindre, pour ne faire perdre la grace à nostre langue, qui a autre phrases et manieres de parler, que l'Italienne: mais je vous puis asseurer, au surplus, que vous la trouverez rendue fidellement, et au plus pres de l'intention de l'Autheur. A Dieu soyez.

2. Translation

The Translator to Seigneur Henri de Mesmes, Jurisconsult

Cousin, in recently revisiting the old compositions of my first youth, I found (without planning to) the present translation, the subject of which, no less honest than pleasurable, moved me to bring it to light along with its Italian source. It will bring more satisfaction to curious souls and more recreation to you, when you are bored of studying austere jurisprudence which demands (or so I have always heard) all of a man's time. However, Cousin, have faith in me and do not put all your faith in it: in this way, every so often tear yourself away from it and you will stroll on Mount Parnassus with the graceful Muses, and especially with the Italians, with whom you are familiar and intimate, even more so than the Greeks and Latins.

To the Readers.

You may find (Reader friends) that at the beginnings and ends of some pages of this comedy, the French does not correspond word-for-word with the Italian. This should not put you off, for the translator did not want to subject nor constrain, so as not to lose the grace of our language, which has phrases and ways of speaking that are different to Italian. Yet I can assure you, moreover, that you will find it faithfully rendered, and as close as possible to the author's intention. May God preserve you.

APPENDIX II

Timeline of Key Dates

c. 1457	The anonymous *La Farce de Maistre Pierre Pathelin* is written
1515	Accession of François I
1540	Charles Estienne begins writing France's first theatrical treatise
1542	Charles Estienne's translation, *L'Andrie*, is printed
1542	Charles Estienne's translation, *Les Abusez*, is printed
1547	Accession of Henri II and Catherine de' Medici
1548	Thomas Sébillet's *Art Poétique* is printed
1548	Bernardo Dovizi da Bibbiena's *La Calandra* is performed in Lyons
1549	Joachim Du Bellay's *Deffence, et illustration de la langue francoyse* is printed
1552	Estienne Jodelle's *L'Eugène* is performed at the French court and the Collège de Boncourt
1554	Agnolo Firenzuola's *I Lucidi* is performed at the French court
1555	Luigi Alamanni's *La Flora* is performed at the French court
1558	Jodelle's *masquarades* are performed at the French court
1559	Jacques Grévin's *La Trésorière* is performed at the Collège de Beauvais
1559	Accession of François II
1560	Accession of Charles IX
1561	Jacques Grévin's *Les Esbahis* is performed at the French court
1562	Outbreak of the first War of Religion
1572	St. Bartholomew's Day Massacre
1574	Accession of Henri III
1579	Pierre de Larivey's *Les six premieres comedies facecieuses* is printed
1580	Odet de Turnèbe's *Les Contens* is written

APPENDIX III

Plot Synopses

Where the comedy under discussion is a French translation, I have provided a synopsis of the original Italian play.

Bernardo Dovizi da Bibbiena: *La Calandra* (*c.* 1507)

A twin boy and girl, Lidio and Santilla, are separated when their father dies in the Turkish invasion of Modon. Santilla is disguised as a boy, taking on her brother's identity, by the servant Fannio and sold to Perillo. Lidio, meanwhile, is saved by a servant and goes to Tuscany. Time passes but Lidio never ceases to look for Santilla, eventually deciding to try to find her in Rome. There he falls in love with the beautiful Fulvia. Since Fulvia is married to the rich merchant Calandro, Lidio dresses up as his sister Santilla to gain access into Fulvia's home and they begin an affair. Calandro mistakes Lidio for a young woman and also arranges an affair with Lidio, who escapes. Fulvia, upset that Lidio now avoids the house, pays a necromancer to make Lidio fall in love with her again. Seeing Santilla dressed as a boy, the necromancer mistakes her for Lidio and sends her to Fulvia's house where, after much chaos, the twins realise that they are brother and sister.

Lodovico Ariosto: *I suppositi* (1509)

Erostrato loves Polinesta, whose father Damonio wants her to marry Cleandro, who is rich but far older than Polinesta. Erostrato and his servant Dulippo both disguise themselves, Dulippo as the master of the house and Erostrato in Dulippo's rags to gain access to Polinesta's home as a labourer. The two men find it difficult to keep up the pretence and are eventually found out by Polinesta. It emerges that Erostrato is the lost son of Cleandro who, delighted that he has found the son he thought he had lost during the Ottoman invasion of Otranto, sanctions the marriage of Erostrato to Polinesta.

Accademia degli Intronati: *Gl'ingannati* (1531)

Lelia and Fabrizio are twins, separated when their father loses Fabrizio in the Sack of Rome. Lelia disguises herself as a man she calls 'Fabio' and serves the handsome Flamminio as a page in order to escape an arranged marriage to Gherardo, an old man, and to win back Flamminio, who is her lost love. But Flamminio is now courting Isabella, and uses Lelia — disguised as Fabio — to deliver love letters to her. Isabella, however, falls in love with Fabio. Exploiting the situation, Lelia pretends to return Isabella's affections, thus inciting Isabella to further rebuke Flamminio's advances. Isabella meets Lelia's twin brother Fabrizio and, thinking him to be Fabio, marries him. When Flamminio sees Fabrizio he too mistakes him for Fabio, and believes his servant has betrayed him, but when Lelia reveals the plot to Flamminio he is sympathetic. Lelia and Flamminio then also marry, through the persuasion of her nurse, Clemenzia.

Agnolo Firenzuola: *I Lucidi* (*c.* 1540)

The play is set in Bologna. Two twins, Lucido Tolto and Lucido Folchetto, the sons of Agabito of Palermo and Madonna Lucrezia, are separated when Lucido Folchetto is lost in Naples. Lucido Folchetto goes to Bologna to find his twin and a series of misunderstandings ensue. Lucido Tolto is cheating on his wife Fiammetta with the next-door neighbour, referred to only as 'Signora', and when she sends him out so that she can cook a dinner for him, his twin brother turns up. Instead the Signora cooks for Lucido Folchetto, who is delighted at his unexpected welcome in Bologna. After the meal he finds himself at the house of the angry Fiammetta, who calls a physician when Lucido Folchetto — mistaken for her husband — fails to recognise her. Finally, Lucido Tolto also reappears at his wife's house and the twins are happily reunited.

Luigi Alamanni: *La Flora* (1549)

Geri has a wife, Clemenza, and a daughter, Porzia. Heading to Sicily on business, he has a relationship culminating in a daughter, Flora. Porzia, meanwhile, dies giving birth to Attilio. Geri eventually returns to Florence, but Flora is captured by pirates en route, eventually sold to Scarabon who takes her to Florence. Simone's son Ippolito is in love with Flora but, being a peasant, cannot afford the high price asked by Scarabon. Flamminia, a prostitute, is in love with Attilio, who is in turn in love with Virginia. Attilio explains to Flamminia Ippolito's predicament, and Flamminia negotiates with Scarabon to get the price lowered. Meanwhile, Ippolito uses the money Simone gives him to buy books to instead free Flora, and Ippolito and Attilio plan to leave Florence to escape the wrath of their fathers. In the end, Geri and Clemenza speak with one another, both finally understanding the true identities of Flora and Attilio. The play ends happily, with the double marriage of Ippolito to Flora, and Attilio to Virginia.

Estienne Jodelle: *L'Eugène* (1552)

[For a scene-by-scene summary can be found in Jeffery, *French Renaissance Comedy, 1552–1630*, p. 172]

The abbot Eugène has engineered the marriage of Alix to the dim-witted shopkeeper Guillaume. Pretending that Alix is his cousin, Eugène's true purpose is to be able to visit and sleep with Alix himself. Meanwhile, Guillaume is delighted that he has found himself such a chaste and honest wife. Florimond is a Gascon soldier back from Germany and intends to marry his beloved Alix: he is, however, unaware that he is loved by Hélène, the sister of Eugène. Chaos ensues as Florimond, furious at Eugène's lascivious intentions for Alix, resolves that he must murder Eugène. Florimond goes with Guillaume and Hélène to Eugène's residence. Eugène is terrified and wants to find nearby sergeants to help him. He is stopped by Hélène, however, and forced quickly to solve the situation. His sister Hélène will marry her beloved Florimond, and Eugène's confessor proclaims that they will be far happier since she has waited so long to be with him. Eugène having paid Guillaume's debts for him, Guillaume decides that he does not mind if Eugène also sleeps with Alix.

Jacques Grévin: *La Trésorière* (1559)

[A scene-by-scene summary can be found in Jeffery, *French Renaissance Comedy, 1552–1630*, p. 173]

Loys loves Constante, wife of the Trésorier, and tells his servant Richard that he hopes to capitalise on the Trésorier's trip out of Paris. During a visit to the Trésorier's residence Richard eavesdrops on Marie, Constante's servant, thereby learning that Constante prefers the Protenotaire to Loys. The Protenotaire is in a precarious financial situation and his servant Boniface is cunningly able to procure a large amount of money from Constante, after eavesdropping on her making arrangements to meet Loys. Richard then witnesses Constante allowing the Protenotaire into her house, and informs Loys. The Trésorier, Loys, and Richard forcibly enter the Trésorier's locked house, and discover Constante in her unfaithfulness. Loys decides that he will be content if the money that he has given to Constante is returned and if the debt he owes to the Trésorier is cancelled. The money lent by Constante to the Protenotaire is also kept and everyone is content.

Jacques Grévin: *Les Esbahis* (1561)

[A scene-by-scene summary can be found in Jeffery, *French Renaissance Comedy, 1552–1630*, p. 174]

Josse is an old man, presumed to be a widower after his wife Agnès left him for another man in Italy. He is extremely smug at now being engaged to Magdalêne, the beautiful young daughter of Gérard, although Josse himself is unattractive, impotent, and in poor health. He boasts of the excellent sex life he will enjoy with his new bride. The Advocat is also in love with Magdalêne, a relationship supported by his servant Julien and the Gentilhomme. Magdalêne has another suitor, the swaggering Italian expatriate Pantaleoné, overblown, parodic, and scorned by the other characters. Pantaleoné attempts to serenade Magdalêne with lines from Ariosto outside her window but only succeeds in infuriating the others. Meanwhile, Gérard is overheard speaking in the town, and he plans to have Magdalêne married to Josse by the very next day. The Advocat decides that he must take matters into his own hands and, in Josse's clothing, breaks into Magdalêne's house to make love to her. He is, however, seen through the keyhole by Gérard and mistaken for Josse. When Josse arrives he denies being there and begins to argue with Gérard, annoyed that his bride is no longer a virgin. Magdalêne is terrified at her actions and wonders what the outcome will be. At the same time Agnès turns up and, recognised by Josse, is invited back into his home. It transpires that Agnès's Italian lover is Pantaleoné, who is driven away by the other characters. L'Advocat and Magdalêne are married.

Odet de Turnèbe: *Les Contens* (1580)

[A scene-by-scene summary can be found in Jeffery, *French Renaissance Comedy, 1552–1630*, p. 178]

Louyse aims for her daughter Geneviefve to marry Eustache. However, Geneviefve has two other suitors who are far more interested in her: Basile and Rodomont, the latter a would-be Italian courtier and soldier. When Basile plots to visit Geneviefve disguised as Eustache, Rodomont decides to follow this same plan, and both borrow a recognisable red suit from Eustache. Eustache, in the meantime, has been told by the bawd Françoise that Geneviefve has deformed breasts, and so he no longer finds her attractive. Françoise also impresses Geneviefve with advice from her confessor and sermons she has heard, thereby convincing Geneviefve to allow Basile to visit her. Rodomont is unable to reach Geneviefve's house, since he is arrested for debt, so Basile gets there first. Geneviefve has managed to stay at home after telling her mother that she has a cold; she lets Basile in and they make love. Louyse returns home from church, sees Basile, and thinks he is Eustache; she locks the door. Basile escapes from the window and instead helps a prostitute named Alix into the room, whom he dresses in the red suit. Louyse is perplexed at finding Alix, and offers Geneviefve to Rodomont, who, since discovering the plot and realising that Geneviefve is no longer a virgin, is also no longer attracted to her. Basile subsequently admits to dressing up as Eustache and Louyse concedes that Basile must marry Geneviefve.

INDEX

Accademia degli Intronati 16, 28, 68
Accursius 75
Advocat (character in *Les Esbahis*) 124, 131
Agnès (character in *Les Esbahis*) 123–24, 128
Agnoletta (character in *L'amor costante*) 29, 125
Ahmed, Ehsan 42
Alamanni, Luigi 77–78, 82–83, 89–94, 102, 109
Alberti, Leon Battista 70
Alfonse (character in *Les Contens*) 166
Alix (character in *Les Contens*) 165
Allen Brown, Pamela 80
Alps 83
d'Amboise, François 4, 154, 180
Ancient Greek comedy 20, 23–24, 44, 48, 96, 154
Andronicus, Livius 136–37
Aneau, Barthélémy 45, 67
Anon *Farce de la Pipée* 45; *La Farce de Maistre Pierre
    Pathelin* 3, 22, 45, 179, 180; *Le Franc-archer de
    Bagnolet* 3, 130; *Le Nouveau Pathelin* 3;
    Le Testament de Pathelin 3
Antoine (character in *Les Esbahis*) 127
Antwerp 7, 35
Apollo 51, 78
Aretino, Pietro 44, 62, 154–56
Argo 102
Argonauts 102 106
Ariosto, Lodovico 8, 18, 41–42, 46–55, 62, 68, 79, 81,
    95, 119, 126, 151, 159, 162
Aristophanes 20
Athena 63–64
Attinger, Gustave 120, 125
Autelz, Guillaume des 55
Aventine Hill 130

Badius, Conrad 121
Baïf, Jean-Antoine de 4, 18, 29, 99–100, 151–52
Baïf, Lazare de 17, 29, 62, 94
ballad 42
Balmas, Enea 5, 106
Balsamo, Jean 6, 62, 122
Bande Nere, Giovanni delle 75
Bardi, Giovanni 76
Barlacchi, Domenico 79–82
Basile (character in *Les Contens*) 164–65, 167–68
Basochiens 3, 45, 83
Bayerische Staatsbibliothek 42
Bazzi, Giovanni Antonio 124

Beccafumi, Domenico 28
Belleau, Rémy 102, 121
Bellenger, Yvonne 155
Belvedere Court 64
Bembo, Pietro 23, 47, 152
Bentivoglio, Ercole 156
Bibbiena, Bernardo Dovizi da 4, 8, 61–62, 66, 68,
    81–82, 154–56, 158, 167, 171
Bienvenu, Jacques 121
Binet, Claude 152
Bizer, Marc 47
Blois 4, 150
Boccaccio, Giovanni 6, 62, 69, 75, 81, 91, 93–94, 100,
    125, 150
Bologna 18, 91
Bolognese 63, 104, 119
Bottasso, Enzo 125
Bowen, Barbara 120
braggart soldier 4, 25, 125, 129–33, 158–64, 180
Brantôme, Pierre de 4, 68–69, 70, 77, 80, 83
Brereton, Geoffrey 1
Bruno, Giordano 180
Bryce, Judith 77
Bunel, François 91
Buonamico, Lazzaro 91
Buonaparte, Niccolò 152
Buondelmonte degli Scolari, Filippo 75
Buoninsegni, Bernardo 93
Buontalenti, Bernardo 76
Burrow, Colin 97

Calais 90, 102
Calandra, Sabino 90
Calandro (character in *La Calandra*) 80–81
Calliope 51
Capitan Malagigi (character in *Alessandro*) 160
captatio benevolentiae 53
Carrefour Saint-Séverin 132–33, 168
Casa, Aldighieri della 91
Castiglione, Baldassare 125–27
Catherine de' Medici 4, 6, 8, 61–70, 73–80, 82, 86,
    91–95, 100, 102, 109, 119, 122–23, 141, 149–51,
    181
Cerreta, Florindo 171
chant royal 42
Chappuys, Claude 62
Charlemagne 75

Charles V 28
Charles VIII 5
Charles IX 4, 122, 150–51
Chartier, Roger 18
Chasble 157
Chasles, Émile 5, 120
Chaussard, Barnabé 67
Cicero 6, 24, 43, 53, 170
Claude (character in *Les Esbahis*) 124
Claudian 75
Clement VII 78
Clément, Michèle 109
Cleopatra 95, 99–100, 102
Coecke van Aelst, Pieter 98
Coligny, Gaspard de 149
Colines, Simon de 23
Collège de Beaumais 129
Collège de Beauvais 119, 121–22
Collège de Boncourt 95, 101–02, 119, 134
Collège de France 159
Colloquy of Poissy 121
comedy:
    accessibility of 19, 33–34, 92, 102, 137, 155
    act and scene division in 20–22, 34, 43, 98–99
    as a grammar-teaching tool 3
    as a language-learning tool 16–17, 44–45, 48, 52–54,
        172, 181
    as a school performance 3, 15–16, 18–19, 34, 45, 181
    as an edifying tool 44–45, 52, 181
    as an example of perfect Latin 3, 15–18, 44–45, 53
    at baptisms 109
    at Christmas 90
    at Epiphany 90, 157
    at weddings 68, 76, 79, 91, 109, 119
    balance of words and action in 20, 34, 43, 47
    costumes in 22, 48, 68, 75–76, 80, 82–83, 93–94,
        102–03, 106, 109–10, 129–30, 150, 162–63, 167,
        172
    in half-round performances 25, 31, 97–98, 104
    in carnival 61, 63, 92, 94, 106, 108, 109
    in parallel-text 42, 52–54
    intervals in 21–22, 25, 34, 43, 55, 61, 75, 78, 82, 94,
        98, 109
    music in 21, 31, 55, 76–78, 98, 106, 108, 110, 126–
        28, 159, 161
    prose vs verse in 15, 19, 22–24, 34–35, 42, 52–54,
        81, 83, 91–92, 97, 99, 109, 172
comic actor types:
    Acrobats 21
    Aretalogi 22
    Fools 21–22, 119
    Ludi 22
    Pantalons 4, 91, 133
    Pantomimi 22, 30
    Zani 4

comic theatre types:
    bergamasque 43
    commedia dell'arte 2, 4, 44, 79, 81, 91, 133, 162
    farce 2–3, 17, 19–22, 25, 42–47, 62, 67, 79, 98–99,
        101–02, 110, 120–21, 134, 179–80, 191
    mascherata 9, 68, 79, 90, 102–10, 119
    mime 43
    mummery 79, 83
    priapeia 43, 44
    satire 3, 27, 91, 107
    saynète 62–63
    sermon joyeux 2–3, 19, 43, 121
    sottie 2–3, 44–45, 47, 67
commedia dell'arte actor types:
    Capitan Spavento 163
    Colombina 91
    Pantalone 4, 91, 133
    Scaramuccia 91
Compagna della Cazzuola 79
Conegrani, Giorgio 73, 77–79
Confrérie de la Passion 3
Conseil de Paris 102–04
Cooper, Richard 61, 63, 68, 74, 77, 108
Corbinelli, Jacopo 150
Corinth 31
Cornacchia (character in *L'amor costante*) 29
Corneille, Pierre 181–82
Costa San Giorgio, Nannoccio della 73–74, 82
Cour de l'Evêché 16

Dante, Alighieri 54, 75, 81, 150
Dassonville, Michel 5
De Capitani Bertrand, Patrizia 5, 155
Diana, Roman goddess 63
Diane de Poitiers 63
Dijon 118
dispositio 19–22, 35, 43, 46, 179
Dolce, Lodovico 23, 152, 154, 156
Dolet, Estienne 24
Dom Dieghos (character in *Les Neapolitaines*) 180
Domenichi, Lodovico 91
Donatus 170
Dorat, Jean 46
Douël Dell'Agnola, Catherine 123, 133
Du Bellay, Joachim 3, 8, 41–55, 62, 95–96, 102, 118,
    127–28, 180
Duke of Mantua 73, 77
Duke of Orléans 68

Edict of Blois 150
elegy 48
Eleanor of Aquitaine 126
Eleonora di Toledo 76
Elizabeth I 122
Enfans-sans-Souci 3, 45

epic 18, 46–49, 51, 131
epic poem 18, 49, 131
epistle 42
Erasmus, Desiderius 6, 44
L'Espine de Pont-Allais, Jean de 3
d'Este, Ercole II 119
d'Este, Ippolito 29, 34, 63, 68–71, 73, 75, 77, 79,
    81–83, 102, 106
d'Este, Isabella 68
Estienne, Charles 2–5, 7–8, 15–35, 41–50, 52–55, 62,
    70, 73, 76–81, 83, 95–99, 102, 109, 118, 125, 129,
    132, 135, 142, 180–81
Estienne, Henri 6, 123, 129, 132, 138, 140–41, 150,
    159–62, 164, 171–72, 179–80
Estienne, Nicole 35, 118, 125
Estienne, Robert 16, 24
L'Estoile, Pierre de 108
Eustache (character in Les Contens) 166, 168

Fantuzzi, Antonio 63–64
Farnese family 66, 131
Ferrara 21, 68, 70, 98
Ferrento 33
Ficino, Marsilio 75
Fiorentino, Rosso 6
Firenzuola, Agnolo 89–92, 152
Florence 34, 66, 69–83, 91, 93–94, 100
Florentine 50, 61, 63, 66–70, 73–83, 91–94, 100, 109,
    123, 150, 152
Folchi, Federico 75
Fontainebleau 6, 29, 63, 66, 68, 70–71, 77, 89–90,
    92–95, 102, 104, 106, 109, 119, 122
François I 3, 6, 29, 62, 66, 77, 81, 150
François II 4, 121
Freeman, Michael 154
Fregoso, Battista 45
Fregoso, Ettore 49

Gabbiani, Vincenzo 152, 156
Gaddi, Niccolò 63
Gelli, Giovanni Battista 47
Gelosi troupe 91
Genette, Gérard 7
Geneviefve (character in Les Contens) 159–61, 164–66
Genoa 77
Gentilhomme (character in Les Esbahis) 123, 139–41
Gentillet, Innocent 6, 123, 125, 129, 141, 150, 159, 172
Geri (character in La Flora) 93
Giglio (character in Les Abusez) 25, 125
Giraldi Cinzio, Giovanni Battista 21
Giunti family 152, 155
gladiators 29, 64
Gondi family 69–70, 75, 82
Gonzaga, Elisabetta 68
Graham, Victor 90, 104

Grands Rhétoriqueurs 42
Grazzini, Antonfrancesco 152, 156
Grévin, Jacques 2, 4, 7, 9, 16, 35, 102, 117–42, 150–51,
    154, 156–59, 161–62, 164–68, 170–73
Gringore, Pierre 3
Guadagni family 69–70, 73–75, 77, 82
Guadagni, Tommaso 73, 77
Guazzo, Stefano 90–94

Hardy, Alexandre 181
Hayes, Bruce 121
Heller, Henry 6
Henri II 8, 61–69, 74, 76–77, 79, 82, 90, 92–94, 102,
    104, 108, 110, 119, 121
Henri II de Navarre 68
Henri III 149, 150
Henri IV 91, 181
d'Herbère, Claude 69
Hoby, Thomas 126
L'Homme, Martin 122
Hope, Thomas 122
l'Hôpital, Michel de 123
Horace 17, 20, 42–43, 136, 137
Hôtel de Bourgogne 181
Hôtel de Guise 119
Hôtel de Reims 95, 98
Hôtel de Ville 102

Imitatio 7, 16, 22–25
Isabel de Requesens 66
Italian acting troupes 4, 19, 67, 79–80, 83, 90–94, 109,
    119
Italian wars (invasions) 5

Janus 104, 119
Jason 106
Jodelle, Estienne 2, 4, 6, 8–9, 16, 48, 89–110, 117–22,
    131–32, 134–35, 137–38, 141, 154, 156, 158, 167,
    170–72, 180
Johnson, Eugene 70–71, 76
Jondorf, Gillian 4
Julien (character in Les Esbahis) 124, 128–31, 138–39

Kenny, Neil 51

La Mothe, Charles de 99
La Ramée, Pierre de 118
La Taille, Jacques de 4
La Taille, Jean de 4, 35, 151
Laelius 170
Landi, Antonio 76
Lando, Ortensio 18
Lapeyre, Élisabeth 120, 139
Larivey, Pierre de 4–6, 9, 149–58, 170, 180–81
Lastricati, Zanobi 74, 82

Lawton, Harold 1
Le Châtelet prison 35
Le Grand Ferrare 70
Lees-Jeffries, Hester 34
Lemaire de Belges, Jean 75
Lenoncourt, Cardinal Robert de 34
Leo X 66
Leonardo da' Vinci 124
Leoquernus 158
Liebault, Jean 118
lily, symbology 74–78, 91–93
Lintilhac, Eugène 168
Lionetto, Adeline 106
Louis XII 3, 5
Louise de Savoie 3, 6
Louyse (character in *Les Contens*) 164, 168, 171
Lucretius 18, 97
Lugdunum 64
Lyons 3, 8, 49, 61–83, 98, 104, 119, 150

Machiavelli, Niccolò 6, 18, 21, 79, 123, 125, 159
MacPhail, Eric 131
Magdalêne (character in *Les Esbahis*) 126–28, 160–61
Magny, Olivier de 49
Malato, Enrico 138
Manetti, Giannozzi 75
Manfredi, Lelio 62
Mantua 21, 70, 73, 77, 90, 150
Manucci, Piero 77–78, 82
Manuzio, Paolo 18
Marguerite de Navarre 5, 49, 62, 68, 79, 80–81, 93
Marguerite de Valois 91, 94–95, 102–03, 109, 118–19
Maria of Spain 68
Marnef, Hierosme de 181
Marot, Clément 42, 46, 51
Marrada, Francisco 125
Martin, Henri-Jean 18
Martin, Jean 27, 34, 45, 107
Massacre of Vassy 121
Masson, Jean-Papire 150
Maupas, Charles 172–73
Maximilian II 68
Mazouer, Charles 5, 76, 99, 151
Mazzei, Francesco 61, 66–67, 70–82
McAllister-Johnson, William 90, 104
McEniry, Grace 70–71
McGowan, Margaret 64
Medici family 62–79
Medici, Cosimo de' 74, 76
Medici, Giovanni di Lorenzo di' 66
Medici, Giulio de' 78
Medici, Lorenzino de' 152–56
Medici, Lorenzo di Piero de' 75
Medici, Lorenzo II de' 79
Medici, Ottaviano de' 73
Meigret, Louis 55

Menander 20, 96, 152
Mesmes, Henri de 51–55
Mesmes, Jean-Pierre de 3, 8, 41–55, 81, 95, 180–81
Michaelangelo 124
Michele, Giovanni 149
Milan 62
Minerva 102
Mitchell, Bonner 77
Mnemosyne 102–03
modesty topos 53
Molière 1, 182
Montaigne, Michel de 152, 171
Münster 133, 169
Muret, Marc Antoine 46, 49, 119, 134–35
muses 51

Neiron, Jean 67
Nivelet (character in *Les Contens*) 160–61, 164–65, 167
Noirot, Corinne 2, 95, 123

ode 42
Orlando (character in Ariosto's *Orlando furioso*) 126, 162
Ovid 44, 48

Padua 18
Pallas 63
Pannonius, Gabriel 150
Pantaleoné (character in *Les Esbahis*) 124–33, 138–41, 158, 160–66, 173
Parabosco, Girolamo 158, 167
paraphrasis 22, 24–25, 31, 52
paratexts 7, 168
Pardessus, Monsieur de 152
Paris 3, 16–17, 29, 35, 45, 67, 90, 102–03, 106–10, 121, 133, 152, 156–57, 160, 167–69, 170, 180
Parlement de Paris 45, 123
Parnassus 41, 51
Pasqualigo, Luigi 155
Pasquier, Estienne 90, 101
Peletier du Mans, Jacques 17, 20, 43, 46, 118, 136, 137
Pellerin, Baptiste 104
Petit de Julleville, Louis 98
Petrarch, Francesco 54, 75, 81, 127, 150
Philibert, Emmanuel 109, 119
Philip II of Spain 109, 199
Piccolomini, Alessandro 28, 125, 128, 130, 132, 138, 152, 154–56, 158, 160, 167
Pico della Mirandola, Giovanni Francesco 23
Picot, Émile 6, 62
Piedmont 63
Pigman, George 137
Pindar 42, 51, 140
Pindarizan 140
Pinvert, Lucien 2, 132
Plague 157

Plantin-Moretus Museum 7, 134
Plautus 44, 48, 92, 109, 155
Pléiade 46, 49, 101, 118, 122
Pliny 18
Poliziano, Angelo 97
Postel, Guillaume de 18
Prato 125
Primaticcio, Francesco 6, 104, 119
Propertius 48
Pula 27, 30, 31

Quintilian 170

Rabelais, François 5, 43
Raphael 66
Ravel, Pierre de 157, 169–70
Razzi, Girolamo 152, 154–56
Ridolfi, Lorenzo di Piero 74
Ridolfi, Lucantonio 69–70, 74, 81–83
Roches, Catherine des 157
Roches, Madeleine des 157
Rodomont (character in Les Contens) 158–67, 172–73
Rodomonte (character in Orlando furioso) 162
Rogé, Anne 152
Roman comedy 16–18, 20, 42–44, 48, 70, 81, 92, 97, 134–36, 151–52, 154, 158, 169–70
Rome 27, 34, 43, 66, 68, 73, 125
Romier, Lucien 90
Ronsard, Pierre de 17, 46, 49, 51, 89, 101, 118, 122, 131, 152
Rouen 3, 83
Rouillé, Claude 69
Ruffo (character in La Calandra) 171

sackings of Prato and Rome 125
Saint-Denis, Antoine de 100
Saint-Gelais, Mellin de 42
Saint-Maixent 180
Saint-Quentin 108
Saône 63
del Sarto, Andrea 72–73, 79
Sauvage, Denis 64
Scève, Maurice 61, 64–69, 73–80
Scipio 169–70
Sébillet, Thomas 3, 8, 41–55, 81, 180
Secchi, Niccolò 155
Serlio, Sebastiano 26–35, 45, 64, 70–74, 77, 82–83, 98, 104, 107
Sidonio, Marcantonio 119
Siege of Calais 102
Siena 51, 108
Sienese 5, 93
Simeoni, Gabriello 109
Simonin, Michel 160
Smith, Helen 7
sonnet 42, 49, 157, 168–71

Sophocles 17, 77, 94
Sozzi, Lionello 6, 62
Spector, Norman 158
Speroni, Sperone 47
sprezzatura 127–28
St Bartholomew's Day Massacre 149–50
Stone, Donald 4
Straparola, Giovanni Francesco 152
Strozzi, Giovanni 75
Strozzi, Palla di Lorenzo 76–77, 79
Strozzi, Piero 70

Tamisier, Pierre 152
Terence 3, 15–17, 19–20, 22, 25, 35, 41–42, 44, 46, 48, 83, 92, 96, 109, 118, 151–52, 155, 158, 169–71
Theatre types (non-comic):
    battagliola 63–64
    morality 17, 21, 47, 55, 62, 120, 124
    mystery 45, 67, 123
    naumachia 63–65
    pastoral 104, 122
    tragedy 4, 17, 21–22, 46–47, 49, 83, 89, 95, 99, 101–02, 119, 134–36, 156
Thespis 136
Thomas (character in Les Contens) 167
Tibullus 48
Tournon 73
translatio 22–25
translatio studii 18
Trechsel, Johannes 25–26
Trissino, Gian Giorgio 4
Troyes 152
Turin 118
Turnèbe, Adrien de 157–59
Turnèbe, Odet de 3–4, 9, 149, 151, 157–73
Tuscany 50, 66, 75–76, 78, 91–92, 100, 138, 150

Uberti, Alessandro degli 69
Uberti, Farinata degli 75
University of Paris 16, 121
Urbino 61, 66

Varchi, Benedetto 94
Vasari, Giorgio 74
Vatican Library 7, 30
Vatican Palace 64
Vauquelin de la Fresnaye, Jean 99
Venice 18, 21, 29–30, 68, 92, 149–50
Verdier, Antoine du 150
via topos 97, 100–02, 137
Villers-Cotterêts 62
Virgil 44, 46–47
Viterbo 33
Vitruvius 26–29, 35
Vivre, Gérard de 181

Wars of Religion 4, 6–7, 9, 122–23, 129, 141, 151,
    160–61
Wildenstein, Georges 104
Wilson, Louise 7

Yver, Jacques 150

Zan Ganassa 91

Milton Keynes UK
Ingram Content Group UK Ltd.
UKHW030417181023
430801UK00004B/34